Single Subject Research

STRATEGIES FOR EVALUATING CHANGE

EDUCATIONAL PSYCHOLOGY

Allen J. Edwards, Series Editor
Department of Psychology
Southwest Missouri State University
Springfield, Missouri

Single Subject Research

STRATEGIES FOR EVALUATING CHANGE

Edited by

[**THOMAS R. KRATOCHWILL**]

Department of Educational Psychology
School Psychology Program
University of Arizona
Tucson, Arizona

ACADEMIC PRESS   New York   San Francisco   London   1978

A Subsidiary of Harcourt Brace Jovanovich, Publishers

ACADEMIC PRESS, INC.
111 Fifth Avenue, New York, New York 10003

United Kingdom Edition published by
ACADEMIC PRESS, INC. (LONDON) LTD.
24/28 Oval Road, London NW1 7DX

Library of Congress Cataloging in Publication Data

Main entry under title:

Single subject research: strategies for evaluating change.

   (Educational psychology)
   Includes bibliographies.
   1. Psychometrics. 2. Longitudinal methods.
I. Kratochwill, Thomas R. [DNLM: 1. Psychology,
Educational. LB1051 S898]
BF39.S86   155   77-6600
ISBN 0-12-425850-6

PRINTED IN THE UNITED STATES OF AMERICA

TO CAROL ANN, MARIAN, AND RUDY

Contents

1

Foundations of Time-Series Research   1

THOMAS R. KRATOCHWILL

2

The Analysis and Presentation of Graphic Data   101

BARRY S. PARSONSON AND DONALD M. BAER

3

N = Nonparametric Randomization Tests   167

JOEL R. LEVIN, LEONARD A. MARASCUILO, AND
LAWRENCE J. HUBERT

4

Analysis of Interrupted Time-Series Experiments   197

JOHN M. GOTTMAN AND GENE V GLASS

5

Sequential Analysis of Observational Data Using Markov Chains   237

JOHN M. GOTTMAN AND CLIFF NOTARIUS

6

Choosing a Statistical Method for Analysis of an Intensive Experiment   **287**

JANET D. ELASHOFF AND CARL E. THORESEN

List of Contributors

Numbers in parentheses indicate the pages on which the authors' contributions begin.

Donald M. Baer (101), Department of Human Development, University of Kansas, Lawrence, Kansas

Janet D. Elashoff (287), Center for Ulcer Research and Education, University of California, Los Angeles, Los Angeles, California

Gene V Glass (197), Laboratory of Educational Research, University of Colorado, Boulder, Colorado

John M. Gottman (197, 237), Department of Psychology, University of Illinois, Champaign, Illinois

Lawrence J. Hubert* (167), Department of Educational Psychology, University of Wisconsin, Madison, Wisconsin

Thomas R. Kratochwill (1), Department of Educational Psychology, School Psychology Program, University of Arizona, Tucson, Arizona

Joel R. Levin (167), Department of Educational Psychology, University of Wisconsin, Madison, Wisconsin

* Present address: Department of Education, University of California, Santa Barbara, Santa Barbara, California.

Leonard A. Marascuilo (167), Department of Education, University of California, Berkeley, Berkeley, California

Cliff Notarius (237), Department of Psychology, Catholic University of America, Washington, D. C.

Barry S. Parsonson (101), Department of Psychology, University of Waikato, Hamilton, New Zealand

Carl E. Thoresen (287), School of Education, Stanford University, Stanford, California

Foreword

The use of single subject research designs has proliferated remarkably in recent years. Although interest in these designs can be traced to divergent historical roots, their current popularity has been stimulated primarily by developments in the areas of the experimental and applied analysis of behavior. These areas include laboratory and applied work in operant conditioning. The experimental branch of behavior analysis investigates variables that control the behavior of individual organisms, usually in animal laboratory research. The applied branch of behavior analysis investigates techniques to alter socially and clinically important behaviors, usually in treatment, educational, and rehabilitation settings. The laboratory and applied areas are experimental endeavors that rely heavily upon single subject research.

Single subject research designs have been a source of continued controversy. For years, and even today in some quarters, it has been debated whether these designs are at all useful relative to traditional large-scale between-group research. The now extensive experimental and applied literature that has generated findings via single subject research would seem to make this debate of historical interest. Although the utility and impact of single subject designs cannot be documented here, they need not be taken on faith either. Articles, books, and even entire journals have shown the viability of these designs and their contribution to experimental methodology in general.

As the use and extension of single subject research have increased, it has become apparent that no central source elaborates the many research options and methods of data evaluation that are available. In particular, the many different methods of examining single subject data and evaluating results statistically have not been detailed elsewhere. Fortunately for those of us involved in this area of research, Kratochwill has brought together an extraordinary collection of papers detailing the methodology of single subject research. The methodology encompasses multiple topics pertaining to assessment of behavior, use of specific experimental designs, and problems in data evaluation and interpretation. The conspicuous void in the available literature on these topics is finally filled with the publication of this volume.

As single subject research has enjoyed increased use, the controversy has shifted to the method of evaluating data generated from such designs. Simply stated, the central issue pertains to the advantages and disadvantages of visual inspection and statistical evaluation of data from single subject research. How should data be evaluated to determine whether a treatment or intervention has effected reliable change? The answers are not at all straightforward. On the one hand, visual inspection of the data has been at the heart of the rationale of intrasubject research. The logic of single subject experimental designs has required continuous assessment of behavior so that conclusions about interventions implemented at different points in time can be drawn. Examining shifts in behavior from visual inspection of graphs has served as a relatively crude but in many ways stringent criterion for determining the variables that are regarded as producing reliable change. Without clear rules of evaluation, visual inspection seems necessarily subjective and unreliable across investigators.

On the other hand, statistical analyses provide a way of assessing intervention effects without simply looking at graphical displays. Presumably, statistical methods afford the advantages of reliably evaluating data and thereby free the interpretive process from the subjectivity that science takes great pains to minimize. Yet, statistical analyses for single subject research are unfamiliar to most investigators in the social and behavioral sciences, and often are seemingly less straightforward than the analyses for group research in the tradition of R. A. Fisher. The data of single subject research often do not meet the assumptions of the more familiar analyses. Also, even accepted or appropriate analyses for single subject research must be used with caution. Statistical analyses require decisions to be made about the data that are not invariably automatic. Constraints of individual statistical tests and the requirements they impose upon the design need to be evaluated carefully.

This volume considers the nature of evaluation of single subject research in considerable detail. Indeed, evaluation of single subject data has not been treated in such depth or with such scholarship elsewhere in the literature. The contributors have elaborated the rationale and weaknesses of various designs and evaluation techniques. Much of the text addresses the lively controversy over the use of statistical techniques. The unique characteristic of the text is the highly constructive approach aimed at providing distinct alternatives for data evaluation. Although the controversy has often pitted visual inspection against statistical evaluation, this greatly oversimplifies the available alternatives. Actually, the rationales for both visual inspection and statistical methods appropriate for single subject research have never been brought together so meticulously or in such detail as Kratochwill has accomplished with this book. From the contributions, it is clear that many different methods of evaluation are available and are subject to a variety of considerations. The method that should be selected in a given investigation is likely to be a function of the purpose of the demonstration, the pattern of the data, the characteristics of the design, and other factors. The blind use of visual inspection or statistical evaluation has led, and will further lead, to interpretive problems.

Single subject research is actively evolving. This book is unique in not only characterizing the present status of this type of research but also in pointing the way to innovative applications of methodological tools in the future. As single subject research is extended to new populations and settings, it cannot help but profit from the increased number of methodological and evaluative options. The breadth of options suggested need not threaten those already proven to be valuable but rather will expand the thrust of single subject research designs.

Alan E. Kazdin
University Park, Pennsylvania

Preface

There is increasing use of and interest in employing single subject and other small group research designs in the behavioral sciences. Moreover, there has been a corresponding interest in and controversy over various data analysis procedures in single subject research, especially the use of inferential statistical tests. This book presents an overview of strategies used to evaluate change in single subject research, a particular approach referring to time-series paradigms in which each subject is used repeatedly. These strategies include research design, graphical analysis, and statistical tests, and it will be apparent that such designs extend beyond those commonly employed in applied behavioral research.

The essential tone of this volume is that of encouraging selection of an appropriate research design and data analysis procedure from one of many available. This is not intended as a comprehensive introduction or a comprehensive review of all problems. The focus is to examine how certain designs and data analysis procedures can be employed and whether or not they are worth doing. Also, no promise is made that the volume will solve all relevant problems, but the focus on methodological issues, available data analysis procedures, and critical guidelines for selecting such procedures should make an impact on future single subject research and further advance it as a credible form of scientific inquiry in the social sciences.

There is a great deal of misunderstanding in the area of data analysis procedures for single subject research. While visual analysis has always played a primary role in single case behavioral and other time-series investigations, it is only recently that methodologists and statisticians have focused major efforts into development of data analysis procedures or refined already existing techniques. Current efforts by the contributors to the volume, as well as a number of other methodologists and statisticians, suggest that appropriate statistical tests can be devised and employed effectively to analyze single subject data.

The present volume expands statistical analysis to novel experimental methodologies. Noteworthy also is the fact that a variety of other statistical analysis procedures are employed for single subject research to unique experimentational questions. While not all of these techniques could be included here, these developments and the content of this book do witness the need to conceptualize single subject statistical analysis beyond the applied behavioral and educational time-series tradition.

The sequence of chapters reflects a reasonable progression from basic research design to various data analysis procedures, to an overview of the issues involved in selecting an appropriate data analysis procedure.

In Chapter 1, "Foundations of Time-Series Research," I present a brief historical perspective of time-series and other small group research. Major sources of internal and external validity are presented in the context of various research designs, and numerous issues involved in the analysis of time-series designs are presented.

Just as there are situations where statistical tests can and should be used, there are circumstances where the major data evaluation technique is the eye and the judgmental aid is the graph. In Chapter 2, "The Analysis and Presentation of Graphic Data." Parsonson and Baer present the analysis of graphic data as being of singular importance in single subject research.

Chapter 3 is entitled "N = Nonparametric Randomization Tests." Levin, Marascuilo, and Hubert suggest that although data from single-subject behavior change experiments are commonly analyzed according to large-sample parametric statistical procedures, such procedures are inappropriate. To address these problems, the units-of-analysis issue is discussed and a nonparametric randomization approach to data analysis is introduced.

Since the publication of Glass, Willson, and Gottman's *Design and Analysis of Time-Series Experiments* in 1975 (Boulder, CO: Colorado Associated University Press), there has been a great deal of interest as well as controversy over analysis of time-series data. In Chapter 4, "Analysis of

Interrupted Time-Series Experiments," Gottman and Glass briefly review their work, underscore some points that have been misunderstood, and update their principles.

In Chapter 5, "Sequential Analysis of Observational Data Using Markov Chains," Gottman and Notarius address a unique and emerging area of data analysis procedures. The authors examine the growing awareness among researchers that understanding the individual characteristics of interacting subjects may be inadequate for understanding the process that has taken place between them.

The design of an experiment and the nature of the response variable are crucial factors in the choice of an appropriate analysis for single case experiments. In Chapter 6, "Choosing a Statistical Method for Analysis of an Intensive Experiment," Elashoff and Thoresen review briefly the advantages and disadvantages of the analytic methods presented in the previous chapters. They demonstrate the close link between the conceptual design of an experiment and the choice of a particular data analytic method.

This volume will be of interest to those individuals actively engaged in educational and psychological experimentation for which single subject research strategies are or may prove to be valuable. Students desiring to supplement their knowledge of a unique and rapidly emerging area of statistical analysis as applied to single subject research designs will also find this volume of importance. Finally, the book will demonstrate to policymakers and critics of educational and psychological experimentation that the single subject research strategy is actively evolving to take its place as a major tool in the quest for scientific knowledge.

Acknowledgments

Many individuals have contributed to the development and preparation of this book. I wish to express my deepest appreciation to my colleague and friend Joel R. Levin for his many discussions with me during the formative stages of this book and for his constructive feedback during its development. A debt of gratitude is also extended to Janet D. Elashoff for her many constructive comments and critical reactions to the chapters prepared for the book.

Preparation of the book was also facilitated by the support of individuals in various roles. My deepest gratitude goes to my wife, Carol Ann, and to my parents, Rudy and Marian Kratochwill, for their faithful assistance. The staff of Academic Press was more than helpful throughout the preparation of this book. I would also like to thank Margaret Patigian,

Sandy Greer, and LeAnn Newman for their typing activities, and especially
Alice Schoenberger for her typing and assistance with the numerous admin-
istrative matters in the Department of Educational Psychology that arose
during the preparation of this book. Finally, I thank the contributors to this
volume for their hard work and scientific contributions.

1

Foundations of Time-Series Research

THOMAS R. KRATOCHWILL

UNIVERSITY OF ARIZONA

The past few years have witnessed an increasing use of various time-series designs in the social sciences. Time-series research is represented as:

> The presence of a periodic measurement process on some group or individual and the introduction of an experimental change into this time series of measurement, the results of which are indicated by a discontinuity in the measurements recorded in the time series [Campbell & Stanley, 1966, p. 37].

A perusal of the psychological literature suggests that time-series designs have been advocated in such diverse areas as behavioral psychology (Baer, Wolf, & Risley, 1968; Bijou, 1970; Kazdin, 1973, 1975c; Hersen & Barlow, 1976), psychiatry (Barlow & Hersen, 1973; Wetzel, Balch, & Kratochwill, 1977), counseling research (Thoresen, 1969, in press; Thoresen & Anton, 1974), developmental psychology (Ashton, 1975; Hoyer, 1974; Risley & Wolf, 1972), school psychology (Bergan, 1977; Kratochwill, 1977), and educational psychology (Glass, Willson, & Gottman, 1975; Kratochwill &

Levin, in press; Snow, 1974). The term "time-series" is used because it is an all-inclusive description that covers diverse methodological orientations in a variety of research areas. Time-series design is to be distinguished from time-series analysis, which refers to a specific form of data analysis that can be applied to a variety of different designs (see Gottman & Glass, Chapter 4). For example, time-series designs can be used to discuss procedures related to research commonly called operant (Sidman, 1960), intensive (Chassan, 1967; Thoresen, in press), idiographic (e.g., Jones, 1971), single case (Du Mas, 1955; Hersen & Barlow, 1976), or other strategies that emphasize $N = 1$ paradigms. However, it can also include group paradigms ($N > 1$) where both within- and between-group comparisons are made. In this context, time-series designs are frequently used in evaluation research (e.g., Anderson, Ball, & Murphy, 1974; Cook & Campbell, 1976). The common benchmark of time-series designs involves the study of individuals and/or groups using time as a variable (Campbell & Stanley, 1966; Glass et al., 1975). This has led some investigators to call such research strategies "longitudinal time designs [Kerlinger, 1973]." While time-series research involves experimental designs in which each subject is used repeatedly (cf. Namboordiri, 1972), they should not be confused with repeated measurement designs commonly used with large group factorial experiments (see Kirk, 1968).

Designs labeled time-series can be best understood in a historical context where methodological issues surrounding their use have been elucidated by researchers over the years. It is in this context that more primitive study of individuals and groups grew into the more formal plans, structures, and strategies that we now call time-series research design.

I. Time-Series Research: A Brief Historical Perspective

Many modern concepts of time-series design originated hundreds of years ago. In fact, they are embedded within the evolution of scientific methodology, which had a number of diverse influences shaping its developments. Generally, five historical influences shaped the evolution of time-series research in the behavioral sciences. These include study of individual differences and corresponding development of inferential statistics, use of case study methodology in psychiatry and applied psychology, controversies over group and individual data in psychotherapy research, development of the experimental analysis of behavior, and development of time-series designs within educational research.

A. Individual Differences and Inferential Statistics

It is generally well documented that study of individual differences through group comparison approaches significantly influenced scientific methodology in the behavioral sciences (Hersen & Barlow, 1976). Such individuals as Cattell, Darwin, Galton, and Pearson emphasized that differences among individuals can be represented by establishing a distribution of differences that ultimately leads to inferences in a population. Study of a specific individual was not of primary importance in this context, but rather individual data represented variability in group data.

Evolving statistical procedures blended quite naturally into this conceptualization since they provided a means from which sampled characteristics could be generalized to target populations. The work of R. A. Fisher was important in this context since he developed properties of statistical tests that helped investigators to make such generalizations (cf. Heermann & Braskamp, 1970). His affiliation with research in the natural sciences (specifically agriculture) led to two other important influences on research design. First, some of his research was concerned with the average performance of crop yield on a particular land plot. Yield of a specific plant was typically irrelevant in the context of the total crop yield. Second, in many designs employed (e.g., split plot), there was an emphasis on measurement at one point in time. Thus, many agricultural investigators were primarily interested in final total yield, rather than the pattern of change over a growth period.

This precedent for group designs and lack of continuous measurement (i.e., frequent measurement over the duration of the study) influenced developing research in the social sciences. Also, a gradual move toward establishing the generality of research findings prompted investigators in the social sciences to study groups and employ group designs. With an emphasis on analysis of group variability and average performance, study of the individual and corresponding development of $N = 1$ time-series methodology declined in popularity (Underwood, 1957). Although the influence of group designs in the social sciences would later be perceived as a narrow perspective and would prompt more nearly continuous measurement in psychotherapy "process research" (e.g., Bergin & Strupp, 1972; Hoch & Zubin, 1964; Kiesler, 1966) and time-series designs in educational research (e.g., Drew, 1976; Gottman, 1973), development of single subject/single group designs lagged behind rapidly evolving between-group designs.

B. Case Study Research

The emphasis placed on the study of individuals by such writers as Allport, Lewin, Shapiro, and Chassan had some influence in shaping $N = 1$

time-series research. Allport was a strong proponent of idiographic (i.e., single subject) research and his writings reflect the notion that certain traits were unique to the individual and that psychology should stress the study of man's unique personality (Allport, 1961, 1962). However, as Hersen and Barlow (1976) observed, Allport was a victim of the lack of an applied research technology and most of his own research was nomothetic (i.e., involved large groups). Similarly, Lewin (1935) was somewhat critical of actuarial approaches in the study of personality and stressed the unique individual (Browning & Stover, 1971), but his method did not have a large impact on specific development of time-series design since correlated measures were frequently used rather than a true functional analysis. For example, some therapeutic variable was correlated with a target response, a procedure Shapiro (1966) referred to as simple or complex descriptive studies.

While not making a large impact on the mainstream of psychological experimentation, both Shapiro (1961, 1966) and Chassan (1962, 1967) made a number of contributions to time-series experimentation. Shapiro emphasized the use of well-defined clinical measures taken over time in one client. In this regard, he went beyond taking correlated measures to more systematically define and manipulate independent variables. For example, one of his early experiments served as a prototype of an *"ABA"* design (see Shapiro & Ravenette, 1959).

Chassan effectively integrated issues involved in extensive (large-N between-group) and intensive (single case) research in a book published in 1967 (Chassan, 1967). Some of his work emphasized use of correlated measures and occasionally a prototype of an *ABAB* design (e.g., Bellak & Chassan, 1964). However, his designs did not meet strict criteria for establishing experimental control.

Unfortunately, advances in $N = 1$ research made by Chassan and Shapiro did not greatly influence future time-series experimentation in psychological research. Hersen and Barlow (1976) cite three reasons for this: (1) many measures used were subjective, (2) changes in client behavior were often not dramatic, and (3) their work was introduced at a time when there was general disillusionment with research in psychotherapy. However, these researchers, as well as others appearing in their tradition (e.g., Davidson & Costello, 1969; Inglis, 1966), kept interest in single-case research in psychotherapy alive.

As individuals from various theoretical orientations gradually became involved in treating people with behavior and personality "disorders," novel and innovative psychotherapeutic techniques were shared in professional journals through "case study" methods (Bolger, 1965; Paul, 1969), which remained the primary methodology of clinical investigation through the first half of the twentieth century. Case study methodology was typically characterized by numerous sources of uncontrolled variation, inadequate description of independent and dependent variables, and was generally difficult to replicate. While this made case study methodology of little scientific value (cf. Boring, 1950; Campbell & Stanley, 1966; Craighead, Kazdin, & Mahoney, 1976; Paul, 1969), it helped to generate hypotheses for subsequent research and undoubtedly facilitated communication of novel psychotherapeutic techniques. For example, Dukes (1965) reviewed over 200 single-case studies over a 25-year period from diverse areas of psychology, noting that in many cases the studies provided instances of "pivotal research."

Other writers also helped to shape the development of single-case research (e.g., Lazarus & Davidson, 1971; Shontz, 1965). Hersen and Barlow (1976) observed that some case studies approached current standards of appropriate design to document experimental control (e.g., Watson & Rayner, 1920). While many of these efforts served to document the importance of single-case studies, they still remain as examples of experimentation that led to rejection of single-case methods by more sophisticated experimental methodologists.

The pervasive use of case study methodology in psychotherapy research had two undesirable consequences for development of time-series research in general. First, investigators operating from diverse theoretical orientations all claimed fantastic success with their particular approaches. More sophisticated investigators rejected these outcomes, and more unfortunately, rejected $N = 1$ experiments generally. Second, the activity of collecting data from many $N = 1$ psychotherapeutic case studies and reporting "percentage of success" (e.g., Eysenck, 1952) had the further negative influence of making various schools of psychotherapy even more isolated (Paul, 1969).

In summary, at a time when a great deal of refinement could have taken place in $N = 1$ time-series methodology, the aforementioned developments served to turn attention away from this strategy and toward group designs that were already formally recognized as a credible form of experimentation in the social sciences.

C. Research in Psychotherapy

Hersen and Barlow (1976) suggest that the appearance of Eysenck's (1952) psychotherapy review paper had two major influences on shaping future research methodology in applied work. First, it encouraged disillusionment with case studies and "percentage of success" groups and increased interest in scientific method in psychotherapy research. Second, it encouraged evaluation of psychotherapy research through large-N between-group strategies, a procedure already well established in experimental psychology.

However, after group designs had been used in various psychotherapeutic research endeavors, their limitations in this research area began to emerge. Bergin (1966) noted that in many of the studies employing group methodology, some clients improved while others either did not improve or even got worse. This led some psychologists to question not only the relationship between various diagnostic categories and psychotherapy (i.e., "psychotherapy works with neurotics") but also to suggest that future research endeavors might well focus on what specific intervention works with what type of client in what circumstances (cf. Paul, 1967).

As reflected in writing of Bergin and Strupp (1972) there were a number of limitations of group psychotherapy research. Hersen and Barlow (1976) summarized these in terms of (1) ethical objections (e.g., withholding treatment in a no-treatment control group), (2) practical problems in collecting large numbers of patients (e.g., obtaining enough subjects to make groups homogeneous with respect to some variable), (3) averaging results over the group (e.g., obscuring individual response to treatment), (4) generality of findings (e.g., results from group data do not reflect behavior change in individual clients), and (5) intersubject variability (e.g., consideration of variability only between subjects). With these considerations aired, $N = 1$ research was perceived as one of the best alternatives to understanding behavior change (Bergin & Strupp, 1972).

D. Behavior Modification: Applied Behavior Theory

During the early 1930s, B. F. Skinner was setting the stage for a new science of behavior. Skinner's (1938, 1953) early works emphasized repeated measurement of a single organism under controlled conditions (see also Skinner, 1963, 1966). Increased interest in principles of operant psychology and publication of Sidman's (1960) major work on experimental methodology helped to promote credibility in single-case experimentation in this area of psychology.

While many of these early efforts were directed at infrahuman research, formation of the *Journal of the Experimental Analysis of Behavior* (1958), which published both infrahuman and human research, and eventually the appearance of the *Journal of Applied Behavior Analysis* (1968), which was devoted to applied human research, further established credibility in this form of experimentation. These influences also led to more formal establishment of behavior modification and behavior therapy.

Behavior therapy consisted of a number of methodological strategies (cf. Krasner, 1971), but study of the single case played an integral role in its development (Yates, 1970). While behavior modification itself has evaded clear definition (Agras, 1973), applied behavior analysis has had less of a definitional problem. As Kazdin (1977b) noted, applied behavior analysis refers to a particular therapeutic focus and methodological stance rather than to a conceptual position. The applied dimension refers to a focus upon clinically or socially significant behavior and an attempt to achieve behavior change of applied significance. The behavior analysis dimension is determined by a methodological stance in implementing and evaluating interventions that derive from the experimental analysis of behavior. The methodology is characterized by a distinct approach toward assessment, design, and evaluation and is not defined by a specific discipline or research area (cf. Kazdin, 1975c).

With the development of behavioral psychology and the growing need for an applied behavioral technology, various research designs came into being (Baer, 1975). Refinement in applied research took place through several publications aimed at $N = 1$ time-series designs (e.g., Baer *et al.*, 1968; Bijou, 1970; Bijou, Peterson, & Ault, 1968). While the methodology of "applied behavior analysis" was advocated in psychotherapy research (cf. Leitenberg, 1973b) and to therapeutic work in psychiatry (Barlow & Hersen, 1973), some degree of isolation existed between behavioral and nonbehavioral psychology (Kazdin, 1975a; Krantz, 1971). Although it is now clear that $N = 1$ methodology in the behavioral tradition is spreading to other areas of psychology (cf. Kazdin, 1975b), it is also noteworthy that it has not spread to some areas of educational research. For example, Kazdin (1975c) found no studies in the *American Educational Research Journal* in the period of 1968 through 1974 that meet design and assessment criteria of applied behavior analysis research.

Single-case methodology has recently achieved even closer scrutiny and elaboration in a major work by Hersen and Barlow (1976). These authors provided an extensive discussion of the historical roots of single-case research as well as excellent discussions of its application in applied therapeutic research.

E. Time-Series Research

With publication of Campbell and Stanley's (1966) major work on educational research design, investigators were introduced to problems in establishing experimental control in the "one shot case study" and the "one-group pretest–posttest design." An extension of these procedures called time-series experiments allowed investigators to establish experimental control more reliably. Campbell and Stanley (1966) advocated use of time-series and equivalent time-samples "quasi-experimental designs" in natural settings where data collection procedures necessary for true experimental designs were not feasible.

Introduction of time-series methodology to educational research has had several major impacts on present-day time-series research. First, it emphasized *repeated measurement* under baseline and intervention conditions in educational experiments. Second, it alerted investigators to a greater range of threats to internal and external validity in such studies. Another important factor was conceptualization of such research in terms of between-group comparisons. This was an important feature since many time-series designs developed in the context of clinical or therapeutic applications to individual clients. A final important influence of Campbell and Stanley's (1966) work on time-series designs is that it set the stage for another important work by Glass *et al.* (1975). Glass and his associates introduced several new time-series designs, extended considerations of various threats to internal validity, and presented a model of data analysis for time-series experiments.

II. Design Considerations

Before discussing specific internal and external validity issues and the various time-series designs, a discussion of some design considerations follows.

A. Notation

To be consistent with the work of Glass *et al.* (1975), identical notational systems will be used: O represents observation of one or more dependent variables, and I designates an intervention into a sequence of observations. Both O and I may be subscripted, to designate time in the former case and distinctness in the latter. The basic design would be listed as follows:

$$O_1\ O_2\ O_3\ I_1\ O_4\ O_5\ O_6$$

In cases where more than one observational unit (subject, group, etc.) is involved in an experiment, their relationship to each other could be either random.

$$R \quad O_1 \, O_2 \, O_3 \, I_1 \, O_4 \, O_5 \, O_6$$
$$R \quad O_1 \, O_2 \, O_3 \, I_1 \, O_4 \, O_5 \, O_6$$

or nonrandom

$$O_1 \, O_2 \, O_3 \, I_1 \, O_4 \, O_5 \, O_6$$
$$\text{- -}$$
$$O_1 \, O_2 \, O_3 \, I_1 \, O_4 \, O_5 \, O_6$$

While random assignment is clearly preferred when multiple groups (multiple N) are involved, most time-series experiments described in this chapter do *not* involve random assignment. Because several behavior modification designs have notational systems that are commonly employed in the literature, these will also be listed.

When two or more interventions are introduced simultaneously, they will be denoted as those listed above. In cases where interventions are introduced sequentially, they will be represented as follows:

$$O_1 \, O_2 \, O_3 \, I_1 \, O_4 \, O_5 \, O_6 \, O_7 \, O_8 \, O_9$$
$$\text{- -}$$
$$O_1 \, O_2 \, O_3 \, O_4 \, O_5 \, O_6 \, I_1 \, O_7 \, O_8 \, O_9$$

In addition, an important notational consideration reflects differences in the type of intervention—continuous or temporary. The differences in such experiments would be represented as follows:

Continuous intervention: $\quad O_1 \, O_2 \, O_3 \, I_1 \, O_4 \, I_1 \, O_5 \, I_1 \, O_6$

Temporary intervention: $\quad O_1 \, O_2 \, O_3 \, I_1 \, O_4 \, O_5 \, O_6$

Thus, an investigator may apply some intervention continuously over several consecutive sessions, as in the application of a new policy or law. On the other hand, the intervention may be applied only once, as in the exposure of a group to a film that purports to change attitudes. The difference between continuous and temporary interventions is important since an intervention may produce a strong or weak effect depending on change in the data series. An example of how possible effects can mediate the strength of the inference from the data is presented in Fig. 1.1. While one would label a temporary

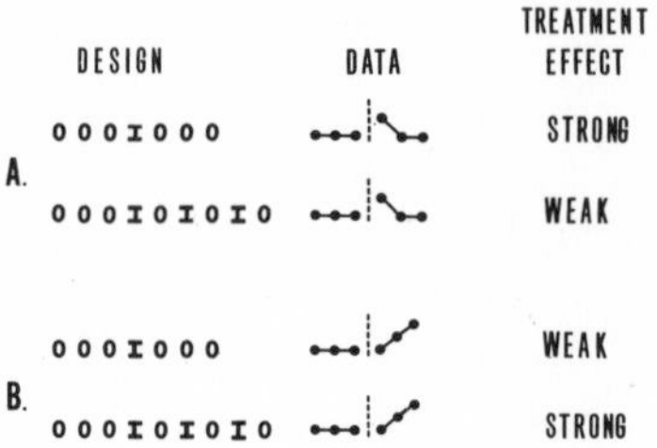

	DESIGN	DATA	TREATMENT EFFECT
A.	o o o ɪ o o o		STRONG
	o o o ɪ o ɪ o ɪ o		WEAK
B.	o o o ɪ o o o		WEAK
	o o o ɪ o ɪ o ɪ o		STRONG

Fig. 1.1. Illustration of how a temporary versus continuous intervention can mediate the strength of evidence for an intervention effect.

intervention effect in "A" as "strong," the same effect with a continuous intervention would likely be "weak."

B. Unit Repetition/Unit Replication

Time-series experimental units can consist of a single subject, group, or social system (e.g., entire school). When some single experimental unit is measured at successive points in time, the design is considered *unit-repetitive*. When the experimental unit is defined conceptually and does not have reference to specific individuals, the design is considered *unit-replicative*. For example, in the former case, investigators may wish to study an intact classroom of first-grade students over a period of several months. Thus measurement is *repeated* on the *same* group of subjects. The unit-repetitive distinction has important methodological considerations since, while investigators would not expect composition of a group to change dramatically in the former case, this is a distinct possibility in the latter case. Furthermore, there is a greater possibility that a selection by change in unit composition bias (to be discussed) could occur in the unit-repetitive case.

C. Time Units Sampled for Measurement

Great diversity exists with regard to the particular time units that are employed in time-series experimentation. Generally, time units that clearly reflect intervention effects should be chosen. For example, an investigator gathering data only in the morning may get a completely different picture of the intervention had afternoon or evening observations been taken. An example of this appears in data presented by Ross, Campbell, and Glass (1970) wherein measurement of traffic fatalities during commuting hours demonstrated no intervention effect but samples of weekend nights clearly showed an effect.

Related to this concern is the issue of how often observations should be made. This is particularly important in therapeutic work using time-series designs. Powell, Martindale, and Kulp (1975) evaluated time-sample measures of behavior by comparing the degree sample measures deviated from a continuous measure. "Measurement error" was a function of the frequency of the sample measurements (e.g., whole-interval versus partial-interval versus momentary time samples) and the criterion used to score an example of the behavior. Thus, an investigator must conceptualize time units such that clear intervention effects are noted and conditions under which no effect occurs can be determined.

III. Time-Series Research: Experimental Validity[1]

Uncontrolled extraneous variables that affect performance of the dependent variable threaten experimental validity. Like any other experiment, a time-series experiment is valid to the degree that obtained results can be attributed to the independent variable and to the degree that results generalize beyond the experiment itself. *Internal validity* refers to the degree of certainty that manipulation of the independent variable is responsible for observed changes in the dependent variable. Internal validity is a basic minimum without which the time-series experiment would remain uninterpretable (Campbell & Stanley, 1966). *External validity* refers to the extent and manner to which results of an experiment can be generalized to different subjects, settings, experimenters, and sometimes tests. Bracht and Glass (1968) extended external validity considerations into those dealing with population and ecological validity. Thus, results of time-series experiments could be generalized to groups (or subjects) and environments outside experimental settings.

Internal and external validity can work in opposition to each other. When internal validity is completely maximized, quite rigid and excessive controls are frequently necessary. When such controls reflect laboratory-like experimentation, results may not generalize to groups or settings where such controls do not exist. On the other hand, many time-series experiments are conducted in naturalistic settings, making it more difficult to establish effective controls to maximize internal validity. Generally, it is better to ensure that the experiment is internally valid, since it would be meaningless to generalize results of an internally invalid study. Thus, it is typically better

---

[1] Representation of various methodological issues in the context of Campbell and Stanley's (1966) internal and external validity was chosen because of many researchers' familiarity with these concepts. However, they represent only one way of dealing with issues relevant to establishing experimental control and establishing the generalizability of experimental results.

to conduct an experiment under more highly controlled conditions, sacrificing external validity, and later to perform experiments in more natural settings, establishing greater external validity. However, one could argue that leads from correlational or ex post facto research could be obtained (exploratory) and that more refined and controlled experimentation could then be conducted (confirmatory). In the former case, many behavioral experiments exploring the effects of reinforcement were conducted in laboratory-like settings where internal validity was maximized. Gradually, external validity of the reinforcement phenomenon was established by demonstrating its effects in more natural environments (e.g., hospitals, schools, and campgrounds).

It is important to consider possible invalidity influences in time-series experiments since designs employed are generally less adequate in dealing with such influences than many conventional designs (Kratochwill & Levin, in press). In contrast to internal validity considerations, there is a paucity of discussion of issues relative to external validity. However, an integration of the work of educational research with those from the behavioral psychology literature will elucidate issues related to external validity of time-series research.

A. Threats to Internal Validity

The several possible threats to internal validity in time-series research include history, maturation, testing, instrumentation, multiple intervention interference, instability, change in unit composition, reactive interventions, and selection and interaction of selection with other sources of invalidity (cf. Campbell & Stanley, 1966; Glass *et al.*, 1975).

1. HISTORY

Events that are extraneous to the independent variable but that occur concurrently with it may produce change in the dependent variable. When such events occur, true intervention effects are confounded with "history." Historical confounding is a major problem in time-series experiments since such experiments extend over time, making the probability of an event extraneous to the treatment higher than in other types of designs.

Historical confounding is highly likely in ex post facto time-series experiments since the investigator did not plan and directly manipulate the intervention. However, this does not mean that the experiment is always historically confounded. An investigator can conduct a careful post hoc analysis of conditions surrounding the intervention and argue that it was likely that the intervention was responsible for observed changes. For example, "qualified conclusions" can be made regarding the unlikelihood of events occurring extraneous to the intervention.

Historical confounding is much less of a threat when the investigator plans an experiment than when it is not planned (i.e., purposely selects a point in the data series when known extraneous events are least likely to occur, and then actively manipulates the independent variable). Glass *et al.* (1975) advise that an investigator should not select an intervention point at random since little control is typically realized under such conditions. However, the decision on what point in the data series to intervene depends somewhat on the type of analysis employed. Glass *et al.* (1975) observed that the investigator should purposely *select* an intervention point least likely to coincide with an extraneous event. It is assumed that random intervention yields little control and the possibility that too few data points could be taken prior to and after the intervention for appropriate determination of intervention effects with the time-series analysis. On the other hand, Edgington (1975) argued that randomization tests should not be applied without random intervention in certain types of designs. As Edgington (1975) observed, random intervention is not typical since more likely an investigator would normally introduce the independent variable when baseline measures are reliable and stable. However, by whatever method stability is determined, introduction of the intervention at a nonrandom time increases the probability that the intervention would be introduced when the data series would have shifted in the direction of the expected intervention effect. Thus, random introduction of the intervention is necessary and provides a sound basis for application of some data-analytic tests discussed in subsequent chapters (see Levin, Marascuilo, & Hubert, Chapter 3, this volume).

Threats of historical invalidity are also lessened in designs that reduce the probability that extraneous events account for changes in the dependent variable (e.g., the "operant" design discussed later). In all time-series research, investigators must examine all possible historical confoundings and control the experimental environment as much as possible. When this is not feasible, an exhaustive analysis of potential confounding historical influences that may have coincided with the intervention should be conducted.

2. MATURATION

Confounding due to maturation occurs when physical and/or psychological changes occur within subjects over a period of time, which may in turn affect their performance on the dependent variable. Especially in time-series experiments, which can extend over long time periods, subjects become older, possibly less motivated, anxious, bored, and so forth. Maturation may be a more likely problem in tasks that require psychomotor abilities, than in, for example, a task consisting of a 25-item spelling test. As with historical influences, investigators cannot always control maturation, but selection of an appropriate design and attention to "procedural" considerations (e.g., monitoring subjects) can minimize potential confounding influences. Also, a careful analysis of preintervention data for the presence of trend can help detect and subsequently help control for its influence (see Parsonson & Baer, Chapter 2, this volume).

3. TESTING

In conventional group designs, confounding due to testing occurs when improved scores on a posttest are, in part, a result of subjects having taken a pretest. In time-series designs, the dependent variable typically consists of a series of pretests (i.e., preintervention or baseline data) and a series of posttests (postintervention data). Testing effects can also occur through reactive measures. Such reactive effects occur when the measurement process itself is a stimulus for change. For example, observers entering a classroom to observe student behavior may cause students to act differently. When possible, nonreactive measures should be employed. Several recommendations offered by Kazdin (1977a), can help applied behavioral researchers deal with this invalidity potential. Investigators employing a time-series design would be also unable to employ "tests" that measure factual information that can be easily recalled from one measure to the next. However, since possible testing confoundings are more likely when time between testings is short, time-series designs that take infrequent measures are less threatened by this confounding.

4. INSTRUMENTATION

Confounding due to instrumentation occurs when unreliable or inconsistent measuring devices are employed. Relatively dramatic changes in a data series can also occur as a function of change in the method of measuring or observing the dependent variable. If an intervention occurs coincident with change in measurement procedures, effects of an intervention are confounded with *instrumentation*. For example, when data are collected through observation, human observers may change their method of recording over the duration of the study (cf. Hopkins & Herman, 1976; Kelly, 1977; Kratochwill & Wetzel, 1977; McNamara, 1975). Observer bias or drift may also occur, causing confounding in recording procedures. Also, mechanical recording devices may malfunction, or preset time intervals may change. Thus, investigators must be careful to select reliable measuring instruments, address issues in the use of human observers, check mechanical devices, and other possible instrument confounding factors. The reader is referred to Kazdin (1976, 1977a) for some useful recommendations in dealing with these confounding factors.

5. MULTIPLE-INTERVENTION INTERFERENCE

Some time-series designs involve two or more interventions into the same data series (e.g., single-N–multiple-I design, discussed later). In designs that employ this strategy, the second or any subsequent intervention may produce effects that are unique to variables that were exposed to previous interventions. Thus false attribution of an effect to the intervention when it was actually due to some combination of the intervention *and* previous interventions or interventions has been labeled "multiple-intervention interference [Glass *et al.*, 1975]."

Applied behavioral investigators have observed that it may be difficult to separate effects of a particular order of conditions from the effect of conditions in certain designs. For example, consider an experiment in which the effects of self-charting and a self-control contingency are being investigated. After baseline is established, a self-charting program is instituted. If self-charting has no appreciable effect on the dependent variable (e.g., weight reduction), a self-control program without charting could be introduced. If a dramatic change occurred, investigators could conclude that the self-control program was effective, but possibly only with clients having had the self-charting intervention first. Only a more refined design would allow statements regarding the pure effects of the self-control program.

6. INSTABILITY

Experiments involving repeated measurement of a single subject or group over time typically evidence some degree of variability. If this "instability" is large, investigators could attribute an effect to the intervention when, in fact, the effectiveness was no larger than natural variation in the data series.

Proposed methods of dealing with instability are currently subject to some debate, especially in some areas of behavior modification research (cf. Kazdin, 1976; Kratochwill, 1977). Some writers have argued that individuals working in applied settings are interested in large effects that are "significant" only in the context of a subject's adequate functioning in society. Such effects are typically large and far surpass those that would be necessary to reach statistical significance. On the other hand, many intervention effects are small and not easily visually apparent. In such cases, statistical tests may be necessary to deal with instability confoundings (see Gottman & Glass, Chapter 4, and Jones, Vaught, & Weinrott, 1977). Because this issue is not completely resolved and since it has numerous implications for future research endeavors, it is discussed in more detail later in the chapter.

7. CHANGES IN EXPERIMENTAL UNIT COMPOSITION

In any group ($N > 1$) experiment some subjects may drop out for various reasons. Attrition in $N > 1$ time-series designs can be a major concern since the experiment may extend over many months or even years. Subjects who leave a group may be less motivated and more anxious, or perhaps subjects who drop out of a group may further share a characteristic such that their absence has a significant effect on results. When this mortality involves a change in composition of the group immediately before (during, or after) introduction of the intervention, the dependent variable could change in the expected direction of hypothesized effects, thereby prompting an investigator to falsely conclude that an effect was due to the intervention. Of course, in $N = 1$ time-series research, the experiment may come to a sudden halt with any attrition.

In time-series designs that employ multiple groups, investigators must ensure that change in unit composition is not related to a factor that could contaminate final results. For example, some factor such as illness may contaminate only those subjects who frequently associate with each other. If subjects share some other characteristics (e.g., low IQ), one cannot assume that attrition was a random phenomenon.

8. REACTIVE INTERVENTIONS[2]

Another possible threat to validity of time-series experiments is that an investigator may intervene into a data series as a *reaction* to either a past or impeding change in that series. Therefore, intervention effects could be confounded with extraneous factors that shift the data series in the expected direction of an intervention effect. Such effects are similar to regression artifacts, which threaten validity of such designs as the pretest–posttest type (cf. Campbell & Stanley, 1966). While a group may not be chosen for its extreme scores, the temptation is to intervene at a time when the *baseline data series* (somewhat equivalent to a pretest) is at its extreme values.

---

[2] Glass *et al.* (1975) introduced this source of internal invalidity. Reactive interventions are not to be confused with Campbell and Stanley's (1966) "reactive arrangements," which refers to a potential *external* validity source stemming from novelty and surveillance effects both in quasi and true experiments.

As an example, consider a situation in which a school psychologist is investigating a special work study program to reduce high school dropout rate. It is possible that the decision to implement a program came during a "crisis" when 10 students decided to drop out in one week. This would, however, be a bad week to establish the program from an experimental design perspective. Even if no intervention were instituted, the dropout rate would probably return (i.e., regress) to a normal level during subsequent weeks. While practical considerations may outweigh concerns over maintaining internal validity, it would have been better for the psychologist to implement the program after the data series stabilized. Careful examination of baseline data can help decide on when to intervene in such situations.

9. SELECTION AND INTERACTION OF "SELECTION" WITH OTHER SOURCES OF INVALIDITY

In time-series designs that involve two or more groups, differential subject selection may occur. This problem typically occurs when already formed groups are employed and refers to the fact that groups may be different before the study begins (i.e., subjects were not randomly assigned). This threat can then interact with other invalidating influences to confound results.

For example, consider an experiment in which an investigator is studying the effect of two types of computer-based instruction on basic statistics course test performance through a multiple-N–multiple-I design. Assuming that groups were not randomly constituted and unknown to the investigator, one group has a disproportionate number of students who "hated" statistics, and several dropped out just prior to the intervention, any sudden change in test scores might support one group over the other. Unfortunately, results would be confounded by selection X change in experimental unit composition.

10. FORMAL RELATIONSHIPS AMONG THREATS TO INTERNAL VALIDITY AND TIME-SERIES DESIGNS

Table 1.1 presents the formal relationships among possible threats to internal validity and various time-series designs. A plus ($+$) is used where the source of internal validity is a possible threat and a minus ($-$) in cases where the design employed precludes an invalidating influence. In the latter case, multiple-intervention interference cannot be an issue in designs where only one intervention is administered to each experimental unit (e.g., multiple-N–single-I or multiple baseline). At first glance, readers may be discouraged to note that for virtually every design there are several major

TABLE 1.1
Possible Threats to Internal Validity in Various Time-Series Research Designs

Design	History	Maturation	Testing	Instrumentation	Multiple intervention interference	Instability	Change in unit composition	Reactive intervention	Selection and interaction with other sources
Single-*N* designs									
A. Case study	+	+	+	+	−	+	+	+	−
B. Basic time series	+	+	+	+	−	+	+	+	−
C. *ABA*	+	+	+	+	−	+	+	+	−
D. Single-*N*-multiple-*I*	+	+	+	+	+	+	+	+	−
E. Operant									
1. Reversal	+	+	+	+	+	+	+	+	−
2. Withdrawal	+	+	+	+	+	+	+	+	−
F. Interaction	+	+	+	+	+	+	+	+	−
G. Multiple baseline									
1. Across behavior	+	+	+	+	−	+	+	+	−
2. Across situations	+	+	+	+	−	+	+	+	−
H. Multiple schedule	+	+	+	+	+	+	+	+	−
I. Multielement	+	+	+	+	+	+	+	+	−
J. Concurrent schedule	+	+	+	+	(+)	+	+	+	−
K. Changing criterion	+	+	+	+	+	+	+	+	−

L. Multiple-N–single-I									
1. Randomized	+	+	+	+	–	+	+	+	–
2. Nonrandomized	+	+	+	+	–	+	+	+	+
M. Multiple baseline									
1. Across N									
a. Randomized	+	+	+	+	–	+	+	+	–
b. Nonrandomized	+	+	+	+	–	+	+	+	+
N. Multiple-N–multiple-I									
1. Randomized	+	+	+	+	+	+	+	+	–
2. Nonrandomized	+	+	+	+	+	+	+	+	+
O. Sequential multiple-N–multiple-I									
1. Randomized	+	+	+	+	–	+	+	+	–
2. Nonrandomized	+	+	+	+	–	+	+	+	+
P. Stratified multiple-N–single-I	+	+	+	+	–	+	+	+	+
Q. Inverted									
1. Randomized	+	+	+	+	+	+	+	+	–
2. Nonrandomized	+	+	+	+	+	+	+	+	+

threats to internal validity. However, Table 1.1 presented only *possible threats;* it should not be interpreted as indicating that an invalidating influence is always present. Such threats should serve to alert investigators that the aforementioned invalidating influences must be considered when using a specific design. As Glass *et al.* (1975) indicated, "No amount of general discussion of invalidating influences in time-series experiments can replace the need for the insight and cleverness one needs to judge the validity of a particular application of a time-series experiment [p. 53]."

B. The External Validity of Time-Series Experiments

After a well-designed and controlled experiment has been constructed, thereby addressing internal validity considerations, investigators are still faced with external validity. As noted earlier, external validity involves population-sample considerations as well as ecological or environmental invalidating influences. Although a time-series experiment should have both internal and external validity, control over one source tends to work in opposition to the other. However, control of internal invalidating influences is absolutely necessary, since, if results are internally invalid, generalization is meaningless.

Relative to other discussions of methodological factors in time-series research, there has been little attention devoted to external validity. However, an evolving literature has helped establish external validity as a central concern in time-series research (Bergin & Strupp, 1972; Bracht & Glass, 1968; Brunswick, 1956; Campbell & Stanley, 1966; Edgar & Billingsley, 1974; Edgington, 1967, 1972; Hersen & Barlow, 1976; Kazdin, 1973; Kiesler, 1971; Medland, Hapkiewicz, & Molidor, 1976; Sidman, 1960; Snow, 1974).

1. ESTABLISHING POPULATION VALIDITY

As noted, time-series designs can involve a single subject ($N = 1$) or a single group ($N > 1$). Such designs can further be conceptualized as involving within-subject(s) or within- and between-subject(s) comparisons. This conceptualization yields four "types" of experiments, which involve somewhat different considerations in generalizing results. The four possible types are depicted in a 2×2 arrangement in Table 1.2.

a. Type I. In Type I time-series experiments a single group (i.e., a single-N design) receives all values of the independent variable(s). There are two steps in making inferences from data in such experiments. The first

TABLE 1.2
**Four "Types" of Experiments That Result from
Employing Various Time-Series Designs**

	$N > 1$	$N = 1$
Within subject(s)	Type I	Type III
Within and between subject(s)	Type II	Type IV

requires generalization from the observed sample to the accessible population from which it was drawn. The next step requires generalization from the accessible population to the target population. The accessible population refers to the population of subjects available to an investigator while the target population refers to the total group of subjects that an investigator hopes to learn something about (Bracht & Glass, 1968; Kempthorne, 1961).

An example will help clarify these points. An investigator involves 25 first-grade children from Cactus Flower School in a single-group time-series experiment. The accessible population can refer to all first-grade children from the school district (e.g., $N = 100$). Since the experiment involves 25 children, the investigator may presumably wish to generalize results to the accessible population and perhaps to all first-grade children in Cactus Junction, the target population. To make such generalizations it would be necessary to draw random samples. Thus, our investigator must randomly sample both accessible and target populations to make such generalizations. In most research endeavors it is rare for random sampling to occur in the first step, and typically it is nonexistent in the second (Bracht & Glass, 1968; Cornfield & Tukey, 1956; Lindquist, 1953; Snow, 1974). Thus it would be typical for our investigator to involve only 25 children from one class and not randomly sample first-grade children from Cactus Junction for purely practical reasons.

Given these issues what options are available? First, one can generalize from the sample to a hypothesized accessible population like those observed. This assumes that an investigator has a thorough knowledge of characteristics of both groups in terms of relevant variables needed to make generalizations (e.g., age, IQ, sex). Thus, in the absence of all relevant data affecting generalizability, statements regarding intervention effects should be restricted to subjects based on logical nonstatistical considerations (Edgington, 1967).

b. Type II. Type II generalizations can be made from time-series designs that employ multiple independent groups ($N > 1$ or multiple N)

with either the same or different interventions applied over experimental units. In such cases, all the considerations discussed in regard to Type I apply to such between-groups comparisons.

In addition to generalizing results from each group, an investigator can make statements about how pervasive the intervention is with similar groups. This is ensured through random assignment of subjects to conditions. Also, in cases where groups have been stratified on some variables (sex, age, etc.) investigators can make statements about how experimental units react differently to the same intervention (as could be done in the stratified multiple-N–single-I design discussed later).

c. Type III. Type III time-series experiments that employ $N = 1$ involve somewhat different considerations in generalizing results. Typically, one cannot generalize to a population from one subject. In basic animal research conducted under highly controlled conditions, some generalization to identical species may be attempted. Likewise, certain basic research on perceptual or other psychological processes could be generalized to the human population (cf. Dukes, 1965; Shontz, 1965).

Means of establishing generalization to subjects other than the one involved in the experiment in such designs can be accomplished in several ways. First, investigators can again depend on logical nonstatistical considerations (cf. Edgington, 1967). For example, subjects with similar characteristics (e.g., age, sex, IQ) may be expected to respond similarly with identical interventions. Another way to establish generality is to identify and control sources of variability (Sidman, 1960). Sidman (1960) argued persuasively that the ultimate test of generality is replication and that unknown and/or uncontrolled sources of variability are potential threats to replication. He noted:

> Tracking down sources of variability is then a primary technique for establishing generality. Generality and variability are basically antithetical concepts. If there are major undiscovered sources of variability in a given set of data, any attempt to achieve subject or principles generality is likely to fail. Every time we discover and achieve control of a factor that contributes to variability, we increase the liklihood that our data will be reproducible with new subjects and in different situations. Experience has taught us that precision of control leads to more extensive generalization of data [p. 152].

Another way to establish generality in $N = 1$ experiments (and in any experiment conducted using time-series designs) is through replication (cf. Smith, 1970). Replication serves to establish the reliability of previous findings as well as to determine the generality of the findings under different conditions. A rather extensive list of experimental procedures can be employed to establish the generality of findings in single-case research. Sidman

(1960) outlined two procedures for replicating single-case experiments in basic research: replication and systematic replication. More recently, Hersen and Barlow (1976) have suggested that clinical replication is relevant in applied research. These concepts are extremely valuable to the applied therapeutic investigator and the interested reader is referred to Hersen and Barlow (1976) for an excellent treatment of replication procedures and for guidelines in conducting replication series.

   d. Type IV. Type IV time-series experiments involve application of one intervention over two or more different individual ($N = 1$) subjects. Essentially such experiments can be categorized as multiple N, but have only one subject in each group. Multiple-baseline designs across N or "time-lagged control" designs (Gottman, 1973; Gottman, McFall, & Barnett, 1969) commonly used in applied behavioral research are an example of this procedure. In such designs the same intervention is applied in sequence across *matched* subjects exposed to nearly identical environmental conditions. Given that consistent findings are obtained, such designs involve a *greater degree* of generalization than the typical Type II experiment since the same intervention is *replicated* over different subjects within the *same* experiment. For example, the finding that some intervention, such as a new drug, demonstrates consistent effects on seizures in children matched on relevant variables allows the investigator more reliable and generalizable findings than if experimental control were demonstrated on one subject (e.g., through an *ABAB* design) in one experiment. However, generalization to subjects (and other settings and variables) must still occur through logical considerations and the replication procedures established for such single-case experiments (see Hersen & Barlow, 1976).

2. GENERALIZATION FROM GROUPS TO INDIVIDUALS

   Just as there are problems in generalizing from $N = 1$ experiments to large groups ($N > 1$), there are problems in generalizing from group experiments to a single subject. Hersen and Barlow (1976) noted that a major shortcoming of a truly random sample is that if all relevant population characteristics are represented, thereby furthering generalizability to other groups, the less relevance findings will have for a specific subject. This could be a major shortcoming of results from group studies that are applied to a single subject in either therapeutic or applied situations.

   As with the "Catch 22" involved in establishing internal and external validity in the same experiment, investigators who do not draw a truly random sample are placed in double jeopardy in trying to generalize results. To the extent that a sample does not represent available or target populations, generalization is limited on the group generalization dimension. To the degree that a sample closely reflects characteristics of subjects involved in accessible and target populations, generalization to any specific individual involved in the experiment is limited. Thus, investigators must make clear what subjects or groups they wish to make generalizations to and design experiments to reflect these considerations.

3. ESTABLISHING ECOLOGICAL VALIDITY

Attention to possible threats to population validity is only part of the process of generalizing research results. Investigators should also know the degree to which interventions generalize to environmental conditions that differ from those in the experiment. Ecological validity refers to the extent to which situations compared in the experiment are representative of the population of situations to which an investigator wishes to generalize (Bracht & Glass, 1968; Snow, 1974). The collection of situations to which an investigator generalizes can be called a universe rather than a "population," and "interventions" can have a broad usage to include any manipulated variable (cf. Snow, 1974).

Some issues discussed in the context of population validity are analogous to those involved in ecological validity. For example, if an investigator wanted to make statements about the effectiveness of an intervention across different experimenters and/or settings, random samples of these variables must also be included in the experiment (Edgington, 1975), a feature rarely accomplished in practice.

Ecological validity has been discussed mainly in the context of conventional group designs (e.g., Bracht & Glass, 1968; Snow, 1974) but an extensive analysis of threats to this source of validity in time-series designs can be addressed. Recently, Hersen and Barlow (1976), drawing on earlier critics of single-case designs (e.g., Kiesler, 1971; Underwood, 1957), noted that even after demonstrating experimental control, investigators will have difficulty inferring that some therapeutic procedure would be equally effective when applied to clients with similar behavior problems ("client generality") or that different therapists employing an intervention will find the same results ("therapist generality"), and that intervention effects would work in different settings. ("setting generality"). While the former is an issue already addressed in population validity, the latter two issues can be discussed in the context of ecological validity. Threats to ecological validity discussed in the next section are common to all time-series designs.

There are at least 11 different threats to ecological validity. Bracht and Glass (1968) specified the following: (1) describing the independent variable explicitly, (2) multiple-intervention interference, (3) Hawthorne effects, (4) novelty and disruption effects, (5) experimenter effects, (6) pretest sensitiza-tion, (7) posttest sensitization, (8) interaction of history and intervention effects, (9) measurement of the dependent variable, and (10) interaction of time of measurement and interaction effects. Snow (1974) proposed that referent generality also be considered as a possible source of ecological validity.

a. Describing the Independent Variable Explicitly. A specific and com-plete description of the independent variable is necessary to estimate the extent to which experimental results can be generalized to other situations. While it may be impossible to replicate an experiment exactly, Kempthorne (1961) suggested that such replication is a matter of *degree.* The degree to which the independent variable is specified typically involves a judgment on the part of the professional community (e.g., colleagues, editors, reviewers).

b. Multiple-Intervention Interference. In the previous section on threats to internal validity it was noted that multiple interventions into the same data series could make it difficult to establish that the second interven-tion had an effect equivalent to subjects' experience with the first interven-tion. Multiple intervention into the same data series could also make it difficult to determine if results will generalize to settings in which only one intervention was administered (Cox, 1958; Kazdin, 1973; Lana & Lubin, 1963).

Multiple-intervention interference can also limit generalizability in cases where a single subject or group has been involved in previous experiments. For example, this could be a problem with "deviant" children, who are fre-quently included in more than one behavioral research program as they progress through school.

c. Hawthorne Effect. It is well known that a subject's knowledge that he/she is participating in an experiment may alter responses to interventions. If subjects' responses are greatly altered, effects of the intervention will not generalize to subjects who do not have such knowledge (Bracht & Glass, 1968). For example, in many behavior modification experiments, teachers may dramatically alter their behavior such that subjects are alerted to the intervention.

Such additional factors as "evaluation apprehension" (Rosenberg, 1965), "social desirability" (i.e., wanting to do the right thing) or deliberately doing the wrong thing (Masling, 1966), and being motivated by a high regard for science (Orne, 1962) can also limit generalization if subjects experience these influences. Another major concern in time-series research involves placebo effects, which are produced if subjects believe that interventions will be effective. Careful attention to both designs and procedural considerations can help rule out these influences.

d. Novelty and Disruption Effects.   When an investigator introduces an unusual or novel intervention, an effect could occur simply as a function of novelty phenomena with effects becoming absent as the intervention progresses. Likewise, an intervention could disrupt normal routines in the experimental environment rendering the intervention less effective during initial stages of the study. It is also possible for novelty and disruption effects to counterbalance each other in the same study.

Bracht and Glass (1968) suggested that an estimate of novelty and disruption effects can be obtained by extending the intervention over time. While this may be difficult in some conventional research designs, it should be less of a threat in time-series designs, where repeated measurement is an integral methodological component.

e. Experimenter Effects.   It is possible that experimenters will intentionally or unintentionally affect behavior to their subjects such that interventions do not generalize to other experimenters. Active effects (e.g., social reinforcement) and passive effects (e.g., age, sex) can dramatically alter the effectiveness or ineffectiveness of interventions, thereby limiting ecological validity (cf. Rosenthal, 1966). Parsons (1974) argued that the Hawthorne effect might even be defined as the confounding that occurs if experimenters fail to realize how the consequences of subjects' performance affect what they do.

In behavior modification research there is growing awareness that observers can be biased (Johnson & Bolstad, 1975; Johnson & Lobitz, 1974; Kass & O'Leary, 1970; Kazdin, 1976; McNamara & MacDonough, 1972; Reid, 1970; Scott, Burton, & Yarrow, 1967), thereby reporting data that do not accurately reflect experimental effects. It appears that experimenter effects can be quite pervasive and limit the ecological validity of experiments (e.g., Boring, 1962; Kaplan, 1964; Kintz, Delprato, Mettee, Parsons, & Schappe, 1965).

f. Pretest Sensitization.   In some time-series experiments it may be necessary to pretest subjects to determine entering behavioral skills, ability levels, personality, and so forth. In such cases it is possible that intervention effects consist of some combination of the intervention and prior sensitization to the intervention. In conventional group studies investigators can design the experiment so as to include a no-pretest group, thus allowing generalization to situations where no pretest will be administered.

This problem is also present in time-series research since repeated baseline data frequently make up the pretest. Relatively few designs do not call for baseline measures (e.g., possibly inverted and multielement baseline time-series designs, described later). To the degree that pretesting sensitizes subjects to interventions, results could possibly be limited to situations where the same pretest is administered under nearly identical conditions.

Bracht and Glass (1968) observed that pretest sensitization effects are most likely to occur when the dependent variable is a self-report measure of behavior. Attention to this issue seems especially relevant in self-control research, where data gathering is accomplished by the subject (Lipinski & Nelson, 1974; Simkins, 1971; Thoresen & Mahoney, 1974).

g. Posttest Sensitization. Under some conditions it is possible for an intervention effect to occur only when a posttest is administered. Thus intervention effects could be either "latent" or incomplete, and appear only when the posttest is administered. For example, if an investigator administered some type of reinforcement survey to a subject some time near the end of an intervention phase, some logical connection between the survey and intervention may be developed, thereby limiting generalizability of the intervention only to those conditions where this type of survey is employed. However, such effects could again be more easily detected in time-series repeated-measurement paradigms. Various unobstrusive measures could also be employed where posttest sensitization is a threat (cf. Webb, Campbell, Schwartz, & Sechrest, 1966).

h. Interaction of History and Intervention Effects. If some extraneous factor occurs concurrently with the intervention, results might be such that the intervention effect would not be found on other occasions. Certain time-series designs discussed later are better at controlling these types of threats.

i. Measurement of the Dependent Variable. Both conceptualization and operational definition of the dependent variable are important considerations in generalizing experimental results. Considerable time should be devoted to exploring the type of variable to be employed. For example, frequency measures may be preferable to duration in some conditions. The manner in which the dependent variable is operationally defined is also important. The variable must also be measured validly and reliably if results of an experiment are to generalize. In applied research employing observers in naturalistic settings, investigators must demonstrate that observers are gathering reliable data (Hartmann, 1977; Hawkins & Dotson, 1975; Johnson & Bolstad, 1975; Kratochwill & Wetzel, 1977; O'Leary & Kent, 1973). The reader is referred to Volume 10, Number 1 (Spring), of the *Journal of Applied Behavior Analysis* for an overview of observer agreement issues.

j. Interaction of Time of Measurement and Intervention Effects. In many conventional designs intervention effects are measured at one or perhaps two points in time (e.g., on an immediate and delayed retention test).

TABLE 1.3

Possible Threats to Ecological External Validity in Various Time-Series Research Designs

Design	Independent-variable description	Multiple-intervention interference	Hawthorne effects	Novelty and disruptive effects	Experimenter effects	Pretest sensitization	Posttest sensitization	Interaction of history and treatment effects	Measurement-dependent variable	Interaction of time of measurement and intervention effects	Referent generality
Single-N designs											
A. Case study	+	−	+	+	+	+	+	+	+	+	+
B. Basic time-series	+	−	+	+	+	+	+	+	+	+	+
C. ABA	+	−	+	+	+	+	+	+	+	+	+
D. Single-N–multiple-I	+	+	+	+	+	+	+	+	+	+	+
E. Operant											
1. Reversal	+	+	+	+	+	+	+	+	+	+	+
2. Withdrawal	+	+	+	+	+	+	+	+	+	+	+
F. Interaction	+	+	+	+	+	+	+	+	+	+	+
G. Multiple baseline											
1. Across behaviors	+	−	+	+	+	+	+	+	+	+	+
2. Across situations	+	−	+	+	+	+	+	+	+	+	+
H. Multiple schedule	+	+	+	+	+	+	+	+	+	+	+
I. Multielement	+	+	+	+	+	+	+	+	+	+	+
J. Concurrent schedule	+	+	+	+	+	+	+	+	+	+	+

Multiple-*N* designs

L. Multiple-*N*–single-*I*												
1. Randomized	+	−	+	+	+	+	+	+	+	+	+	+
2. Nonrandomized	+	−	+	+	+	+	+	+	+	+	+	+
M. Multiple baseline												
1. Across *N*												
a. Randomized	+	−	+	+	+	+	+	+	+	+	+	+
b. Nonrandomized	+	−	+	+	+	+	+	+	+	+	+	+
N. Multiple-*N*–multiple-*I*												
1. Randomized	+	+	+	+	+	+	+	+	+	+	+	+
2. Nonrandomized	+	+	+	+	+	+	+	+	+	+	+	+
O. Sequential multiple-*N*–single-*I*												
1. Randomized	+	−	+	+	+	+	+	+	+	+	+	+
2. Nonrandomized	+	−	+	+	+	+	+	+	+	+	+	+
P. Stratified multiple-*N*–multiple-*I*	+	−	+	+	+	+	+	+	+	+	+	+
Q. Inverted												
1. Randomized	+	+	+	+	+	+	+	+	+	+	+	+
2. Nonrandomized	+	+	+	+	+	+	+	+	+	+	+	+

29

This could limit the ecological validity of an experiment since it is possible for an intervention either to show or not to show an effect had the investigator added additional measurement occasions. In time-series designs repeated measurement of the dependent variable generally increases the ecological validity of results. However, when possible, investigators should include followup checks after the intervention has been terminated. Effects measured during followup sessions may provide leads as to how programs are to be designed to maintain lasting effects.

k. Referent Generality. Snow (1974) introduced "referent generality" to designate the range or pervasiveness of possible experimental outcomes measured in a given study. In most educational experiments, outcomes should be conceptualized on many dimensions (i.e., multivariate). Such outcomes not only refer to the external validity of the experiment, but also possibly to its value in understanding the phenomenon under study. For example, an investigator studying the effects of some reinforcement program on cooperative behavior could employ multiple dependent variables to explore how other social behaviors are influenced by the program. After reviewing the operant literature, Kazdin (1973) noted that many observations have been restricted to a single target behavior. He argued that there are distinct advantages in using measures of nontarget behaviors as well as the usual target response (e.g., such assessment would allow examination of response generalization).

l. Relationship of Possible Threats and Ecological Validity and Various Time-Series Experimental Designs. Relationships among various designs and ecological validity are presented in Table 1.3. As noted earlier, a plus is used where the source of ecological validity is a possible threat and a minus in cases where the design employed precludes an invalidating influence. While a plus indicates that a specific factor is a *possible* invalidating influence, it should not be used to judge the external validity of a time-series design in an absolute sense. Use of a particular design is an integral part of the *experimental* procedures used during the study. However, "design" and "procedures" are not independent components in an experiment, as some authors have argued (cf. Medland, Hapkiewicz, & Molidor, 1976). These authors incorrectly observed that if one views the "design" as the problem confounding interpretation of results, then one fails to examine procedure. Many threats to ecological validity are procedural issues but as examination of Table 1.3 clearly indicates, some specific threats are nonexistent as a function of the design employed.

IV. Time-Series Research Design

This section includes a description of various time-series designs, some examples of their application, and specification of some considerations in their use. Both designs employed in educational research and commonly labeled "time-series" and those developed in the context of behavioral psychology and commonly labeled "intrasubject" will be discussed. As noted earlier, the mutual isolation between behavioral and nonbehavioral psychology led to the development of different names and notational systems for sometimes identical design procedures. However, a particular design title may reflect certain basic theoretical assumptions about the way individuals behave as a function of certain environmental influences (e.g., reinforcement). Thus, for example, some behavioral designs developed in the context of therapeutic applications to a single subject or group. This is not to say that they are limited to this orientation, but rather that they developed and are used primarily in this context. Names given these designs reflect this orientation (e.g., "multiple schedule" to reflect differing schedules of reinforcement in therapeutic research). At this point a further distinction will be made between planned and ex post facto types of time-series experiments. The distinction is important in further drawing inferences from experimental data (see Levin, Marascuilo, & Herbert, this volume, for a related discussion).

A. Planned versus ex post facto Experiments

Educational investigators frequently draw cause–effect conclusions from events that occurred in the past. However, post hoc assumptions can yield misleading interpretations of research data, especially when there is no direct control over independent and dependent variables. In ex post facto research an investigator does not have direct control over independent variables because they have already occurred or cannot be manipulated. Thus, inferences about relationships between the independent and dependent variable are not made from direct intervention, but rather from concomitant variation (Kerlinger, 1973).

Glass et al. (1975) suggested that concomitant variation is actually the most primitive level of causal inference. When two variables (e.g., sunspots and thunderstorms; cf. Huntington, 1945) demonstrate nearly parallel concomitant variation it is possible to generate hypotheses of relationship. Such inference consists of explorations in negative instances (i.e., if two data series are uncorrelated, it is unlikely that they are causally connected).

The next level of inference involves generating post hoc hypotheses to account for fluctuations of a system by some historical log assumed to be causal in nature and looking for shifts in the data series (Glass *et al.*, 1975). There are two essential differences between quasi-experimental (and experimental) types of research and such ex post facto approaches: Neither experimental manipulation nor random assignment can be employed by the investigator in ex post facto experiments. Thus, in ex post facto research direct control is not possible and invalidating influences are higher in probability. While many time-series designs do not allow random assignment, they do involve a planned intervention, making the *probability* of establishing a relationship higher since many rival hypotheses can be eliminated. However, it cannot be too strongly emphasized that while a planned experiment allows a greater *degree* of confidence that some relationship is present in most instances, it is probably unwarranted to assume that a causal relationship has been established.

In summary, the most important difference between experimental research and ex post facto research is the degree of control. In planned time-series experiments, investigators have an active variable in manipulative control. If an experiment is a "true" experiment, an investigator may also employ randomization to exercise a greater degree of control. To further elaborate on the parameters of ex post facto research an example experiment is presented below.

1. EX POST FACTO RESEARCH: AN EXAMPLE

Ex post facto experiments involve situations where an investigator could have manipulated a variable but did not, or where a variable could not be manipulated, possibly due to practical and ethical considerations. Under some conditions ex post facto research can help explain certain phenomena or generate future more controlled experimentation. Schnelle and Lee (1974) demonstrated how ex post facto quasi-experimental methodology can be applied in a situation where data, otherwise lost, can be retrieved and whereby qualified conclusions from data can be developed. These authors employed a basic time-series design (described later) and "quasi-experimental logic" to assess behavioral effects of a prison disciplinary intervention on a population of approximately 2000 adult male inmates incarcerated at the Tennessee State Prison for men in Nashville, Tennessee, for all or part of a period extending from January, 1959, to June, 1971. On July 28, 1969, the Tennessee State Prison initiated a new policy whereby all prisoners who were considered behavioral problems were transferred to Brushy Mountain State Prison, a maximum security institution located in a remote area of East Tennessee. Schnelle and Lee (1974) con-

ceptualized transfer to Brushy Mountain as a "time-out from positive reinforcement" and the policy change as a "threat" to use this time-out procedure. Simultaneously with this transferral policy, the Tennessee State
Prison discontinued a restricted diet procedure, which consisted of an un-
seasoned mixture of vegetables and meat. The dependent variable consisted
of prison behavioral offenses entered into a log book as they were observed
by prison guards.

    This research was then a retrospective attempt to describe behavioral
changes among a prison population that may have resulted from adoption
of the Brushy Mountain Policy and simultaneous discontinuance of the
restricted diet policy. Figure 1.2 illustrates the average number of daily
offenses for all inmates not transferred to Brushy Mountain, graphed over
each month of the study. A change in level calculated from the IMA(1,1)
time-series analysis (Glass et al., 1975) suggested a significant decrease in
frequency of all behavioral offenses after July, 1969, which coincided with
the two aforementioned "interventions." However, the "significant" effect
only tells the investigator that there was a real (rather than a chance) difference and not why there was one.

    As Schnelle and Lee (1974) observed, the major contribution of the
experiment lies in the description of quasi-experimental logic to retrospective data to prevent unwarranted conclusions, definition of limits of data
interpretation, and application of a model by which qualified statements
can be made. However, plausible explanations for the "intervention effects"

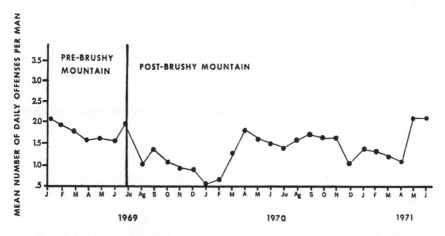

Fig. 1.2 Average number of offenses per inmate over a 30-month period. Brushy Mountain
policy introduced July 28, 1968. Monthly data multiplied by a constant of 1000. [Source:
Schnelle, J. F., & Lee, J. A quasi-experimental retrospective evaluation of prison policy change.
Journal of Applied Behavior Analysis, 1974, 7, 483–496. Copyright by Society for the Experimental Analysis of Behavior, Inc. Reproduced by permission.]

must be made in the context of such invalidating influences as history, instrumentation, and regression (cf. Kratochwill & Levin, in press, for further discussion of methodological consideration in the study). Finally, the study does provide guidelines for future efforts to evaluate prison policies under a well-planned and systematic design format.

B. Design Variations

In this section some major time-series designs are reviewed. No attempt is made to exhaust all possible designs that could be constructed. Rather, the subsequent discussion will draw heavily on the work of Glass *et al.* (1975), for a review of time-series designs, as well as on a recent book on design

TABLE 1.4
**Notational Representation for Various Single-N
and Multiple-N Time-Series Research Designs**

Design	Notation
Single-N designs	
A. Case study	I_1 *000* or *B*
B. Basic time-series	*000 I_1 000* or *AB*
C. *ABA*	*000 I_1 000 000* or *ABA*
D. Single-N–multiple-I	*000 I_1 000 I_2 000* or *ABC*
E. Operant	*000 I_1 000 000 I_1 000* or *ABAB*
F. Interaction	*000 I_1 000 I_2 000 I_1 I_2 000*
G. Multiple baseline	
1. Across behaviors	a *000 I_1 000 000 000*
	b *000 000 I_1 000 000*
	c *000 000 000 I_1 000*
2. Across situations	a *000 I_1 000 000 000*
	b *000 000 I_1 000 000*
	c *000 000 000 I_1 000*
H. Multiple schedule	I_1 *O* I_2 *O* I_1 *O* I_2 *O*
	I_2 *O* I_1 *O* I_2 *O* I_1 *O*
I. Multielement	*000 I_1 00 I_1 00 I_1 00 I_1 000*
J. Concurrent schedule	I_1 *000*
	000 I_2 000, I_1 000 or *I_2 000* or *I_3 000*
	I_3 *000*
	—*B*
	or *A*——*C B* or *C* or *D*
	—*D*
K. Changing criterion	*000 I_1 000*
	I_1 *000*
	I_1 *000*
	I_1 *000*

methodology by Hersen and Barlow (1976) for a review of single-case behavior modification designs. After discussing basic rationales of a particular
design, major considerations in their use are presented. Table 1.4 presents
a notational representation of the various time-series designs. Designs presented in Table 1.4 and those subsequently discussed in the text are categorized as single N or multiple N. As noted, single-N designs involve the
measurement of a single subject or group and allow a within subject (or
group) comparison of intervention effects in the time-series framework.
Multiple-N designs involve both a *within*-group (or subject) and a *between*-
group (or subject) comparison. Thus, such designs would be included in the
Type II and Type IV cells of Table 1.2. As discussed, this is an important
consideration in time-series research since a design over different subjects or
groups typically allows a greater degree of generalization (see also, Simonton,
1977). Also, when different groups are involved, subjects can be randomly

TABLE 1.4 (Continued)

Design	Notation
Multiple-N designs	
L. Multiple-N–single-I	$OOO\ I_1\ OOO$

	$OOO\ I_1\ OOO$

	$OOO\ I_1\ OOO$
M. Multiple-N–multiple-I	$OOO\ I_1\ OOO$

	$OOO\ I_2\ OOO$

	$OOO\ I_3\ OOO$
N. Multiple-baseline across n	$OOO\ I_1\ OOO\quad OOO\quad OOO$

	$OOO\quad OOO\ I_1\ OOO\quad OOO$

	$OOO\quad OOO\quad OOO\ I_1\ OOO$
O. Sequential multiple-N–multiple-I	$OOO\ I_1\ OOO\quad OOO$

	$OOO\quad OOO\ I_2\ OOO$
P. Stratified multiple-N–single-I	Type A units $OOO\ I_1\ OOO$

	Type B units $OOO\ I_1\ OOO$

	Type C units $OOO\ I_1\ OOO$
Q. Inverted design	$OOO\ I_1\ OOO\ I_2\ OOO$

	$OOO\ I_2\ OOO\ I_1\ OOO$

assigned to different interventions, eliminating selection bias interactions with other internal invalidating influences (see also Kratochwill & Levin, in press).

1. SINGLE N DESIGNS

a. Case Study. As previously discussed, case study research was used extensively to evaluate and document various therapeutic endeavors in both psychology and psychiatry, and likely set the stage for more well controlled and designed time-series experiments in educational and behavior modification research. While case study methodology can involve a "one shot" measurement (e.g., posttest administered after some intervention), measurement occasions can extend over a period of time, reflecting the nearly continuous measurement characteristic of time-series research. Many case studies conducted in behavior modification reflect this strategy.

Norman and Broman (1970) treated a 12-year-old "elective mute" (a child who talks only in a few select situations) using positive reinforcement procedures in a case study format. Visual feedback from a volume-level meter was used to induce sounds and to raise speech volume. Reinforcement was also employed to increase rate of speech and generalize it to other situations. The sound meter contained a background divided into red (loudest sounds) and black (low or no sounds) regions. Intervention procedures consisted of 44 sessions and anywhere from 40 to 400 trials per session. Dependent variables (reported in percentage) consisted of three measures: The child's voice either moved the meter needle into a black or red region, or no response was made. Data on these measures are reported in Fig. 1.3. The authors increased responses in the red and decreased the percentage of no responses. Black region responses also gradually decreased over sessions. During the last session the child responded to 80% of the questions from the adult (HB) and 54% from a new person.

While the study suggests that various treatment procedures were successful, it would have been greatly strengthened by inclusion of baseline measures as well as a withdrawal of the intervention. In the context of studies like these, several advantages and limitations of case study research can be described.

In psychotherapeutic interventions, Hersen and Barlow (1976), drawing on the work of Lazarus and Davidson (1971), suggest that case studies can (1) foster clinical innovation, (2) cast doubt on certain theoretical assumptions, (3) permit study of rare phenomena, (4) develop new technical skills, (5) buttress theoretical views, (6) promote refinement in technique, and (7) provide clinical data that can be used to design more highly controlled research.

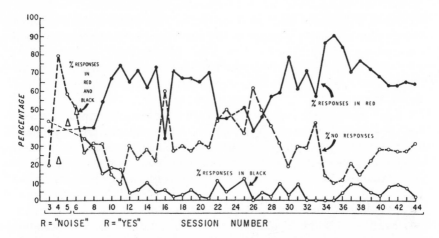

Fig. 1.3. A record of subject's responses to HB with no one else in the room. Note the "all-or-none" pattern of responding in most sessions; subject either gave a reinforced response (red) or did not respond. In sessions 4, 5, and 6, responses in "red" and "black" were accidently combined during recording the data and are represented by triangles. [Source: Norman, A., & Broman, H. J. Volume feedback and generalization techniques in shaping speech of an electively mute boy: A case study. *Perceptual and Motor Skills,* 1970, *31,* 463–470. Reprinted with permission of authors and publisher.]

Browning and Stover (1971, p. 80) presented a case study procedure in the context of a *B* design. This procedure consists of well-controlled observations of some intervention without a formal baseline measure. While well aware of its limitations, these authors suggest that it is popular because it (1) is easy to administer, (2) is compatible with traditional methods of assessing psychotherapy effectiveness, (3) is inexpensive, and (4) provides a compromise to clinicians who gradually make transitions to behavior-therapy procedures.

As another variation on the time-series case study paradigm, an investigator may wish to examine some variable(s) in a purely descriptive fashion. Such a design may not involve any formal intervention and could be notationally represented with a series of measurements (e.g., 000) or labeled an *A* design. However, such a case study may be characterized by the same degree of methodological rigor as any other design (e.g., as reflected in the reliability of measurements).

Case study methodology can also be used to study concomitant variation. Researchers may wish to describe fluctuations of a social system over time and examine how changes in that system are influenced by variables free to vary (e.g., crime rate and temperature). Such "case study" formats in time-series research have appeared from time to time (Fisher, 1921; Huntington,

1945; Box & Jenkins, 1970). For example, an investigator can generate post hoc hypotheses to account for fluctuations of a system by employing historical logs of events and scanning for shifts in the data series (Glass *et al.*, 1975). Weisberg and Waldrop (1972) used such a format to study the fixed-interval pattern at which Congress passed bills during its legislative session. For example, in eight Congresses sampled from 1947 to 1968 the rate of passage was extremely low three to four months after commencement, but was followed by a positively accelerated growth rate that continued until time of adjournment. While such "ex post facto" studies can again be useful to generate hypotheses in subsequent research, a strong argument for an intervention effect is not possible without conducting a *planned* experiment.

Investigators employing case study methodology should address several considerations. Campbell and Stanley (1966) note that basic to scientific evidence is the process of comparison. Because a case study does not involve a true comparison of an intervention with no intervention, scientific credibility is lost. Although a case study can be used to generate hypotheses for subsequent research (cf. Bolgar, 1965; Lazarus & Davidson, 1971), such research involves "misplaced precision" in that while considerable effort goes into a typical case study, time would be better spent on a well-controlled experiment wherein appropriate comparison techniques are involved.

Finally, case study methodology is subject to all major threats to establishing internal validity. In addition, subjective dependent variables are frequently employed making it unclear if bias or "placebo" effects were responsible for change.

b. Basic Time-Series or AB Design. The basic time-series design represents the foundation of quasi-experimental designs. In this strategy, well-controlled observations are taken repeatedly over some time period. At a planned point in the data series some intervention is introduced and changes in the dependent variable are noted. The design differs from the case study in that a "baseline" or pretest data series is taken. The design can further be conceptualized as an improved form of the pretest–posttest design in that more frequent measurement of the dependent variable occurs.

The Schnelle and Lee (1974) study referred to earlier employed a basic time-series design in an ex post facto fashion. Repp and Deitz (1974) used a planned basic time-series design to evaluate a program to reduce aggressive and self-injurious behavior in a severely retarded 13-year-old male child in experiment III of their research project. Phase I of the study lasted 28 sessions. Aggressive and self-injurious behavior varied between .00 and .22 responses per minute, with a mean of .08. In Session 29 (phase II) a program began in which for every 15-minute interval in which no inappropriate responding occurred, five stars were placed in a small notebook carried by the child. An inappropriate response was followed by three events: The child was informed that he was wrong, all stars were taken from the book, and a timer was reset. Thus, differential reinforcement of other behaviors (DRO) was combined with response cost (removal of stars) and a mild punishment ("wrong"). The effect of these combined intervention procedures was quite dramatic, as Fig. 1.4 shows. The authors concluded that DRO combined with other techniques was quite manageable for the teacher and successful on three other subjects involved in these experiments.

There has been considerable attention directed toward the advantages and limitations of the basic design in both the educational (e.g., Campbell, 1969; Campbell & Stanley, 1966; Drew, 1976; Glass *et al.*, 1975; Gottmen, 1973; Gottman, McFall, & Barnett, 1969) and behavioral literature (e.g., Risely & Wolf, 1972; Wolf & Risley, 1971). The basic time-series design can help control some but not all sources of internal invalidity. In cases where a conventional comparison or control group cannot be employed the design can provide better control than either the one-shot case study or one-group pretest–posttest design. For example, rather than taking a single measure of the dependent variable, a series of pretest–posttest measures is taken. Such

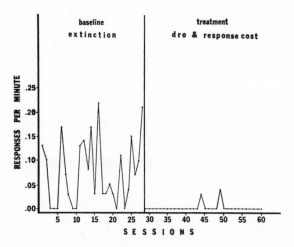

Fig. 1.4. The rate of aggressive responses by subjects. During baseline, the inappropriate behaviors were ignored (extinction). During treatment, response cost was combined with the DRO procedure, where the absence of these behaviors for 15 minutes earned exchangeable tokens. [Source: Repp, A. C., & Deitz, S. M. Reducing aggressive and self-injurious behavior of institutionalized retarded children through reinforcement of other behaviors. *Journal of Applied Behavior Analysis*, 1974, 7, 313–325. Copyright by Society for the Experimental Analysis of Behavior, Inc., reproduced by permission.]

repeated measurement helps control threats of maturation and, to some degree, history—two major threats to validity of case studies and pretest–posttest designs. Testing effects are, in part, also controlled since repeated exposure to a single pretest is likely to lead to possible adaptation. Thus, testing effects that do not occur on pretesting would not be expected to also occur through the posttest series.

Another important feature of the basic design and its variations is that such an approach to research involves continuous or nearly continuous measurement (Drew, 1976; Namboodiri, 1972). This is in contrast to many research designs where few data points are taken. Even in repeated measure-ANOVA, fewer data points are taken than is characteristic of most time-series designs. In this context, it is also possible to *study* the influence of historical confounding. The possibility of some extraneous uncontrolled event occurring during the repeated data series offers investigators more opportunity to study this phenomenon than in designs that involve only one or two measurement occasions. Possible confounding influences could then be controlled in subsequent investigations.

The basic design has been used to good advantage in psychotherapeutic research. Hersen and Barlow (1976) document its utility when used with (1) a single target measure and extended follow-up, (2) multiple target measures, and (3) follow-up and booster treatments. Use of the design in these situations has generated fruitful areas for further research where some of these factors are subsequently controlled.

Despite these advantages, investigators using basic time-series designs should consider that it is impossible to rule out historical confoundings. For example, it is possible for change in the B phase to have occurred regardless of an intervention. Under some conditions, there may also be great difficulty in interpreting an intervention effect with baseline trend. The baseline series must be stable, or exhibit a significant shift in the series, or be in the opposite direction from trend in baseline (see Parsonson and Baer, Chapter 2 of this volume). This problem relates to most of the time-series designs to be discussed in more detail in Section VI.

A further difficulty in use of the basic time-series design is that data in the experimental condition are compared to a "forecast" from baseline measures (Risley & Wolf, 1972). Any relationship between the intervention and change in the data series depends heavily on such a forecast. Stronger support for the intervention could only be accomplished by adding another phase to the experiment where the intervention is withdrawn (e.g., an *ABA* design).

Tuckman (1972) suggested that one major limitation of the design is the possibility of unavailability of data to serve as multiple pretest observations (O_1-O_k). Such practical considerations as the manner in which school systems keep records on achievement data could be a problem since such data are gathered relatively infrequently. Also, to implement a research program that requires repeated measurement may prove impractical since investigators would have to plan well in advance for data collection.

In summary, the basic time-series design is truly limited in advancing strong conclusions for experimental control. It has some application to situations where the purpose of experimentation is purely exploratory or where other design options cannot be used. It has been useful in the experimental therapeutic literature and offers better experimental control than conventional case study methodology.

c. The ABA Time-Series Design.   The *ABA* design strengthens analysis of controlling effects by including an intervention withdrawal, which allows a greater *degree* of certainty that the intervention was responsible for change. As Hersen and Barlow (1976) observed: "Unless the natural history of the behavior under study were to follow identical fluctuations in trends, it is *most improbable* that observed changes are due to any influence (e.g., some correlated or uncontrolled variable) other than the treatment variable that is systematically changed [p. 176]." However, the confounding influence is *not* completely ruled out.

Twardsoz, Cataldo, and Risley (1974) used an *ABA* design in one of their experiments, which investigated various aspects of an open environment design for infant and toddler day care. In the third experiment, they examined what effect light and noise had on infant sleep, compared to a closed dark room. Alternate conditions of noise and light (door left open so that noise from other activities could be heard and some activities were audible and light was allowed to enter from a window) and quiet and dark (door in the sleep area was closed, and the window covered with foil to make the room dark) were created in a sleep room. The dependent variables consisted of the percentage of sleep and crying per day for 13 children. Results reported in Fig. 1.5 indicated that quiet and dark, and noise and light room conditions made no difference on sleeping or crying. The authors further reported that group data also reflected individual children's sleep.

In addition to advantages of *AB* designs, the *ABA* design is clearly preferable since a greater likelihood of experimental control is established. Replication of the *ABA* design on different subjects further strengthens conclusions about intervention effects. The *ABA* design may also be quite useful for applied investigators in situations where a client cannot complete a program or where experimental changes are necessary.

If baseline reflects absence of some treatment variable importance for a client or group, a major problem in the use of the *ABA* design is that the experiment ends on a baseline phase. This may involve practical as well as

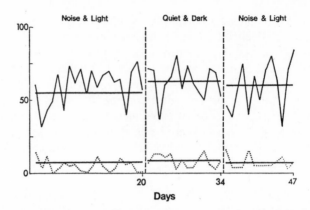

Fig. 1.5. Percentage of crib time babies spent sleeping and crying in the sleep room of the Infant Center during conditions of noise and light, when the door was left open and the room was light, and quiet, and dark, when the door was closed and the room was very dark. Solid curves, sleeping; dotted curves, crying. Heavy solid lines indicate means for each condition. [Source: Twardosz, S., Cataldo, M. F., and Risley, T. R. Open environment design for infant and toddler day care. *Journal of Applied Behavior Analysis*, 1974, 7, 529–546. Copyright by Society for the Experimental Analysis of Behavior, Inc. Reproduced by permission.]

ethical considerations. In the former case, an investigator may find few situations in which removing an intervention is acceptable to individuals in the natural environment. Also, it would seldom be justifiable to complete a research project with no treatment for a client.

In studying certain learning phenomena an investigator may be unable to retrieve original baseline levels. Browning and Stover (1971) also observed that in applied therapeutic situations an investigator seldom returns to the original baseline level. This militates against the logic of the design and would not allow investigators to establish experimental control.

A third problem in the use of the *ABA* design is that it is susceptible to multiple-intervention interference and sequential confounding (Bandura, 1969; Campbell & Stanley, 1966; Kazdin, 1973). Effects observed in the final baseline phase may not be the same as those observed under conditions where no intervention had been introduced into the series.

d. Single-N–Multiple-I Design. In the single-N–multiple-I design an investigator successively introduces two or more interventions into one experimental unit. Any abrupt change in level or direction of the data series coincident with the intervention is the intervention effect. While the design has been described by some educational writers (e.g., Glass *et al.*, 1975), Browning and Stover (1971) have also presented a discussion of this "*ABC* design" in the behavior modification area. It has not been used extensively in the educational and psychological literature.

Chadwick and Day (1971) investigated the effects of contingent tangible and social reinforcement on academic performance of an experimental classroom of 25 selected underachieving students. During the first intervention, a point system with tangible backup reinforcers was combined with contingent social reinforcers dispensed by teaching staff. During the second intervention contingencies for tangible reinforcers were terminated while social reinforcement was continued to see if effects of I_1 would occur. Thus, the design also involved components of a partial treatment *withdrawal* in forming I_2. Three dependent variables were used: percentage of time at work (number of minutes spent actually working on assignments divided by the total time assigned to the task); rate of work output (number of exercises and problems done divided by the number of minutes); and accuracy of output (number of problems and exercises done correctly divided by total attempted). The authors noted that results reported in Fig. 1.6 show that combined tangible and social reinforcers increased students' work time, rate of output per hour, and accuracy. Termination of tangible reinforcement demonstrated a maintenance of high rates of output per hour and accuracy, but total amount of work time returned to baseline level.

As can be observed from this experiment, one main advantage of the design is economy. Several hypotheses can be tested successively, as for example in treating rare behavior disorders. Browning and Stover (1971) suggested that the design is of great value in experimental–clinical settings when one finds that the B phase fails to produce desired results. In such cases data under the B condition can help formulate hypotheses that can be incorporated in a revised treatment and subsequently labeled C or I_2.

Even though an investigator sacrifices some degree of internal validity in the design, it also has application to situations in which simultaneous comparison of different treatments is politically unfeasible or impossible (Campbell, 1969; Glass et al., 1975).

A major disadvantage of the design is that it is confounded by "multiple–intervention interference" (cf. Campbell & Stanley, 1966; Kazdin, 1973). For example, a change in the data series that occurs under I_2 may be due to the initial effect of I_1, or to some combination of I_1 and I_2. For example, a "time-out" program under I_1 may consist of one minute in an area removed from peers. If I_2 consists of an additional one minute (i.e., two minutes total) an investigator does not know to what extent the effectiveness of I_2 was due to I_1, which preceded it.

While the design has many major internal validity threats, several modifications in procedure can strengthen its validity. Glass et al. (1975) observed that interventions that are abrupt and applied for a single unit of time lessen multiple-intervention interference. Glass et al. (1975) also suggested that when single-group–multiple-I designs are employed with an

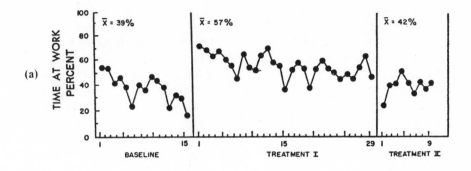

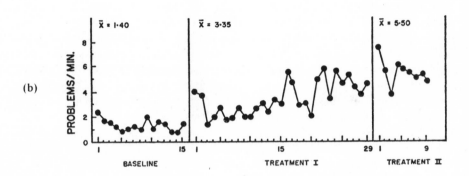

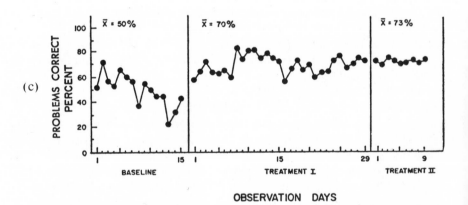

OBSERVATION DAYS

Fig. 1.6. (a) Percentage of time at work: the number of minutes spent actually working on assignments divided by the total time assigned to the task. (b) Rate of work output: the number of exercises and problems done divided by the number of minutes. (c) Accuracy of output: the number of problems and exercises done correctly divided by the total attempted. [Source: Chadwick, B. A. & Day, R. C. Systematic reinforcement: Academic performance of under-achieving students. *Journal of Applied Behavior Analysis*, 1971, *4*, 311–319. Copyright by Society for the Experimental Analysis of Behavior, Inc. Reproduced by permission.]

experimental group of interchangeable subunits, it more easily protects against such potential threats as multiple-intervention interference, repeated testing effects, and some instrumentation errors. Thus investigators could randomly sample a small number of units from a larger group at each point in time for measurement and/or exposure to the intervention. However, this procedure could no longer be conceptualized as a single-N experiment.

e. The Operant or ABAB Design.   The *ABAB* design is employed most frequently in $N = 1$ behavior modification research. Its affiliation with behavioral psychology has led some writers to label it the "operant" design (cf. Glass *et al.*, 1975). However, commonly labeled the *ABAB* design (Hersen & Barlow, 1976), it has also been referred to as a replication design in that the last two phases replicate the first two. In this context, the *ABAB* design is an extension of the *ABA* design in that an additional *B* phase is included.

The design has at least three major variations, although actual variations are numerous and are tailored to applied research needs. Leitenberg (1973b) described two variations in the design as used in the context of a "reversal" and "withdrawal." In the reversal variation baseline measures are taken prior to an intervention. Subsequently, an intervention is introduced into the data series. In the next phase a therapeutic reversal takes place. Leitenberg (1973b) indicates:

> If a particular procedure that has been applied to one behavior to make it increase and to make the behavior opposite it decrease, this operation is reversed in Phase 3. As a result, if the therapeutic procedure were really responsible for the observed effects in Phase 2, then in Phase 3 one should see the behavior that was formerly increased now decrease and the behavior that formerly decreased now increase. Phase 4 is a reinstatement of the conditions present in Phase 2. In summary, this sequence can be characterized as a "baseline, ABA" design [p. 89].

An example of the design is reported in Allen, Hart, Buell, Harris, and Wolf (1964) in the modification of isolate behavior of a nursery school child. Data reported in Fig. 1.7 show that the child spent approximately 45% of the time interacting with adults and only approximately 10% interacting with children. Allen *et al.* (1964) speculated that adult attention was being made contingent on the child's isolation, and baseline data confirmed this. In Phase 2, adult attention was redirected in a contingent manner such that when subject was in contact with other children, she and other children were attended to and praised for their activities; when she was alone or tried to approach adults, she was ignored. Figure 1.7 shows that after this procedure, she now spent approximately 60% of the time with other children and only 15% with adults. During phase 3, a "reversal" took place in that "isolate behavior" received adult attention and play with other children was ignored. In accordance with the reversal procedures, frequencies of behaviors reversed (i.e., percentage of interaction with adults increased and percentage of interaction with children decreased). The Phase 2 procedure was again implemented during Phase 4, and examination of Fig. 1.7 shows that behavior formally existent was reestablished. Follow-up measures were also taken after the experiment.

The withdrawal form of the *ABAB* design is probably used more frequently in behavior modification research than the reversal form (cf. Kazdin, 1977a). The major difference between the two designs is actually in the third phase. As in the reversal design, Phase 1 involves some baseline measures and Phase 2 consists of some intervention. However, Phase 3 consists of simply withdrawing or discontinuing the intervention rather than applying it to an alternative incompatible behavior. In the withdrawal design the major concern is what happens to a single relevant dependent variable when a single intervention is instituted, withdrawn, and then reinstated.

The *ABA* design employed by Twardosz *et al.* (1974) was actually a withdrawal *ABA* design since the second phase consisted of a withdrawal of quiet and dark conditions and a return to baseline or noise and light conditions. Twardosz *et al.* (1974) also employed a withdrawal *ABAB* design to investigate another aspect of the day care environment. The day care center consisted of an open environment with 24 children. During baseline (Days 1 to 5), a sleep area was separated from the rest of the center by a sheet hung from the ceiling to the floor (i.e., partition). On Day 6, the sheet was removed and remained down until Day 15. On Day 16 this intervention was withdrawn by returning to the partition condition established during baseline. The "open" condition was again reinstated on Day 23. Results reported in Fig. 1.8 suggest that the intervention had no effect on sleep. The "crying" dependent variable was slightly lower during the "open" or intervention phases.

In summary, the major difference between the reversal and withdrawal design is the third phase. In the reversal design, the second intervention is now applied to an alternative but incompatible behavior. In contrast, the second *A* phase of the withdrawal design simply involves removal of the previous intervention and return to baseline or no intervention conditions.

In yet another version of the *ABAB* design, a contingency between some behavior and environmental consequences is removed in the second phase. That is, consequences previously presented during the intervention phase continue to be in effect, but they are no longer contingent on performance (cf. Hall, Lund, & Jackson, 1968; Kazdin, 1977b). For example, a child may be contingently praised for playing with peers during *B* phases and a removal of these contingencies might consist of continued noncontingent praise (i.e., praising the child independently of his or her performance).

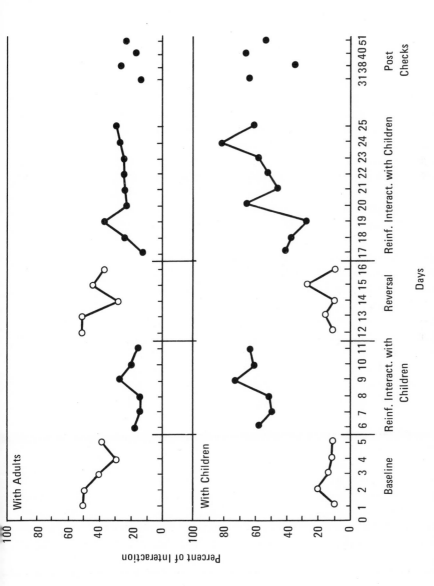

Fig. 1.7. Percentage of time spent in social interaction with children and adults during approximately two hours of each morning session. [Reprinted with permission from an article by Allen, K. E., Hart, B. M., Buell, J. S., Harris, F. R., & Wolf, M. M., published in *Child Development*, 1964, Vol. 35. Copyright by the Society for Research in Child Development.]

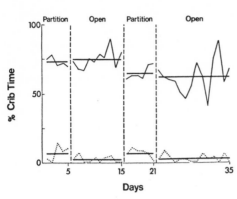

Fig. 1.8. Percentage of crib time the babies spent sleeping and crying during conditions when the sleep area of the open environment Infant Center was not separated from the rest of the Center (open conditions), and when the sleep area was separated by a partition from the rest of the center. Solid curves, sleeping; dotted curves, crying. Heavy solid lines indicate means for each condition. [Source: Twardosz, S., Cataldo, M. F., and Risley, T. R. Open environment design for infant and toddler day care. *Journal of Applied Behavior Analysis*, 1974, 7, 529–546. Copyright by Society for the Experimental Analysis of Behavior, Inc. Reproduced by permission.]

Alteration of this contingency may further revert behavior to prior baseline levels. Thus, when an investigator wishes to argue that some consequences do not control behavior except under response contingent conditions, this variation of the *ABAB* design is useful.

Other variations of the *ABAB* design include employing several interventions across phases before reinstating the second *A* phase or beginning with the intervention in an *BABA* fashion (e.g., Kazdin & Polster, 1973). More detailed accounts of the *ABAB* design variations can be found in Kazdin (1977b) and Hersen and Barlow (1976).

Few designs have received as much attention as the *ABAB* design and its variations. The subsequent considerations are primarily confined to its major uses in behavioral psychology. The *ABAB* design has considerably more validity than the basic design in that the intervention effect is replicated, thus *reducing* the probability of historical confounding. As noted, it can be used in applied research in the context of either withdrawal or reversal of experimental intervention. Leitenberg (1973b) observed that the reversal design, although showing dramatic effects, can be more cumbersome than the more common withdrawal design.

Investigators employing *ABAB* designs must achieve nearly identical levels of the dependent variable during the third or "return to baseline" phase, but this is sometimes difficult to achieve. To deal with this concern, Bijou, Peterson, Harris, Allen, and Johnson (1969) proposed that the second phase intervention be of relatively short duration (i.e., just long enough to demonstrate treatment effects). Glass *et al.* (1975) suggested that the logic of the *ABAB* design is too stringent in that some data series have no formal baseline (i.e., they are nonstationary). However, an investigator can still argue that an intervention had an effect, even though the data series did not return to baseline. Some of the issues will be discussed later in data evaluation.

Like the *ABA* design, logic of the withdrawal *ABAB* design is that intervention effects will occur under *I* and "go away" when *I* is removed. Clearly, this design could not be employed to study phenomena where *I* produces irreversible change in behavior (e.g., as in skill acquisition). Failure to return to baseline allows less confidence in experimental control. Hersen and Barlow (1976) noted that withdrawal designs are much better suited for investigations that do not emanate from the operant or reinforcement paradigm.

Arguing from a behavioral orientation, Browning and Stover (1971) indicated that successive replications of intervention and no intervention could encourage a client (perhaps especially children) to retrieve undesirable habits more quickly and possibly make such habits more durable. However, empirical research demonstrating this speculation is needed.

When applied investigators wish to determine the effects of some intervention relatively quickly, the *ABAB* design may prove impractical. Investigators must ensure that a second baseline is achieved and this may take considerably more time than one of the other designs (e.g., multielement, described later). Return to baseline phases may also be quite aversive to individuals involved in an applied program, particularly where they suffer direct consequences of a child's behavior (e.g., aggresion). It is also possible for staff to resist return to a baseline phase (cf. Hanley, 1970), thereby directly or indirectly sabotaging the program.

A final consideration in the use of the *ABAB* design involves ethical implications. After eliminating some behavior (e.g., self-mutilation, academic failure), there may seldom be justification to reestablish behavior under no treatment conditions to satisfy design requirements. To deal with the problem of an external withdrawal of treatment the investigator can employ brief probes (Bijou *et al.*, 1969) in which an intervention is terminated for only a short period. Unfortunately investigators may still object to such minireversals (Stoltz, 1976).

f. Interaction-Type Designs.   In some cases an investigator may wish to evaluate the interaction of two (or more) variables since these variables may have different effects when interacting with each other or interventions. In this case, a variety of "interaction" type designs can be employed (Glass *et al.*, 1975; Hersen & Barlow, 1976; Leitenberg, 1973a). Ideally, such a design should allow investigators to estimate the independent and interactive effects of two different interventions. However, to do this an investigator must be careful not to change more than one variable at a time when proceeding from one phase to the next (Hersen & Barlow, 1976). That is, when the investigator simultaneously manipulates two variables, it is impossible to know which of the two components (or how much of each) contributes to change in the data series. Noteworthy also is the fact that the manipulation of one-variable rule also holds regardless of the particular phase that is being evaluated. A published example will elucidate some of the options available to the investigator employing one interaction type design.

Broden, Hall, and Mitts (1971) used an interaction type design extension from an *ABAB* design to investigate the effects of self-recording on classroom behavior of an eighth-grade student. Results of their experiment reported in Fig. 1.9 show that they used an interactive component during the last four phases. These phases would be conceptualized as follows:

	I_1	Not I_1
Not I_2	Self-recording only (phase IV or B_2)	Neither self-recording nor praise (phase VIII or A_3)
I_2	Self-recording and praise (phase V or BC_1)	Praise only (phase VII or C_1)

Technically the Broden *et al.* (1971) study is not capable of isolating interactive (or additive effects) since the investigators manipulate more than one variable at a time. Their complete design is essentially represented as a $000I_1000\ 000\ I_1000\ I_1I_2000I_2000\ 000$ design (or *A–B–A–B–BC–C–A*), where I_2 or *C* is a different variable (i.e., praise).

From the *A–B–A–B* portion of their experiment, it is possible to assess the effect of self-recording. However, the extended design (i.e., *BC–C–A*) presents some problems of interpretation. If the investigators desired accurate evaluation of the interactive effects of self-recording and praise (i.e., *BC*) the following extended design would be necessary: *A–B–A–B–BC–B–BC*. Thus when this strategy is employed, the interactive effects of self-recording and praise can be examined systematically by comparing differences in trends between the adjacent *B* (self-recording) and *BC* (self-recording and praise) phases. Subsequent return to *B* and reintroduction of the combined *BC* phase would allow analysis of the additive and controlling effects of Praise. This does assume that the expected changes in the data series occur. However, the cardinal rule is to change one variable at a time when proceeding from one phase to the next.

The Broden *et al.* (1971) study does present another issue in the application of praise (*C*) following self-recording and praise (*BC*). Relabeling of

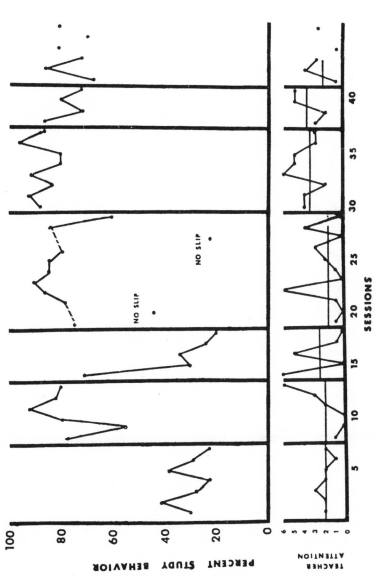

Fig. 1.9 A record of Liza's study behavior and/or teacher attention for study during: *Baseline*—before experimental procedures; *Self-Recording*—Liza recorded study or non-study on slips provided by counselor; *Baseline₂*—Self-recording slips withdrawn; *Self-Recording₂*—Self-recording slips reinstated; *Self-Recording Plus Praise*—Self recording slips continued and teacher praise for study increased; *Praise-Only*—Increased teacher praise maintained and self-recording withdrawn. *Baseline₃*—Teacher praise decreased to baseline levels (Source: Broden, M., Hall, R. V., & Mitts, B. The effect of self-recording on the classroom behavior of two eighth-grade students. *Journal of Applied Behavior Analysis,* 1971, *4,* 191–199.)

the last four phases yields an $A–B–C–A$ design. Hersen and Barlow (1976) note that if an investigator can show that A (now self-recording) and B (now self-recording and praise) do not differ, equivalence of A and B can be assumed (i.e., $A = B$). If one then collapses data across these two phases, an $A–C–A$ design emerges, which allows evaluation of C (praise only). Inclusion of a return to C phase (yielding an $A–C–A–C$ design) would further add credibility to the experimental analysis. However, the practice of combining data across phases could be questioned since there are no clear guidelines for suggesting when they are the same. Moreover, the possibility that the observed changes in behavior resulted from unrecognized factors that happen to covary with the manipulated one is rarely considered (Bandura, 1976). It would appear that even a statistical test showing lack of significant effects would not be appropriate since even a difference at the .05 level of confidence does not mean that they are not different in some other important ways, or that other controlling factors are operating.

Glass $et\ al.$ (1975) further noted that in their form of the interaction design, investigators are presented with the issue of what orders to introduce interventions. In the I^2 factorial design, there are 24 (4!) orders in which $I_1 I_2$, not I_1, and not I_2 can be arranged. Thus, effects may be specific to a particular arrangement of Is. One option to deal with this problem is to combine the interaction and inverted designs (the latter to be discussed), thus forming a multiple-N procedure. Although it would be impossible to use all possible combinations for practical reasons, a combined design like the following one could help tease apart some questions regarding the efficacy of a particular intervention employing interacting components:

$$OOO\ I_1\ OOO\ I_2\ OOO\ I_1,\ I_2\ OOO$$

$$OOO\ I_2\ OOO\ I_1\ OOO\ I_1,\ I_2\ OOO$$

$$OOO\ I_1,\ I_2\ OOO\ I_1,\ OOO\ I_2\ OOO$$

$$OOO\ I_1,\ I_2\ OOO\ I_2\ OOO\ I_1\ OOO$$

   $g.\ Single-N–Multiple-Baseline\ Designs.$ Multiple-baseline designs have been used quite extensively in behavior modification research. The design actually has three variations, one of which involves application of some intervention over different individuals or groups (Kazdin & Kopel, 1975). This multiple-N–multiple-baseline design will be discussed later in the chapter, since it involves somewhat different considerations when discussing internal and external validity (cf. Kratochwill, LeBlanc, & Piersel, 1977). In all variations of the multiple-baseline design, data are collected simultaneously across two or more baseline series. An intervention effect is demonstrated by showing that change in the data series accompanies introduction of the intervention at different points in time. In the two forms of the design to be discussed, a single subject or group receives some value of an independent variable over separate behaviors or situations.

(1) *Multiple baseline designs across behaviors.* Multiple baseline designs across behaviors allow investigators to assess two or more behaviors or responses in a single client or group. After a stable baseline is established on two or more behaviors, an intervention is introduced to only one behavior. It is expected that the intervention will change only the series to which it has been applied, with the other series remaining stable. After stability is achieved in all series, the intervention is applied to the second behavior series with remaining responses continued on baseline. This sequential introduction of interventions is continued until all behaviors have received the intervention. Thus, the design is like a series of *AB* designs with the same intervention introduced sequentially. An intervention effect is said to occur when each behavior changes only when the intervention is introduced.

Christopherson, Arnold, Hill, and Quilitch (1972) investigated the effects of a parent-administered token reinforcement program to reduce children's behavior problems. In the part of the experiment that will concern us, baseline measures were recorded for each of three children on some relevant social behaviors. In the case of Dollie, whining, bickering, and later, jumping on furniture were chosen for modification. Like the other children, Dollie had been introduced to a point-earning program (i.e., she could earn points for various tasks such as emptying trash). Through a point fine system, baseline data were taken for three behaviors with the point fine consequence scheduled for a specific behavior. One parent would approach Dollie and tell her that she had been fined and for which behavior she was fined. After approximately 2 weeks, point fines were begun for a second behavior, and 2 weeks subsequent, a point fine was initiated for the third behavior. Results reported in Fig. 1.10 suggest that the program was quite successful in reducin the frequency of problem behaviors.

(2) *Single-N–multiple baseline designs across situations, settings, or time.* Single-*N*–multiple-baseline design across situations, settings, or time can also be employed to change some response across separate situations, settings, or time periods, in a single subject or group. Procedural considerations are essentially the same as in the design's applications across separate behaviors. In an experiment reported by Hall, Cristler, Cranston, and Tucker (1970) a fifth-grade teacher concurrently measured the *same behavior* in three stimulus *situations* (i.e., after morning, noon, and afternoon recesses) on a group of 25 students. Posting names of pupils on a chart titled "Today's Patriots" was made contingent on being on time to noon

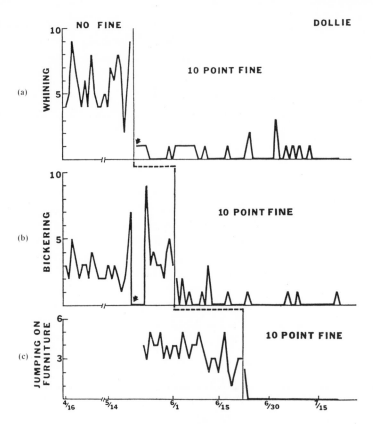

Fig. 1.10 Multiple Baseline analysis of the effects of introducing point fines on social behaviors of an 8-year-old girl. The arrows indicate when the point system was instituted for maintained behaviors (Source: Christopherson, E. R., Arnold, C. M., Hill, D. W., & Quilitch, H. R. The home point system: Token reinforcement procedures for application by parents of children with behavior problems. *Journal of Applied Behavior Analysis,* 1972, *5,* 485–497.)

recess, then sequentially to morning and afternoon recesses. An examination of Fig. 1.11 shows that tardiness was reduced to near zero rates at the points where the interventions were applied. While the remainder of the design variations added credibility to the experiment they need not concern us here.

There has been a rather extensive discussion of variations of multiple-baseline designs in the literature, and advantages and considerations surrounding their use are generally well known. The potential application of the design to different individuals (or groups), situations, or behaviors, and possible combination with other designs promotes flexibility and a variety

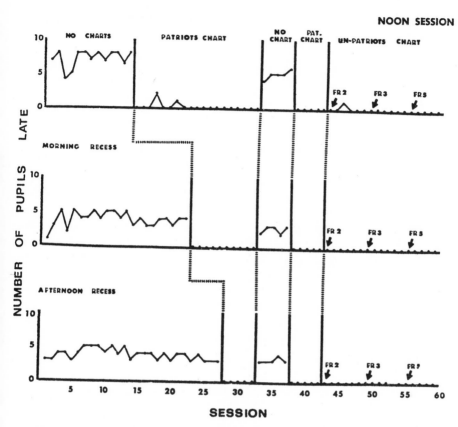

Figure. 1.11 A record of the number of pupils late in returning to their fifth-grade classroom after noon, morning, and afternoon recess. *No Charts*—baseline, before experimental procedures. *Patriots' Chart*—posting of pupil names on "Today's Patriots" chart contingent on entering class on time after recess. *No Chart*—Posting of names discontinued. Patriots' Chart— return to Patriots' Chart conditions. *Un-Patriots' Chart*—posting of names on "Un-Patriots'" chart contingent on being late after recess (FR 2) every two days, (FR 3) every three days, and (FR 5) every five days (Source: Hall, R. V., Christler, C., Cranston, S. S., & Tucker, B. Teachers and parents as researchers using multiple baseline designs. *Journal of Applied Behavior Analysis,* 1970, *3,* 247–255.)

of options for applied researchers (cf. Hall *et al.,* 1970). While no withdrawal of the intervention is typically instituted in the design, this feature could be added to strengthen its validity.

A major advantage of the design is that it promotes simultaneous measurement of several concurrent target measures. This is important because monitoring of concurrent behaviors allows a closer approximation to naturalistic conditions wherein numerous responses typically occur simultaneously and an examination of concurrent behaviors leads to analysis of behavioral covariation.

In situations where it is impossible or impractical to retrieve the initial baseline level of performance (as is necessary in the *ABAB* design), the multiple-baseline design provides an alternative. Relative to other designs that are used in applied therapeutic settings, the multiple-baseline design may also be more likely accepted by individuals in natural settings since no return to an aversive baseline is necessary.

Some writers have noted that inference may be weaker in the multiple-baseline design than in within-subject replications as occur in the *ABAB* design (Hersen & Barlow, 1976), since replications occur on different rather than the same experimental units (i.e., different behaviors or situations). Another considerations relates to the number of replications necessary to document experimental control. Although a minimum of *two* replications across behaviors and situations (and subjects or groups) provides modest evidence for an intervention effect, there is some consensus that a minimum of three replications be conducted (cf. Wolf & Risley, 1971). Hersen and Barlow (1976) recommend a minimum of three to four replications if practical and if experimental considerations permit. Typically, the more replications across behaviors or situations, the greater the likelihood that change is due to the intervention. However, this is a complex issue and depends on such factors as baseline duration, presence of trends or excessive variability in the data series, rapidity of series change after introduction of the intervention, as well as magnitude of change in the series (cf. Kazdin, 1977b). Therefore, when baselines are stable and intervention effects are both stable and reliable, few replications may be necessary. However, investigators must make an educated "guess" regarding how many replications are necessary and monitor data closely to make necessary changes as the experiment proceeds. The number of baselines used in the experimental literature has been quite variable, ranging from two (e.g., Milby, 1970) to nine (e.g., Clark, Boyd, & Macrae, 1975).

Another concern relates to the consistency of intervention effects over different behaviors and situations. Under these two conditions it must be assumed that a particular intervention will affect behaviors or situations similarly. Gelfand and Hartmann (1975) noted that it could be difficult to find two or more behaviors that are typographically or functionally similar so that when the same intervention is applied, change in the dependent variable is dramatic enough to document change as related to the intervention. While such factors threaten experimental validity, they are best considered procedural issues rather than design components per se (cf. Medland et al., 1976).

Like many time-series designs, the multiple-baseline procedures requires that a stable baseline series be established. Since a stable baseline must be established on two or more data series, considerably more time may be spent gathering data before an intervention can be introduced. Continuation of a stable baseline on the third or fourth situation, behavior, or individual may be difficult especially if measurement is reactive with the dependent variable. Related to this consideration is the probability that intervention effects may not be immediate, thereby necessitating continuation of baseline measures. Such factors may cause considerably more expense and time, especially when observational data are gathered.

Another potential limitation of these designs is that when an intervention is applied to the first behavior or situation, it could have widespread effects and alter more than the first target-dependent variable (cf. Kazdin & Kopel, 1975). Such effects have been noted when interventions are applied to different behaviors (e.g., Buell, Stoddard, Harris, & Baer, 1968) and across situations (e.g., Bennett & Maley, 1973). While the appearance of such generalized effects does not always mean that the intervention was not responsible for change in the series, it does militate against a strong claim because historical invalidating influences cannot be ruled out. To address this consideration, Kazdin and Kopel (1975) suggest that (1) baseline behaviors or situations should be as independent as possible, (2) four or more baselines should be used rather than less, and (3) programming for a temporary withdrawal of the intervention on one (but not necessarily all) data series could be used. Such recommendations clearly reflect some contrasts between design requirements and applied or therapeutic considerations for practitioners in natural settings (cf. Hartmann & Atkinson, 1973). For example, a practitioner may be unable to replicate the intervention over four separate behaviors and may have initially chosen the design to circumvent the necessity of withdrawing the intervention.

While the multiple-baseline design is frequently employed as an alternative to the ABAB design for ethical reasons, it can be argued that in subjecting only one behavior (or setting or individual) to treatment sequentially is temporarily denying treatment for some aspects of the client's behavior (or other client's behavior). Thus, denying treatment through the multiple-baseline design might be construed as unethical under some contitions (Stoltz, 1976).

h. Multiple-Schedule Designs. Multiple-schedule designs have been used relatively infrequently in applied research. Leitenberg (1973b) provided a description of such a design:

> This design is based on discrimination learning principles; that is, if the same behavior is treated differently in the presence of different physical or social stimuli, it will exhibit different characteristics in the presence of these stimuli [p. 93].

Hersen and Barlow (1976), in contrasting the multiple-baseline and multiple-schedule designs, suggested that whereas the multiple-baseline across behaviors involves interventions into each behavior individually in sequence, the multiple-schedule design involves intervention on the same behavior, but differentially under varying stimulus conditions. Thus, the logic of the design is that the same behavior treated differently in two different stimulus situations will follow two distinct patterns of performance.

O'Brien, Azrin, and Hersen (1969) used a multiple-schedule design to examine communications of 13 chronic mental patients housed on a token economy hospital unit. Patients were initially quite passive and exhibited a low rate of interaction–communication patterns. During various experimental phases patients were involved in a series of daily meetings with two group leaders (A or B). During each meeting a group leader directed three questions separately to each patient in attendance in order to prompt comments and suggestions. Over various phases two group leaders alternated in either following (I_1) or not following (I_2) suggestions made by patients.

Results reported in Fig. 1.12 suggest that while an equal number of suggestions were initially made in the presence of the two leaders, the subsequent number of suggestions made in the presence of leader A increased, whereas the number of suggestions offered in the presence of leader B decreased. During the second phase the role of the two leaders was reversed such that the number of suggestions made in the presence of B increased while those made in the presence of A decreased. A slight modification in procedure took place during phase 3 such that B followed 75% of the suggestions and A followed 25% of the suggestions. The next eight sessions demonstrated that responsiveness of the patients decreased for A and increased for B. The final phase involved having a naive leader conduct the meetings; however, the number of suggestions increased for A, who now granted 100%, whereas suggestions decreased under B, who now granted 0%. Thus results suggest that when group leaders follow suggestions made by patients, their responsiveness to suggestions increases the number of suggestions presented by the same patients during subsequent meetings. In a design context the experiment also shows that patients can discriminate

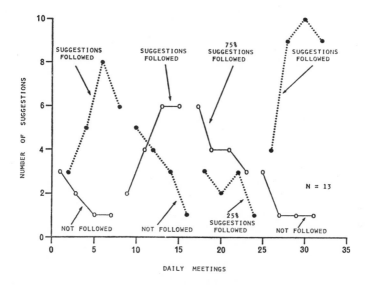

Fig. 1.12. The number of suggestions made by 13 mental patients daily, during the multiple schedule of experiment III. The schedule stimuli were the two meeting leaders *A* and *B*, who conducted the meetings and reacted to the suggestions. On days 25 to 33, a third person conducted the meetings during which group leaders *A* (●) and *B* (○) reacted to the suggestions as noted. [Source: O'Brien, F., Azrin, N. H., & Hersen, K. Increased communication of chronic mental patients by reinforcement and by response. *Journal of Applied Behavior Analysis*, 1969, *2*, 23–29. Copyright by Society for the Experimental Analysis of Behavior, Inc. Reproduced by permission.]

between group leaders in terms of their changing roles of reinforcing and nonreinforcing of suggestions.

Because the design has not been used frequently in applied research, its parameters are not as well known as other designs (see Agras, Leitenberg, Barlow, & Thompson, 1969; Leitenberg, 1973a; Wahler, 1969). The multiple-schedule design obviates the necessity for withdrawing treatment procedures. In this respect it has definite advantages over the *ABAB* design. The multiple-schedule design is also useful under conditions where an investigator cannot achieve complete independence of behaviors, as is necessary in the multiple-baseline design. Leitenberg (1973a) noted that one of the reasons for the infrequent use of the multiple-schedule design is that it is difficult to have independence of experimental procedures and/or two stimulus conditions. As a practical consideration, the design also requires very specific control of experimenters in the natural environment. Under some conditions this is difficult to achieve. Finally, the design may consist of a somewhat artificially structured approximation to naturalistic conditions (Hersen & Barlow, 1976).

Multielement-baseline design. The term multielement-baseline design was used by Sidman (1960) as an option to traditional procedures of using different groups of subjects for each baseline as in evaluating the effects of experimental extinction. For many years application of this design was primarily confined to basic research. Recently its potential usefulness for the applied researcher has been described by Ulman and Sulzer-Azaroff (1975). These authors also labeled the procedure "alternating conditions design" to reflect repeated measurement of some behavior under alternating conditions of the independent variable. Baseline and experimental conditions are presented in alternation in either a consistent or unpredictable (random) schedule, either within and/or from one session to the next. The multielement design is actually a type of the multiple-schedule design discussed above. Technically, the major difference between the two procedures is that the multiple-schedule design, when used with a particular reinforcement contingency, has a specific *schedule* attached with each stimulus component, whereas the multielement does not.

An example of the design with hypothetical data is shown in Fig. 1.13. Note that after a baseline is first established, experimental conditions are alternated (e.g., every other day or session) independent of behavior change. The degree of correlation between behavior and intervention can be observed from higher performance under the experimental conditions. If change is reliable after repeated alternations of baseline and intervention, experimental control is likely. Figure 1.13a represents a possible outcome from the same experiment had the multielement design not been employed. Note that appearance of trend in Fig. 1.13a militates against an intervention effect.

Since this design was introduced to applied investigators only recently, there are few examples in the literature. Examples provided by Ulman and Sulzer-Azaroff (1975) are more illustrative of either the multiple-schedule design (e.g., O'Brian *et al.*, 1969) or the concurrent-schedule design to be discussed (Browning, 1967). A definite advantage of the multielement-baseline design is that it does not require an investigator to retrieve the original baseline level established before the intervention is introduced. Thus the design has special application to study of learning phenomena where certain experiences during intervention may produce irreversible change in behavior (cf. Bandura, 1969). For example, if an investigator studies a child's performance in reading, certain skills induced by the intervention (e.g., ability to sound out words) obviously cannot be reversed or withdrawn. As the intervention proceeds it may be having an effect over the previous skill levels. Alternation of baseline and intervention may show the

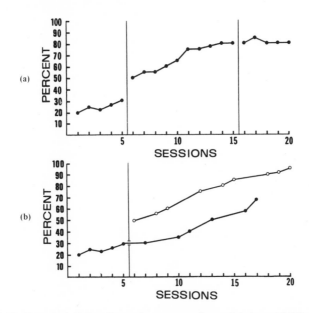

Fig. 1.13. Hypothetical data illustrating two experimental designs. (a) When the intervention was withdrawn, data did not reverse to original baseline level. Presence of trend also militates against an intervention effect. (b) A multielement-baseline design showing data over 20 sessions. Closed circles represent baseline conditions and open circles represent intervention sessions. The multielement-baseline design demonstrates experimental control despite trend.

efficacy of the intervention procedure when these conditions are graphed separately (as in Fig. 1.13b).

In some designs it is necessary to continue the experiment after some potentially useful and, from an investigator's perspective, clear intervention effects have occurred. For example, even after the successful first *B* phase in an *ABAB* design, one must still return to baseline and intervention phases to demonstrate reliable experimental control. In contrast, the multielement-baseline design can be terminated as soon as control is demonstrated. Furthermore, it may not be necessary to discard data if the study must be terminated prematurely. Relative to other design options, enough time may have elapsed in which the number of alternations stands as convincing evidence for experimental control.

Unstable baselines can be a major problem in time-series research. They can be a special problem in educational research because learning sets, reactive influences, and variation in task difficulty (e.g., 20 versus 30 item test responses) all potentially cause variability and sometimes trend. The multielement-baseline design would appear quite useful in these situations since intervention effects can be evaluated if they are reliably larger than baseline phases. This can occur in the presence of trend and when variability is not greater than the magnitude of intervention and baseline differences.

Frequent alternation of baseline and intervention characteristic of the multielement-baseline design adds credibility to the hypotheses that change in the dependent variable is functionally related to the independent variable. Ulman and Sulzer-Azaroff (1975) suggested that this feature is especially important in the use of complex behavior analysis (i.e., component analysis of multiple intervention procedures, comparative analysis of different interventions, and parametric analysis of single independent variables). The authors observe:

> Especially with complex behavior analysis, the more often the independent variables are manipulated, the more believable is the demonstration of experimental control. Thus, when conducting a complex behavior analysis, it is better to manipulate the independent variables repeatedly rather than only once, and it is better to vary the order of their presentation than not to do so [p. 384].

In this regard, there may be situations in which an investigator wishes to run more frequent alternation of the *AB* phases than is possible in the *ABAB* design. For example, some type of stability must be achieved within phases of the *ABAB* design. Several consecutive sessions may be necessary to achieve stability, which in turn takes additional time. More frequent alternations of baseline and intervention may also allow an investigator to include more independent variables than would be practical in other time-series designs.

The problem of multiple-intervention interference that occurs in the *ABAB* design is minimized in the multielement-baseline design since each condition occurs only briefly. This is based on the logic that a short exposure to the intervention would be less interfering than a long exposure (O'Brian, (1968). Such problems could also be minimized by counterbalancing order of intervention and baseline over the duration of the study. Since alterations are more frequent, more counterbalancing is possible than would be typical in *ABAB* designs.

The multielement-baseline design helps to deal with another problem prevalent in behavioral research—contrast effects. Reynolds (1968) described contrast as occurring when behavior changes under one set of circumstances are caused by changes in the behavioral consequences under a different set of circumstances (pp. 45–46). Contrast effects could possibly be controlled by (1) counterbalancing, (2) programming only one condition per session, or (3) assessing their existence (cf. Sidman, 1960), all of which could be accomplished in the multielement-baseline design (see Ulman & Sulzer-Azaroff, 1975, pp. 388–389).

Although the multielement-baseline design has been used in basic animal research, it has not been used often in applied research, making its limitations relatively unknown. Like the *ABAB* design, it requires return to baseline phases, albeit brief. While it is possible that relatively brief returns to baseline phases will be less objectionable to staff in applied settings, there may still be conditions under which it would be better to employ multiple-baseline or changing-criterion designs (discussed later).

Frequent alternation of baseline and intervention characteristic of multielement designs may also militate against intervention effects, which might otherwise occur if the intervention were carried for several consecutive sessions. Therefore, the *ABAB* or multiple-baseline designs could be more advantageous under conditions where an investigator expects an intervention effect only after more extended repeated application of the independent variable. Furthermore, research must elucidate situations under which such "false negatives" could appear.

Finally, the multielement design may have a potentially greater chance of training subjects to retrieve undesired habits than the *ABAB* design. Also, it can be noted that short intervention phases may not promote strong generalization effects and may further extinguish weakly acquired treatment effects. It remains for future research to determine how closely it will approximate an "ideal" experimental design.

i. Concurrent-Schedule Designs. Concurrent-schedule designs present a contrast to multiple-schedule designs; whereas the multiple-schedule strategy treats the same behavior differently under different stimulus conditions (i.e., stimuli presented individually in alternation), the concurrent-schedule design *simultaneously* exposes the same subject to different stimulus conditions (Hersen & Barlow, 1976). The design has been referred to by various names. Ulman and Sulzer-Azaroff (1975) referred to this procedure as the "multielement-baseline" design, but as we shall see, the concurrent-schedule design can be discriminated from this procedure. The design was introduced by Browning (1967) and subsequently discussed in Browning and Stover (1971) in the context of a "same-subject design for simultaneous comparison of three reinforcement contingencies" and has been labeled the "simultaneous treatment" design (cf. Kazdin, 1977a,b; McCullough, Cornell, McDaniel, & Mueller, 1974). The term concurrent-schedule design will be used to be consistent with Hersen and Barlow (1976).

The design has been used in basic laboratory research (e.g., Catania, 1968; Hernstein, 1970; Honig, 1966; Reynolds, 1968) but less frequently in applied research. An examination of Table 4 shows that the *A* phase represents baseline performance while *B*, *C*, and *D* in the vertical arrangement refer to different intervention conditions, which are administered simultaneously and successively in counterbalanced order. The B, C, or D phase is continued, depending on which was initially the most effective. The design combines the repeated measurement feature of time-series with a procedure, where each subject serves as his/her own control (cf. Benjamin, 1965). Thus the logic in the design involves a repeated measure methodology in which each subject receives all interventions.

McCullough et al. (1974) compared two interventions in the modification of cooperative behavior in a 6-year-old child. Condition A paired social reinforcement with cooperative behavior, while uncooperative behavior was ignored. Condition B paired social reinforcement with cooperative behavior, but administered a time-out procedure for uncooperative behavior. After baseline, a teacher and teacher aide alternated between a.m. and p.m. sessions for 2 days with a teacher administering intervention A and an aide administering intervention B.

During the next 2 days, procedures were reversed. A teacher administered intervention B and an aide administered A, while A and B were alternated between a.m. and p.m. The teacher (T) and aide (A) interventions are counterbalanced over Days 1–4. The design arrangement is as follows:

$$AM \quad A_{T_1} \quad B_{A_2} \quad A_{A_3} \quad B_{T_4}$$
$$PM \quad B_{A_1} \quad A_{T_2} \quad B_{T_3} \quad A_{A_4}$$

Data are presented in Fig. 1.14. Based on an analysis of variance of data from the first 2 days of intervention, McCullough et al. (1974) concluded that intervention B facilitated cooperative behavior. Visual analysis of Fig. 1.14 also suggests that B is the more effective. Based on these findings, the authors decided to continue B during phase 3.

A major advantage of the concurrent-schedule design is that it allows applied researchers to evaluate an intervention program in which two or more independent variables are presented simultaneously (Browning & Stover, 1972; Hersen & Barlow, 1976; McCullough et al., 1974). Compared to the $ABAB$ and multiple-baseline procedures, the concurrent-schedule design may also take less time to implement if only two or three interventions are compared. McCullough et al. (1974) reported that the design was efficient timewise since "in a matter of four days, two sets of treatment conditions were compared in such a way as to partially control for sequence and experimenter effects [p. 292]."

Like multielement-baseline designs, concurrent-schedule designs have not been used extensively enough for their limitations to be fully known and very few applications of the procedure have appeared in the applied literature. The design would seem to require great effort in planning and

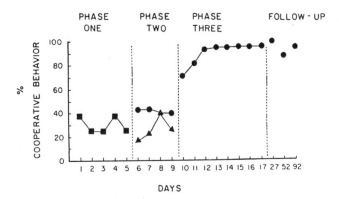

Fig. 1.14. Percentage of observation periods in which Cedric emitted cooperative behavior. The sudden jump in cooperative behavior during phase 3 is an artifact of combining cumulative percentage totals from phase 2 over the two conditions. However, the authors were not able to explain why the target rate increased as it did during the remainder of phase 3. ■, baseline; ▲, condition *A*; ●, condition *B*. [Source: McCullough, J. P., Cornell, J. E., McDaniel, M. H., & Mueller, R. K. Utilization of the simultaneous treatment design to improve student behavior in a first-grade classroom. *Journal of Consulting and Clinical Psychology*, 1974, *42*, 288–292. Copyright (1974) by the American Psychological Association. Reprinted by permission.]

monitoring of individuals responsible for implementing a program. However, this may depend on program complexity as well as resources available. It would appear that when three or more interventions are compared, confounding of experimenters, time employed for the intervention, or a comtion of these influences could be difficult to eliminate (cf. Kazdin, 1977b). It may also be difficult for subjects to discriminate different interventions. For example, a subject must discriminate that experimenters and time periods are not consistently correlated with a specific intervention because the intervention varies across each of these dimensions. This may be especially difficult for brief time periods. There is also a possibility that an intervention effect will be determined by other interventions introduced immediately before or concurrently with another intervention. Thus, effects of administering each intervention in the same phase may differ from situations in which interventions are administered in separate phases.

McCullough *et al.* (1974) suggested that an advantage of the design is that it "lends statistical support to the therapy decision-making process [p. 289]." Unfortunately, some applications of the concurrent-schedule design have involved a statistical procedure that is based on questionable validity for $N = 1$ data (cf. Kratochwill, Levin, & Benjamin, 1977). However, use of a statistical test is not necessary for successful use of the design (see Kazdin, in press b, for an example).

j. Changing-Criterion Design. Among the applied research procedures, the changing-criterion design is one of the most recent strategies developed. The design was first named by Hall (1971) and illustrated by Weis and Hall (1971). The design was described, but left unnamed, by Sidman (1960, pp. 254–256) and has recently been discussed in more detail (Hall & Fox, 1977; Hartmann & Hall, 1976). As conceptualized, the design requires initial baseline observations on a single target behavior. Subsequent to baseline, an intervention program is implemented in each of a series of intervention phases. A stepwise change in criterion rate for a target behavior is applied during each intervention phase. Thus, each phase of the design can be conceptualized as a baseline for each subsequent phase. Experimental control is demonstrated through successive replication of change in the target behavior, which changes with each stepwise change in criterion.

Hall and Fox (1977) employed the changing-criterion design on a child (Dennis) who refused to complete arithmetic assignments. In order to establish baseline measures he was given a worksheet with nine subtraction problems and one example over four sessions. The teacher worked an example and then told him to work as many problems as he could before recess. Feedback regarding correct problems was provided. The number of problems correct at the end of a 45-minute session formed the dependent variable.

During intervention phases, Dennis was required to correctly complete a specified number of problems each session. He was also told that if he worked these problems correctly by the end of the session he could take recess and play with a basketball. Failure to complete the problems by recess time resulted in remaining in his room until they were correctly computed. The criterion for each step was determined by computing a mean for the four baseline conditions and setting criterion at the next highest whole problem. The criterion was advanced only after he had achieved three consecutive days at a specified level of performance. A final goal was to shape (i.e., gradually move toward a goal in small steps) and maintain completion of textbook assignments.

Results reported in Fig. 1.15 show that Dennis correctly computed an average of 4.25 problems per session during baseline. When the first criterion was set at five problems with the opportunity to go to recess and to play basketball contingent on meeting criterion, Dennis met criterion in a minimum number of days for the next and all remaining criterion changes. During the sixth criterion change phase, criterion was held at 10 problems for 5 days to establish further that behavior was functionally related to the intervention. The final criterion change involved transferring Dennis to a formal textbook. Criterion was met on seven of nine days. Other examples and discussion of the application of the changing-criterion design to aca-

Fig. 1.15. A record of the number of math problems correctly solved by Steve, a "behavior disordered" boy during baseline, with recess, and the opportunity to play basketball contingent on changing levels of performance and return to textbook phases. [Source: Hall, R. V. & Fox, R. G. Changing-criterion designs: An alternate applied behavior analysis procedure. In C. C. Etzel, G. M. LeBlanc, & D. M. Baer (Eds.) *New developments in behavior research: Theory, method, and application. In honor of Sidney W. Bijou.* Hillsdale, N. J.: 1977, Lawrence Erlbaum Associates, in press. Reproduced by permission of the authors and publisher.]

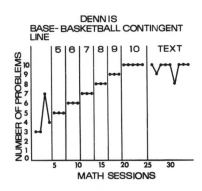

demic and behavioral problems can be found in several sources (e.g., Craighead *et al.*, 1976; Thorensen & Mahoney, 1974; Kazdin, 1975, 1977b).

When change in the dependent variable neatly conforms to an established criterion the design can be conceptualized as a series of repeated basic time-series or *AB* designs in that the effect is replicated consecutively with criterion changes. Hartmann and Hall (1976) observed that criterion changes function analogously to the sequential changes in behavior or situation (or individual) to which an intervention is applied in variants of the multiple-baseline design. However, the design does not require multiple independent behaviors or situations as is required in multiple-baseline designs.

The changing-criterion design seems especially advantageous in those situations in which an investigator wishes to gradually shape behavior over a period of time (Hall & Fox, 1977). The shaping feature helps to assure that a subject does not deteriorate in performance as might happen when an initial large change is scheduled. Hartmann and Hall (1976) observed that, in general, the design should be useful for evaluating acceleration problems in which stepwise increases in such measures as accuracy, frequency, duration, latency, or magnitude are therapeutic goals. Likewise, deceleration problems (e.g., eating and smoking) could be effectively evaluated using this design.

Hartmann and Hall (1976) indicated that changing-criterion designs require attention to three factors: (1) length of baseline and intervention, (2) magnitude of criterion changes, and (3) number of intervention or criterion changes. First, as in any design that employs a baseline phase, data should not change in the direction of an expected intervention effect (i.e., zero slope) or should be changing in the opposite direction of expected change due to the intervention. The authors suggest that the baseline phase should include more observations than each of the separate intervention phases to assure that stepwise changes in the rate of the target behavior are not naturally occurring in synchrony with criterion changes. With regard to intervention phases, the authors observe that:

> The length of each treatment phase and the magnitude and number of criterion changes are independent and should vary as a function of the total length of treatment, the variability of the target behavior, and the difference between baseline and anticipated terminal rate of the target behavior. Each phase must be long enough to allow the rate of the target behavior to restabilize at a new (and lower/changed) rate; it is stability after change has been achieved and before introduction of the next criterion change in the criterion, that is crucial to producing a convincing demonstration of control [p. 531].

For example, in the case of Dennis, stability was achieved in each phase before the next stepwise change in criterion was introduced.

In addition to this consideration, the magnitude of stepwise criterion changes must be large relative to such factors as ensuring detection of change in the behavior and variability in the data. When variability is large, investigators should consider both larger criterion changes and longer intervention phases. This must, of course, be balanced against a client's therapeutic needs.

With regard to the number of criterion changes needed to argue for experimental control, a general recommendation would be to follow guidelines advanced for the multiple-baseline design. While Hartmann and Hall (1976) suggested that *two* replications may be adequate, it is here recommended that at least four be employed. In addition, investigators could establish stronger inference for control by leaving criterion at an established level for several sessions beyond the normal stability criterion (cf. Hall & Fox, 1977) and/or return to a former criterion for a short time period. This does not assume, however, that complete withdrawal of the contingency will be necessary, as typically occurs in the *ABAB* withdrawal-type design. Both of these latter features appear essential when correspondence between criterion and behavior is not clear.

Hartmann and Hall (1976) suggested that visual data analysis can provide the best demonstration of experimental control. However, since changes from one phase to the next represent those in typical *AB*-type designs, statistical analysis appropriate for such data could be employed.

Finally, changing-criterion designs have not been used extensively in the applied research area for their useful parameters and limitations to be fully known. Increased application of the procedures will help fill the gaps in knowledge regarding their use.

2. MULTIPLE-N DESIGNS

a. Multiple-N–Single-I-Design.   In the multiple-N-single-I design investigators simultaneously apply an intervention into separate time-series observed on two or more experimental units "not distinguished by type" (Glass *et al.*, 1975). The design is a more primitive form of the multiple-N–multiple-baseline design, where single interventions are staggered rather than introduced simultaneously (discussed on pages 71–73).

While the design has not been used extensively as an independent experimental procedure, it has been employed as part of more adequate research designs. An example of how the design could be employed in applied research can be examined in an experiment by Kazdin and Klock (1973), who actually used an *ABAB* design. These authors investigated the effect of contingent nonverbal teacher approval on attentive behavior of 12 retarded children. After baseline data were recorded on contingent verbal and nonverbal teacher approval and student attentive behavior, a teacher was instructed to increase contingent nonverbal approval (e.g., smiles and physical contact) and to maintain her baseline level of verbal approval. A replication of the former phases was also instituted.

Results for the children's behavior suggested that the percentage of attentive behavior increased during the increase of nonverbal attentive behaviors by the teacher. While the authors first presented results for the mean of the group ($N = 12$), it is data reported for individual subjects that concern us here. An examination of Fig. 1.16 shows the attentive behavior for individual subjects (7 through 12). The first three phases of the design could be conceptualized as a multiple-N–single-I design.

Kazdin and Klock (1973) noted that of the 12 subjects, only Subject 11 was unaffected by the alteration in contingencies. This study shows how group means may obscure performance of a particular subject. The practice of displaying individual data is to be encouraged when an investigator suspects that intervention effects are not consistent over all subjects.

In the context of the above study, the multiple-N–single-I design permits an investigator to examine the pervasiveness of an intervention over groups or individual subjects. In this respect it provides a modest attempt to deal with experimental generalizability. The design may further lead to the characterization of experimental units that react differently to an intervention (as Subject 11). However, a problem occurs when a large group composes the experimental unit since individual reactions to the intervention may be obscured. As noted, it is advisable that the investigator who uses groups should examine individual effects to determine the pervasiveness of the intervention.

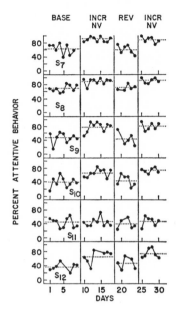

Fig. 1.16. Attentive behavior for individual subjects (7 through 12). Missing data points on individual figures represent absences on the part of the subject. [Source: Kazdin, A. E. & Klock, J. The effect of nonverbal teacher approval on student attentive behavior. *Journal of Applied Behavior Analysis*, 1973, *6*, 643–654. Copyright by Society for the Experimental Analysis of Behavior, Inc. Reproduced by permission.]

Perhaps the major shortcoming of the design is that intervention effects could occur as a function of a mere historical coincidence. Such historical confounding could be addressed by staggering the interventions, thereby replicating effects across time. This type of design is then actually a form of the multiple-baseline design.

b. Multiple-N–Multiple-I Design. The multiple-*N*–multiple-*I* design is similar to the multiple-*N*–single-*I* design with the exception that the former applies different interventions over separate subjects or groups while the latter employs only one and the same intervention.

Glass (1968) presented an example of the design in evaluating the effects of traffic fatalities in the Connecticut "crackdown" on speeding. On December 23, 1955, Abraham Ribicoff, then Governor of the State of Connecticut, announced that as of January 1, 1956, convicted speeders would have their licenses suspended for 30 days at the first offense, 60 days at the second offense, and indefinitely upon a third offense. Data from before and after the policy from the State of Massachusetts (as well as three other nearby states) supplemented the Connecticut data series to form a multiple-*N*–multiple-*I* design. Data reported in Fig. 1.17 show results for two of the five-state comparisons. Data are in the form of monthly adjusted fatalities per 100,000 driver miles for 60 months prior to and 48 months after January 1, 1956. Glass (1968) concluded that there was a statistically significant reduc-

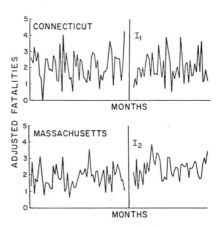

Fig. 1.17. Fatalities/100,000,000 driver miles minus monthly average plus two for Connecticut and Massachusetts, before and after the January 1956 crackdown on speeding in Connecticut. [Source: Glass, G. V. Analysis of data on the Connecticut speeding crackdown as a time-series quasi-experiment. *Law and Society Review,* 1968, *3,* 55–76. Reproduced by permission.]

tion as of January 1956 for Connecticut as compared with the four control states. However, regression effects possibly contributed to the intervention effect (cf. Campbell & Ross, 1968; Glass, 1968; Glass *et al.,* 1975).

In addition to advantages of the multiple-*N*–single-*I* design, Glass *et al.* (1975) suggested that multiple-*N*–multiple-*I* designs can have a large measure of validity in that the threat of multiple-intervention interference does not occur since a between-group rather than a within-group evaluation of the intervention effect is made. The design can be used for either randomized or nonrandomized groups. Random assignment of experimental units to interventions greatly improves the design. Matching of experimental units can also be employed, but appears more desirable when there are few experimental units (Glass *et al.,* 1975).

The design shares disadvantages of the multiple-*N*–single-*I* design. In addition, application of two or more distinct interventions may prove quite cumbersome and accrue more research time and expense than the multiple-*N*–single-*I* design. It is difficult to gauge this since it has not been employed extensively in research. Finally, the design does not allow examination of the influences of two or more interventions when applied to a single group.

c. Multiple Baseline across N. The logic of the multiple baseline across *N* is essentially the same as the application of the design across behaviors and situations. Baseline data are collected on some variable across at least two individuals or groups (*N* units). After a stable baseline is apparent over each unit, the intervention is applied to one unit. After a change in the data series is noted, the intervention is extended to the next unit, with this sequential introduction of the intervention continuing for all units for whom baseline data were gathered. Experimental control is likely if the dependent variable of each unit changes only when the intervention is introduced.

Wilson and Hopkins (1973) employed a multiple-baseline design to investigate the effects of quiet-contingent music on general noise levels of four seventh- and eighth-grade classrooms. Following baseline, popular radio music was used to reinforce maintenance of noise below an acceptable level of intensity (70 dB) in three of four classes. In the fourth class, an *ABAB* design was added to show that contingent presentation of radio music was inportant to control noise produced by students. Results were quite dramatic, as Fig. 1.18 shows.

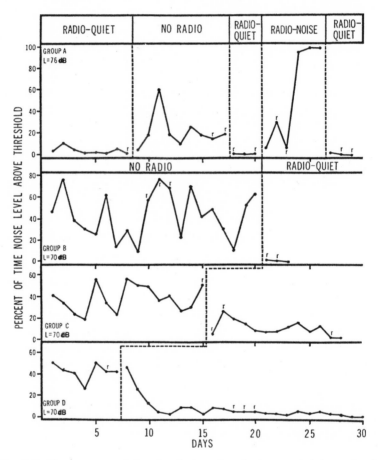

Fig. 1.18. The percentage of time that the intensity of noise exceeded the teacher-deter-mined threshold for all four classes. (Source: Wilson, C. W. & Hopkins, B. L. The effects of contingent music on the intensity of noise in junior high home economics classes. *Journal of Applied Behavior Analysis*, 1973, *6*, 269–275. Copyright by Society for the Experimental Analysis of Behavior, Inc. Reproduced by permission.)

Application of the multiple-baseline design across N has several unique considerations relative to the design's application within subjects. Relative to the multiple-N–single I design it allows stronger inference for experimental control since sequential introduction of interventions helps eliminate historical invalidating influences (cf. Kazdin & Kopel, 1975). Successful demonstration of an intervention across subject or groups also helps to establish the external validity of research results.

Generally, all considerations in the use of the design across behaviors and/or situations apply to its use across N. An additional concern is that the logic of the design assumes that the intervention will affect each N unit similarly. However, this is not always tenable since individuals may react in different ways. For example, a number of studies have demonstrated that changing behavior of one individual may alter behavior of other subjects who were "maintained" under baseline conditions (e.g., Broden, Bruce, Mitchell, Carter, & Hall, 1970; Kazdin, Silverman & Sittler, 1975; Kounin & Gump, 1958). Thus an investigator must ensure that subjects (or groups) do not communicate with each other regarding intervention procedures, intent of the study, and other features that would likely influence baseline stability. This is actually a procedural consideration rather than a design problem per se.

When different *groups* compose the experimental units, an investigator must consider "differential change in experimental unit composition" as a possible invalidating influence. When possible, subjects should be randomly assigned to conditions to eliminate an interaction of selection bias with other potentially invalidating influences (Kratochwill & Levin, in press).

d. Sequential Multiple-N–Multiple-I Design. The sequential multiple-N–multiple-I design combined features of the multiple-N–multiple-I and multiple-baseline design in that *different* interventions are introduced sequentially. Deese and Carpenter (1951) used such a design to explore the relationship between learning and drive level under which it occurs. Rats (Group I) were deprived of food for 22 hours (high drive) before each of 24 trials that involved running a short alley for food; during the final eight trials, these same rats were fed for one hour (low drive) before each trial. Group II received the high-drive/low-drive states in reversed order. The dependent variable was "latency" or the time between when the rat was placed in the apparatus and when it began to traverse the alley.

Results reported in Fig. 1.19 are expressed in terms of starting speeds (the reciprocal of the average of the logs of the latencies). Data have been coalesced by graphing them with respect to "trials" within each experiment rather than "time" across experiments. Maguire and Glass (1967) subjected these results to time-series statistical analysis. While the significance of the

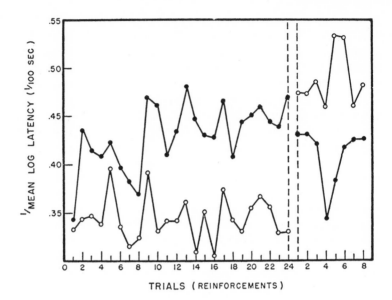

Fig. 1.19. Reciprocal of mean log latencies for a running response as a function of training under low and high hunger drive and test under reversed drives. ○, low drive/high drive; ●, high drive/low drive. (Source: Deese, J. & Carpenter, J. A. Drive level and reinforcement. *Journal of Experimental Psychology*, 1951, *42*, 236–238. Copyright (1951) by the American Psychological Association. Reprinted by permission.)

effect of shifting from a low- to a high-drive state (Group II) is visually apparent and typically would not be enhanced by statistical analysis, Group I data do *not* indicate a statistically significant shift downward after the 24th trial when subjected to time-series analysis.

The design has advantages over procedures in which multiple-intervention interference is a problem (e.g., single-*N*–multiple-*I* design). Glass *et al.* (1975) observed that in research with reactive social systems (e.g., schools) there may be difficulty instituting different interventions at the same point in time since they may be perceived as discriminatory by individuals with a priori knowledge of possible outcomes. The sequential multiple-*N*–multiple-*I* design can be employed to deal with such situations.

However, inference for experimental control is weaker in this sequential design than either in the simultaneous multiple-*N*–multiple-*I* design or the multiple-baseline design, since the possibility of historical confounding is greater. That is, the *same* intervention effect is *not replicated* since different *I*s are used in the sequential design.

  e. Stratified Multiple-N–Single-I Design. This design is essentially an extension of the multiple-*N*–single-*I* design and permits examination of different effects of the same intervention on stratified experimental units. In previous designs experimental units were not distinguished with respect to type. Glass *et al.* (1975) discussed a study originally reviewed by Glass, Tiao, and Maguire (1971) that presents an example of the design. For purposes of discussing a design application let us consider a hypothetical investigation conducted by a school psychologist to determine the effects of an 8-series 20-minute educational television program designed to teach social skills (e.g., cooperative behavior) to elementary school children. One constraint is that the program is broadcast at 10:00 a.m. from the local university station, making sequential introduction of the "intervention" to separate groups impossible. The program will be viewed by all children in grades one through four. Rather than combine data to form a basic design, the psychologist decides to stratify data on the basis of the four grades. Teachers are directed to record cooperative behavior during eight school days prior to the program and the 8 days during the program.

Hypothetical data reported in Fig. 1.20 show that the program had differential effects on the four grades chosen for the program. While some effect on cooperative behavior was noted in the first and third grades, effects are not so clear for the second- and fourth-grade children. A careful post hoc search for plausible causes for these results would be in order.

Use of the stratified multiple-*N*–single-*I* design represents further refinement in experimentation over designs where units are not distinguished by type. For example, demonstration that the intervention is effective by type promotes greater external validity. However, in addition to sharing disadvantages of the multiple-*N*–single-I design, the stratified multiple-*N*–single-*I* design may prove more difficult to implement due to diversity in group composition. Historical invalidating influences are also quite prob-

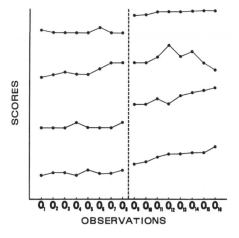

Fig. 1.20. Hypothetical data illustrating the impact of a 20-minute TV program designed to increase cooperative behavior in subjects stratified by grade (one through four). The first eight sessions represent "continuous" intervention.

SCORES

O_1 O_2 O_3 O_4 O_5 O_6 O_7 O_8 O_9 O_{10} O_{11} O_{12} O_{13} O_{14} O_{15} O_{16}

OBSERVATIONS

able. Consider, for example the possibility that teachers in grades one and four instituted a time-out from TV viewing for children who fail to exhibit cooperative behavior during the actual TV program. Such change in unit Composition × History interaction would then be a likely source of internal invalidity.

f. Inverted Design. In the inverted design two separate subjects or groups are observed under baseline conditions until a stable pattern of performance is established. I_1 is then introduced into the first series, followed by I_2 at a later point in time. The order of introduction of the two interventions is "reversed" in the second subject or group. Although the design has been labeled the "reversal" design by Glass *et al.* (1975) the term inverted is used here to avoid confusion over the use of reversal to refer to the *ABAB* design in the behavioral literature. The design has been described by Glass *et al.* (1975) but has few applications in the literature (e.g., Gottman & McFall, 1972; Tyler & Brown, 1968).

Tyler and Brown (1968) employed an inverted design to compare effects of contingent and noncontingent reinforcement on 15 court-committed delinquent boys ages 13 to 15. Their design represents a slight variation in that no baseline measures were taken:

Group I $R\,I_1\,OOO\,I_2\,OOO$ $(N = 9)$
Group II $R\,I_2\,OOO\,I_1\,OOO$ $(N = 6)$

During the first 17 days Group I received varying amounts of money, which increased as their score increased on a multiple-choice test over the previous night's Huntley–Brinkley news broadcast. Group II received 21¢ per day for the first 17 days for completing the test regardless of their score. The reinforcement schedules were switched on the eighteenth day. Results reported in Fig. 1.21 supported the hypothesis that test scores would be higher under contingent reinforcement on both between- and within-subject comparisons.

The inverted design can be conceptualized as two simultaneous single-N–multiple-I designs with the order of interventions inverted or switched. In this context it allows control of multiple-intervention interference, which threatens designs where multiple interventions occur within a single data series. As demonstrated in Tyler and Brown (1968), the inverted design can also be used without a baseline phase. In such cases I_1 is introduced immediately into the first group while I_2 is introduced into the second group. However, in this short form of the design an investigator cannot evaluate effects of I_1 and I_2 in isolation or without possible confounding of the multiple-intervention threat. Thus including the baseline phase provides a much stronger design and is recommended.

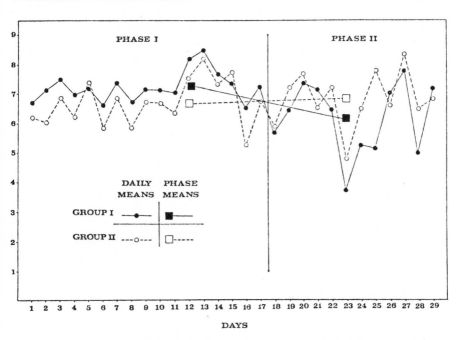

Fig. 1.21. The effect of contingent and noncontingent token reinforcement on true-false test performance. [Source: Tyler, V. O. & Brown, M. D. Token reinforcement of academic performance with institutionalized delinquent boys. *Journal of Educational Psychology*, 1968, *59*, 164–168. Copyright (1968) by the American Psychological Association. Reproduced by permission.]

Glass *et al.* (1975) noted that the design can be extended to include J interventions. However, to match design logic, $J!$ groups would be required to evaluate all possible orders of I. Thus, three Is would require 3! (or 6 groups) to have one of 6 possible orderings of interventions I_1, I_2, and I_3. In this regard, a major consideration of the inverted design is the cumbersome nature of ordering interventions that would be necessary to evaluate three or more interventions (e.g., 4! = 24 different orderings).

V. Considerations in the Choice of a Time-Series Design

In the aforementioned discussion of various time-series designs, many examples consisted of a single design. While an investigator may employ a single design, in actuality some combination of designs could be employed.

Factors surrounding the choice of a particular design relate to five considerations: ex post facto designs, planned single designs, revised single–combined designs, planned combined designs, and planned combined time-series designs with conventional designs.

A. Ex post facto Designs

Often an investigator must gather data in a retrospective fashion. In such cases data may already exist and the research is conceptualized post hoc. Such was the case in the Schnelle and Lee (1974) and Glass (1968) experiments. It has already been noted that such ex post facto experiments do not enjoy the degree of validity of planned experiments. Thus in many cases an investigator would have to settle for a more basic design since one could not typically expect "nature" to come up with a procedure that promotes high-quality methodology (e.g., multiple baseline).

B. Planned Single Designs

In many situations designs that promote a good deal of validity as well as answer specific research questions can be employed. For example, one may select an *ABAB* design because it promotes greater control for historical invalidating influences and the particular variable examined is clearly expected to reverse effects once the intervention is removed. Thus, experimental control may be clearly demonstrated with the choice of a single design.

C. Revised Single Designs

Investigators often initially select some design strategy but find that experimental control cannot be fully demonstrated. This may then lead to the decision to combine the design with another to add experimental credibility. For example, one may initially employ a single-N–multiple-I design, but to further document experimental control, I_1 may be withdrawn to determine its impact on the dependent variable. This is an important feature of time-series research since in some design variations it would allow continuation of the experiment. This option is often not available in more conventional large-N between-group designs (e.g., pretest–posttest designs).

D. Planned Combined Designs

Investigators may initially select some combined designs to ensure experimental control. For example, an investigator employing a multiple-baseline design across different groups may withdraw the intervention at some point after experimental control has been documented through the logic of the multiple-baseline design. Such a combined feature would greatly add credibility to the experiment.

E. Combined Time-Series and Conventional Designs

When the option is available and when it is desirable, time-series designs can be combined with more conventional designs. Although this feature of combined designs has not been prevalent, it has been suggested by a number of writers (e.g., Bandura, 1976; Kazdin, 1977b; Jones, 1974; Kratochwill, 1977; Shine, 1975a) and seems to be increasing in behavior modification research (Kazdin, 1975b,c). An example of designs combined on this dimension will help clarify potential advantages of this approach.

Herman, deMontes, Dominguez, Montes, and Hopkins (1973) evaluated the efficacy of an incentive procedure to increase punctuality of workers in an industrial setting in Mexico by combining an *ABAB* and between-group design procedure. An experimental ($N = 6$) and control group ($N = 6$) were formed from $N = 12$ individuals who were frequently tardy at work. The experimental group received daily monetary reinforcers during the intervention, which was presented in an *ABAB* design format. The control subjects received no reinforcers. Results reported in Fig. 1.22 demonstrate that in the experimental group, the intervention reduced tardiness relative to baseline while tardiness in the control group increased slightly.

While use of the *ABAB* design documented the reinforcer effect (i.e., assessed the magnitude of change *within* the experimental group), inclusion of a control group provided the investigators with information on the absolute levels of the dependent variable on subjects who were never exposed to the treatment (Kazdin, 1977b).

It should be noted that this is only one variation of the possible ways to combine time-series and conventional design strategies. Such combined designs can be used to evaluate different interventions (e.g., Kaufman & O'Leary, 1972) or can be nested within the cells of conventional group factorial designs (cf. Snow, 1974).

VI. Measuring Change in Time-Series Research

Generally, there are two procedures that can be employed to measure change in time-series experiments. The investigator can plot the data graphically and visually judge the pattern and level of change. In addition to this

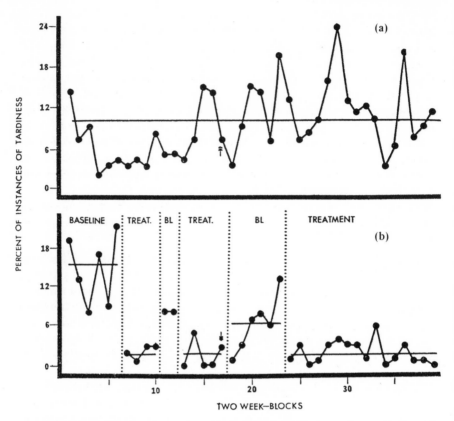

Fig. 1.22. (a) The percentage of instances of tardiness of the control group. (b) The same data from the treatment group. The arrows indicate that the points are based on one week instead of two weeks of data collection. Horizontal lines represent means for each condition. (Source: Herman, J. A., deMontes, A. I., Dominguez, B., Montes, F., & Hopkins, B. L. Effects of bonuses for punctuality on the tardiness of industrial workers. *Journal of Applied Behavior Analysis*, 1973, *6*, 563–570. Copyright by Society for the Experimental Analysis of Behavior, Inc. Reproduced by permission.)

strategy one of several inferential statistical tests can be employed to complement visual inspection. Both methods of analysis are actually statistical in nature since even with graphical analysis, statistical concepts (i.e., stability, variability, overlap, and numbers of scores) form the basis for data inference (cf. Jones *et al.*, 1977). Thus, visual and statistical analysis lie on a continuum with regard to the degree to which scores from the experiment are transformed.

While statistical analysis of time-series experiments was used in many areas of social science research for over a decade, visual analysis has been most pervasive in $N = 1$ applied behavior research (see Parsonson and Baer, Chapter 2 of this volume). There has also been a corresponding rejection of inferential statistical analysis of $N = 1$ data in some sectors of behavior modification research (e.g., Michael, 1974a), although many of the arguments advanced against statistics have been discussed in the context of problems with statistical inference in general (i.e., its use in large-N between-group methodology). The decision to employ a particular data analytic technique depends on numerous considerations that are detailed in the following sections and in subsequent chapters (see Elashoff & Thoresen, Chapter 6). Because visual analysis has been the most common form of evaluation in time-series research, this technique and issues surrounding its use are discussed first.

A. Visual Data Analysis

Psychologists have long depended on visual inspection to make conclusions from experimental data in time-series experiments. As Parsonson and Baer note in Chapter 2, in this form of analysis, data are transformed to line or bar graphs and plotted over different design phases. Sidman (1960) referred to this form of analysis as "criterion-by-inspection" and noted that one of the basic requirements for "success" of this method is that experimental manipulations produce large effects. In addition, the reader will see that successful visual analysis also depends on careful data presentation and aids available for interpretation. In recent years a number of considerations have been raised in visual analysis. These include trend, variability, and autocorrelation. The existence of trend, excessive variability, and autocorrelation can make visual analysis a complex endeavor.

1. TREND

In designs that employ a baseline phase (e.g., *ABAB*) data should ideally remain stable over the length of the phase. However, appearance of a trend may pose problems. Two types of trends are possible. First, baseline data may demonstrate a systematic shift in a direction opposite to that expected when an intervention is introduced. For example, if the investigator expects the intervention to increase in a certain direction, a trend could develop in the opposite direction. This situation may not be problematic if the intervention alters both the trend and level of the data series.

On the other hand, a trend in the same direction of the expected intervention effect could be quite problematic. The intervention would have to be quite dramatic to demonstrate that the change in the series was due to the intervention and not to an already existing tendency for change. Thus existence of trend in the direction of expected change due to the intervention is a major threat to the internal validity of the experiment.

To deal with this problem, several possible alternatives exist (Kazdin, 1977b). First, an investigator can wait for the baseline to stabilize prior to intervening (e.g., Baer et al., 1968). In some cases, the data series may stabilize and/or shift in the opposite direction. Unfortunately, this may take considerable time and often cannot be done for practical reasons, as in therapeutic endeavors.

A second alternative is to employ a design (e.g., ABAB) in which a procedure for changing the data series in the opposite direction can be repeatedly alternated with the intervention. For example, an intervention initiated after baseline could be withdrawn and a behavior incompatible with a target response could be reinforced. This recommendation is most useful for applied behavioral research, but even then, there may be difficulties in reversing or withdrawing certain behaviors.

A third possible solution is to employ a design in which trend is generally irrelevant to evaluation of the intervention. Some designs (e.g., concurrent-schedule or multielement design) allow examination of two or more separate interventions. An intervention could reveal the extent to which one procedure has more impact than another on an existing trend.

Another method to deal with trend is to employ one or more of the procedures to fit trend lines to time series data. These include the freehand method, semiaverage method, method of least squares, and a method for "ratio charts." All of these procedures are described in more detail in Parsonson and Baer (Chapter 2, this volume).

A final solution to deal with problematic trend is to employ a statistical test where the intervention effect can be tested against baseline level. These options are described in later chapters. In addition, Gelfand and Hartmann (1975) proposed that a procedure described by Freidman (1968) can provide a useful guideline for determining whether or not a statistical test is needed. A demonstration of this procedure appears in their book (see pp. 274–275).

2. VARIABILITY

As noted, variability can threaten the internal validity of the experiment. Generally, the greater the variability, the greater the difficulty in demonstrating change in the data series as a result of the intervention. With great variability the intervention effect must be large; if it is not large, an investigator cannot argue for an effect. In their work, Glass et al. (1975) noted that data from time-series experiments have frequently shown no effect through visual analysis, but when statistically analyzed, showed clear effects of the intervention. The converse can also be true in that effects that appear visually apparent are not when statistically analyzed (see also Gottman and Glass, Chapter 4 of this volume).

Depending on the particular focus and theoretical orientation of the research, variability can emanate from a variety of sources. Kazdin (1977b) observed that variability may result from behavior being controlled from a variety of stimuli, which results in drastically varying performances in their presence, cyclical events (both physiological and learned), unreliable recording by observers, as well as from naturally occurring variability in behavior.

Various techniques have been employed to deal with problematic variability. First, an investigator can reduce variability by averaging data points across consecutive days or sessions. Such averaging or transformation may reduce fluctuations and render data more stable (see Gottman & Leiblum, 1974). While this procedure distorts the actual picture of behavior change, it does clarify level and trend so that a reasonable estimation of intervention effects can be made. However, it would be better to control sources of variability than to transform scores statistically.

Another procedure that can be used as an adjunct judgmental aid to evaluate intervention effects from graphical displays is the mean line. Such mean lines are constructed by averaging data points within phases and then displaying the mean of that phase with a horizontal line. This procedure has been used relatively infrequently in some areas of time-series research (e.g., a little over 20 experiments using line graph reporting procedures were found in the *Journal of Applied Behavior Analysis* between 1968 and 1976). While this procedure clarifies the *level* of performance relative to each design phase, it may misrepresent trend. Such mean lines are different from trend lines computed from split middle or split median techniques (cf. Kazdin, 1976b; White, 1972, 1974).

3. AUTOCORRELATION

Autocorrelation refers to a correlation(s) among successive data points separated by different time intervals (lags) in the series (see Levin, Marascuelo, and Hubert, Chapter 3 of this volume, for further discussion). Kratochwill, Alden, Demuth, Dawson, Panicucci, Arntson, McMurray, Hempstead, and Levin (1974) demonstrated that in a typical observation of a child's time-on-task, temporally ordered scores in the time-series are highly related to each other (i.e., highly correlated in that a score for one observation point will predict subsequent points.) Thus, serial dependency is a typical characteristic of time-series data (see Gottman and Glass, Chapter 4 of this volume). Jones *et al.* (1977) suggested that unlike stability, variability, overlap, and number of scores, serial dependency is a property of behavioral data that heretofore has not been recognized as an important influence on visual judgment of graphical data. In contrast to other statistical properties of time-series scores, Jones and his associates argue that serial dependency cannot be appraised visually. They advocate application of time-series analysis as an alternative and present data to support their contention. Jones, Vaught, and Weinrott (1975) also noted that visual analysis is unreliable when compared to a statistical analysis of data, which is perfectly reliable (assuming no computational or clerical errors). Gottman and Glass also reach the same conclusion (see Chapter 4, this volume).

4. CRITERIA EMPLOYED FOR DATA ANALYSIS IN APPLIED BEHAVIORAL RESEARCH

Two criteria have been proposed for data analysis in applied behavioral time-series research, namely, experimental and therapeutic (cf. Kazdin, 1977c, in press b; Risley, 1970). The experimental criterion involves comparison of the dependent variable before and after the independent variable has been introduced. Actually, this data analysis consideration extends to all time-series designs and is not limited to those conventionally affiliated with applied behavioral analysis. Thus, the investigator must establish that there was a change from baseline to intervention either through visual and/or statistical analysis criteria. For example, in cases where data distributions in baseline and intervention phases do not overlap and where a credible design is employed, demonstration of experimental control is typically acceptable through visual analysis. In cases where data distributions do overlap to a large extent (as with trend or variability problems) demonstration of experimental control is more difficult. As Sidman (1960) noted, change due to the intervention must be large enough to override "baseline noise." All the aforementioned considerations relating to visual data analysis must then be considered. Also the investigator is presented with the issue of whether to depend on visual analysis or employ a statistical test.

It should be noted that investigators employing conventional between-group designs are also guided by experimental criteria. Typically, this has involved application of an inferential statistical test where certain significance levels are employed, as in hypothesis testing approaches. Rarely has a visual analysis of results from group experiments been employed to determine the experimental criterion.

In recent years applied behavior research has been guided by therapeutic or clinical criteria, in addition to experimental criteria. Increasingly, applied behavioral investigators have been concerned with determining the clinical significance of behavior change, a procedure referred to as social validation (cf. Kazdin, in press). Two procedures have been advanced to socially validate treatment outcomes. First, behavior of the subject is compared to peers who are not considered deviant. Second, subjective evaluations of the subject's performance are solicited from individuals in the natural environment. Selection of certain criteria also suggests that the behavior selected for change is itself of clinical or social significance (e.g., eliminating disruptive behavior in classrooms). Achieving behavior change of clinical significance presupposes a criterion toward which interventions can develop and against which program outcomes can be evaluated. For example, research conducted by Wolf and his associates at Achievement Place has used social validity criteria in evaluating various programs for predelinquent youth (e.g., Maloney, Harper, Braukmann, Fixsen, Phillips, & Wolf, 1976). Thus some researchers have used social validation of intervention effects by demonstrating the extent to which behavior change places subjects within an acceptable range when judged by the social community (see also Kazdin, 1977 for an excellent treatment of the topic for token economy research).

It should be observed that applied behavior investigators have argued that their data base is still at the stage where large effects are most important in advancing the science of applied behavior analysis (cf. Baer, 1977). The degree to which clinical criteria will influence future research remains to be determined. With the increased emphasis on large effects, future data in published reports would be predicted to far surpass that required by conventional experimental criteria, visual or statistical analyses not withstanding.

Some writers have chosen statistical analysis as a point of departure to contrast clinical and experimental criteria. However, *both* visual and/or statistical analysis, as discussed in this chapter, represent experimental criteria. Thus statistical analysis of data may add credibility to the experimental criterion. While therapeutic criteria would typically far surpass those required to reach statistical significance, such criteria would also typically far surpass acceptable experimental criteria based on visual analysis. This can easily be demonstrated in the case of a behavioral program designed to eliminate self-mutilation in autistic children. Reduction of the problem behavior from 80% to 20% may be both visually and statistically significant (vis à vis experimental criteria), but not reach clinical criterion (zero frequency as established by the investigator and the child's parents). Thus, the issue seems to be more of one of relative versus absolute level of change.

It should be observed that researchers employing large-N between-group designs have also addressed the issue of significant (typically statistical) and meaningful change (cf. Levin, 1975). For example, in some educational and psychological experiments employing null hypothesis testing approaches, much research has been based on such vague theoretical grounds that between-group point estimates of what should happen, given certain treatments, cannot be made. Thus some experiments are designed for significant differences rather than meaningful differences. However, power and sample size can be taken into consideration and statistical significance conceptualized in the context of meaningful differences between groups, as in choosing some N subjects to reach significance when the difference between groups is one-half a standard deviation. Furthermore, the percentage of variance accounted for can be determined and sample size based on this consideration. Short of a certain percentage of variance accounted for, results may be statistically significant but not meaningful.

In applied behavioral research employing time-series designs, experimental criteria can be considered ancillary to clinical criteria. Failure to achieve clinical criterion would probably lead the investigator to redesign or reconstruct the intervention program, even though an experimental criterion was established. An investigator might also exercise this option in conducting a large-N between-group experiment. However, exclusive use of clinical criteria in applied behavioral research may be shortsighted. First, an investigator must consider that a given change of therapeutic significance may be difficult to specify under some conditions since, for example, deviant behavior is defined in different ways by different individuals. Also, small intervention effects should not be overlooked since they may be important in future research endeavors (Hartmann, 1975) or show large effects in replication series. Finally, variables that initially produce small effects could combine to produce large effects in subsequent research (Kazdin, 1975a). Such combined variables may have great therapeutic significance in future applied research.

B. Statistical Analysis: General Considerations

One of the most remarkable features in the evolution of science has been the development of statistical theory and technique. While modern statistical theory guides many of the data analytic procedures in the social sciences, there has always been considerable controversy over the value of the statistical significance test in psychological research (e.g., Morrison & Henkel, 1970). Like Pearson, Fisher suggested that a close relationship between statistical theory and its application to specific scientific areas was necessary. In his classic text, the *Design of Experiments* he wrote "Statistical procedure and experimental design are only two different aspects of the same whole, and the whole comprises all the logical requirements of the complete process of adding to natural knowledge by experimentation [Fisher, 1935, p. 95]." As research inexorably drifted to subjects exhibiting increased variability, the problem of design of experiments taking this variability into account became more and more urgent (Neyman, 1970). Fisher played a primary role in this endeavor.

On the other hand, data-analytic procedures developing within the context of the experimental analysis of behavior challenged the value of large group designs and the corresponding use of statistical tests as a formal method of scientific inquiry on both practical and theoretical grounds (e.g., Sidman, 1960; Skinner, 1953). Over the years a number of writers have discussed disadvantages of employing inferential statistical procedures (e.g., Kazdin, 1976; Hersen & Barlow, 1976; Michael, 1974b; Skinner, 1956; Sidman, 1960). Some of these issues also reflect considerations in the use of inferential statistics in time-series research. The reader is referred to several sources for an introduction to these issues (e.g., Baer, 1977; Craighead *et al.*, 1976: Hartmann, 1975; Kazdin, 1976; Michael, 1974a).

1. STATISTICAL ANALYSIS FOR TIME-SERIES
   EXPERIMENTS

Statistical analysis of time-series experiments has been used relatively infrequently in psychological research. Part of this is due to the fact that development of statistical procedures for $N = 1$ time-series research has lagged behind procedures developed in the tradition of Fisher. This is ironic because Fisher (1935) may have been the first statistician to describe a statistical test for an $N = 1$ experiment. The hypothetical situation involved application of a randomization test to examine a claim that an individual could determine by tasting a cup of tea whether tea or milk was first put into the cup.

Over the years, there has been increased attention to $N = 1$ statistical tests. Some tests developed from diverse areas of science, and like some ANOVA procedures developed by Fisher, were not conceptualized specifically for psychological experiments. For example, time-series procedures were used extensively in economic research (e.g., Box & Jenkins, 1970) and Markov matrix analysis to the ecological study of birds (see Gottman and Notarius, Chapter 5 of this volume). There are a variety of statistical procedures that have been applied to $N = 1$ experiments. Some of these involve application to a particular time-series design previously discussed, while others are uniquely suitable to a specific methodological technique. The list includes variations of the conventional t test and ANOVA (Browning, 1967; Browning & Stover, 1971; Gentile, Roden, & Klein, 1972; McCullough *et al.*, 1974; Shine & Bower, 1971), multiple-regression procedures (Kelly, McNeil, & Newman, 1973), time-series analysis (Holtzman, 1963; Campbell & Stanley, 1966; Gottman, 1973; Glass *et al.*, 1975; Jones, Vaught, & Reid, 1975; Gottman, McFall, & Barnett, 1969; Box & Tiao, 1965), the p technique (e.g., Cattell, 1966; Coan, 1966; Nesselroade, 1970), cluster analysis (cf. Johnson, 1977), Markov matrix analysis (e.g., Stuart, 1971), the R_n

statistic (Revusky, 1967; Kazdin, 1976), and randomization tests (e.g., Edgington, 1967, 1975; Kazdin, 1976). All of these statistical tests have their unique application to certain data evaluation problems, and as we shall see, not all have been applied appropriately.

Investigators employing the aforementioned statistical procedures should consider two factors, namely, validity of the test employed and practicality or relevance of the procedure. First, a statistical test could be employed in a certain design, but fail to meet certain assumptions necessary in the appropriate use of the test (e.g., independence of error components). Some statistical tests employed in the analysis of $N = 1$ behavior modification research have been employed inappropriately.

The second issue is that application of a particular test may prove impractical in terms of design requirements (e.g., number of data points within a phase must be large to use a test appropriately) or potentially redundant to the design (e.g., large intervention effects occur making visual analysis valid and reliable). With regard to practicality, the statistical test should serve as a measurement tool and not dictate design (cf. Michael, 1974a). Application of a statistical test under conditions of large effects where variability and trend are not problematic is ancillary and is left up to the discretion of the investigator.

2. STATISTICAL TESTS IN $N = 1$ BEHAVIOR
MODIFICATION RESEARCH

If one were interested in examining various statistical procedures applied to $N = 1$ research, he/she would examine research areas in which the methodological approach to data evaluation involves a single case. Research in applied behavioral psychology provides such an area with its emphasis on the experimental analysis of individual organisms. It has also been within some sectors of behavior modification research where there has been controversy over application of inferential statistics to both large-N and $N = 1$ research paradigms. While one might expect few applications of statistics to $N = 1$ experiments because of arguments against group methodology, where statistical inference is typically necessary, Kratochwill and Brody (in press) found that this was not the case.

We observed that the controversy over statistical tests has two dimensions. First, a criticism of statistics has been leveled in the context of large-N between-group research where individual performance is obfuscated by statistical analysis (Kazdin, 1976; Sidman, 1960; Skinner, 1956). A second issue relates to the use of statistics in $N = 1$ research. The case against statistics has centered on the irrelevance over its use when experimental and therapeutic criteria are applied to the data (cf. Kazdin, 1976). The reader is referred to Levin, Marascuilo, and Hubert (Chapter 3 of this volume) for another dimension.

It is only recently that controversy over the use of statistical tests in $N = 1$ time-series applied behavioral research has come to the forefront. While statistical tests were employed in $N = 1$ behavior modification research prior to 1974 (e.g., Browning, 1967; Browning & Stover, 1971; Kelly et al., 1973; Stuart, 1971; Revusky, 1967; Weiss, Laties, Siegel & Goldstein, 1966), it was the publication of a paper by Gentile, Roden and Klein (1972) and series of rejoinders to their ANOVA procedure applied to an *ABAB* design (Hartmann, 1974; Keselman & Leventhal, 1974; Kratochwill et al., 1974; Michael, 1974a; Thoresen & Elashoff, 1974) that prompted increased interest in and debate over statistical tests in behavior modification research in general. However, even before these issues were raised it was generally accepted that statistical inference was not needed in $N = 1$ behavioral studies (e.g., Leitenberg, 1973b).

To examine the actual frequency and type of inferential statistical tests employed in behavior modification research, Kratochwill and Brody (in press) assessed four major behavior modification journals from their inception through 1974. Results suggested that *Behavior Research and Therapy* (BRT) contained the highest percentage of articles using inferential statistical tests. However, these journals and the remaining three [*Journal of Applied Behavior Analysis* (JABA), *Behavior Therapy* (BT), *Journal of Behavior Therapy and Experimental Psychiatry* (JBTEP)] all contained some between-group experiments that relied on some form of inferential statistic. Analysis-of-variance and nonparametric tests were generally the most commonly employed statistical test used in the five major journals. In addition, all journals contained some number, though small, of $N = 1$ experiments that used a statistical test to evaluate intervention effects. Kratochwill and Brody's (in press) findings suggested that a distinction between various practices within behavior modification in terms of design requirements is becoming increasingly blurred, since, for example, some journals that initially published $N = 1$ experiments are increasingly publishing large-N between-group studies (see also Kazdin, 1975a).

Kratochwill and Brody (in press) also suggested that a number of statistical procedures employed in $N = 1$ behavioral studies have been used inappropriately. Specifically, the ANOVA procedure developed by Gentile et al. (1972) for *ABAB* designs and the ANOVA for the "simultaneous treatment design" by Browning (1967) have been inappropriately applied in $N = 1$ experiments [see Epstein, Hersen, & Hemphill, 1974; and McCullough et al. (1974) for inappropriate applications, respectively]. On the other hand, some statistical tests have been applied quite appropriately, though infrequently, such as time-series analysis (e.g., Schnelle & Lee, 1974;

Schnelle, Kerchner, McNees, & Lawler, 1975), nonparametric (e.g., Revusky, 1967), and Markov analysis (e.g., Stuart, 1971).

A major issue raised in this context is that the use of statistics in time-
series or other small- or single-N experiments should be perceived as a
separate and distinct issue from application of inferential tests in conventional large-N designs. This point has been obscured in some of the writings
and discussions over issues related to statistical analysis of time-series or
other $N = 1$ experimental paradigms. In the chapters that follow, the authors
discuss their own perception of the issues in the application of various data-
analytic techniques. The reader must determine their parameters of usefulness in scientific research based on the presentation of their advantages and
limitations.

C. In Closing

In this chapter, I have presented a brief historical perspective on time-
series research, discussed major sources of internal and external validity in
various time-series designs, presented some major time-series designs, and
described some issues relevant to data analysis. The advances in this area as
well as controversies over various issues suggest that time-series methodology
is actually evolving. This chapter along with the specific introductions of
data-analytic techniques in subsequent chapters should promote more refined methodological tools in the conduct of time-series and other small-N
research. The positive achievements of this endeavor will be empirically determined in future scientific research.

ACKNOWLEDGMENTS

The author gratefully acknowledges the contributions of Drs. Joel R. Levin, David H.
Barlow, John R. Bergan, Sidney W. Bijou, Janet D. Elashoff, Alan E. Kazdin, and Carl E.
Thoresen to his thinking and for the constructive feedback in the preparation of this chapter.

REFERENCES

Agras, W. S. Toward the certification of behavior therapists? *Journal of Applied Behavior
Analysis*, 1973, *6*, 167–173.
Agras, W. S., Leitenberg, H., Barlow, D. H., & Thompson, L. Instructions and reinforcement
in the modification of neurotic behavior. *American Journal of Psychiatry*, 1969, *125*, 1435–
1439.
Allen, K. E., Hart, B. M., Buell, J. S., Harris, F. R., & Wolf, M. M. Effects of social reinforcement on isolate behavior of a nursery school child. *Child Development*, 1964, *35*, 511–518.

Allport, G. W. *Pattern and growth in personality*. New York: Holt, Rinehart, & Winston, 1961.

Allport, G. W. The general and unique in psychological science. *Journal of Personality*, 1962, *30*, 405–422.

Anderson, S. B., Ball, S., & Murphy, R. T. *Encyclopedia of educational evaluation*. San Francisco: Jossey-Bass, Inc., 1974.

Ashton, P. T. Cross-cultural Piagetian research: An experimental perspective. *Harvard Educational Review*, 1975, *4*, 475–506.

Baer, D. M. In the beginning there was the response. In E. Ramp & G. Semb (Eds.). *Behavior analysis: Areas of research and application*. Englewood Cliffs, N.J.: Prentice-Hall, 1975.

Baer, D. M. Perhaps it would be better not to know everything. *Journal of Applied Behavior Analysis*, 1977, *10*, 167–172.

Baer, D. M., Wolf, M. M., & Risley, T. R. Some current dimensions of applied behavior analysis. *Journal of Applied Behavior Analysis*, 1968, *1*, 91–97.

Bandura, A. *Principles of behavior modification*. New York: Holt, Rinehart, & Winston, 1969.

Bandura, A. Self-reinforcement: Theoretical and methodological considerations. *Behaviorism*, 1976, *5*, 135–155.

Barlow, D. H., & Hersen, M. Single case experimental designs: Use in applied clinical research. *Archives of General Psychiatry*, 1973, *29*, 319–325.

Benjamin, L. S. A special Latin square for the use of each subject "as his own control." *Psychometrika*, 1965, *30*, 499–513.

Bennett, P. S., & Maley, R. S. Modification of interactive behavior in chronic mental patients. *Journal of Applied Behavior Analysis*, 1973, *6*, 609–620.

Bergan, J. R. *Behavioral consultation*. New York: Charles E. Merrill, 1977.

Bergin, A. E. Some implications of psychotheraphy research for therapeutic practice. *Journal of Abnormal Psychology*, 1966. *71*, 235–246.

Bergin, A. E., & Strupp, H. H. *Changing frontiers in the science of psychotherapy*. Chicago: Aldine–Atherton, 1972.

Bijou, S. W. What psychology has to offer education—now. *Journal of Applied Behavior Analysis*, 1970, *3*, 65–71.

Bijou, S. W., Peterson, R. F., & Ault, M. H. A method to integrate descriptive and experimental field studies at the level of data and empirical concepts. *Journal of Applied Behavior Analysis*, 1968, *1*, 175–191.

Bijou, S. W., Peterson, R. F., Harris, F. R., Allen, K. E., & Johnston, M. S. Methodology for experimental studies of young children in natural settings. *The Psychological Record*, 1969, *19*, 177–210.

Bolger, H. The case study method. In B. B. Wolman (Ed.), *Handbook of Clinical Psychology*. New York: McGraw-Hill, 1965.

Boring, E. G. *A history of experimental psychology*. New York: Appleton-Century-Crofts, 1950.

Boring, E. M. Newton and the spectral lines. *Science*, 1962, *136*, 600–601.

Box, G. E. P., & Jenkins, G. M. *Time series analysis: Forecasting and control*. San Francisco: Holden-Day, 1970.

Box, G. E. P., & Tiao, G. C. A change in level of non-stationary time series. *Biometrika*, 1965, *52*, 181–192.

Bracht, G. H., & Glass, G. V. The external validity of experiments. *American Educational Research Journal*, 1968, *5*, 437–474.

Broden, M., Bruce, C., Mitchell, M. A., Carter, V., & Hall, R. V. Effects of teacher attention on attending behavior of two boys at adjacent desks. *Journal of Applied Behavior Analysis*, 1970, *3*, 199–203.

Broden, M., Hall, R. V., & Mitts, B. The effects of self-recording on the classroom behavior of two eighth-grade students. *Journal of Applied Behavior Analysis*, 1971, *4*, 191–199.

Browning, R. M. A same-subject design for simultaneous comparison of three reinforcement contingencies. *Behavior Therapy*, 1967, *5*, 237–243.

Browning, R. M., & Stover, D. O. *Behavior modification in child treatment: An experimental and clinical approach*. Chicago: Aldine-Atherton, 1971.

Brunswick, E. *Perception and the representative design of psychological experiments*. Berkeley: University of California Press, 1956.

Buell, J., Stoddard, P., Harris, F., & Baer, D. M. Collateral social development accompanying reinforcement of outdoor play in a preschool child. *Journal of Applied Behavior Analysis*, 1968, *1*, 167–173.

Campbell, D. T. Reforms as experiments. *American Psychologist*, 1969, *24*, 409–429.

Campbell, D. T., & Ross, H. L. The Connecticut crackdown on speeding: Time series data in quasi-experimental analysis. *Law and Society Review*, 1968, *3*, 33–53.

Campbell, D. T., & Stanley, J. C. *Experimental and quasi-experimental designs for research*. Chicago: Rand McNally, 1966.

Catania, A. C. (Ed.). *Contemporary research in operant behavior*. Glenview, Ill.: Scott, Foresman, 1968.

Cattell, R. B. The data box: Its ordering of total resources in terms of possible relational systems. In R. B. Cattell (Ed.), *Handbook of multivariate experimental pshcyology*. Chicago: Rand McNally, 1966.

Chadwick, B. A., & Day, R. C. Systematic reinforcement: Academic performance of underachieving students. *Journal of Applied Behavior Analysis*, 1971, *4*, 311–319.

Chassan, J. B. Probability processes in psychoanalytic psychiatry. In J. Scher (Ed.), *Theories of the mind*. New York: Free Press of Glencoe, 1962.

Chassan, J. B. *Research designs in clinical psychology and psychiatry*. New York: Appleton-Century-Crofts, 1967.

Christopherson, E. R., Arnold, C. M., Hill, D. W., & Quilitch, H. R. The home point system: Token reinforcement procedures for application by parents of children with behavior problems. *Journal of Applied Behavior Analysis*, 1972, *5*, 485–497.

Clark, H. B., Boyd, S. B., & Macrae, J. W. A classroom program teaching disadvantaged youths to write biographic information. *Journal of Applied Behavior Analysis*, 1975, *8*, 67–75.

Coan, R. W. Child personality and developmental psychology. In R. B. Cattell (Ed.), *Handbook of multivariate experimental psychology*. Chicago: Rand McNally, 1966.

Cook, T. D. & Campbell, D. T. The design and conduct of quasi-experiments and true experiments in field settings. In M. D. Dunnette & J. P. Campbell (Eds.), *Handbook of industrial and organizational research*. Chicago: Rand McNally, 1976.

Cornfield, J., & Tukey, J. Average values of mean squares in factorials. *Annals of Mathematical Statistics*, 1956, *27*, 907–949.

Cox, D. R. *Planning of Experiments*. New York: John Wiley & Sons, 1958, 308.

Craighead, W. E., Kazdin, A. E., & Mahoney, M. G. *Behavior modification: Principles, issues, and applications*. Boston: Houghton Mifflin, 1976.

Davidson, P. O., & Costello, C. G. $N = 1$: *Experimental studies of single cases*. New York: Van Nostrand–Reinhold, 1969.

Deese, J., & Carpenter, J. A. Drive level and reinforcement. *Journal of Experimental Psychology*, 1951, *42*, 236–238.

Drew, C. J. *Introduction to designing research and evaluation*. Saint Louis: The C. B. Mosby Co., 1976.

Dukes, W. F. $N = 1$. *Psychological Bulletin*, 1965, *64*, 74–49.

Du Mas, F. M. Science and the single case. *Psychological Reports*. 1955, *1*, 65–76.

Edgar, E., & Billingsley, F. Believability when $N = 1$. *Psychological Record*, 1974, *24*, 147–160.

Edgington, E. S. Statistical inference from N = 1 experiments. *Journal of Psychology*, 1967, *65*, 195–199.

Edgington, E. S. N = 1 experiments: Hypothesis testing. *The Canadian Psychologist*, 1972, *2*, 121–134.

Edgington, E. S. Randomization tests for one-subject operant experiments. *The Journal of Psychology*, 1975, *90*, 57–68.

Epstein, L. H., Hersen, M., & Hemphill, D. P. Music feedback in the treatment of tension headache: An experimental case study. *Journal of Behavior Therapy and Experimental Psychiatry*, 1974, *5*, 59–63.

Eysenck, H. J. The effects of psychotherapy: An evaluation. *Journal of Consulting Psychology*, 1952, *16*, 319–324.

Fisher, R. A. Studies in crop variation. *Journal of Agricultural Science*, Part II, 1921, *11*, 8–35.

Fisher, R. A. *The design of experiments*. London: Oliver & Boyd, 1935.

Freidman, H. Magnitude of experimental effect and a table for its rapid estimation. *Psychological Bulletin*, 1968, *70*, 245–251.

Gelfand, D. M., & Hartmann, D. P. *Child Behavior: Analysis and therapy*. New York: Pergamon Press, 1975.

Gentile, J. R., Roden, A. H., & Klein, R. D. An analysis of variance model for the intrasubject replication design. *Journal of Applied Behavior Analysis*, 1972, *5*, 193–198.

Glass, G. V. Analysis of data on the Connecticut speeding crackdown as a time-series quasi-experiment. *Law and Society Review*, 1968, *3*, 55–76.

Glass, G. V., Tiao, G. C., & Maguire, T. O. Analysis of data on the 1900 revision of German divorce laws as a time-series quasi-experiment. *Law and Society Review*, 1971, *4*, 539–562.

Glass, G. V., Willson, V. L., & Gottman, J. M. *Design and analysis of time-series experiments*. Boulder: University of Colorado Press, 1975.

Gottman, J. M. N-of-one and N-of-two research in psychotherapy. *Psychological Bulletin*, 1973, *80*, 93–105.

Gottman, J. M., & Lieblum, S. R. *How to do phychotherapy and how to evaluate it*. New York: Holt, Rinehart, & Winston, 1974.

Gottman, J. M., & McFall, R. M. Self-monitoring effects in a program for potential high school dropouts: A time-series analysis. *Journal of Consulting and Clinical Psychology*, 1972, *39*, 273–281.

Gottman, J. M., McFall, R. M., & Barnett, J. T. Design and analysis of research using time-series. *Psychological Bulletin*, 1969, *72*, 299–281.

Hall, R. V. (Ed.). *Behavior management series: Part II, Basic principles*. Lawrence, KS: H. & H. Enterprises, 1971.

Hall, R. V., Cristler, C., Cranston, S., & Tucker, B. Teachers and parents as researchers using multiple baseline designs. *Journal of Applied Behavior Analysis*, 1970, *3*, 247–255.

Hall, R. V., & Fox, R. G. Changing-criterion designs: An alternative applied behavior analysis procedure. In C. C. Etzel, G. M. LeBlanc, & D. M. Baer (Eds.), *New Developments in behavioral research: Theory, method, and application*. In honor of Sidney W. Bijou. Hillsdale, NJ: Lawrence Erlbaum Associates, 1977.

Hall, R. V., Lund, D., & Jackson, D. Effects of teacher attention on studying behavior. *Journal of Applied Behavior Analysis*, 1968, *1*, 1–12.

Hanley, E. M. Review of research involving applied behavior analysis in the classroom. *Review of Educational Research*, 1970, *40*, 597–625.

Hartmann, D. P. Forcing square pegs into round holes: Some comments on "An analysis-of-variance model for the intrasubject replication design." *Journal of Applied Behavior Analysis*, 1974, *7*, 635–638.

Hartmann, D. P. Some dangers of methodological intolerance in applied behavioral research.

In A. E. Kazdin (Ed.), *Use of statistics in N = 1 research.* Symposium presented at the American Psychological Association, Chicago, August, 1975.

Hartmann, D. P. Considerations in the choice of interobserver reliability estimates. *Journal of Applied Behavior Analysis,* 1977, *10,* 103–116.

Hartmann, D. P., & Atkinson, C. Having your cake and eating it too: A note on some apparent contradictions between therapeutic achievements and design requirements in N = 1 studies. *Behavior Therapy,* 1973, *4,* 589–591.

Hartmann, D. P., & Hall, R. V. A discussion of the changing criterion design. *Journal of Applied Behavior Analysis,* 1976, *9,* 527–532.

Hawkins, R. P., & Dotson, V. A. Reliability scores that delude: An Alice in Wonderland trip through the misleading characteristics of interobserver agreement scores in interval recording. In E. Ramp & G. Semb (Eds.), *Behavior analysis: Areas of research and application.* Englewood Cliffs, NJ: Prentice-Hall, 1975, pp. 359–376.

Heermann, E. F., & Braskamp, L. E. (Eds.). *Readings in statistics for the behavioral sciences.* Englewood Cliffs, NJ: Prentice-Hall, 1970.

Herman, J. A., deMontes, A. I., Dominguez, B., Montes, F., & Hopkins, B. L. Effects of bonuses for punctuality on the tardiness of industrial workers. *Journal of Applied Behavior,* 1973, *6,* 563–570.

Hernstein, R. J. On the law of effect. *Journal of the Experimental Analysis of Behavior,* 1970, *13,* 243–266.

Hersen, M., & Barlow, D. H. *Single case experimental designs: Strategies for studying behavior change in the individual.* New York: Pergamon Press, 1976.

Hoch, P. H., & Zubin, J. (Eds.). *The evaluation of psychiatric treatment.* New York: Grune & Stratton, 1964.

Holtzman, W. H. Statistical models for the study of change in the single case. In C. W. Harris (Ed.), *Problems in measuring change.* Madison: University of Wisconsin Press, 1963.

Honig, W. K. (Ed.). *Operant behavior: Areas of research and application.* New York: Appleton-Century-Crofts, 1966.

Hopkins, B. L., & Hermann, J. A. Evaluating inter-observer reliability of interval data. *Journal of Applied Behavior Analysis,* 1977.

Hoyer, W. J. Aging as intraindividual change. *Developmental Psychology,* 1974, *10,* 821–826.

Huntington, E. *Mainsprings of civilization.* New York: John Wiley & Sons, 1945.

Inglis, J. *The scientific study of abnormal behavior.* Chicago: Aldine, 1966.

Johnson, S. M., & Bolstad, O. D. Reactivity to home observation: A comparison of audio recorded behavior with observers present or absent. *Journal of Applied Behavior Analysis,* 1975, *8,* 181–185.

Johnson, S. M., & Lobitz, G. K. Parent manipulation of child behavior in home observations: A methodological concern. *Journal of Applied Behavior Analysis,* 1974, *7,* 23–31.

Jones, H. G. In search of an idiographic psychology. *Bulletin of the British Psychological Society,* 1971, *24,* 279–290.

Jones, R. R. Design and analysis problems in program evaluation. In P. O. Davidson, F. W. Clark, & L. A. Hammerlynck (Eds.), *Evaluation of behavioral programs.* Champaign, IL: Research Press, 1974.

Jones, R. R., Vaught, R. S., & Reid, J. B. Time-series analysis as a substitute for single-subject analysis of variance designs. In G. R. Patterson, I. M. Marks, J. D. Matarazzo, R. A. Myers, G. E. Schwartz, & H. H. Strupp (Eds.), *Behavior change.* Chicago: Aldine, 1975.

Jones, R. R., Vaught, R. S., & Weinrott, M. *Visual versus statistical inference in operant research.* Paper presented in a symposium entitled "Use of statistics in N = 1 research" at the American Psychological Association, Chicago, August, 1975.

Jones, R. R., Vaught, R. S., & Weinrott, M. Time-series analysis in operant research. *Journal of Applied Behavior Analysis*, 1977, *10*, 151–166.

Kaplan, A. *The conduct of inquiry: Methodology for behavioral science.* San Francisco: Chandler Publishing Co., 1964.

Kass, R. E., & O'Leary, K. D. *The effects of observer bias in field-experimental settings.* Paper presented at a symposium entitled "Behavior analysis in education" at the University of Kansas, Lawrence, April, 1970.

Kaufman, K. F., & O'Leary, K. D. Reward, cost, and self-evaluation procedures for disruptive adolescents in a psychiatric hospital school. *Journal of Applied Behavior Analysis*, 1972, *5*, 293–304.

Kazdin, A. E. Methodological and assessment considerations in evaluating reinforcement programs in applied settings. *Journal of Applied Behavior Analysis*, 1973, *6*, 1–23.

Kazdin, A. E. *Behavior modification in applied settings.* Homewood, IL: Dorsey Press, 1975. (a)

Kazdin, A. E. Characteristics and trends in applied behavior analysis. *Journal of Applied Behavior Analysis*, 1975, *8*, 332. (b)

Kazdin, A. E. The impact of applied behavior analysis on diverse areas of research. *Journal of Applied Behavior Analysis*, 1975, *8*, 212–229. (c)

Kazdin, A. E. Statistical analysis for single-case experimental designs. In M. Hersen & D. Barlow (Eds.), *Single case experimental designs: Strategies for studying behavior change.* New York: Pergamon Press, 1976.

Kazdin, A. E., Artifact, bias, and complexity of assessment: The ABC's of reliability. *Journal of Applied Behavior Analysis*, 1977 *10*, 141–150. (a)

Kazdin, A. E. Methodology of applied behavior analysis. In T. A. Brigham & A. E. Catania (Eds.), *Social and instructional processes: Foundations and application of a behavioral analysis.* New York: Irvington/Naiburg–John Wiley & Sons, 1977. (b)

Kazdin, A. E. *The token economy: A review and evaluation.* New York: Plenum Press, 1977. (c)

Kazdin, A. E. The influence of behavior preceding a reinforced response on behavior change in the classroom. *Journal of Applied Behavior Analysis*, in press. (a)

Kazdin, A. E. Assessing the clinical or applied importance of behavior change through social validation. *Behavior Modification*, in press. (b)

Kazdin, A. E., & Klock, J. The effect of nonverbal teacher approval on student attentive behavior. *Journal of Applied Behavior Analysis*, 1973, *6*, 643–654.

Kazdin, A. E., & Kopel, S. A. On resolving ambiguities in the multiple-baseline design: Problems and recommendations. *Behavior Therapy*, 1975, *6*, 601–608.

Kazdin, A. E., & Polster, R. Intermittent token reinforcement and response maintenance in extinction. *Behavior Therapy*, 1973, *4*, 386–391.

Kazdin, A. E., Silverman, N. A., & Sittler, J. L. The use of prompts to enhance vicarious effects of nonverbal approval. *Journal of Applied Behavior Analysis*, 1975, *8*, 279–286.

Kelly, F. J., McNeil, K., & Newman, I. Suggested inferential statistical models for research in behavior modification. *The Journal of Experimental Education*, 1973, *41*, 54–63.

Kelly, M. B. A review of the observational data collection and reliability procedures reported in the *Journal of Applied Behavior Analysis*. *Journal of Applied Behavior Analysis*, 1977, *10*, 97–101.

Kempthorne, O. The design and analysis of experiments, with some reference to educational research. In R. O. Colliar & S. M. Elas (Eds.), *Research design and analysis: The second annual Ohio Delta Kappa symposium on educational research.* Bloomington, IN: Phi Delta Kappa, 1961.

Kerlinger, F. N. *Foundations of behavioral research.* New York: Holt, Rinehart, & Winston, 1973.

Keselman, H. J., & Leventhal, L. Concerning the statistical procedures enumerated by Gentile et al.: Another perspective. *Journal of Applied Behavior Analysis*, 1974, *7*, 643–645.

Kiesler, D. J. Basic methodological issues implicit in psychotherapy process research. *American Journal of Psychotherapy*, 1966, *20*, 135–155.

Kiesler, D. J. Experimental designs in psychotherapy research. In A. E. Bergin & S. L. Garfield (Eds.), *Handbook of psychotherapy and behavior change: An empirical analysis*. New York: John Wiley & Sons, 1971.

Kintz, B. L., Delprato, D. J., Mettee, D. R., Parsons, C. E., & Schappe, R. H. The experimenter effect. *Psychological Bulletin*, 1965, *63*, 223–232.

Kirk, R. E. *Experimental design: Procedures for behavioral sciences*. Belmont, CA: Brooks/Cole Publishing Co., 1968.

Krantz, D. L. The separate worlds of operant and non-operant psychology. *Journal of Applied Behavior Analysis*, 1971, *4*, 61–70.

Krasner, L. Behavior therapy. *Annual Review of Psychology*, 1971, *22*, 483–532.

Kratochwill, T. R. N = 1. An alternative research strategy for school psychologists. *Journal of School Psychology*, 1977, *15*, 239–249.

Kratochwill, T. R., Alden, K., Demuth, D., Dawson, D. L., Panicucci, C., Arntson, P. H., McMurray, N. M., Hempstead, J. O., & Levin, J. R. A further consideration in the application of an analysis of variance model for the intrasubject replication design. *Journal of Applied Behavior Analysis*, 1974, *7*, 629–633.

Kratochwill, T. R., & Brody, G. H. Single subject designs: A perspective on the controversy over employing statistical inference and implications for research and training in behavior modification. *Behavior Modification*, in press.

Kratochwill, T. R., LeBlanc, C. P., & Piersel, W. C. *Further consideration in the use of the multiple baseline design across subjects*. Paper presented at the annual meeting of the American Educational Research Association, New York, April, 1977.

Kratochwill, T. R., & Levin, J. R. What time-series designs may have to offer education. *Contemporary Educational Psychology*, in press.

Kratochwill, T. R., Levin, J. R., & Benjamin, L. S. *On the applicability of the Benjamin special Latin square design to single subject research*. Paper presented at the annual meeting of the American Educational Association, New York, April, 1977.

Kratochwill, T. R., & Wetzel, R. J. Observer agreement, credibility, and judgement: Some considerations in presenting observer agreement data. *Journal of Applied Behavior Analysis*, 1977, *10*, 133–139.

Kounin, J. S., & Gump, P. V. The ripple effect in discipline. *Elementary School Journal*, 1958, *59*, 158–162.

Lana, E., & Lubin, A. The effect of correlation on the repeated measures design. *Educational and Psychological Measurement*, 1963, *23*, 729–739.

Lazarus, A. A., & Davidson, G. Clinical innovation in research and practice. In A. E. Bergin & S. L. Garfield (Eds.), *Handbook of psychotherapy and behavior change: An empirical analysis*. New York: John Wiley & Sons, 1971.

Leitenberg, H. *Interaction designs*. Paper presented at the meeting of the American Psychological Association, Montreal, August, 1973. (a)

Leitenberg, H. The use of single-case methodology in psychotherapy research. *Journal of Abnormal Psychology*, 1973, *82*, 87–101. (b)

Levin, J. R. Determining the sample size for planned and post hoc analysis of variance comparisons. *Journal of Educational Measurement*, 1975, *12*, 99–108.

Lewin, K. *A dynamic theory of personality selected papers*. New York: McGraw-Hill, 1935.

Lindquist, E. F. *Design and analysis of experiments in psychology and education*. Boston: Houghton-Mifflin, 1953.

Lipinski, D. & Nelson, R. O. The reactivity and unreliability of self-recording. *Journal of Consulting and Clinical Psychology*, 1974, *42*, 118–123.

Maguire, T. O., & Glass, G. V. A program for the analysis of certain time-series quasi-experiments. *Educational and Psychological Measurements*, 1967, *27*, 743–750.

Maloney, D. M., Harper, T. M., Braukmann, C. J., Fixsen, D. L., Phillips, E. L., & Wolf, M. M. Teaching conversation-related skills to pre-delinquent girls. *Journal of Applied Behavior Analysis*, 1976, *9*, 371.

Masling, J. Role-related behavior of subject and psychologist and its effects upon psychological data. In D. Levine (Ed.), *Nebraska Symposium on Maturation* (Vol. 14). Lincoln: University of Nebraska Press, 1966.

McCullough, J. P., Cornell, J. E., McDaniel, M. H., & Mueller, R. K. Utilization of the simultaneous treatment design to improve student behavior in a first-grade classroom. *Journal of Consulting and Clinical Psychology*, 1974, *42*, 288–292.

McNamara, J. R. Ways by which outcomes measures influence outcomes in classroom behavior modification research. *Journal of School Psychology*, 1975, *13*, 104–113.

McNamara, J. R., & MacDonough, T. S. Some methodological considerations in the design and implementation of behavior therapy research. *Behavior Therapy*, 1972, *3*, 361–378.

Medland, M., Hapkiewicz, W. G., & Molidor, J. *Strong designs for behavior analysis*. Paper presented at the annual meeting of the American Educational Research Association, San Francisco, April, 1976.

Michael, J. Statistical inference for individual organism research: Mixed blessing or curse? *Journal of Applied Behavior Analysis*, 1974, *7*, 647–653. (a)

Michael, J. Statistical inference for individual organism research: Some reactions to a suggestion by Gentile, Roden, & Klein. *Journal of Applied Behavior Analysis*, 1974, *7*, 627–628, (b).

Milby, J. G. Modification of extreme social isolation of contingent social reinforcement. *Journal of Applied Behavior Analysis*, 1970, *3*, 149–152.

Morrison, D. E., & Henkel, R. E. (Eds.). *The significance test controversy*. Chicago: Aldine, 1970.

Namboodiri, N. K. Experimental designs in which each subject is used repeatedly. *Psychological Bulletin*, 1972, *77*, 54–64.

Nesselroade, J. R. Application of multivariate strategies to problems of measuring and structuring long-term change. In L. R. Goulet & P. B. Baltes (Eds.), *Life-span developmental psychology: Research and theory*. New York: Academic Press, 1970.

Neyman, J., R. A. Fisher (1890–1962): In appreciation. In E. F. Heermann & L. A. Braskamp (Eds.), *Readings in statistics for the behavioral sciences*. Englewood Cliffs, NJ: Prentice-Hall, 1970.

Norman, A., & Broman, H. J. Volume feedback and generalization techniques in shaping speech of an electively mute boy: A case study. *Perceptual and Motor Skills*, 1970, *31*, 463–470.

O'Brien, F. Sequential contrast effects with human subjects. *Journal of the Experimental Analysis of Behavior*, 1968, *11*, 537–542.

O'Brien, F., Azrin, N. H., & Hersen, K. Increased communication of chronic mental patients by reinforcement and by response priming. *Journal of Applied Behavior Analysis*, 1969, *2*, 23–29.

O'Leary, K. D., & Kent, R. Behavior modification for special action: Research tactics and problems. In L. A. Hammerlynck, L. C. Handy, & E. J. Mash (Eds.), *Behavior change: Methodology concepts and practice*. Champaign, IL: Research Press, 1973.

Orne, M. T. On the social psychology of the psychological experiment: With particular reference to demand characteristics and their implications. *American Psychologist*, 1962, *17*, 776–783.

Parsons, H. M. Reexamining the Hawthorne effect. *Science*, 1974, *183*, 922–932.

Paul, G. L. Strategy of outcome research in psychotherapy. *Journal of Psychology*, 1967, *31*, 104–118.

Paul, G. L. Behavior modification research: Design and tactics. In C. M. Franks (Ed.), *Behavior therapy: Appraisal and status*. New York: McGraw-Hill, 1969.

Powell, J., Martindale, A., & Kulp, S. An evaluation of time-sample measures of behavior. *Journal of Applied Behavior Analysis*, 1975, *8*, 463–469.

Reid, J. B. Reliability assessment of observation data: A possible methodological problem. *Child Development*, 1970, *41*, 1143–1150.

Repp, A. C., & Deitz, S. M. Reducing aggressive and self-injurious behavior of institutionalized retarded children through reinforcement of other behaviors. *Journal of Applied Behavior Analysis*, 1974, *7*, 313–325.

Revusky, S. H. Some statistical treatments compatible with individual organism methodology. *Journal of the Experimental Analysis of Behavior*, 1967, *19*, 319–330.

Reynolds, G. S. *A primer of operant conditioning*. Glenview, IL: Scott, Foresman, 1968.

Risley, T. R. Behavior modification: An experimental–therapeutic endeavor. In L. A. Hammerlynck, P. O. Davidson, & L. E. Acker (Eds.), *Behavior modification and ideal mental health services*. Alberta, Canada: University of Calgary, 1970.

Risley, T. R., & Wolf, M. M. Strategies for analyzing behavioral change over time. In J. Nesselroade & H. Reese (Eds.), *Life-span developmental psychology: Methodological issues*. New York: Academic Press, 1972.

Rosenberg, M. *Society and the adolescent self-image*. Princeton, NJ: Princeton University Press, 1965.

Rosenthal, R. *Experimenter effects in behavioral research*. New York: Appleton-Century-Crofts, 1966.

Ross, H. L., Campbell, D. T., & Glass, G. V. Determining the social effects of a legal reform: The British "breathalyzer" crackdown, 1967. *American Behavioral Scientist*, 1970, *13*, 493–509.

Schnelle, J. F., Kerchner, R. E., McNees, M. P., & Lawler, J. M. Social evaluation research: The evaluation of two police patrolling strategies. *Journal of Applied Behavior Analysis*, 1975, *8*, 353–365.

Schnelle, J. F., & Lee, J. F. A quasi-experimental retrospective evaluation of a prison policy change. *Journal of Applied Behavior Analysis*, 1974, *7*, 484–496.

Scott, P., Burton, R. B., & Yarrow, M. Social reinforcement under natural conditions. *Child Development*, 1967, *38*, 53–63.

Shapiro, M. B. The single case in fundamental clinical psychological research. *British Journal of Medical Psychology*, 1961, *34*, 255–262.

Shapiro, M. B. The single case in fundamental clinical-psychological research. *Journal of General Psychology*, 1966, *74*, 3–23.

Shapiro, M. B., & Ravenette, P. T. A preliminary experiment of paranoid delusions. *Journal of Mental Science*, 1959, *105*, 295–312.

Shine, L. C. Five research steps designed to integrate the single-subject and multisubject approaches to experimental research. *Canadian Psychological Review*, 1975, *16*, 179–184. (a)

Shine, L. C., & Bower, S. M. A one-way analysis of variance for single-subject designs. *Educational and Psychological Measurement*, 1971, *31*, 105–113.

Shontz, F. C. *Research methods in personality*. New York: Appleton-Century-Crofts, 1965.

Sidman, M. *Tactics of scientific research*. New York: Basic Books, 1960.

Simkins, L. The reliability of self-recorded behavior. *Behavior Therapy*, 1971, *2*, 83–87.

Simonton, D. K. Cross-sectional time-series experiments: Some suggested statistical analyses. *Psychological Bulletin*, 1977, *84*, 489–502.

Skinner, B. F. *The behavior of organisms*. New York: Appleton-Century-Crofts, 1938.

Skinner, B. F. *Science and human behavior*. New York: Macmillan, 1953.

Skinner, B. F. A case history in scientific method. *American Psychologist*. 1956, *11*, 221–233.

Skinner, B. F. Operant behavior. *American Psychologist*, 1963, *18*, 503–515.

Skinner, B. F. Operant behavior. In W. K. Honig (Ed.), *Operant behavior: Areas of research and application*. New York: Appleton-Century-Crofts, 1966.

Smith, N. C. Replication studies: A neglected aspect of psychological research. *American Psychologist*, 1970, *25*, 970–975.

Snow, R. E. Representative and quasi-representative designs for research in teaching. *Review of Educational Research*, 1974, *44*, 264–291.

Stoltz, S. B. Evaluation of therapeutic efficacy of behavior modification in a community setting. *Behaviour Research and Therapy*, 1976, *14*, 479–481.

Stuart, R. B. Behavioral contracting within the families of delinquents. *Journal of Behavioral Therapy and Experimental Psychiatry*. 1971, *2*, 1–11.

Thoresen, C. E. *Let's get intensive: Single case research*. Englewood Cliffs, NJ: Prentice-Hall, in press.

Thoresen, C. E. Relevance and research in counseling. *Review of Educational Research*, 1969, *39*, 263–281.

Thoresen, C. E., & Anton, J. L. Intensive experimental research in counseling. *Journal of Counseling Psychology*, 1974, *21*, 553–559.

Thoresen, C. E., & Elashoff, J. D. An analysis-of-variance model for intrasubject replication design: Some additional comments. *Journal of Applied Behavior Analysis*, 1974, *7*, 639–641.

Thoresen, C. E., & Mahoney, M. J. *Behavioral self-control*. Monterey, CA: Brooks/Cole Publishing Co., 1974.

Tuckman, B. W. *Conducting educational research*. New York: Harcourt Brace Jovanovich, 1972.

Twardosz, S., Cataldo, M. F., & Risley, T. R. Open environment design for infant and toddler day care. *Journal of Applied Behavior Analysis*, 1974, *7*, 529–546.

Tyler, V. O., & Brown, M. D. Token reinforcement of academic performance with institutionalized delinquent boys. *Journal of Educational Psychology*, 1968, *59*, 164–168.

Ulman, J. D., & Sulzer-Azaroff, B. Multi-element baseline design in educational research. In E. Ramp, & G. Semb (Eds.), *Behavior analysis: Areas of research and application*. Englewood Cliffs, NJ: Prentice-Hall, 1975.

Underwood, R. G. *Psychological research*. New York: Appleton-Century-Crofts, 1957.

Wahler, R. G. Setting generality: Some specific and general effects of child behavior therapy. *Journal of Applied Behavior Analysis*, 1969, *2*, 239–246.

Watson, J. B., & Rayner, R. Conditioned emotional reactions. *Journal of Experimental Psychology*, 1920, *3*, 1–14.

Webb, E. J., Campbell, D. T., Schwartz, R. D., & Sechrest, C. *Unobtrusive measures: Non-reactive research in the social sciences*. Chicago: Rand McNally, 1966.

Weis, L., & Hall, R. V. Reduction in smoking behavior through avoidance of punishment. In R. V. Hall (Ed.), *Behavior management series: Part III, applications in school and home*. Lawrence, KS: H. & H. Enterprises, 1971.

Weisberg, P., & Waldrop, P. B. Fixed-interval work habits of Congress. *Journal of Applied Behavior Analysis*, 1972, *5*, 93–97.

Weiss, B., Laties, V. G., Siegel, L., & Goldstein, D. A computer analysis of serial interactions in spaced responding. *Journal of Experimental Analysis of Behavior*, 1966, *9*, 619–626.

Wetzel, R. J., Balch, P., & Kratochwill, T. R. Behavioral counseling: The environment as client. In J. D. Noshpitz (Ed.), *Basic handbook of child psychiatry*. New York: Basic Books, 1977.

White, O. R. *A manual for the calculation and use of the median slope—a technique of progress estimation and prediction in the single case.* Eugene, OR: Regional Resource Center for Handicapped Children, University of Oregon, 1972.

White, O. R. *The "split middle"—a "quickie" method of trend estimation.* Experimental Education Unit, Child Development and Mental Retardation Center, University of Washington, 1974.

Wilson, C. W., & Hopkins, B. L. The effects of contingent music on the intensity of noise in junior high home economics classes. *Journal of Applied Behavior Analysis*, 1973, 6, 269–275.

Wolf, H. M., & Risley, T. R. Reinforcement: Applied research. In R. Glaser (Ed.), *The nature of reinforcement.* New York: Academic Press, 1971.

Yates, A. J. *Behavior therapy*, New York: John Wiley & Sons, 1970.

2

The Analysis and Presentation of Graphic Data

BARRY S. PARSONSON
UNIVERSITY OF WAIKATO

DONALD M. BAER
UNIVERSITY OF KANSAS

I. Introduction

A. A Tale of Two Paradigms

Experimental discovery or verification has been pursued within both of two great design paradigms throughout the history of science. One of these paradigms, the group design, is very well known to students of behavioral science: it is the method always taught, except for a very small minority of social scientists called operant conditioners. It can be instructive to examine that paradigm as if it were to be explained to a bright child whose curiosity is just ready for formalization and discipline—not because any likely reader of this chapter requires such an examination, but because, curiously enough, that type of explanation can serve as one of the most basic justifications of the other great paradigm, single-subject design. To a bright child, suitable explanation of proof by means of the group design paradigm is offered then as follows:

I think that people would behave very differently than usual, if only one important thing were done to them—if only they were told a certain thing.

What thing? Never mind for a moment—I'll tell you later. For right now, let's just call it the "very important thing." See—I want you to consider the possibilities without being influenced by any opinion you already might have about that very important thing. Okay? Thanks.

What we need to do is pick somebody who would be handy for us to study, and then tell that somebody the very important thing, and then watch to see if that somebody behaves differently as a result.

(What do you mean, why do I call "him" "somebody"? How do you know we're going to study a "him"? Haven't you learned yet that it's just as important that girls be "somebodies" as boys? Okay, don't forget again.)

So, we're going to pick somebody, and tell somebody the very important thing, and then watch to see if somebody behaves differently. Wouldn't that be the way to do it?

You want to know how the somebody would behave differently? Never mind that either for a moment—I'll tell you later, when I tell you what the very important thing is. It's the same as a minute ago—I want you to consider the possibilities without being influenced by any opinion that you might already have about that kind of behavior and what should make it happen or stop happening. For now, let's just call it the "behavior." Okay? Thanks.

Now—wouldn't you agree that if you had a hard time believing that somebody's behavior would be different if only they were told the very important thing, then the way to see whether it was really true would be to watch somebody's behavior after they were told the very important thing?

"Behave" different from what? Good question! The answer is, different from somebody who hasn't been told the very important thing. Good—you're really understanding it: we need to study two somebodies: one who has been told and one who hasn't. We could use your friend Mary for the one who gets told and your friend Joe for the one who doesn't. We'll see if Mary behaves differently from Joe. Okay?

Mary already behaves differently from Joe in a lot of ways and she hasn't even been told yet? You're right, that's the problem. So, what we'll do is . . . .

What? Mary doesn't listen a lot of the time? So we could tell her the very important thing and it might not change her behavior because she didn't listen to it? Hmmm. Well, do you have any friends who do *listen? I mean, most of the time?*

You can't think of anybody who always listens? You know, you're right; neither can I. Look, here's the idea: we get a whole bunch of your friends, and tell each one of them the very important thing, and we get another whole bunch and we don't *tell any of them, see? And then we'll see if, on the average, the bunch who got told behave differently from the bunch who didn't. We'll call the first bunch the Told Group and the second bunch the Not Told Group. There must be some kids in the Told Group who'll listen when we tell them the very important thing, so we've got a chance of seeing it in action in that group. And I know that Mary already behaves differently from Joe in a lot of ways, but with a whole bunch of differently behaving kids in the Told Group and another bunch in the Not Told Group we'll have examples of all sorts of behavior in* both *groups, see—not just Mary versus Joe—so it'll be fair. It's just like choosing up sides for a game: the thing to do for a good game is to get some real talent on each team, and some just average kids on each team, and some real no-goods on each team. Then the game should be fair; you know,* on the average, *each team should make about the same number of points. In the long run, you know.*

You've been thinking? About what? Oh, you've thought of some kids who are pretty good listeners. You want all of them in the Told Group, so we'll really *have a chance to see the very important thing in action? That's smart thinking, sort of. But . . . look, if you wanted a fair game, you wouldn't put all the talent on one team, would you? No, I wouldn't think you would. Then we'd better not put all the good listeners in the Told Group. Maybe good listeners already behave differently than the Not Told Group, without even being told the very important thing. After all, they already all listen better; maybe they behave better, too. It's the same point* you *made to* me, *when you told me that Mary already behaved differently from Joe and she hadn't even been told yet, remember? Right. We need two groups that are all mixed up, no differences between them, on the whole, just like two fair teams. Then, we can tell one group, and see if that makes them different from the group that we don't tell—on the whole, of course, on the whole.*

I knew you'd ask that—how do we decide if a bunch of kids behave differently from another bunch "on the whole"? What we've got to do is measure each kid's behavior, and then we can figure the average score for each group, for the Told Group and for the Not Told Group. You know

*averages, don't you? Sure—I thought so. Believe me, you can measure
this behavior: each kid will have a score somewhere between 0 and 100.
So you figure the average in each group, and see if I'm not right—you just
see if the Told Group doesn't have a different average than the Not Told
Group.*

*In fact, kid, I can draw you a picture of what I think you're going to
find. Suppose that we draw the measuring scale of the behavior, on which
every kid will get a score that's somewhere between 0 and 100, like so
[see Fig. 2.1] . . . .*

*And suppose that we draw each of the Told Group kids on that scale,
as a dot like this ●, wherever their scores happen to be. And then we'll
draw the Not Told Group kids on the same scale, as open dots like this ○,
each one wherever that kid's score happens to be. I bet the picture will
look like this [see Fig. 2.2] . . . .*

*You can see that the Told Group got mainly high scores, and that the
Not Told Group got pretty much lower scores. You can see that telling
them the very important thing changed their behavior, in fact, increased
it. And I've drawn in the average for the Told Group—it's about 83—and
the average for the Not Told Group—it's about 35. You could see that's
about where they'd be, anyway, without figuring them, but now you've
got a really precise number description of each group—on the average,
of course, on the average.*

*You like the picture better than the averages? Sure, you can see
everything, and you can see that some Not Told kids actually do better
than some Told kids—but there are some neat things you can do with averages. For example, I know that you're about to ask me whether those two
groups of kids might not have got that different from one another by
chance, instead of being Told or Not Told.*

Fig. 2.1. The measuring scale of the "behavior."

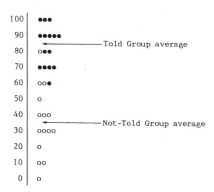

Fig 2.2. The distribution and average of scores for the Told Group and for the Not Told Group.

You weren't going to ask that? You should have. You can see that they're different? Well, look, there's this really neat formula that you can use, if you've got the means and each kid's score. Suppose that we call the Not Told Group's average M_{nt}, and the Told Group's average M_t, and the general score for each kid in the Not Told Group x_{nt}, and for each kid in the Told Group x_t, then—look right here there's this neat formula you can use. . . . Hey, kid, come back! Kid? KID?

Let us suppose that, indeed, the kid does come back. Remember that this is a very bright child, who, while fleeing from the formula for t, will be thinking hard about the original problem. Upon returning, the child might now attempt to explain something to the proof-explainer, perhaps as follows:

You know, I bet that you're right: I bet that some people would behave differently just because they were told the very important thing. I thought of a particular very important thing that makes me behave differently just about every time that I hear it. The reason I thought of it is that my friend Susie also behaves differently every time that she hears it, but she behaves in just the opposite way that I do. Let me show you how to prove that for each of us.

What? You want to know what you could tell me and Susie that would cause us to behave differently from one another? Uh . . . would you mind, uh, if I didn't tell you for a moment? I'll tell you later. See, I don't want you to be influenced by any opinion that you might already have about how Susie and I ought to behave when we hear this particular thing. Okay? Really, I'm not trying to be sassy, I hope you understand. (Mom would kill me! Backtalk to an inferential statistician! Wow!) But I've got this problem . . . let me show you.

First, you look at how I behave, and then you tell me the very important thing, and then you look again at how I behave; and what you're looking for, see, is a change in the behavior from before when you tell me to after you tell me.

Okay, sure, I knew you'd say that: I know that I behave differently from minute to minute in lots of ways, even without anyone telling me any big deal in between. So if I behave differently after you tell me from how I behaved before you tell me, it might not be because you told me, but because I was going to behave differently then, anyway. Sure, I see that. So, what we need to do is watch me do this behavior a lot of times, one after another, before you tell me the very important thing, and then watch to see if I behave differently from that a lot of times again, after you tell me. It's just like Mary being different from Joe in lots of ways, even without being told; I'm different from myself in lots of ways, without being told, just from minute to minute. The way you fixed that problem, your way, was to get lots of kids to go with Mary and Joe, and make a fair pair of teams out of them, and then tell one team and not tell the other. Well, I'm going to do the same thing with myself: I'm going to let you look at lots of my behavior before you tell me, and then look at lots of my behavior after you tell me. Instead of lots of Marys and Joes (you know what I mean), there'll be lots of mes, some before, some after. You know, what you were doing was let the funny Marys and Joes average out in big groups of kids; what I'm going to do is let my funny minutes average out in lots of minutes—of me. I know that you can't depend on just one look at me, any more than you can depend on just one Mary versus just one Joe. Same problem. And, you know, this is just about the same answer. I'm going to compare two groups—of me.

Hey, I'll even draw a picture. This behavior of mine is measured on a 0 to 100 scale, too. I'm going to draw you my Before scores, one after another in the order I behaved them, and then my After scores, one after another, same way, Okay? Like this [see Fig. 2.3] . . . .

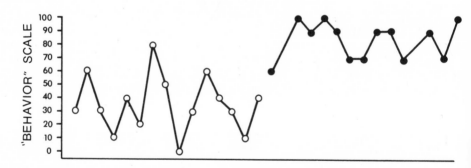

Fig. 2.3. Minutes of my "behavior," one after another.

You know? That's the very same set of dots that you drew, with open ones like this ○ for my behavior before I was told, and dark ones like this ● for my behavior after I was told. All I've done differently is show you the order they came in. Since they all came from me, see, they had to come in an order. What you're watching is me change over time. So I connected the points with a line, see, to suggest that it's like, you know, a . . . process. And what you see is that after I'm told the very important thing, I give much higher scores than before I was told. That's what I think you'd see from me, if you were trying to prove this thing about my behavior.

But Susie's case—oh, boy! Is she different! I'll draw you her picture. Here [see Fig. 2.4] . . . .

How come Susie has such a different picture from mine? Look, I'll have to tell you what the behavior is, and what the very important thing is that we get told. The behavior is being in the dining room: 100 means we're seated at the table, 90 means we're almost seated, 80 means we're in the room, and so on. So, 0 means we're nowhere even near the dining room. And the very important thing is Mom announcing that a meal's served and ready to eat. You can see that being told that really turns me on. Of course, I'm kind of a bouncy kid—I don't get just 100 scores all the time while a meal's being served, 'cause I have to be up and around. I help serve a little, and I remember things that I have to do, and I answer the phone (it rings a lot, sorta), and such like. . . . Susie? Oh! What you don't know is that Susie and her father just hate *one another. She'll do anything not to eat with him, so she's always finding things that keep her away from the dining room. But that's so, only when her Mom announces a meal—'cause that's the only time her father is ever in the dining room, just about. So, you can see Susie spends a lot of time in the dining room before her Mom calls everybody to eat, just sort of borrowing some of the food—'cause she's hungry, you know, and there's usually something to*

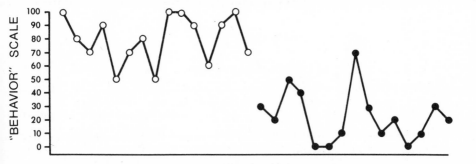

Fig. 2.4. Minutes of Susie's "behavior," one after another.

*eat on the table just before her Mom calls everybody officially (ha ha).
But when the announcement comes, Susie usually can find something she's
just got to do somewhere else. She spends a lot of time calling that she'll
"be right there"—but she almost never gets there until her father's
finished. I think it's probably the way he wants it too. They really don't
like each other.*

*Yeah, that is too bad. But I wanted you to see that it might be kind
of hard to make two fair teams if you had a lot of Susies to assign to them.
You know—if you put her in the Not Told Group, she'll give a big score
when the rest of them, mainly, are giving low scores. And if you put her
in the Told Group, she'll give a low score when the rest of them are giving
high scores, mainly.*

*Yeah, Susie would get averaged out in a big group. At least, she
would, if there's only the one of her, or maybe a couple. It would be kind
of tough if there were a lot of Susies—at least, it would be tough making
up fair teams—I mean groups.*

*How do you know that there aren't a lot of Susies in the world? I
guess there better not be—an average of me and Susie wouldn't exactly
represent either of us, would it? It would be a funny proof, if you proved
something about that average, wouldn't it? 'Cause our average isn't the
way that either of us works.*

*You know, I always thought that a t table was what Mom served
tea on.*

This bright child may seem suspiciously like Rousseau's child of nature,
replete with the innate wisdom of curiosity, unsullied by the sophistries of
abstruse formulas and hidden assumptions of unknown gravity, and determined to remain so. The remainder of this chapter is devoted to all bright
children.

B. Graphics as a Form of Data Analysis

1. A RATIONALE FOR GRAPHIC ANALYSIS

The literature of experimental and applied behavior analysis contains
ample evidence of the generality of data from single-subject designs, that is,
from procedures intended to establish precise behavioral control in single
organisms. This emphasis on achieving and demonstrating direct individualized experimental control must be regarded as a major factor in the success
of the functional analysis of behavior (Baer, 1977; Michael, 1974). Experimental designs and data analyses that prescribe direct, individualized, and

responsive behavioral control may possess certain benefits not offered by those that impose greater limitations on the freedom of action of the researcher. Some of these potential benefits are outlined below.

Graphic analysis of data and flexible, pragmatic research designs combine in a unique way to produce responsive experimental and treatment programs. The behavior of the subject(s) controls the pace and procedures of the programs through the data, which are continuously available to the experimenter when graphed after each session. Judgments, decisions, and changes can be made as the program proceeds, providing a degree of adaptibility essential in applied research (also see Kratochwill, Chapter 1 of this volume). Programs that can be modified to produce, intensify, or moderate changes in the ongoing behavior of subjects, or be altered in response to unplanned events, such as the loss of some subjects or changes in staffing or institutional procedures, and still give rise to valid data, meet the realities of research in applied settings.

The close and continuing data contact that results from graphic analysis allows for diversity in research endeavor. Both Skinner (1956) and Sidman (1960) appreciate the value of indulging one's curiosity as part of the scientific enterprise. Skinner's unformalized principles of scientific practice reflect the fact that important scientific advances are not always the product of an intentional search. Close, ongoing contact with data allows those events and results that arouse interest and curiosity to be noticed and subsequently investigated systematically. Thus experimental designs and forms of data analysis that do not isolate researchers from direct, continuing contact with their subject matter, or smooth out interesting variations in performance, may broaden the scope of scientific discovery.

Operant research designs, with their emphasis on replication (Baer, Wolf, & Risley, 1968) and graphic analysis of data, increase the capacity for independent evaluation of research. As experimental procedures and equipment become increasingly sophisticated and costly, the likelihood of direct replication is reduced. This is especially so where procedures developed in the laboratory are transferred to applied settings where research activity is limited by lack of time, money, personnel, and facilities. Consequently, there is an emphasis on the believability of the results of published research; and the ease with which the data may be independently interpreted, analyzed, and judged becomes an important consideration. Persons confronted with graphed operant data usually have access to the primary data as well as a direct replication. They can perform their own data analysis and reach their own conclusions, because the details necessary to do so often have not been obscured, coalesced, or dissolved via mediation by computer or statistical tables.

By contrast, the statistical analysis of the significance of the controlling effect of experimenter-imposed variables is a post hoc process; thus it is not a parallel to ongoing graphic analysis and responsive experimental procedures. The functional analysis of behavior is functional only as long as the analysis is a responsive process. For example, if a variable has a weak but interesting effect, then systematic investigation should be undertaken to discover whether it is possible to increase its power. Weak variables and moderate effects are not strengthened by the ritual administration of algebra; rather they indicate the need for further more extensive (or intensive) functional analysis.

Perhaps the most compelling reason for retaining current operant methodology is the fact that it has been successful in the systematic investigation of the variables controlling the behavior of single organisms. Hogben (1957), in discussing the pressure on social scientists to design and analyze their research in ways prescribed by inferential statistics, states that

> it is not the obligation of the research worker to bow to the dictates of statistical theory until he or she has conclusively established its relevance to the technique of inquiry. On the contrary, the onus lies on the exponent of statistical theory to furnish irresistible reasons for adopting procedures which still have to prove their worth against a background of three centuries of progress in scientific discovery accomplished without their aid [p. 344].

The costs of alternative data analytic procedures may outweigh their reputed benefits when compared with the above advantages, both direct and indirect, of ongoing graphic data analysis. Horton (1970) reached similar conclusions with respect to the advantages of visually analyzed wall-charts over computer printouts in certain managerial applications.

2. THE RELATIVE INSENSITIVITY OF GRAPHS
COMPARED WITH STATISTICAL ANALYSES

Operant baseline logic, and the experimental designs based on it, has been viewed with some skepticism by members of the several generations of behavioral scientists trained to follow experimental procedures espoused by statisticians (e.g., Fisher, 1942). Plutchik (1968) probably reflects their opinion quite accurately in regarding operant baseline methodology as interesting, though possessing certain weaknesses and a limited applicability beyond the study of rates of bar-pressing.

It is perhaps ironic that the development of a functional, technologically applicable, and effective analysis of behavior is in part attributable to the fact that Skinner (1956, 1969) and his followers (e.g., Sidman, 1960) eschewed the hypothetico-deductive method, group designs, and inferential statistics so highly favored by Fisher (1942) and his successors. Instead, they developed flexible and pragmatic single-subject procedures that permitted demonstration of reliable control of observable behaviors. The data from these procedures were plotted as rates of responding across time. The demonstration of reliable control was achieved by showing, graphically, that visible, reliable changes in the plotted response rate were correlated with the repeated introduction and removal of the independent variable. Thus, in the functional analysis of behavior, the graph attained particular importance as a comprehensive means of recording and storing data, and more important, analyzing it for evidence indicative of a functional relationship.

It is this analytic function of the graph that has become of particular significance. In behavior analysis ongoing research decisions, judgments of the adequacy and meaningfulness of data, and the conclusions drawn from research are all based on the analysis of graphed data. The analysis is essentially a visual process; determination of change is dependent on the change being of sufficient magnitude to be apparent to the eye. Compared with the potential algebraic sophistication of statistical tests of significance (not always realized in practice), the above procedure usually is relatively insensitive, yet that very lack of refinement may have important and valuable consequences for the analysis of behavior (Baer, 1977).

The outcome of studies employing traditional statistical data analyses usually is judged in accordance with conventions established for determining the p-levels beyond which it is assumed that the null hypothesis safely can be rejected. In the behavioral sciences the 5% (.05) level is widely accepted, which means that the chance probability of a Type I error, i.e., of having erroneously rejected the null hypothesis, is no more than 1 in 20.

If there is a probability that a result will, by chance, be statistically significant 1 out of every 20 replications, it is necessary to know the outcome of studies that are, at the very least, similar, in order to determine whether or not any current result is itself a product of chance. However, studies with findings that are not statistically significant are rarely published because, according to McNemar (1960), they are either rejected by editors, not submitted for publication by researchers, selectively excluded from submitted studies, or rejected by investigators because they do not fit the theory the experiment was designed to support. The high proportion of published studies reporting statistically significant outcomes, coupled with the small number of published replications, contributes to a biased literature in which an essential body of reference material is missing, either unpublished, unsubmitted, or unattempted (Craighead, Kazdin, & Mahoney, 1975).

Bakan (1967) points out that a major sociological side-effect of Type I errors is that "significant" findings tend to inhibit rather than facilitate direct replication. Consequently, a Type I error may go undiscovered or uncontested as research moves on to new fields of endeavor or until systematic replications fail to produce effects, thus initiating direct replication studies. Lubin (1957) and Lykken (1968) have both suggested that more emphasis should be placed on evidence of replicability than on statistical significance as a criterion of acceptance for publication. This would help reduce the incidence of Type I errors.

The chance probability of a Type II error, i.e., accepting the null hypothesis when it should have been rejected, is not usually known. In effect, the only way to ascertain whether a Type I or Type II error has been made in a given instance is through a series of direct replications, apparently an uncommon procedure in group design studies (Sterling, 1959). The probability of a Type II error is higher when the sample size is small, and even quite powerful effects may well remain undetected (Wallis & Roberts, 1956). Consequently, it is common for researchers to be advised to increase the size of their samples when their experimental results trend in the expected direction, but fail to exceed the .05 level. Yet, given a suitably large sample, a statistically significant result may be obtained even though the interaction between the independent and dependent variables is weak. For example, Nunnally (1960) quoted a study with an N of 700 in which many "significant" correlations were obtained between a variety of factor scores and individual-difference variables, such as age, income, education, and sex. With an N of 700, correlations of .08 were significant at the .05 level, and he reported that many of those obtained in the study were of "no theoretical or practical importance [p. 643]." Nunnally commented that, given enough data, the null hypothesis would generally be rejected and that if its rejection was the real goal of psychological experimentation, "there usually would be no need to gather data [p. 643]."

According to Bakan (1967), editorial policies are such that Type II errors have less of an inhibiting effect on further investigation than do Type I errors because they are not at issue in the published field. Consequently, variables with sufficient power are likely to be given further opportunities to make their presence felt. A Type II error seems the lesser of the two evils.

In the visual analysis of graphed data, differences between baseline and experimental conditions have to be clearly evident and reliable for a convincing demonstration of stable change to be claimed, and audiences will differ in whether or not they are convinced. In order to produce a visible change in the data, an effect would probably have to be more powerful than that required to produce a statistically significant change. Glass, Willson, and Gottman (1975) comment that data from time-series experiments that do not appear statistically significant when inspected visually, often prove to be significant when "appropriately tested [p. 62]." While they also note that on occasion some nonsignificant effects may appear significant (see Chapter 4, this volume), their observation does suggest that the probability of Type I error is likely to be much lower in visual analysis than when statistical analyses are used. Also, Jones, Weinrott, and Vaught (1975) found that judges employing visual analysis were most "accurate," when compared against the standard of a time-series analysis, at identifying operant studies with low autocorrelations and nonsignificant effects. They concluded that this indicated visual appraisal to be more conservative than statistical analysis. Furthermore, since it is almost mandatory for acceptable research designs in applied behavior analysis to include at least one replication (Baer, Wolf, & Risley, 1968), the probability of a Type I error is reduced even further. The applied behavioral researcher, unlike the traditional behavioral scientist, has access to a literature in which the majority of studies include at least one direct replication.

The use of the less sensitive visual data analysis in behavior analysis also means that the probability of a Type II error could be higher than is the case in studies employing statistical analyses. This is because small effects do not show up as readily, unless graphs are distorted, and are more likely to be rejected as no effect (Baer, 1977). As noted previously, Type II errors are less of a problem to science than Type I errors, since further investigation is likely to reveal any actually effective variables.

The preceding argument leads to the conclusion that the less sensitive measurement technique has been advantageous in the development of a functional analysis of behavior, in that it has a built-in bias against the selection of weak and unstable variables. As a result, the basic and fundamental variables of behavior are those possessing sufficient power and generality to be seen through graphic analysis. Undoubtedly, these same variables would have emerged from statistical analyses, but so too would many weak and unstable variables, which may have served only to confound, complicate, and delay the development of a functional analysis of behavior (Baer, 1977).

3. THE ADVANTAGES OF INSENSITIVITY AT CERTAIN STAGES IN THE DEVELOPMENT OF AN AREA

If, in the early stages of the investigation of a phenomenon, important information about its controlling variables can be discovered using primitive measuring instruments, then those variables are likely to be powerful. Their potency is such that their effects are measurable despite the relative insensitivity of the measurement process. A powerful variable is also likely to be a basic variable, one with a widespread sphere of influence with respect to the phenomenon of interest. Thus, basic variables have powerful and generalized effects, and their discovery provides the impetus for the development of an area of scientific inquiry.

The robustness of powerful variables is also valuable at other stages of development. If a variable is weak or unstable, is measurable only under the most exacting laboratory conditions, and then only by the most delicate of instruments, the phenomenon under investigation probably will remain in the laboratory. Its applicability may be proscribed by its delicacy. In possessing powerful and generalized effects, basic variables are resilient. They may be found operating effectively under less than optimal conditions and are likely to continue to be effective when applied by technicians, paraprofessionals, and relatively unskilled operators. They permit the establishment of an effective, widely applicable technology. These arguments are directly applicable to the analysis of behavior. Those variables whose operation was repeatedly and generally apparent in the graphed data from animal studies were those that were fundamental to the control of behavior. They survived the transfer from the animal laboratory to the less hospitable environment of the human social milieu, and that from the highly trained behavior analyst to the briefly instructed teacher or parent, because they possessed the power and generality of basic variables.

II. Visual Analysis of Graphic Data[1]

A. Basic Design and Data Presentation in Applied Behavior Analysis

Experiments in applied behavior analysis can be identified as interrupted time-series experiments (Glass, Willson, & Gottman, 1975); they employ designs designated as *quasi-experimental* by Campbell and Stanley (1966), although behavior analysts typically follow Sidman's (1960) terminology and identify them as intrasubject replication designs. The most important attribute of these designs is that they permit the demonstration of both reliable experimental control of behavior and the generality of that control across time and/or a range of environmental stimuli (Baer *et al.*, 1968). Interrupted time-series experiments have two basic components: (1) a number of observations made in the absence of the independent variable(s),

---

[1] This section makes reference to parts of graphs and to graphic forms with which most readers will be familiar. However, in the event of any uncertainty, the reader is directed to Section III and to Fig. 2.23.

constituting the *baseline* or *A* condition, and (2) a number of observations made after the introduction of the independent variable(s), which form the *treatment, experimental,* or *B* condition of the design. The different designs used in applied behavior analysis are characterized by replications employing different arrangements and elaborations of this basic *AB* sequence. The unreplicated *AB* sequence alone is generally considered an inadequate design because any changes in behavior coincident with the introduction of the independent variable could be attributed either to concurrent extraneous events or to the experimental manipulation (Campbell, 1963). As Kratochwill (Chapter 1) has provided detailed outlines of the variety of replication designs derived from the basic *AB* sequence, we will not elaborate further here.

Behavioral data are gathered across time, which can be expressed as chronological time (e.g., minutes, hours, days, weeks), occasional time (e.g., successive sessions, treatment days), or as successive blocks of responses regardless of interresponse times.

The recording and reporting of the data may take one of a number of forms. They may be expressed in terms of *frequency of occurrence*, usually the proportion of recording intervals in which the target behavior occurred at least once:

$$\frac{\text{intervals in which response occurred}}{\text{total intervals available}} \times \frac{100}{1}$$

rate of occurrence, the ratio of the number of times the target behavior occurred per unit of observation time:

$$\frac{\text{number of responses}}{\text{time unit}}$$

duration of occurrence, the total time of occurrence of the behavior as a proportion of the total observation time:

$$\frac{\text{time of behavior}}{\text{time of observation}} \times \frac{100}{1}$$

or *percentage of responses*, usually expressed as the proportion of times the behavior occurs per opportunity:

$$\frac{\text{number of responses}}{\text{number of opportunities}} \times \frac{100}{1}$$

Graphic representation of the obtained data provides visual evidence of whether or not there is a temporal association between changes in target behavior(s) and an experimenter's manipulation of the independent variable(s). Replication is intended to exclude more firmly any alternate explanations of the obtained effect, and to provide data on the generality of the phenomenon of interest (Sidman, 1960).

B. Checking the Presentation and Format[2]

Before evaluating graphic data, a thorough and critical assessment of their purpose and format should be made. The graph should have been presented so that it represents, summarizes, and describes the data independently of the accompanying text.

1. The title should provide a concise description of the nature and purpose of the figure.

2. The scale captions should establish the identity and meaning of the independent and dependent variables.

3. The X and Y scales and their scale units should represent the appropriate type and range of scales, whether arithmetic (single or multiple) or logarithmic scales.

If the Y scale divisions are much larger (or smaller) than those of the X scale, vertical changes are likely to be distorted. For behavioral data, vertical changes usually express change in the dependent variable and often such changes are those which authors want to emphasize visually. There may be occasions when socially or scientifically important, but relatively small, changes in behavior need to be stressed. For example, Fig. 2.5a portrays the effects of sequences of treatment over extended follow-up periods, on the verbal behavior of a retarded child. The changes in percentage occurrence of appropriate verbal behavior, although small in terms of the percentage change, may be important with respect to the norms of language acquisition in retarded children.

Whether or not we are impressed, the amount of control demonstrated in any given instance may well be determined by normative assessments of just how much control could reasonably be expected in such an instance. The clinical importance of certain changes may well outweigh statistical considerations in some instances (Risley, 1970).

---

[2] The graphs prepared for this chapter are stylized representations. Although they were in many instances derived from actual examples in the literature, their data are fictitious, as are the "experiments" they represent. Often, only those details essential for illustrative purposes have been included. Many figures have been left without scale numbering or precise labels. Correct labeling format is illustrated on Fig. 2.23.

The locations of similar figures, found in the behavioral literature, are referenced in the text as follows: (see also Fig. 6, Smith, 1974); the full reference is listed in the References.

However, Fig. 2.5a has certain faults. For instance, the reader should have been made aware that the Y axis had been attenuated, some 90% of that scale having been pruned. Also, the use of a line graph to represent discrete data, when the actual data path between temporally distant plotted points is unknown, is inappropriate. Figure 2.5b shows how the data may have been better represented. A scale break between the 10 and 100% divisions of the Y axis draws the reader's attention to the fact that the Y scale has been abbreviated. Representation of the data using a bar graph format avoids giving the impression of linear changes between data points (see also Fig. 8, Lovaas, Koegel, Simmons, & Long, 1973).

In Fig. 2.6a, the Y axis has not been taken down to its zero origin (there is no scale break to indicate this), has scale divisions that are much larger than those along the X axis, and data points in adjoining conditions have been linked. These factors combine to produce a visual impression of large vertical changes in the data path.

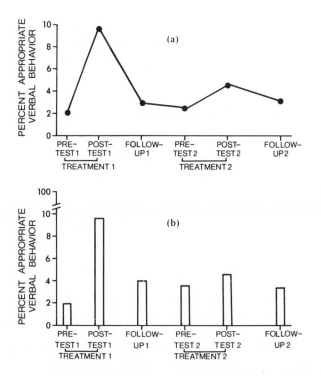

Fig. 2.5. (a) Discrete data in line graph format, no scale break on an attenuated Y axis. (b) Identical data in bar graph format, with scale break.

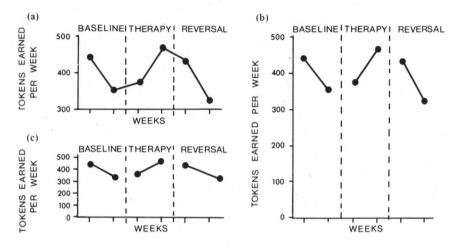

Fig. 2.6. (a) Visual distortion produced by attenuated Y axis and continuous data path. (b) Identical data on an undistorted graph. (c) The effects of reducing the scale on the Y axis.

Figure 2.6b shows how the data would have looked if the entire graph had been presented; this gives a different visual impression by deemphasizing the vertical changes to some degree. Figure 2.6c shows the same data in a revised version of Fig. 2.6a in which the Y scale intervals have been made smaller than those of the X scale. When compared with Fig. 2.6a, the visual impression is that the changes between and within conditions are comparatively small (see also Fig. 5, Winkler, 1970).

The bars or columns of a "bar" graph may appear longer if they are drawn so that they begin far below the zero origin (Fig. 2.7). A less exaggerated form of this procedure is legitimate when an author wishes to discriminate, on a bar graph, between those occasions on which data are missing (i.e., no data were gathered) and those when the relevant behavior was not displayed by the subject in a session or phase (i.e., frequency of occurrence = 0). In such an instance no column would be shown for the missing data, while zero scores would be indicated by a vestigial column extending up to the zero line from a point just below that line.

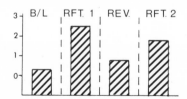

Fig. 2.7. Visual distortion of column length on a bar graph by displacing the abscissa well below the zero line.

4. The different experimental phases should be labeled on the graph and should establish the experimental design used in the study.

5. All of the relevant data should be shown in an appropriate form. For example, the reader is unlikely to be able to imagine the location of the data points showing "percent time in-seat" on Fig. 2.8a, yet comparison between in-seat and on-task behaviors may be relevant to the analysis of the graph and to drawing conclusions from it. Figure 2.8b shows how the data look when both sets are plotted. Now, instead of having to accept the author's interpretation of the data, as readers might have done when confronted with with Fig. 2.8a, they are able to make their own judgments (see also Fig. 2, Barlow & Agras, 1973).

Because visual impressions are susceptible to influence from distortions, it is important to check the foregoing aspects of graphs thoroughly before analyzing and judging the data they present. If a graph appears to be distorted or misconstructed in any way, it may be worthwhile to sketch out a more accurate alternative, to see whether its conclusions are very different. It is often worth the effort.

C. Analyzing Graphic Data

The statistical properties of data that are relevant to visual analysis are outlined below. Items 1–5 were identified by Jones, Vaught, & Weinrott

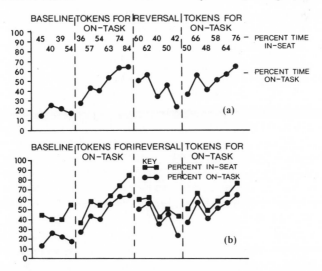

Fig. 2.8. (a) Impending analysis of graphic data by replacing a data path with numerical information. (b) The same data in graphic form.

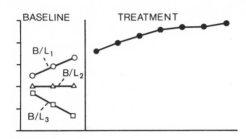

Fig. 2.9. Baseline data that drift in the direction of improvement are less impressive than those that are stable or trend in the opposite direction.

(1977), and Items 7 and 8 by Kazdin (1976) and Glass, Willson, & Gottman (1975).

1. STABILITY OF BASELINE

When baseline (B/L) data drift in the direction of improvement (e.g., B/L_1), it is difficult to sustain claims identifying the treatment procedure as the major change agent in an adjacent treatment phase (see Fig. 2.9).

Stable baselines (e.g., B/L_2), or those which drift in the direction opposite to improvement (e.g., B/L_3), provide a better basis for attributing change to the effects of treatment.

2. VARIABILITY WITHIN PHASES

Baselines that are initially variable but later stabilize (e.g., Data Path 1 in Fig. 2.10) suggest that there may have been an initial, sometimes transitory effect of introducing the observational process. When treatment data approximate Data Path 1, it might be assumed that they indicate a good technique (i.e., stable control), but that the components being acquired in this program themselves need analysis, if smoother acquisition is desired, or a more complete understanding is required.

A highly variable baseline, like Data Path 2 in Fig. 2.10, suggests that potentially controlling variables occasionally were in effect. Cyclic or recurring patterns are suggestive of some systematically recurring environmental event. Thus, systematic scrutiny of environmental variables in an effort to identify the causes of these effects is indicated. Their identification may lead to the discovery of potentially useful treatment variables. Treatment data resembling Data Path 2 would signal occasional control attributable to variables other than, or in addition to, the experimental variable. Given that these variables could be identified, then if the peaks occurred when the occasional variables were in effect, one would wish to harness these potentially powerful treatment variables. If the valleys occurred when they were in effect, one would be faced with excluding them from the environment

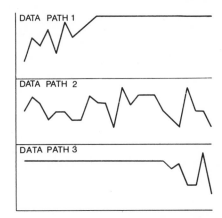

Fig. 2.10. Analysis of variability within phases can provide important information on programming and experimental control.

and/or extinguishing their effect and/or finding ways to convert them into effective treatment variables.

Baseline or treatment data that, like those in Data Path 3 of Fig. 2.10, become unstable after an extended period of stability would raise suspicions about the intrusion of some extraneous variables into a stable process. For example, the instability might be found to result from loss of reinforcer effectiveness through satiation or inhibition.

Data paths like 2 and 3 (Fig. 2.10) suggest that more data are needed in order to see whether stability eventually could be achieved or if more convincing evidence of the nature of the controlling variables could be obtained from further analysis.

3. VARIABILITY BETWEEN PHASES

When relatively stable treatment-phase data follow variable baseline data (see S_1 data, Fig. 2.11) the achievement of a degree of experimental control is apparent.

When baseline data like those of S_2 are followed by a stable treatment phase, the level of which approximates the baseline peaks, the indications are that the occasional variables of the baseline perhaps *are* the treatment variables, or else that the treatment variables override and cancel the occasional baseline variables. Evidence of control is less impressive when the baseline and treatment data are both variable (e.g., S_3), and changes in level (suggested by phase trends) may be too small, and the overlap in scores too great, to be convincing. A reader would probably conclude from S_3s data, that although a weak treatment effect was suggested, further investigation was required to establish both the effectiveness of the variable and the believability of any claims made for it.

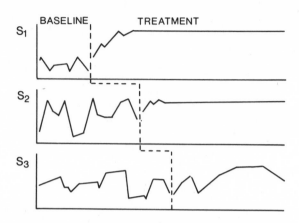

Fig. 2.11. Comparison of variability between experimental phases can give indications of the effect of introducing the experimental variable and its power over time.

4. OVERLAP BETWEEN SCORES OF ADJACENT PHASES

The parallel lines, drawn through both baseline and treatment phases of Fig. 2.12, give an indication of the extent to which scores overlap between phases.

Although there are no established criteria of excessive or acceptable amounts of overlap, the less overlap, the more convincing the treatment effect. Overlap between baseline and treatment phase scores only in the initial sessions of treatment clearly is more acceptable than overlapping scores occurring throughout, or at the end of, treatment.

5. NUMBER OF DATA POINTS IN EACH PHASE

As a general rule, more data points are necessary when there are clear indications of variability, overlap, or drift in the data. For example, the data of Baseline and Reinforcement 1 (Fig. 2.13) indicate a treatment effect, but the Reversal (REV) and Reinforcement 2 (RFT 2) phases do not constitute a convincing replication. Part of the fault lies in the fact that both reversal

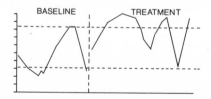

Fig. 2.12. Overlap in data between baseline and treatment phases early in treatment is less critical than overlap later in treatment.

Fig. 2.13. Too few data points in a phase make judgment difficult, especially if behavior is unstable.

phase data points fall within the range of Reinforcement 1 data points. Additional reversal data points may (or may not) have supported an effective demonstration of control. Since the data are not available the reader can only remain unimpressed.

Further problems are raised by the RFT 2 data. Although two of three points fall within the upper range of Reinforcement 1 phase scores, the final trend is downward. Additional data points, within the upper range of Reinforcement 1 scores, would have been more supportive of claims for successful and durable treatment effects.

6. CHANGES IN TREND WITHIN PHASES

While the overall trend of the first six data points in baseline of Fig. 2.14 is very slightly upward, there is some variability. However, the evidently stable upward trend of the last three baseline points raises suspicions. That final trend might have continued and eventually washed out the apparent treatment effect had baseline observations been extended. Similarly, taken overall the treatment data trend upward, but there is a downward trend in the final two data points, which rasises the question of loss of control, or no control. For both sets of data, analysis is influenced by changes in trend within phases. Readers analyzing similar data would prefer additional data points in each phase so that they could reach firmer conclusions on the effectiveness of the treatment procedure.

7. CHANGES IN TREND BETWEEN ADJACENT PHASES

The representative data from S_1 (Fig. 2.15) indicate an upward trend over baseline and a change to a downward trend over treatment. The data

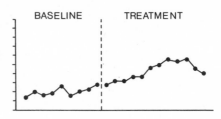

Fig. 2.14. Changes in trend within phases may indicate the need to delay changes in experimental procedure and obtain more data.

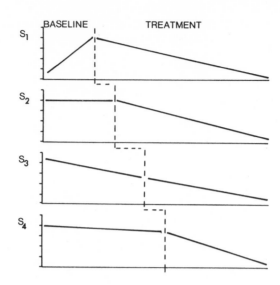

Fig. 2.15. Changes in trend between phases indicate the effect of introducing or withdrawing experimental variables. The amount and direction of trend change are relevant to judgment.

of S_2 show no trend in baseline and change to a downward trend during treatment. Such between-phase trend changes offer strong indications of treatment effects.

The S_3 data show a baseline trend that continues unchanged through treatment. Such uninterrupted linear trends indicate that the treatment variable is either ineffective or, at best, no more efficacious than variables not under the control of the experimenter. Data for S_4 show a moderate downward trend through baseline, which then becomes slightly steeper following the introduction of treatment. These data may suggest that, in the absence of treatment, a linear trend would have continued and that, given more time, the treatment effect could have resulted without intervention. Thus, treatment may have been effective in terminating the problem rather earlier than could otherwise have been expected. A reversal in which there were changes in both trend and level (see Subsection 8), or data from a number of subjects in a multiple-baseline design showing similar increases in trend following the introduction of the treatment, could indicate a treatment effect. Whether such a treatment would be considered worthwhile, compared to waiting out the natural course of events, would depend on the nature of the problem. Data like those of S_4 might also be interpreted as approximating a curvilinear or exponential function, and indicative of the operation of variables other than those introduced by the experimenter. Experimental procedures such as the reversal or multiple-baseline designs suggested above might then be employed in an effort to establish the nature of the controlling variables.

Figure 2.16 shows four types of trend change identified by Glass, Willson, and Gottman (1975).

Treatment data from S_1 illustrate the immediate change from baseline trend, termed an *abrupt* change. If data such as these (abrupt but gradual change) were obtained in the first treatment phase of a reversal design, one might anticipate a slow reversal and, consequently, a somewhat long reversal phase. If they represented the first baseline of a multiple-baseline design, it is likely that a long wait would be necessary before intervening in the second baseline. In Fig. 2.16, the S_2 intervention has been introduced much too soon to be viewed as that second baseline.

The S_2 data illustrate a *delayed* change in the treatment phase trend. Experimental data taking this form may simply indicate that a number of sessions are required before the effects of a particular program are evident. Alternately, they might suggest that revision of the programming is required if a more abrupt effect is sought. For instance, the delay in effect may be reflecting the presence of inputs or training steps that are redundant and simply waste time without contributing to the behavior the experimenter wants to establish. They could also indicate that the current procedures need refinement since they are failing to program the necessary prerequisites of the behavior of interest. The subject may be spending the first few sessions struggling, on a trial-and-error basis, to meet the requirements of the program before finally making appropriate responses. Either or both of these factors could contribute to delayed change, their identification being dependent on a systematic attempt to discover the cause of the effect. The consequences, for gradually changing data like those depicted for S_2, in a

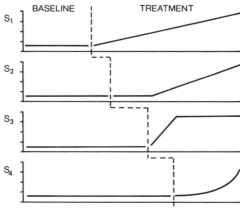

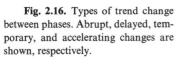

Fig. 2.16. Types of trend change between phases. Abrupt, delayed, temporary, and accelerating changes are shown, respectively.

reversal or multiple-baseline design could be similar to those suggested above for S_1.

In the case of the S_3 data, a *temporary* change is apparent. After a brief period of rapid change a ceiling or plateau is reached. Such data may show either that a behavior has reached its maximum level or that the current program has attained its maximal effectiveness. In the latter case, if further change is sought, the data probably suggest that modification of the program, e.g., addition of further training procedures or introducing more powerful reinforcing contingencies, is necessary. Data of the form shown for S_3 pose no special problems in either reversal or multiple-baseline designs.

Data from S_4 illustrate an *accelerated* change in which there is an initial, gradual treatment effect that subsequently changes to a curve indicative of a rapidly increasing level of performance. Recommendations here would be similar to those given for S_2 data with respect to the possibility of reprogramming initial components of the program. This curve may reflect a natural exponential function; either reversal or multiple-baseline designs may aid verification.

8. CHANGES IN LEVEL BETWEEN PHASES

The S_1 data in Fig. 2.17 show no change in trend between baseline and treatment phases, but an abrupt change in level is evident. Data for S_2

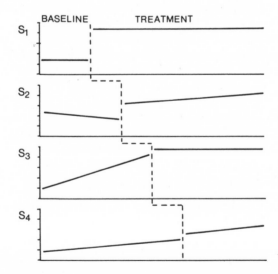

Fig. 2.17. Changes in level between phases indicate the impact of manipulation of experimental variables. Level changes like these are termed abrupt.

show changes in both trend and level between phases. Changes like these are generally more impressive to the eye than the changes in level illustrated in the data for S_3 and S_4.

Typically, the greater and more abrupt the change in level, the more convincing the data appear. Since some procedures do not produce abrupt changes in behavior, and some behavioral phenomena do not change abruptly, large and abrupt changes in level should not be regarded as a necessary criterion of "good" data.

In addition to *abrupt* changes in level like those illustrated in Fig. 2.17, Glass, Willson, and Gottman identify three other types of level change, as shown in Fig. 2.18.

The data from S_1 demonstrate a *temporary* change in level, in which there is an initial abrupt change following intervention that, after a brief period of stability, subsequently fades until baseline is recovered. Data reflecting changes of this nature suggest an initial treatment effect that is later counteracted by more powerful competing contingencies. Discovery and harnessing of those variables might prove useful in reestablishing the treatment effect. Alternately, such data might be indicative of temporary effects in some way correlated with the start of treatment, but not due to variables intentionally introduced by the experimenter, e.g., more obtrusive recording procedures after intervention. Systematic analyses of such apparently transient effects could be performed using a multiple-baseline design across subjects, thus providing the means of establishing whether the effect is subject specific, a problem in the experimental procedure, or a component of the extraexperimental environment.

Data from S_2 show *delayed* change in level, in which it takes a number of sessions before the experimental effect begins to appear. Such data may

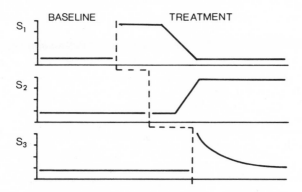

Fig. 2.18. Changes in level between phases. Temporary, delayed, and decaying changes (respectively) provide a basis for data analysis.

simply reflect latency in the emergence of an effect. They may also indicate a need for better programming of the initial treatment phase in an effort to produce a more abrupt change in trend.

The S_3 data are indicative of a *decaying* change in level. There is a transient "treatment" effect that could be due either to the intrusion of variables other than the intended treatment or to effects such as might be obtained in a program where the subject is invited to change behavior but is not provided with any feedback on or consequences for the performance of the new behavior. A multiple baseline across subjects could serve to probe the nature of this type of transient effect. The appearance of an unusual effect such as this in a program often necessitates temporarily abandoning the intended study in order to analyze the new phenomenon systematically. The flexibility of single-subject designs makes this possible.

9. ANALYSIS OF DATA ACROSS SIMILAR PHASES

While assessment of data within phases and between adjacent phases forms a major part of the visual analytic process, judgment of the congruity of data across experimentally similar phases is also important. A convincing replication involves more than a demonstration that a similar baseline-treatment change can be approximated on subsequent occasions.

With reversal designs, it is meaningful both when scores in the reversal-to-baseline phase(s) return within range of the original baseline scores and when they fail to do so. Successful replication of all levels is indicative of full experimental control and a complete analysis of the controlling variable(s). Failure to recover completely, in reversal, may indicate either that more data should have been obtained in that phase, or that a degree of control has been lost. For example, in Fig. 2.19 the reversal data have come to approximate those obtained in the two treatment conditions. The effect may be due to the fact that the target behavior is increasingly coming under the control of contingencies other than those arranged by the experimenter. Such a consequence is exemplified by "trapping" (Baer & Wolf, 1970; Baer, Rowbury, & Goetz, 1976), in which available natural contingencies take control of the

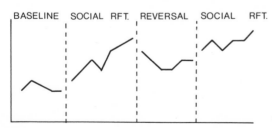

Fig. 2.19. Reversal phase behavior may not return to baseline levels due to effects such as "trapping" or resistance to extinction.

behavior. Alternately, the reinforcement schedule employed during the preceding treatment phase may have been such that the target response became increasingly resistant to extinction (e.g., Kale, Kaye, Whelan, & Hopkins, 1968), and a brief reversal was insufficient to demonstrate any effects resulting from removal of the experimental variable. Identification of the variables responsible for the above effect can follow only from systematic investigation. The phenomenon may be more apparent after repeated reversals (see also Fig. 2, Kirby & Shields, 1972).

Another apparent consequence of reversal that is sometimes noted is an intensification of the target behavior when experimental contingencies are reintroduced subsequent to reversal. The effect is apparent in the final "tokens" phase in Fig. 2.20. It may result from enhanced discrimination of the essential components of a behavior as a function of reversal and recovery, or from changes in the topography of a response as a result of exposure to extinction during reversal. The specific causes of postreversal intensification have yet to be investigated [see also Fig. 2 ("Kim"), McKenzie & Rushall, 1974].

In the case of the multiple-baseline design, comparisons across baseline conditions provide information on the occurrence of generalized treatment effects in untreated baselines or on the presence of varying trends in the different baselines. The generality of the experimental variable is assessed, at least in part, by comparing the effects of its sequential introduction into the various baselines. This form of replication is less complete than that from a successful reversal, to the extent that it is carried out under somewhat different circumstances (different behaviors, subjects, or settings) and involves the assumption that the variable will be (or has been) equally effective across all baselines. The experimenter cannot be certain that a full reversal would be achieved even if attempted, and so the degree of control demonstrated is less complete.

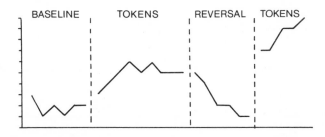

Fig. 2.20. Post reversal intensification may indicate enhanced discrimination or changes in topography resulting from reversal.

10. EVALUATION OF THE OVERALL PATTERN
OF THE DATA

The impact of the data as a whole serves as a basis for judgment of the success or failure of an experiment. Analysis of data within or between phases may draw attention to one or two equivocal elements, yet it might be unrealistic to regard these as invalidating the experiment as a whole. The overall pattern may prove convincing despite some isolated faults. Conversely, one good demonstration of control is unlikely to impress if the overall pattern of the data fails to generate confidence in the findings.

D. Determining Trends in the Data

As noted previously, visual analysis of data includes determination of changes in trend and changes in level between conditions. The methods by which trend lines may be fitted to time-series data are outlined below.

1. FREEHAND METHOD

Trend lines can be fitted freehand by drawing a line that bisects the data points, but the reliability of judgments of best-fit may be low when this method is used (Edwards, 1967).

2. SEMIAVERAGE METHOD

Straight-line trends may be fitted more rapidly and more reliably by the semiaverage method. The data in the phase are divided into two equal groups; if there are an unequal number of entries the middle one is usually omitted. The mean of each group of data is calculated to give two values, which can then be located on the Y axis. The two values of X are represented on the X axis by the midpoint of the range of each group. The points at which the respective XY pairs intersect are marked on the graph and a straight line is drawn through them. This process is useful if a rapid tentative estimate of trend is required (Neiswanger, 1956).

3. METHOD OF LEAST SQUARES

The method of least squares has the advantage of offering procedures for establishing logarithmic, parabolic, or straight-line trends in time-series data (Dubois, 1964).

   The procedure for establishing straight-line trends by the method of least squares is given below in a step-by-step form and is illustrated in Fig. 2.21.

   This procedure may be employed when inspection of the data indicates that a straight-line trend is appropriate. The data for the analysis can be

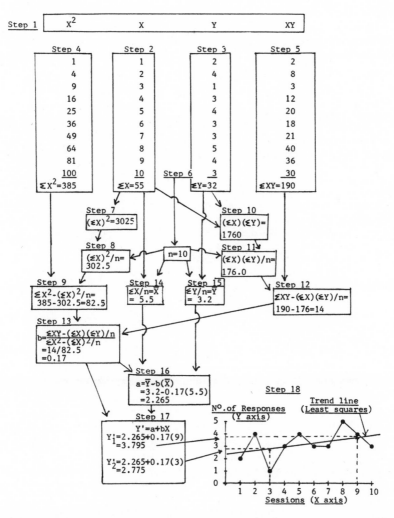

Fig. 2.21. Step-by-step procedure for calculation of linear trend by the method of least squares.

obtained directly from a graph. The X data consist of the number of days, sessions, or trials in the phase being analyzed, they are simply entered in numerical order (1, 2, 3, etc.). The Y data are obtained by reading off the value (e.g., number of responses, percentage of appropriate responses, etc.) of each of the data points in the phase from the Y scale. Once these data are obtained, the procedure outlined below may be followed.

Step-by-step outline of procedure for fitting a straight-line trend by the method of least squares.	Examples of computation using data from Fig. 2.21.

1. Head four columns as follows: X^2, X, Y, XY.

2. Fill out the X column with the number of days, sessions, or trials—in ascending numerical order—in the phase being analyzed, and their sum ($\sum X$). $\sum X = 55$

3. In the Y column, enter the scores obtained on each successive day, session, etc., and and their sum ($\sum Y$). $\sum Y = 32$

4. Fill out the X^2 column with the *square* of each of the corresponding X entries, and their sum ($\sum X^2$). $\sum X^2 = 385$

5. The XY column is composed of the cross products obtained by multiplying each Y column entry by its paired X column entry, and their sum ($\sum XY$). $\sum XY = 190$

6. The number of *pairs* of X and Y entries, n, is obtained by counting the number of entries in either the X or Y columns. $n = 10$

7. Square $\sum X$ to obtain $(\sum X)^2$. $(\sum X)^2 = 3025$

8. Divide $(\sum X)^2$ by n. $(\sum X)^2/n = 302.5$

9. Subtract $(\sum X)^2/n$ from $\sum X^2$. $\sum X^2 - (\sum X)^2/n = 385 - 302.5 = 82.5$

10. Multiply $\sum X$ and $\sum Y$ to obtain $(\sum X)(\sum Y)$. $(\sum X)(\sum Y) = 1760$

11. Divide $(\sum X)(\sum Y)$ by n. $(\sum X)(\sum Y)/n = 176.0$

12. Subtract $(\sum X)(\sum Y)/n$ from $\sum XY$. $\sum XY - (\sum X)(\sum Y)/n = 190 - 176 = 14$

13. Divide $\sum XY - (\sum X)(\sum Y)/n$ by $\sum X^2 - (\sum X)^2/n$ (Step 9) to obtain b. $b = 14/82.5 = 0.17$

14. Divide $\sum X$ by n to obtain mean of X, $\bar{X}$. $\bar{X} = 5.5$

15. Divide $\sum Y$ by n to obtain mean of Y, $\bar{Y}$. $\bar{Y} = 3.2$

16. To obtain a, multiply $\bar{X}$ by b and subtract $b(\bar{X})$ from $\bar{y}$. $a = \bar{Y} - b(\bar{x}) = 3.2 - 0.17(5.5)$ $= 2.265$

17. The regression equation $Y' = a + bX$ is solved by substituting the values of a and b, and values of X from the X column. Two solutions, for different values of X, give two values of Y'. $Y_1' = 2.265 + 0.17(X)$ Let $X = 9$ (ninth X entry); $Y_1' = 2.265 + 0.17(9) = 3.795$ Let $X = 3$ (third X entry): $Y_2' = 2.265 + 0.17(3) = 2.775$

18.   Locate Y_1' on the Y axis of the graph and
      the selected value of X on the X axis of
      the graph and mark the point at which
      they intersect. Similarly, locate Y_2' on
      the Y axis, and its paired X value on the
      X axis, and mark their point of intersec-
      tion. A straight line drawn through the
      two points is the line of best-fit and de-
      scribes the trend in the data.

4. TREND ANALYSIS OF DATA ON RATIO CHARTS

Several authors have outlined procedures for determining trends and making projections on the Standard Behavior Chart (Koenig, 1972; Penny-packer, Koenig, & Lindsley, 1972; White, 1972, 1973, 1974; Koorland & Martin, 1975). A description of these procedures is provided by Kazdin (1976).

While it is apparent that behavior analysts develop considerable skills in the visual analysis of graphic data, the means by which this skill is transmitted appears to rely on an oral, rather than a written, tradition. This is an unusual state of affairs, considering the undoubted prominence of visual analysis in the field of behavior analysis and the complexity of the procedures involved. This section has attempted to provide the beginnings of a systematic approach to the analysis of graphic data.

III. Forms of Graphic Representation

A. The Function of Graphs

The old Chinese proverb, "One picture is worth a thousand words," aptly represents the value of the graph in data presentation.

Three major functions can be identified. First, graphs present summaries of data, giving such information as the relationships between variables, trends over time, and the effect of new variables, in a form that permits rapid assimilation and assessment by the reader.

Second, graphs provide detailed descriptions. The range and stability of the data, the sequence of events over time, the degree of control achieved, and other similar information can be ascertained more effectively than would be possible from a table of figures.

Third, graphs can function as a compact analysis of data. In behavior analysis the graph is the primary form of data processing; research decisions, judgments, and conclusions are based almost exclusively on graphed data.

In essence, the function of the graph is to communicate, in a readily assimilable and attractive manner, descriptions and summaries of data that enable a rapid and accurate analysis of the facts.

Factors that help graphs to serve their function are *clarity*—data paths and data points should be distinctive and discriminable; *simplicity*—too many data paths and data points, too many scales or complex scale transformations inhibit information transfer; *explicitness*—brief, legible, and descriptive labeling of title, scale variables, and data paths aid the reader; and *good design*—selection of the most appropriate form of graph (e.g., line, bar), suitable scales, and good proportion so as to present the data clearly and without deception.

B. Types of Graphs

1. LINE GRAPHS

The line graph has the advantage of being easy to construct, simple and attractive in appearance, and widely adaptable. It is best employed to portray continuous data, trends, and/or the behavior of a set of variables over time or during different experimental conditions.

The line graph is based on a quadrant, known as the cartesian plane or field, in honor of the French mathematician and philosopher, Rene Descartes (1596–1650), who is credited with its invention.

This development permitted pictorial representation of mathematical functions on a two-dimensional plane divided into four quadrants by horizontal (X) and vertical (Y) axes. The portion of the vertical axis above the intersection by the horizontal axis has positive scale values; the portion below this point has negative scale values. The horizontal scale to the left of the vertical axis carries negative scale values; that on the right has positive scale values. Using this system, a point of any given positive or negative value of X and Y can be located in the quadrants. Figure 2.22 illustrates the cartesian plane.

2. THE PARTS OF THE LINE GRAPH

Line graphs share three common components: a whole or partial rectangle, horizontal and vertical scales, and at least one data path showing changes in the dependent variable (Meyers, 1970). The major components of the line graph are shown in Fig. 2.23 and described below.

The *rectangle* is formed, on two sides, by the horizontal X *axis*, or *abscissa* and the vertical Y *axis*, or *ordinate*. The common intersection of

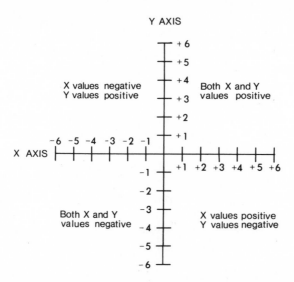

Fig. 2.22. The cartesian plane, the development of which made possible graphic presentation.

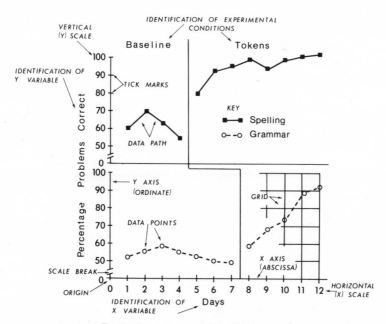

Fig. 2.23. The component parts of a line graph.

these two orthogonal axes is termed the *origin*. The length of the axes, and the consequent dimensions of the rectangle, is determined by the range of the variables represented on the *horizontal* and *vertical scales*. The numbers on the horizontal scale usually represent successive numerical values for the independent variable(s) and those on the vertical scale represent successive numerical values for the dependent variable(s). *Scale-breaks* should be used when scales are abbreviated to maintain the proportion of the rectangle.

The origin, on conventional arithmetic graphs, represents the zero point for the numerical values of both horizontal and vertical scales.

At those points along the scales where values are given or indicated, *tick marks* are made on or through the axes. These represent a vestige of the *grid* on which the data were originally plotted. Arithmetic graph papers are usually printed with a grid of regularly spaced vertical and horizontal lines, which aid in the preparation of the graph and the plotting of data. This grid is usually omitted in published figures in the interests of simplicity and clarity.

Data points are located within the rectangle by reference to their respective values on the X and Y scales. The point of intersection on the grid of the coordinates of the values determines the location of the data point within the quadrant, e.g., for the upper baseline of Fig. 2.23, 60% of words were spelled correctly in Session 1, 70% in Session 2, 63% in Session 3, etc. The relevant data points were plotted at the intersections of the relevant X and Y scale values, i.e., Session 1, $X = 1$, $Y = 60$; Session 2, $X = 2$, $Y = 70$; etc.

The line linking the data points obtained from successive observations is called the *data path* and represents the imaginary course taken by the datum point across time. The data path expresses the functional relationship between the independent and dependent variables. Since data are not usually continuously recorded, the data path rarely describes their actual path, but it does represent the closest available approximation (Meyers, 1970).

3. TYPES OF LINE GRAPHS

Line graphs may take any of a large number of forms. The choice of format depends on the type of data being presented and on the clarity and accuracy of portrayal offered by a particular graph type. Some examples of different types of line graph appear below.

a. Simple Line Graphs. Figure 2.24 shows a simple line graph, this example having multiple data paths. The data paths are clearly discernible and are identified by a key. The changes in experimental conditions have been emphasized by breaks in the data path and vertical dashed lines between conditions, and by labeling of each phase.

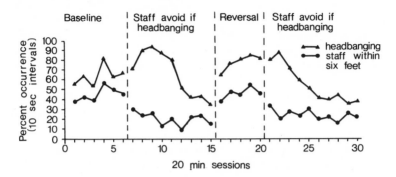

Fig. 2.24. A simple line graph with multiple data paths.

The clarity and simplicity of this type of graph aid the reader in assessing the data it presents, but this is not always so. The communicative function of the line graph can be inhibited by a profusion of different data paths and data points (e.g., Fig. 1, Packard, 1970). As a rule three separate data paths represent a maximum for an uncluttered line graph. Data analysis may also suffer when the data path is omitted (e.g., Fig. 2, Hopkins, 1968).

b. Subdivided Line Graphs. It is sometimes necessary to present complex part–whole relationships graphically, and the subdivided line graph provides a vehicle for separate and simultaneous display of such relationships within the one rectangle.

In Fig. 2.25 the proportion of "delusional conversation" and the proportion of "normal conversation" have been summed to provide a sessional record of "total conversation." When reading this graph note that the data path of delusional conversation serves as the abscissa for normal conversation (see also Fig. 2, Reynolds & Risley, 1968).

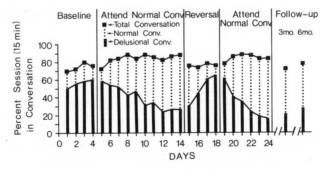

Fig. 2.25. A subdivided line graph showing component and total data. Note that the "delusional conversation" data path serves as the abscissa for locating "normal conversation" data.

138   Barry S. Parsonson and Donald M. Baer

c. Surface Charts. In this adaptation of the line graph the data path is indicated by the upper and lower limit of the shading, rather than by a line linking distinct data points.

Figure 2.26 shows a stratified surface chart that is functioning in much the same way as a line graph with multiple data paths (see Fig. 2.24). The surface chart format can also be adapted to serve the functions of the simple line graph with a single data path or the subdivided line graph (Fig. 2.25) (see also Fig. 1, Clark, Boyd, & Macrae, 1975).

d. Step Charts. The step or staircase chart (Fig. 2.27) is often classed as a bar graph, but it is in fact a form of line graph. Spear (1969) noted that it was a useful format for the display of frequency distributions, data with abrupt fluctuations, and data gathered over differing time periods.

One limitation is that multiple data paths can be shown clearly only when these different data paths do not share the same coordinates. This problem may be overcome by superimposing a simple line graph on the step chart (e.g., Fig. 2.39) (see also Fig. 1, Herbert & Baer, 1972).

e. Three-Dimensional Charts. Charts such as that shown in Fig. 2.28 are not widely used, but they do offer an economy of space and an interesting format for emphasizing similarity of experimental effects across a number of subjects, settings, or behaviors.

Difficulty in reading off the scale values may be a disadvantage.

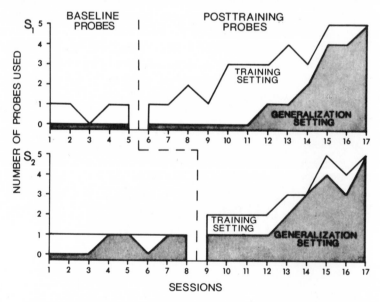

Fig. 2.26. A surface chart, stratified to accommodate multiple data paths.

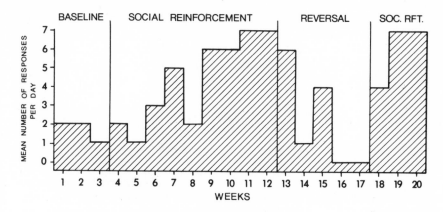

Fig. 2.27. A step or staircase chart.

These charts can be drawn easily and accurately using *isometric* graph paper (see also Fig. 2, Blough, 1961).

f. Range Graphs. The range of scores obtained from an individual, a group, or different reliability observers can be plotted on a line graph such as the idealized example shown in Fig. 2.29 (see also Fig. 1, Reynolds & Risley, 1968).

The lower limit of the range serves as the source of one data path and the upper limit is used to establish the other. The closer together the two data paths, the narrower the range. Kratochwill and Wetzel (in press) discuss the value of such graphs in the analysis of observer agreement.

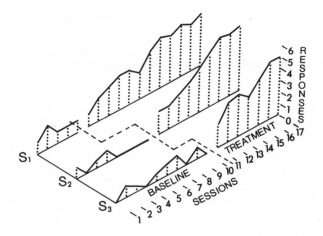

Fig. 2.28. A three-dimensional chart.

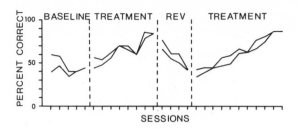

Fig. 2.29. A range line graph.

g. Multiple-Scale Line Graphs. This form of line graph allows comparison of data based on dissimilar units within the one rectangle. The location of the data points from each set of data, within the rectangle, is made
possible by establishing a separate vertical scale for each set of data. The
usual practice is to place the scales at opposite ends of the rectangle (e.g.,
Fig. 2.30a) (see also Fig. 3, Schroeder, 1972).

In reading Fig. 2.30a, note that the left vertical scale relates to number
of operations per minute and that the scale is divided into two-unit intervals.
The right vertical scale, units completed per minute, has scale intervals of
only .2 units. The reader is required to associate the squares and broken-line
data path (ops. per min.) with the left vertical scale, and the dots and solid-
line (units comp.) with the scale on the right.

Multiple-scale graphs should be used with caution as they are easily
misinterpreted. It is important to associate each data path with its related
scale, and to alert the reader that multiple-scales are in use, especially when
the visual impression given by the data paths makes judgment difficult. For
example, in Fig. 2.30a the "units completed per minute" data path appears to

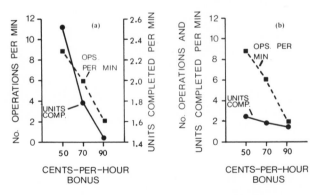

Fig. 2.30. (a) A multiple-scale line graph. Graphs of this type require careful reading. (b)
Identical data plotted on single scale format give a different impression.

parallel that of "operations per minute." The decrement in "units completed-per-minute" is emphasized by the fact that the data path slopes steeply right down to the abscissa, but inspection of the right vertical scale reveals that it has no zero origin.

A more accurate assessment of these data might be obtained from Fig. 2.30b, which shows the same graph converted to a single vertical scale encompassing both variables. The impression given by Fig. 2.30b is different from that provided by Fig. 2.30a, hence the need for caution in reading multiple-scale graphs. Comparison of relative rates of change, such as those in Fig. 2.30a, may also be appropriately analyzed using semilogarithmic charts (see Fig. 2.42c).

h. Trend Lines. Sometimes generalizations are sought from data that, because of their variability, are difficult to integrate. Under such circumstances there are available a number of trend-plotting procedures, ranging from freehand estimates to the method of least squares. The choice of an appropriate procedure is dependent on its applicability to the data at hand and the use to be made of the information it produces. (Details of various trend-fitting procedures can be found in Section II,D.)

Figure 2.31a illustrates the use of lines, other than a data path, to establish trends in data. In this instance the trends were obtained by the method of least squares. It should be remembered that a trend line represents the data in only a generalized way, and that the trend line need not pass through any of the obtained data points, even though it can be regarded as representative of the trend in those obtained data. All of the data points should be plotted and shown along with a trend line, even though the actual data path may be omitted, so that the reader can appreciate the deviation of those points from the trend line and their general pattern. The manner in which the trend line was determined should also be reported since some methods of estimation are more reliable than others.

The data in Fig. 2.31b are identical to those represented in Fig. 2.31a, but the dashed line through each condition is not a trend line: it indicates the level of the condition mean. As with a trend line, a mean line represents the data only in a generalized way, and none of the data points may actually fall on the line. The addition of mean lines to Fig. 2.31b gives the impression of an abrupt and evident change in level between baseline and treatment, whereas the change in least-squares trend in Fig. 2.31a is less impressive.

The practice of adding mean lines to a graph may prove misleading when there is considerable variability in the data or when there are only small changes in trend between conditions. They may, by emphasizing mean changes, imply changes in level that suggest a greater degree of experimental control than had actually been achieved (see also Kratochwill, Chapter 1 of this volume).

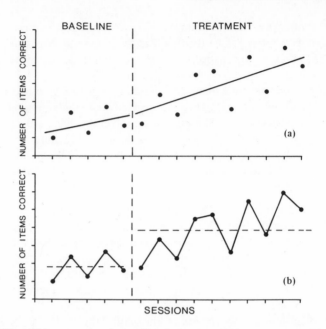

Fig. 2.31. (a) Linear trends calculated by the method of least squares. (b) Identical data with the phase means indicated by dashed horizontal lines. These give an impression of experimental effect not supported by trends in the data.

4. BAR GRAPHS

The bar graph offers simplicity of construction, clear presentation of information and, because of its many forms, versatility. It can be used to present either continuous or discrete data (although, puristically, the latter are most appropriate); to display comparative information, such as the values of one or more variables obtained simultaneously or the values of the different contributions of components; and to present blocks of data.

Like the line graph, the bar graph is based on the cartesian plane and most of its components are like those in Fig. 2.23. The major difference is in the replacement of the data points and data path with horizontal bars, or vertical columns, that extend from the relevant axis to the appropriate intersection of the X and Y values on the grid. The length of the bar or height of the column indicates the magnitude of the data at that point. It is important that the width of each bar be identical. If not, an erroneous impression of change can arise from the additional comparison provided by a simultaneous two-dimensional change in area as a variable changes in magnitude.

While bar graphs with horizontal bars (see Fig. 2.32a) are always called *bar graphs*, those with vertical bars (see Fig. 2.32b) are often termed *column*

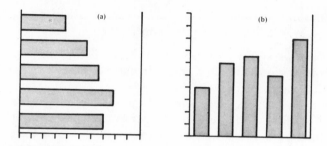

Fig. 2.32. (a) A simple bar graph in bar format with horizontal bars. (b) A simple bar graph in column format with vertical bars.

graphs. This distinction is only a spatial one; there are no technical differences. The generic term "bar graph" will be used to refer to both forms, although, where relevant, they will be identified as *bar* or *column* graphs.

5. TYPES OF BAR GRAPHS

The versatility of the bar graph format is evidenced by the variety in which it is found in the behavior analytic literature. A sampling follows.

a. Simple Bar Graphs. There are two types of simple bar graphs, the single bar, shown in both bar and column form in Fig. 2.32, and the grouped bar, seen in grouped column format in Fig. 2.33.

The single bar graph provides for neat and simple presentation, but it is limited in that it can be used only to communicate the simplest forms of data.

The grouping of bars (e.g., Fig. 2.33) permits the display of more complex data and allows the reader to make direct comparisons between a

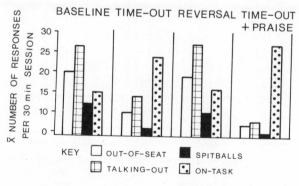

Fig. 2.33. A simple bar graph with grouped bars.

number of variables over a series of sessions and a variety of conditions (see also Fig. 1, Wasik, Senn, Welch, & Cooper, 1969).

b. Subdivided Bar Graphs. Subdivision allows the expression of part–whole relationships in bar graphs in much the same way as in the subdivided line graph (see Fig. 2.25).

Figure 2.34a shows requests made by a child, for play materials during preschool sessions. A proportion of requests were made through gestures (e.g., pointing) and others were verbal in nature. Summing these two components—reading across the top of each column—provided an index of total requests per block of sessions. When reading this graph, note that the top of the "gesture" component of the column serves as the origin of the "verbal" component, that is, for the first baseline column, number of gesture requests = 65, verbal requests = 5, total = 70 (see also Fig. 4, Hall, Lund, & Jackson, 1968).

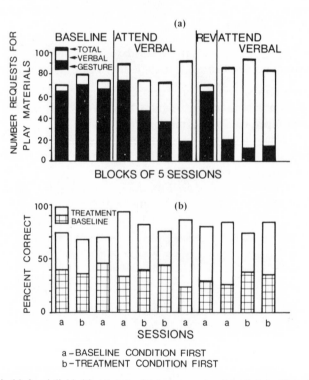

Fig. 2.34. (a) A subdivided bar graph with component and total data. Note that the tops of the "gesture" columns serve as the abscissa for the "verbal" columns. (b) A subdivided bar graph showing multiple data. Both baseline and treatment data share the same abscissa.

   The subdivided bar format can also be used to present multiple data in stratified form, as shown in Fig. 2.34b. Each of the columns shown in Fig. 2.34b has the abscissa of the graph as its base, so that for the first column percentage correct in baseline = 40%, treatment = 74%. This form of subdivision represents an alternative to the line graph with multiple data paths (e.g., Fig. 2.24) and the grouped bar format (e.g., Fig. 2.33). However, it is satisfactory only if the different data do not have the same coordinates (see also Fig. 4, O'Leary, Becker, Evans, & Saudargas, 1969).

   c. Proportion Bar Graphs. The extent to which each of a number of components contributes to the whole can be expressed as a proportion of that total. A proportion bar graph provides graphic expression of these relationships, as seen in Fig. 2.35.

   In this figure, the relative contribution of each of four categories of specific playground behavior to the total amount of playground behavior is shown. From such a figure a reader can quickly ascertain which classes of behavior were predominant in each phase of the experiment (see also Fig. 1, Boer, 1968).

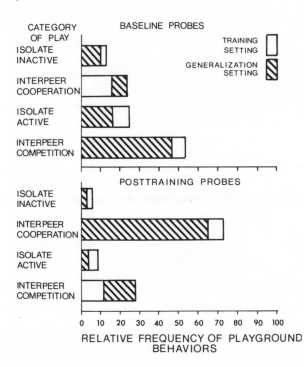

Fig. 2.35. A proportion bar graph. The proportion that each component contributes to the whole is reflected in the length of the bar.

Where relevant, the proportionate contributions can be set out in rank-order to produce an orderly and pleasing visual effect.

d. Deviation Bar Graphs.   Changes in a dependent variable as a consequence of intervention may be in either a positive or negative direction from a previously established baseline or standard. These changes can be expressed graphically by plotting the deviations from the standard, which serves as the point of origin.

Figure 2.36 shows mean change in caloric intake per meal over a series of experimental phases. Presume that the zero point was determined on the basis of calculations of the mean caloric intake per meal necessary for the subject to maintain stable weight. Intake over and above that amount was likely to contribute to weight gain, intake below that amount would contribute to weight loss. Assume that the obese subject wished to lose weight and that the program trained control of caloric intake. Baseline and reversal data show that the mean per-meal intake was above the "stable weight" limit (zero on the scale). The treatment data show reduction in mean intake to below the stable weight limit.

Representation of these deviations necessitated the use of the upper right and lower right quadrants of the cartesian plane (see Fig. 2.22). Had the bar format been used instead of the column, the upper left and right quadrants would have been employed.

Schroeder and Baer (1972) found that use of the deviation bar format made possible the identification of important experimental effects that might otherwise have gone undetected (see also Fig. 2, Mann, 1972).

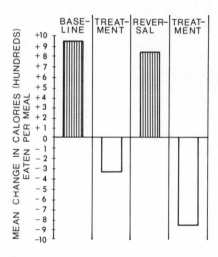

Fig. 2.36. A deviation bar graph indicates the extent to which behavior deviates, in a positive or negative direction, from a baseline or standard.

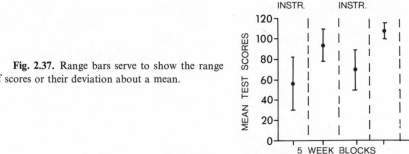

Fig. 2.37. Range bars serve to show the range of scores or their deviation about a mean.

e. Range Bar Graphs. These, like their line graph equivalents (see Fig. 2.29), can be used to display the range or variation of a set of scores. The graph in Fig. 2.37 has data points indicating mean test scores with range bars at each point to show the standard deviations about each mean. Range bars allow a reader to see the variation in scores and to estimate overlap between scores obtained under different conditions. When grouped data are presented graphically, these relationships can be seen more clearly than would be the case if these same data were to appear instead on an accompanying table (see also Fig. 4, Semb, 1974).

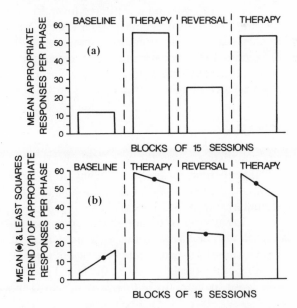

Fig. 2.38. (a) A typical bar graph with column tops indicating condition means. (b) A trend bar, with least-squares linear trend of each phase shown to aid analysis.

f. Trend Bar Graphs.   Trend line graphs (e.g., Fig. 2.31a) can provide the reader with useful information. This same information is not generally available when data are plotted in bar graph form, especially if the bars represent blocks of time rather than discrete sessions.

Figure 2.38a represents data as typically shown on a bar graph. Figure 2.38b displays those same data but the mean is now represented by a dot rather than by the top of the column. The least-squares trend over each phase is represented in the slope in each column, the height of the left upright being determined by $Y' = a + b(1)$ and that of the right upright by $Y' = a + b(15)$—each column representing a block of 15 sessions. The reader can now examine the trends in each phase and may, as a consequence, come to different conclusions about the data than would have been the case if simply confronted with Fig. 2.38a. This type of graph may distort apparent trend if data, obtained from a large number of sessions and showing a steep trend, are represented on narrow columns.

6. COMBINATION LINE AND BAR GRAPHS

Complex information can be presented graphically by combining different types of graphic form within the one rectangle. By this means a variety of data can be presented in a clear and uncluttered form, free from a mass of interwoven data paths and crowded data points. Figure 2.39 shows a bar graph–surface chart–step chart–line graph combination (see also Fig. 1, Clark, Boyd, & Macrae, 1975). A combination of line graph and step chart formats have been successfully employed by Herbert and Baer (1972), while Guess (1969) has used a combination of line and grouped-column formats.

7. CUMULATIVE CURVES

One form of cumulative curve, the cumulative record, historically was synonymous with the experimental analysis of behavior. In experiments using automated equipment, the responses on the manipulandum typically were fed through a cumulative recorder. This instrument produced on a moving chart paper, a cumulative curve of the number of responses (ordinate) over time (abscissa). Each response stepped the response pen one unit "up" the paper, which was moving at a constant rate. The rate of responding thus was expressed in the slope of the resultant curve: the higher the rate, the steeper the curve, and the lower the rate, the more nearly the curve approximated a horizontal line.

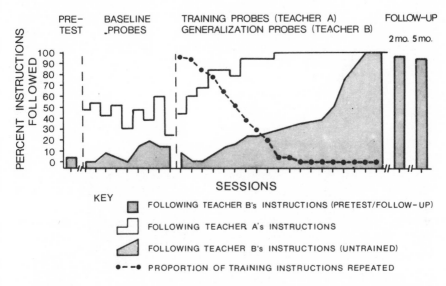

Fig. 2.39. A combination of bar graph, surface chart, step chart, and line graph shows how complex data may be presented graphically.

Reinforcer delivery usually was indicated by hatch marks on the curve, and additional events noted during a session could be marked on the paper margin by an event marker (Reynolds, 1968).

The cumulative record provided an immediate, compact, and continuous record of reinforcer delivery data; response data, such as number of responses, local and overall response rates, changes in response rate, and interresponse times; plus any additional data from the event recorder. Thus it was a remarkably complete and accurate record. Oddly enough, it is rarely used today in applied work, perhaps because instrument recording is much less common than in the experimental analysis, persons unfamiliar with it find it difficult to read, and many of those involved in the applied field have little or no background in the experimental analysis of behavior where the cumulative record originated.

Cumulative curves can be produced from any data by accumulating the scores or number of responses from succeeding sessions across time.

Figure 2.40a and b shows, respectively, cumulative curves presented in line graph, and step chart form. Bar graphs may also be used (see also Fig. 3, Schroeder & Holland, 1968; Fig. 2, Lloyd & Knutzen, 1969; Fig. 3, Risley, 1968; Fig. 2, Goetz & Baer, 1973; and Fig. 2, Wulbert, Nyman, Snow, & Owen, 1973).

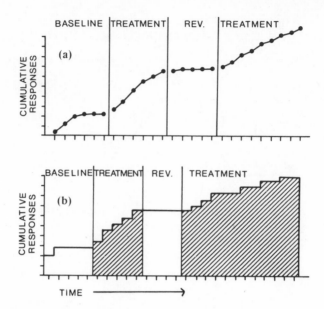

Fig. 2.40. (a) A cumulative line graph. (b) A cumulative step chart. Note that cumulative data never decline below the horizontal.

8. SCALE TRANSFORMATIONS

Two major types of scale transformation are used in presenting data from behavior analyses: reciprocal scales and logarithmic scales. These are employed for a number of reasons. The data may be more accurately represented and interpreted if scales are transformed; comparison of data based on dissimilar scales may be made possible through scale transformation; or the data may "look better" if transformed.

Scale transformations using reciprocals simply produce a mirror image of the data path that would have been derived from the original untreated data. The purpose of such a transformation would be largely cosmetic, in that a decelerating curve could be represented as an accelerating curve, or vice versa (see Fig. 2, Franchina, Hauser, & Agee, 1975).

Logarithmic scales exist in two forms. Logarithmic, log–log, double-log, or double-ratio charts, as they are variously called, employ logarithmic scales along both the X and the Y axes. Since most behavioral studies involve the measurement of behavior over time, which is elapsing at a constant rate, this form is not frequently encountered in behavior analysis.

Semilogarithmic, or ratio, charts have a logarithmic Y scale, with one or more logarithmic cycles along the Y axis, but an arithmetic (equal-interval)

X scale along the abscissa. When semilogarithmic chart paper is used the numbering along both scales is arithmetic, but the Y scale has no zero origin (see Fig. 2.41a).

If the graph is plotted on regular arithmetic paper, the Y scale units are transformed into their logarithmic equivalents and located on the equi-distant grid scale. The arithmetic X scale is not transformed (see Fig. 2, Bellack, 1973). Logarithmic scales have no zero origin, nor do they have any scale units with negative values.

Advocates of ratio charts (e.g., Lindsley, 1971; Smith, 1938) consider them to be ideal for expressing relative or comparative rates of change in data. For example, in Fig. 2.41a the first "treatment" data point is on 1.1, the second on 2.2, the third on 4.4, and the fourth on 8.8. Clearly, the rate is doubling in each successive session. The ratio of change is a constant $1:2$ over these sessions, a 100% increase in each instance. The equal magnitude

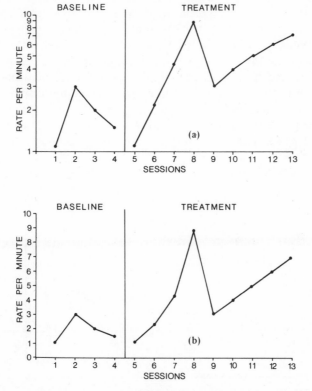

Fig. 2.41. (a) Data plotted on a semilogarithmic chart. Note the absence of a zero on the Y scale. (b) Identical data plotted on an arithmetic chart. Compare the visual impression given by each chart.

of these changes is represented, on the ratio chart, as a straight line. These same data have been reproduced on the accompanying arithmetic chart (Fig. 2.41b) and appear as an exponential curve, rather than as a straight line. Conversely, the "treatment" data obtained for sessions 9–13 (Fig. 2.41a) are not changing at a constant ratio, but rather the ratio is decreasing between each succeeding pair of data points: hence the asymptotic curve. These same data appear as a straight line on the arithmetic chart (Fig. 2.41b).

Smith argues that comparative rates of change are more easily, and more accurately, determined from ratio scales than from arithmetic scales and that, with a small amount of practice, absolute changes in rate can be accurately read from ratio charts.

Figure 2.42a,b,c, respectively, shows the same data presented on multiple-scale and single-scale arithmetic graphs and on a single-scale ratio chart. On the multiple-scale graph (Fig. 2.42a) the rates of change in operations per minute and units completed per minute appear approximately equal. Presented on a single-scale arithmetic graph (Fig. 2.42b), the impression is that although the rate of operations per minute is declining rapidly, the rate of units completed per minute is falling off more slowly. The ratio chart (Fig. 2.42c) retains the impression of a rapid decline in operations per minute, while the decrement in units completed appears to fall between the steep decline shown on the multiple-scale graph and the more shallow fall-off on the single-scale arithmetic graph. For operations-per-minute, the rate at 50 cents per hour compared with that at 90 cents per hour stands at a ratio of 4.5:1, while the ratio for units completed is almost 2:1. Although these ratios could be calculated from any of these graphs, Fig. 2.42c would, under these circumstances, present the more accurate visual impression of relative slope.

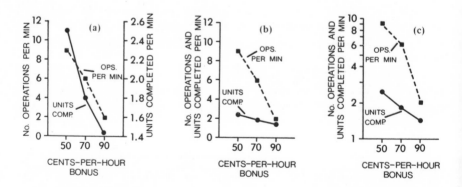

Fig. 2.42. A comparison of the visual impressions from identical data plotted on (a) multiple scale and (b) single scale, arithmetic charts, and (c) on a semilogarithmic chart.

In developing the Standard Behavior Chart (Koenig, 1972; Koorland & Martin, 1975; Lindsley, 1971; Pennypacker, Koenig, & Lindsley, 1972), Lindsley has sought to provide a standardized and useful analytic tool for persons involved in the systematic recording of behavior.

The Standard Behavior Chart (SBC) arose out of the view that frequency (rate of responding) was a universal and well-proven measure of behavior. The fact that semilogarithmic scales were capable of expressing both comparative rates of change and percentages (Koenig, 1972) meant that they were the best available mode of recording and analyzing the frequency data.

The six-cycle logarithmic Y scale of the SBC (see Koorland & Martin, 1975) represents "counts per minute" (frequency) of behavior. It has sufficient counting periods to allow for 24 hours of continuous recording of daily frequencies ranging from 1000 responses per minute to one response per 24 hours. The arithmetic X scale represents 140 successive calendar days and is conveniently subdivided into 7-day blocks.

Procedures have been developed that permit simple linear analyses of the changes in the plotted frequencies over time. These changes, referred to under the generic title of *celeration*, represent increases (*acceleration*) or decreases (*deceleration*) in response frequency. The linear analyses permit precise representation of current trends in data and, it is claimed, provide relatively accurate projections of future trends (Koenig, 1972).

A frequently raised objection to the use of semilogarithmic charts is that they are often used inappropriately and, even when used properly, are often misinterpreted (Lutz, 1949). The provision of programmed self-instruction manuals for the SBC (Pennypacker, Koenig, & Lindsley, 1972; Koorland & Martin, 1975), and the demonstration that children *can* use the chart accurately (Lindsley, 1971), seem to have done little to encourage widespread use of the SBC in research reported in specialist behavioral journals. The restriction to rate of responding as the measure of behavior as well as the fact that logarithmic scales are unable to accommodate zero rates of responding adequately, may be factors in the resistance to their widespread adoption.

A perusal of published applied studies shows frequency of occurrence measures, such as number/proportion of intervals in which the target response occurs at least once, are among the most widely used.

While this selection of graphic formats is not exhaustive, it does draw attention to the variety of methods of data presentation available to behavior analysts. Careful selection of graphic format should permit display of data in accurate, interesting, and attractive form. Even relatively complex data may be presented by combining different formats (e.g., line, column, and surface chart). Considering its significance in behavior analysis, we should be encouraged to explore to the full the potential of the graphic form.

IV. The Construction and Presentation of Graphs

In the preparation of graphic material, the constructor must constantly bear in mind the fact that the primary function of the graph is one of communication. A graph should be designed and presented in a fashion that provides the reader with a clear, complete, and accurate summary, description, and representation of the data. It should be able to do so without assistance from the accompanying text.

As graphs are expensive to publish, they should be used selectively. Relevant data that can be presented in simple graphic form have the best cost:benefit ratio. When preparing graphs for publication, obtain details of the format preferred by the editors. The *Publication Manual of the American Psychological Association* (2nd ed.) has detailed guidelines (pp. 50–55) on the preparation of figures for the publications it sponsors. Since these guidelines have also been adopted by a large number of non-American Psychological Association journals (see Appendix B of the Manual), it is a useful addition to one's professional library. The editors of the *Journal of Applied Behavior Analysis* (*JABA*) have provided additional instructions on the preparation of graphs for intending authors (see *JABA*, 1976, *9*, 24).

A. Proportions

Factors contributing to the determination of the proportions of a graph's rectangle are the accuracy with which particular dimensions represent changes in the variable(s) of interest, the data to be displayed, the type of graph chosen to portray those data, and the space available for the display of the graph.

Behavioral data are usually plotted as changes in the dependent variable over time as a function of the systematic introduction and/or withdrawal of the independent, experimental variable. The magnitude of these changes is expressed vertically on a line or column graph, and horizontally on a bar graph. Distortion of the relative magnitude of the data points is likely to result if the scale (usually the *Y* scale) representing the dependent variable(s) is longer or has more widely spaced scale graduations than that for the independent variable(s). Distortion can also result when the *Y* scale is foreshortened or attenuated, since vertical changes are emphasized when the data path fluctuates sharply close to the baseline (see Fig. 2.6). A scale-break should be used to notify a reader that the scale has been abbreviated.

The dimensions of the rectangle, and thus the amount of the available display area that it will occupy, are partly determined by the type of data to be displayed and the type of graph selected to represent it.

For instance, data from studies employing reversal or multiple-component designs will usually be plotted over a considerable time span and are likely to generate broad, shallow figures. Multiple-baseline studies are more likely to produce broad, deep figures that absorb much of the available display space. Line and column graphs tend to have X axes longer than their Y axes, and so will generally be broad and shallow, while bar graphs may require deep, narrow spaces.

Obviously, such a variety of factors make the determination of rules of proportion difficult. However, the Y axis to X axis ratio of 2:3 represents a proportion that limits distortion and has generalized applicability to the spaces within which graphs of behavioral data are most frequently displayed (see Table 2.1).

Although graphs may be specifically prepared to fit a particular space, it is possible to submit the completed figures on letter-size (8.5 × 11 in.)

TABLE 2.1

The Dimensions of Paper, Journal Pages, and 35 mm Slide Frames within Which Behavior-Analytic Graphs Are Often Displayed

Mode of display	Outside dimensions in inches (centimeters in parentheses)	Maximum display area in inches (centimeters in parentheses)
Letter-size paper	8.50(21.6) × 11.00(28.0)	Variable, depends on margins, etc.
A4 (metric) paper	8.25(21.0) × 11.75(30.0)	Variable, depends on margins, etc.
Journal of Applied Behavior Analysis	6.88(17.5) × 9.88(25.1)	Double column 5.81(14.8) × 8.25(21.0) Single column 2.81(7.2) × 8.25(21.0)
Journal for the Experimental Analysis of Behavior	6.88(17.5) × 9.88(25.1)	Double column 5.88(14.9) × 8.38(21.3) Single column 2.81(7.2) × 8.38(21.3)
Behavior Therapy	5.88(14.9) × 8.88(22.6)	4.50(11.5) × 7.38(18.8)
Behavior Research and Therapy	7.38(18.8) × 10.69(27.1)	5.25(13.4) × 7.75(19.7)
35 mm slide		0.88(2.3) × 1.31(3.4)

paper and have the printer reduce the proportions to fit the given space [*Publication Manual of the APA* (2nd ed.), 1974].

B. Titles, Labels, and Presentation of Data

The degree to which a graph achieves its communicative function is very dependent on concise, descriptive figure titles, clear identification of the scale variables and scale units, and data presentation that emphasizes clarity, precision, and ease of assimilation. The careful planning that these factors require is emphasized by the following aspects of presentation, which have to be considered when constructing a graph (see Fig. 2.23).

The title and scale captions are important because they will inform a reader about the graph. They should not be too long nor contain irrelevant detail as these defeat the purpose of graphic presentation of data. Succinct and accurate description is most effective.

Scale numbering, tick-marks, and the units of which a scale is composed should be clearly apparent to a reader. Scale transformations should be reported in the scale captions. Broken or abbreviated scales should be marked by scale breaks, and where data paths or bars cross them they too should be broken to conform with the scale breaks.

It is also important, when planning a graph, to take into account any changes in scale from the originally drafted form to the graph as finally displayed. For instance, a graph to be published in a journal will probably be reduced in size for presentation. Consequently, the lettering, numerals, and symbols will also be reduced in scale. A graph projected from a 35 mm slide may be increased in scale by projection, but the details will have to be read from a distance. In both cases, the original lettering, numerals, and symbols must be sufficiently large to remain legible after the scale changes.

Multiple data paths and grouped or subdivided bars should be clearly identified by discriminably different types of data path (e.g., solid, broken, dotted), data points (e.g., open or closed squares, triangles, circles), or bars (e.g., shaded, cross-hatched, dotted). The separate components should be clearly labeled and/or identified by symbols on a key.

The essence of graphic presentation is simplicity and clarity. Attempts to convey complex information may overload the capacity of the graphic form. If data are complex, yet suited to graphic presentation, the best mode of display may be through a combination of graphic formats, such as that illustrated in Fig. 2.39, or on subdivided line (Fig. 2.25), surface (Fig. 2.26), or bar (Fig. 2.34) graphs. Alternately, a number of separate graphs could be presented individually or reproduced on thin transparent sheets overlaying each other so that they can be read either independently or super-imposed.

Presentation of trivial or unimportant data should be avoided since they add nothing but confusion, but all relevant information should be included (see Fig. 2.8).

C. Techniques of Graph Construction

1. GENERAL EQUIPMENT

Every skilled task generates an array of specialized equipment that, although not always absolutely necessary, can contribute to a good quality product. The accompanying list is one of equipment that is not highly expensive (many of the items can be purchased at "dime" stores) and that will contribute to better graphs. Items of general equipment useful in graph construction: small T-square, plastic triangles (90° and/or 30–60°), bevel-edged plastic rule, a selection of graph papers, tracing paper, adhesive tapes (double-sided and "invisible"), No. 3 pencils, pencil-sharpener, soft eraser, and typing correction fluid (useful for correcting errors). A firm laminated-plastic or glass-topped table can serve as a suitable working surface if a back-lit charting table is not available. The work area should be uncluttered and well lit.

2. PLANNING THE LAYOUT

The keynote to the production of good graphs is careful attention to detail at all stages of construction, from the selection of the type of graph to the finished product.

The selection of the type of graph will be influenced by the forms of data to be displayed and the information they will be required to convey. Simplicity, clarity, and accuracy of communication are desirable characteristics of graphic design, wording, and presentation.

A draft, drawn up on an appropriate graph paper, will help in the assessment of the adequacy of the chosen format. The layout should be centered on the paper and proportioned to approximate the intended display space and should include any wording, numerals, and key symbols that may appear on the finished product in their intended location and of an approximate size (off-the-graph lettering for scale captions, experimental conditions, etc., is usually of a bigger size than that used inside the rectangle to label a key or data paths). The draft layout should be done lightly in No. 3 pencil so that components can be erased and altered if necessary.

As the size of lettering, numerals, and symbols and the weight of lines will be affected by changes in scale in publication or projection, careful choices should be made during preparation. [See Figs. 2-11 and 2-14 in Spear (1969) for template letter and pen line sizes and the effects of reduction upon them, and Fig. 2, Publication Manual of the APA (2nd ed.) (1974), for similar information on press-on materials.]

Once the layout is deemed satisfactory, spelling of all wording should be checked for errors and the accuracy of numerals, symbols, and labels should be ensured. The location of data points and data paths, or the magnitude of bars, should be rechecked for accuracy. The draft is now ready for transfer to its final form.

3. DRAFTING PROCESSES

Whatever the process (pen, typewriter, press-on materials) selected to produce the graph in its final form, it is necessary to transfer the figure from graph paper on to plain paper.

When tracing paper is employed, the draft should first be firmly and squarely fixed to the working surface. (The invisible-type adhesive tape seems to peel off easiest, without tearing the paper, when the job is finished. The tape is also easier to peel off later if a small section is folded back on itself before being applied to the working surface).

A sheet of tracing paper is then overlaid on top of the draft, the graph is centered in relation to its future location on the tracing paper, and then the tracing paper is also firmly and squarely attached to the working surface with tape.

The details of the figure may then be traced from the draft using a pen or direct application of press-on materials. The X and Y axes are traced first. Next the tick-marks (correctly spaced and of equal length) are added to the axes and the data points, data paths, or bar lines are traced within the rectangle. (If press-on materials are used for line graph construction, data path tapes can be applied first and then the data points overlaid to cover the joins in the tape. Solid data points are much easier to apply neatly than the open types). When tracing graphs with multiple data paths, surfaces, or subdivided bars, separate completion of each data path, surface, or bar level, will ensure greater accuracy.

If the location, size, and/or spacing of lettering and numerals have been worked out on the draft, the relevant details can be reproduced on the top copy. The grid lines of the underlying graph paper can be used as guides to spacing, and vertical and horizontal location of lettering.

Before removing the completed top copy from the draft, carefully check that all details to be traced or copied have in fact been accurately reproduced, it may not be easy to line everything up again. Also check out for spelling errors, letter reversals, or inappropriate wording, since these are easier to rectify while the figure is firmly taped down over a grid, which can be used as a reference in making alterations.

The most commonly employed drafting processes are discussed next:

a. Pen. With practice and the right equipment effective and professional-looking graphs can be drafted with pen and ink. The available equipment ranges from the relatively inexpensive drafting pen and a collection of different nibs to a collection of reservoir pens. The reservoir-type pen produces fine work but a set of these may be a worthwhile investment only if frequent use justifies the outlay. Used carefully, the nib-type pen can provide a satisfactory result. Felt-tipped pens can be used, but they are not suitable for use with templates and tend to produce lines of variable quality and definition. Advice and supplies of pens, nibs, inks, and templates can be obtained at most stores that specialize in supply of drafting materials.

Care is required when using pen and ink as spillage, blots, smudges, or marks are easily produced and difficult to remedy. Make sure the ink bottle is securely located in a place where, if it is knocked over, it is unlikely to spill on the work. Using rules with beveled edges, templates that are raised above the surface of the paper, and only a minimum of ink on the nib, are precautions that help avoid blots. To avoid smudging, it is best to work from the top of the sheet down so that already completed work is not marred, and blotting paper can be used to dry the work quickly if a slow-drying ink is used.

Marks are sometimes made by the residue of ink left on equipment after prior use, so keep it clean at all times. Errors or small marks may be covered with typewriter-correcting fluid or pasted over so that they will not be visible when the graph is reproduced on a copier.

b. Typewriters. Accurate and effective graphs can be produced with a typewriter equipped with a carbon ribbon, a rule, and a felt-tipped pen. Paper in a typewriter can be moved, in calibrated units, in two directions. The horizontal spacing on most standard machines is 12 spaces per inch (per 2.55 cm) for *elite* type and 10 spaces per inch for *pica*. Vertical spacing is generally 6 spaces per inch but there are variations. To check your machine, type a row and a column of letters and measure with a rule.

Lettering, numerals, axes, scale breaks, tick marks, and data points can all be accurately reproduced on a graph with a typewriter. The letter-space markings on the paper bail provide an accurate guide for calibration of the graph and placement of data points.

Many typewriters have guide holes in the line indicator through which a pencil or felt pen can be inserted. Horizontal lines then can be produced by moving the carriage from left to right, vertical lines, by rolling the platen. Alternately, solid, dashed, or dotted horizontal lines can be produced using the appropriate keys and similar vertical lines can be made by placing the paper in the machine sideways.

Scale breaks can be made with the "slant" key, while tick marks can be applied using the hyphen/underline key. Data points can be identified with symbols such as asterisk, o, or appropriate code letters, and joined using a rule and pen.

A typewriter can also be used to construct portions of bar and column graphs (see Meyers, 1970) and for producing lettering and numbering, either directly onto the final copy or for cutting out for a "paste-up," which is then reproduced on a copying machine. Note that some journals will not accept graphs with typed lettering because it does not reduce well for publication. However, an IBM Selectric typewriter with an Orator element produces a large, bold type that may prove acceptable.

c. *Press-on Materials.*   These offer many advantages, they are clean, simple to use, and a wide range of styles, sizes, and weights of lettering and numerals is available, as are lines of different thickness, weight, and form (solid, dashed, dotted), a variety of shadings for bar graphs and surface charts, and an array of symbol sizes and shapes for data points.

Typefaces should be selected for clarity and legibility and the one type used throughout the figure. The height of the type is measured in "points," but there are differences between *pica* (American) and *didot* (European) point units, the latter being slightly larger than the former. Most good materials will provide both "point" data and the metric linear equivalents on the sheet. Drafting equipment suppliers usually have sample materials available and they are usually willing to advise on purchases.

Care is needed in handling and applying these materials as they are easily damaged and may be difficult to remove cleanly once in place, although they can be lifted off on carefully applied adhesive tape or removed with a soft eraser. Damage may result during application if a sharp or fine-pointed instrument is used to press the material onto the tracing paper or if they are pressed on too hard. A blunt soft-lead pencil or a gently applied ball-point pen are satisfactory if the appropriate type of stylus is not available. After the graph is completed it can be covered with another sheet of tracing paper and all of the press-on materials can be rubbed over with a smooth, flat stylus to aid firm adhesion. To avoid damage during storage the materials should be stored flat and kept separated from other sheets with the waxed-paper interleaves supplied. Also separate completed graphs with interleaves and store them flat so that the press-ons are not damaged after application.

Whatever the method employed to prepare the graph, the finished product will reflect the care that went into its planning and construction.

As with any product of time and effort, ensure that the masterpiece is not unique by reproducing a few copies for your files; it's no fun starting over.

D. Useful References on Graphing

Cooper, J. O. *Measurement and analysis of behavioral techniques.* Columbus, Ohio: Charles E. Merrill, 1974.

Provides an introduction to measurement and data presentation in applied behavior analysis. The chapter on preparing graphs for printing contains useful information on materials and procedures.

Koorland, M. A., & Martin, M. B. *Elementary principles and procedures of the Standard Behavior Chart* (3rd. ed.). Gainsville, Florida: Learning Environments Inc., 1975.

A systematic introduction to the Standard Behavior Chart, a data analysis system based on plotting rates of responding on a specially prepared six-cycle semilogarithmic chart. Also has a glossary of terms developed for use with these charts.

Meyers, C. H. *Handbook of basic graphs: A modern approach.* Belmont, California: Dickenson, 1970.

A thorough and well-written text that covers the principles, presentation, and format of all types of graph. It contains a wealth of information on all aspects of graphic presentation.

Publication manual of the American Psychological Association (2nd ed.). Washington, D.C.: American Psychological Association, 1974.

This contains essential information on the preparation of graphs for publication.

Spear, M. E. *Practical charting techniques.* New York: McGraw-Hill, 1969.

A text that covers the gamut of graphic formats in a thorough fashion. While it is probably directed more toward professional draftspersons, this text is a useful reference on drafting techniques and different styles of presentation.

V. Summary and Conclusions

The functional analysis of behavior is very dependent on a responsive interaction between the behavior of the subject and the behavior of the experimenter. This requires continuous monitoring of subject behavior and experimental procedures that are adaptable to changes in that behavior. On-going graphic data analysis and a responsive research methodology have evolved to serve this functional analysis.

The lack of refinement of the visual analysis of graphic data contributed to the discovery of powerful, generalized, and resilient variables. In order to be apparent to the eye the effects had to be dramatic, and weak or unstable variables were winnowed out. These powerful variables made possible the expansion of the functional analysis into the applied field by remaining effective under the less than optimal conditions of the social milieu.

In order to increase the believability of data from single subjects, replication designs were developed. As a result, the literature of behavior analysis is singular in the behavioral sciences, in that the majority of published research articles contain a direct replication.

As yet, there are no undisputed alternatives to graphic presentation and visual data analysis of single-subject data. The accuracy of that analysis, and the validity of subsequent judgments and decisions, rests heavily on clear, concise, and accurate data presentation. Thus, the selection of the appropriate graphic format and the honest representation of the data are maximally important considerations. The reliability of visual analysis may be lower than could be achieved using time-series analysis (Jones *et al.*, 1975; Chapter 4, this volume), but time-series analysis usually is a post hoc procedure, and the functional analysis of behavior requires ongoing analysis. In an effort to promote the establishment of some standardized criteria of judgment that could contribute to improved reliability, this chapter has attempted to describe some of the factors involved in the analytic process.

Regardless of any other statistical procedures that are brought into play, visual analysis of graphic data must remain the primary source on which on-going research decisions are based. It represents the most rapid, reactive, and economical data analysis procedure, capable of being used and understood by persons with differing levels of technical skill in a wide variety of applied and research settings. Before adopting new, largely untried forms of data analysis, we should attempt to exploit to the full those procedures that have contributed so positively to the functional analysis of behavior and the technology based on it.

REFERENCES

Baer, D. M. Perhaps it would be better not to know everything. *Journal of Applied Behavior Analysis*, 1977, *10*, 167–172.

Baer, D. M., Rowbury, T. G., & Goetz, E. M. Behavioral traps in the preschool: A proposal for research. In A. Pick (Ed.), *The Minnesota symposia on child psychology* (Vol 11). Minneapolis: University of Minnesota Press, 1976.

Baer, D. M., & Wolf, M. M. The entry into natural communities of reinforcement. In R. Ulrich, T. Stachnik, & J. Mabry (Eds.), *Control of human behavior* (Vol. 2): *From cure to prevention*. Glenview, IL: Scott, Foresman, 1970.

Baer, D. M., Wolf, M. M., & Risley, T. R. Some current dimensions of applied behavior analysis. *Journal of Applied Behavior Analysis*, 1968, *1*, 91–97.

Bakan, D. *On method: Toward a reconstruction of psychological investigation*. San Francisco: Jossey-Bass, 1967.

Barlow, D. H., & Agras, W. S. Fading to increase heterosexual responsiveness. *Journal of Applied Behavior Analysis*, 1973, *6*, 355–366.

Bellack, A. Reciprocal inhibition of a laboratory conditioned fear. *Behaviour Research and Therapy*, 1973, *11*, 11–18.

Blough, D. S. The shape of some wavelength generalization gradients. *Journal of the Experimental Analysis of Behavior*, 1961, *4*, 31–40.

Boer, A. P. Application of a simple recording system to the analysis of free-play behavior in autistic children. *Journal of Applied Behavior Analysis*, 1968, *1*, 335–340.

Campbell, D. T. From description to experimentation: Interpreting trends as quasi-experiments. In R. W. Harris (Ed.), *Problems in measuring change*. Madison: The University of Wisconsin Press, 1963.

Campbell, D. T., & Stanley, J. C. *Experimental and quasi-experimental designs for research*. Chicago: Rand-McNally, 1966.

Clark, H. B., Boyd, S. B., & Macrae, J. W. A classroom program teaching disadvantaged youths to write biographic information. *Journal of Applied Behavior Analysis*, 1975, *8*, 67–75.

Cooper, J. O. *Measurement and analysis of behavioral techniques*. Columbus, Ohio: Charles E. Merrill, 1974.

Craighead, W. E., Kazdin, A. E., & Mahoney, M. J. *Behavior modification: Principles, issues, and applications*. Boston: Houghton Mifflin, 1976.

Dubois, E. N. *Essential methods in business statistics*. New York: McGraw-Hill, 1964.

Edwards, A. L. *Statistical methods* (2nd ed.). New York: Holt, Rinehart & Winston, 1967.

Fisher, R. A. *The design of experiments* (3rd ed.). Edinburgh: Oliver & Boyd, 1942.

Franchina, J. J., Hauser, P. J., & Agee, C. M. Persistence of response prevention effects following retraining of escape behavior. *Behaviour Research and Therapy*, 1975, *13*, 1–6.

Glass, G. V., Willson, V. L., & Gottman, J. M. *Design and analysis of time-series experiments*. Boulder: University of Colorado Press, 1975.

Goetz, E. M., & Baer, D. M. Social control of form diversity and the emergence of new forms in children's block building. *Journal of Applied Behavior Analysis*, 1973, *6*, 209–217.

Guess, D. A functional analysis of receptive language and productive speech: Acquisition of the plural morpheme. *Journal of Applied Behavior Analysis*, 1969, *2*, 55–64.

Hall, R. V., Lund, D., & Jackson, D. Effects of teacher attention on study behavior. *Journal of Applied Behavior Analysis*, 1968, *1*, 1–12.

Herbert, E. W., & Baer, D. M. Training parents as behavior modifiers: Self-recording of contingent attention. *Journal of Applied Behavior Analysis*, 1972, *5*, 139–149.

Hogben, L. T. *Statistical theory: The relationship of probability, credibility, and error. An examination of the contemporary crisis in statistical theory from a behaviourist viewpoint*. New York: W. W. Norton & Co., 1957.

Hopkins, B. L. The effects of candy and social reinforcement, instructions, and reinforcement schedule leaning on the modification and maintenance of smiling. *Journal of Applied Behavior Analysis*, 1968, *1*, 121–129.

Horton, W. G. *Data display systems: Their use as visual planning aids for management in the age of computerization*. Princeton, NJ: Brandon/Systems Press, 1970.

Jones, R. R., Vaught, R. S., & Weinrott, M. Time-series analysis in operant research. *Journal of Applied Behavior Analysis*, 1977, *10*, 151–166.

Jones, R. R., Weinrott, M., & Vaught, R. S. Visual *v* statistical inference in operant research. In A. E. Kazdin (Ed.), *The use of statistics in N = 1 research*. Symposium presented at the annual convention of the American Psychological Association, Chicago, September, 1975.

Journal of Applied Behavior Analysis. Instructions to authors: Preparation of graphs for *J.A.B.A. Journal of Applied Behavior Analysis*, 1976, *9*, 24.

Kale, R. J., Kaye, J. H., Whelan, P. A., & Hopkins, B. L. The effects of reinforcement on the modification, maintenance, and generalization of social responses of mental patients. *Journal of Applied Behavior Analysis*, 1968, *1*, 307–314.

Kazdin, A. E. Statistical analyses for single-case experimental designs. In M. Hersen & D. H. Barlow (Eds.), *Single-case experimental designs: Strategies for studying behavior change*. Oxford: Pergamon Press, 1976.

Kirby, F. D., & Shields, F. Modification of arithmetic response rate and attending behavior in a seventh-grade student. *Journal of Applied Behavior Analysis*, 1972, *5*, 79–84.

Koenig, C. H. *Charting the future course of behavior*. Unpublished doctoral dissertation, University of Kansas, 1972.

Koorland, M. A., & Martin, M. B. *Elementary principles and procedures of the Standard Behavior Chart*. Gainesville, FL: Learning Environments Inc., 1975.

Kratochwill, T. R., & Wetzel, R. J. Observer agreement, credibility, and judgment: Some considerations. *Journal of Applied Behavior Analysis*, in press.

Lindsley, O. R. An interview. *Teaching Exceptional Children*, 1971, *3*, 114–119.

Lloyd, K. E., & Knutzen, N. A. A self-paced programmed undergraduate course in the experimental analysis of behavior. *Journal of Applied Behavior Analysis*, 1969, *2*, 125–133.

Lovaas, O. I., Koegel, R., Simmons, J. Q., & Long, J. S. Some generalization and follow-up measures on autistic children in behavior therapy. *Journal of Applied Behavior Analysis*, 1973, *6*, 131–166.

Lubin, A. Replicability as a publication criterion. *American Psychologist*, 1957, *8*, 519–520.

Lutz, R. R. *Graphic representation simplified*. New York: Funk & Wagnalls, 1949.

Lykken, D. T. Statistical significance in psychological research. *Psychological Bulletin*, 1968, *70*, 151–159.

Mann, R. A. The behavior therapeutic use of contingency contracting to control an adult behavior problem: Weight control. *Journal of Applied Behavior Analysis*, 1972, *5*, 99–109.

McKenzie, T. L., & Rushall, B. S. Effects of self-recording on attendance and performance in a competitive swimming training environment. *Journal of Applied Behavior Analysis*, 1974, *7*, 199–206.

McNemar, Q. At random: Sense and nonsense. *American Psychologist*, 1960, *15*, 295–300.

Meyers, C. H. *Handbook of basic graphs: A modern approach*. Belmont, CA: Dickenson Publishing Co., 1970.

Michael, J. Statistical inference for individual organism research: Mixed blessing or curse? *Journal of Applied Behavior Analysis*, 1974, *7*, 647–653.

Neiswanger, W. A. *Elementary statistical methods as applied to business and economic data* (rev. ed.). New York: Macmillan, 1956.

Nunnally, J. The place of statistics in psychology. *Educational and Psychological Measurement*, 1960, *20*, 641–650.

O'Leary, K. D., Becker, W. C., Evans, M. B., & Saudargas, R. A. A token reinforcement program in a public school: A replication and systematic analysis. *Journal of Applied Behavior Analysis*, 1969, *2*, 3–13.

Packard, R. G. The control of "classroom attention": A group contingency for complex behavior. *Journal of Applied Behavior Analysis*, 1970, *3*, 13–28.

Pennypacker, H. S., Koenig, C. H., & Lindsley, O. R. *Handbook of the Standard Behavior Chart.* Kansas City: Precision Media, 1972.

Plutchik, R. *Foundations of experimental research.* New York: Harper & Row, 1968.

Publication manual of the American Psychological Association (2nd ed.). Washington, D.C.: American Psychological Association, 1974.

Reynolds, G. S. *A primer of operant conditioning.* Glenview, IL: Scott, Foresman, 1968.

Reynolds, N. J., & Risley, T. R. The role of social and material reinforcers in increasing talking of a disadvantaged preschool child. *Journal of Applied Behavior Analysis*, 1968, *1*, 253–262.

Risley, T. R. The effects and side-effects of punishing the autistic behaviors of a deviant child. *Journal of Applied Behavior Analysis*, 1968, *1*, 21–34.

Risley, T. R. Behavior modification: An experimental-therapeutic endeavor. In L. A. Hamerlynck, P. O. Davidson, & L. E. Acker (Eds.), *Behavior modification and ideal mental health services.* Calgary, Alberta: University of Alberta Press, 1970.

Schroeder, G. L., & Baer, D. M. Effects of concurrent and serial training on generalized vocal imitation in retarded children. *Developmental Psychology*, 1972, *6*, 293–301.

Schroeder, S. R. Parametric effects of reinforcement frequency, amount of reinforcement, and required response force on sheltered workshop behavior. *Journal of Applied Behavior Analysis*, 1972, *5*, 431–441.

Schroeder, S. R., & Holland, J. G. Operant control of eye movements. *Journal of Applied Behavior Analysis*, 1968, *1*, 161–166.

Semb, G. The effects of mastery criteria and assignment length on college student test performance. *Journal of Applied Behavior Analysis*, 1974, *7*, 61–69.

Sidman, M. *Tactics of scientific research.* New York: Basic Books, 1960.

Skinner, B. F. A case history in scientific method. *American Psychologist*, 1956, *11*, 221–233.

Skinner, B. F. *Contingencies of reinforcement: A theoretical analysis.* New York: Appleton-Century-Crofts, 1969.

Smith, H. G. *Figuring with graphs and scales.* Stanford, CA: Stanford University Press, 1938.

Spear, M. E. *Practical charting techniques.* New York: McGraw-Hill, 1969.

Sterling, T. D. Publication decisions and their possible effects on inferences drawn from tests of significance—or vice versa. *Journal of the American Statistical Association*, 1959, *54*, 30–34.

Wallis, W. A., & Roberts, H. V. *Statistics: A new approach.* New York: The Free Press, 1956.

Wasik, B. H., Senn, K., Welch, R. H., & Cooper, B. R. Behavior modification with culturally deprived children. *Journal of Applied Behavior Analysis*, 1969, *2*, 181–194.

White, O. R. *The prediction of human performances in the single-case: An examination of four techniques.* Working paper No. 15, Regional Resource Center for Handicapped Children, University of Oregon, Eugene, OR, 1972.

White, O. R. *A manual for the calculation of the median slope: A technique of progress estimation and prediction in the single-case.* Working paper No. 16, Regional Resource Center for Handicapped Children, University of Oregon, Eugene, OR, 1973.

White, O. R. *The "split middle": A "quickie" method of trend estimation* (3rd revision). Unpublished manuscript, Experimental Education Unit, Child Development and Mental Retardation Center, University of Washington, Seattle, WA, 1974.

Winkler, R. C. Management of chronic psychiatric patients by a token reinforcement system. *Journal of Applied Behavior Analysis*, 1970, *3*, 47–55.

Wulbert, M., Nyman, B. A., Snow, D., & Owen, Y. The efficacy of stimulus fading and contingency management in the treatment of elective mutism: A case study. *Journal of Applied Behavior Analysis*, 1973, *6*, 435–441.

3

N = Nonparametric Randomization Tests

JOEL R. LEVIN
UNIVERSITY OF WISCONSIN

LEONARD A. MARASCUILO
UNIVERSITY OF CALIFORNIA, BERKELEY

LAWRENCE J. HUBERT*
UNIVERSITY OF WISCONSIN

I. Introduction

It is no secret that there currently exists a controversy over the "proper" treatment of data from single-subject ($N = 1$) and other small-sample (where $N > 1$) behavior change experiments (see Chapter 1, this volume, for an overview). Unfortunately, what complicates the controversy is not simply that inappropriate statistical procedures have been proposed (e.g., Gentile, Roden, & Klein, 1972). In addition, misguided criticisms of these procedures have been offered (e.g., Hartmann, 1974; Keselman & Leventhal, 1974); and, as has been recently pointed out by Kratochwill, Levin, and Benjamin (1977), erroneous applications of various procedures have appeared in the literature.

Furthermore, there are really two controversies in one that should be distinguished: (1) whether or not any type of inferential statistical procedure should be summoned up to analyze the data from such experiments, in con-

*Present address: Department of Education, University of California, Santa Barbara, Santa Barbara, California.

trast to clinical judgments or visual analyses (based on specified criteria or graphical plots, respectively; see Chapter 2, this volume); and (2) given an affirmative response to the inferential statistical question, which of a variety of statistical procedures is (are) appropriate. Our concern here is primarily with the second of these issues, as are most of the chapters in this volume.

Before dispensing with the preliminaries, some additional comments are in order. We are focusing on a particular type of data analysis strategy that seems to make sense in the present context. This is not to say that other strategies are unreasonable, for indeed merits can be ascribed to alternative ones as well (see the other chapters in this volume). The attractiveness of our strategy stems from its comparative simplicity, in terms of both the logic behind it and the mathematical demands associated with it. (As might be expected, in comparison to more complex strategies—time-series analysis, for example—there may be compensating "sensitivity" losses, however.) In considering our special type of strategy we will be purposely selective, with regard to previously recommended statistical procedures as well as to those developed here. This is in contrast to our including a detailed treatment of the enormous number of possibilities that could be recommended within this framework (for a commendable beginning, see Kazdin, 1976). To focus our illustrative intentions even further, we will concentrate on $N = 1$ designs of the $AB \cdots AB$ variety (see Chapter 1, this volume), although the present rationale can be easily applied to other designs as well. In sum, we will propose what we consider to be a reasonable course of action, along with a few candidate exemplars, rather than provide a compendium of statistical tests with its associated pros and cons, do's and don't's, and the like.

In Section II, we introduce our *randomization* approach to data analysis. As Edgington (e.g., 1967) has done before us, we highlight the basic assumptions underlying this approach while pointing out the shortcomings of previously offered solutions. In Section III, we illustrate certain randomization schemes for the analysis of data from $N = 1$ $AB \cdots AB$-type designs.

II. A Randomization Framework for Small-Sample Behavior Change Experiments

In order to develop our case, it will be helpful to contrast the present approach with previously recommended data analysis procedures for small-sample behavior change experiments. In particular, let us consider the analysis-of-variance (ANOVA) recommendation of Gentile *et al.* (1972), and see how it differs from the present approach and why it cannot be considered an appropriate solution. Following Edgington's (1975a) lead, we will capitalize on the Campbell and Stanley (1966) distinction between internal and external validity as a convenient point of departure.

A. External Validity Considerations

External validity refers to the ability to generalize the findings of an experiment conducted with one group of *subjects* in one *stimulus situation* to others. These two components of external validity have been termed *population* and *ecological* validity respectively (Bracht & Glass, 1968).

1. EXTERNAL VALIDITY AND LARGE-SAMPLE DESIGNS

It should be pointed out that most experimental (typically laboratory) studies—even those with large samples—are sorely lacking in external validity inasmuch as a random sampling of subjects and stimulus situations (the necessary condition for generalizing on a statistical basis from some to all) almost never occurs. Fortunately, however, individual externally invalid experiments may be collectively externally valid to the extent that findings are replicated with different subject populations and under different stimulus situations (see also Hersen & Barlow, 1976; Chapter 1, this volume).

2. EXTERNAL VALIDITY AND $N = 1$ DESIGNS

In the case of $N = 1$ designs, the external validity problem becomes exacerbated. Not only does one not typically randomly sample the single subject to be investigated, nor the stimulus-situational factor from the unlimited number of possibilities available, but there is an additional within-subject external validity consideration that is virtually never met as well. To illustrate this, suppose that the intent of a study is to assess the efficacy of a particular reinforcement procedure on students with a particular type of behavior problem. First, a given student exhibiting the behavior problem is nonrandomly selected from some typically ill-defined population. Next, that student is administered the reinforcement in a highly prescribed manner within a highly structured context. Finally, the investigator is surely not interested in the efficacy of the treatment for that small slice of the student's life happening to coincide with the duration of the experiment; consequently, failure to sample randomly other times from the student's life represents a *within-subject* generalizability limitation.

It is important that behavior change researchers recognize each of these sources of external invalidity in $N = 1$ contexts. Without a random sampling of subjects, situations, *and* slices of behavior, generalizability certainly cannot proceed on *statistical* grounds; and, for that reason, *logical* bases for generalizability must be considered (see, for example, Edgington, 1975a).

B. Internal Validity Considerations

Internal validity refers to the soundness of the experiment, in terms of the conclusions that can be legitimately drawn from it. Thus, an experiment is internally valid if and only if all extraneous variables (i.e., those apart from the treatment) have been ruled out as plausible contributors to the results.

1. INTERNAL VALIDITY AND LARGE-SAMPLE DESIGNS

For example, in a simple one-group pretest–posttest design in which a treatment has intervened between the pretest and the posttest, any number of extraneous variables could account for an observed mean change in performance. Time has passed and the world has changed, individuals have gotten older, they have benefited from practice on the pretest, to name only a few. Without a proper control group (or groups) the results of such an experiment are completely uninterpretable. And as Campbell and Stanley (1966) have forcefully noted, random assignment of subjects to treatment groups is the *sine qua non* of an internally valid experiment. Indeed, several years later Cook and Campbell (1975) express the regret that Campbell and Stanley's extensive treatment of a certain class of nonrandom assignment designs ("quasi-experiments") seems to have undeservedly elevated the status of such designs in the minds of researchers.

2. INTERNAL VALIDITY AND $N = 1$ DESIGNS

When there is only one experimental subject, one obviously cannot randomly assign subjects to treatments. However, if A represents a subject's baseline performance (control) and B represents performance during or following the administration of some treatment such as positive reinforcement or punishment (experimental), then one can certainly use aspects of the randomization notion. For example, instead of automatically administering the two phases in an AB order, one could randomly determine which phase should come first.[1] Under this scheme, half of all potential experiments would be expected to be conducted in an AB order, and half in a BA order. While this is clearly better than adopting a blanket AB order-of-administration strategy for every experiment thus conducted, it nonetheless has its associated problems. For one, it is not possible to separate treatment effects from time-related effects within the confines of a single experiment. Although it is true that these problems would cancel one another out over several replications of the experiment (i.e., with $N > 1$) or over several experiments, it is of little consolation to the $N = 1$ researcher who is interested in interpreting the results of a one-time experiment.

Second, there is the problem of carryover effects. Just as the administration of one drug can interact with a subsequently administered drug and influence its effect, in most behavior change experiments it is reasonable to expect that the administration of a reinforcer in the initial phase of an experiment will "carry over" to some extent into the subsequent phase. In fact, it can be argued that baseline performance following the B phase is not even "baseline" any more but rather an "extinction" phase (see also Chapter 1, this volume). Thus, for these reasons, something better has to be done than simply randomizing single A and B phases.

The advent of the $ABAB$ design reduces the likelihood that the passage of time *per se* is a "plausible rival hypothesis" in the Campbell and Stanley (1966) sense, since each phase appears both early and late in the game. Neither is there as extensive a carryover problem as before, for with A preceding B in both early and late phases, a "return to baseline" criterion can be assessed, as can the subsequent "return to treatment level" criterion. Even with this going for the $ABAB$ design, however, *systematic* assignment (A preceding B in each pair) is not the same as *random* assignment (either within each pair or within the entire experiment). This has important implications for the statistical analysis of the $ABAB$ design, as will be noted shortly.

It is also worth mentioning that neither does the $ABAB$ design escape certain other internal validity criticisms of the simple AB design. For example, a subject's awareness of the reinforcement contingency could give rise to Hawthorne/novelty effects as a competing extraneous variable (see Glass, Willson, & Gottman, 1975, and Chapter 1, this volume, for further discussion). However, since the $ABAB$ design has found favor with applied

---

[1] In this chapter, "phase" will refer to an uninterrupted interval associated with any given condition. Thus, in an AB design there are two phases, in an $ABAB$ design there are four, and so on.

behavioral researchers, for now we will have to accept it as a given and do
the best with it we can, despite its limitations.

C. Statistical Conclusion Validity Considerations

The statistical conclusions derived from any piece of research may also
be viewed as a validity issue (Cook & Campbell, 1975). Moreover, the issue
in the present context overlaps somewhat with previously discussed internal
and external validity issues.

1. STATISTICAL CONCLUSION VALIDITY AND $N = 1$ DESIGNS

Let us consider the statistical analysis for *ABAB* designs proposed by
Gentile *et al.* (1972), which exemplifies attempts by others (e.g., Shine &
Bower, 1971; Keselman & Leventhal, 1974) to generalize classical statistical
procedures based on designs with moderately large numbers of subjects
to designs in which there is only one subject. Conclusions that follow from
such analyses are invalid, however, as a result of both implicit and explicit
assumptions underlying the statistical model adopted.

Recall, for example, the previously discussed external validity issues
associated with $N = 1$ designs. In adapting classical ANOVA procedures
to such designs, Gentile *et al.* (1972) and others are implicitly arguing that
inferences can be made about other (unobserved) behavior samples of the
subject under consideration. This, of course, is unwarranted, due to the nonrandomly selected time slice that comprises the experiment proper. Moreover, even when the experiment is extended over several days, weeks, or
months (which is the case with long-term behavior change investigations)
the type of analysis proposed by these authors does not allow for a comparison of between- and within-phase variability in order to assess the
reliability/generalizability of the statistical conclusions. Thus, one can question the assumptions made by those who have advocated the use of classical
ANOVA procedures in $N = 1$ contexts, since they are implicitly concerned
with a generalizability that is clearly different and/or ignored in the analysis.

There is also an explicit (and fundamentally more important) statistical
conclusion validity problem with such analyses that can be related to our
previous discussion of internal validity. Apart from the well-known assumptions of normality and variance homogeneity, classical ANOVA procedures—and, for that matter, common regression procedures—require
that the *errors* in the statistical model are uncorrelated (read "independent"
if the normality assumption holds). By errors (or *residuals*) is meant that
which is left of an observation after it has been deviated about the model's

parameters (e.g., a grand mean, a treatment effect, a slope). The reason that the uncorrelated errors assumption must be spelled out is because it is often confused with the unneeded assumption that the *observations* themselves are uncorrelated. At the same time, it should be mentioned here that in many applications correlated observations *will* be sufficient to guarantee correlated errors. For example, in ANOVA models in which a constant treatment effect is applied to all within-condition observations (e.g., Gentile *et al.*, 1972), the observations themselves may be examined for autocorrelation. The same is true for simple linear regression approaches as applied to a series exhibiting no systematic drift (i.e., when the slope of the regression line is zero), as will be the case in many baseline conditions. Nonetheless, it is possible to conceive of situations in which errors will be uncorrelated even though observations are not and so the errors/observations distinction should be kept in mind.

As far as $N = 1$ behavior change research is concerned, both observations *and* errors are believed to be influenced by previous responses in a manner described by time-series methodologists (e.g., Box & Jenkins, 1970; Glass *et al.*, 1975). While it certainly can be debated whether or not the uncorrelated errors assumption is violated in *all* $N = 1$ applications, we will proceed under the supposition that it is violated in *many* of them. For those situations in which a researcher can demonstrate that the correlation among the lagged errors (deviations from the best-fitting model) is zero or near zero (see Chapter 4, this volume), a case can be made for ANOVA- and regression-type procedures. At the same time, notice the use of the word "demonstrate" in the preceding sentence, since we are of the firm conviction that in situations where correlated errors are likely, the burden of proof is on the investigator. As one final comment on this issue, the interobservation interval surely comprises an important determinant of whether or not the assumption is likely to be met; that is, with all else constant, the further apart in time that observations are made, the greater the probability that the lagged errors will be uncorrelated.

The Gentile *et al.* (1972) ANOVA model for the *ABAB* design includes as an explicit assumption that the errors discussed above are, in fact, uncorrelated, and they apply their model to a set of real $N = 1$ data for which the validity of the assumption has not been demonstrated. The impact of behaving in this fashion is serious, for as has been pointed out by Glass, Peckham, and Sanders (1972) in a related context, the use of ANOVA procedures when such model assumptions are not met can result in vastly inflated Type I error probabilities. That is, researchers will conclude that there is a treatment effect *when in fact there is none* far more frequently than they should be doing (for empirical evidence, see the recent paper by Nicolich & Weinstein, 1977). Gentile *et al.* (1972) believe that the countless degrees of freedom in their example reflect "independent" estimates of error, which, as might be surmised on the basis of our previous arguments, we do not (see also Kratochwill, Alden, Demuth, Dawson, Panicucci, Arntson, Mc-Murray, Hempstead, & Levin, 1974). With several repetitions of the AB sequence (e.g., $A_1B_1, \ldots, A_{10}B_{10}$) it might be possible to use an ANOVA-type procedure as an approximate statistical test, but as will be discussed later, this requires quite a different orientation from that proposed by Gentile *et al.* (1972). Specifically, what their proposed test fails to maintain is a degree of consistency between the randomization scheme employed in the experimental design and that assumed by the test itself.

To be somewhat more concrete, within each phase of an $ABAB$ design, suppose that $k = 24$ successive observations are taken. The actual design itself is assumed to consist of *four* randomized "units," the two A and the two B phases. On the other hand, the Gentile *et al.* (1972) analysis would view the design as consisting of 96 randomized units, which is clearly not so. The situation is somewhat analogous to administering two treatments, A and B, to students in four different classrooms. In this case, if two classrooms of 24 students apiece are randomly assigned to Treatment A and two to Treatment B, the proper "unit" of analysis is *classrooms* and not *students*. Unfortunately, educational and behavioral researchers are not well attuned to problems of using individuals rather than classrooms or other aggregates as the correct unit of analysis (Page, 1965); however, the consequences of not doing so can be most severe (cf. Peckham, Glass, & Hopkins, 1969) and it is about time that researchers exhibit a behavior change. The same goes for the analysis of $N = 1$ designs, and we will return to this analogy shortly.[2]

D. Randomization Tests as a Possibility

In order to overcome the major difficulties associated with previously offered $N = 1$ statistical strategies, a fundamentally different approach must be recommended; in particular, one that maintains an internally valid correspondence between the randomization units associated with the experimental design and those of the test itself.

A class of procedures, namely, *permutation* (or *randomization*) tests, can be drawn from to satisfy these conditions. As an important aside, con-

---

[2] There are situations (emanating from the approach to be proposed here) in which individual within-phase observations can, in fact, comprise the proper units of the analysis. However, this requires a radically different conceptualization and randomization scheme than are typically adopted (see Edgington, 1975a).

cerning the generalizability (external validity) question, the usual randomization approach does not pretend that random samples of either subjects or a single subject's behavior are available—but see our later discussion of Lehmann's (1975) two models. A randomization test simply answers the question, *For the particular set of scores (or observations) obtained,* how likely is it that the differences between treatment groups (e.g., baseline and experimental phases) could have been at least as large as the one observed? The obtained data are regarded as a *population* and the no-difference hypothesis is assessed by referring to the conditional probability distribution associated with all theoretically possible assignments of *these data* to treatments. Thus, this type of randomization approach is particularly well suited to the $N = 1$ design with its previously acknowledged nonrandomly sampled components, insofar as one's basic inference question changes from "other subjects and situations" to "other treatment-control differences, given the data." Examples of the approach in action will be provided in Section III. (See also Hubert and Levin, 1976, for a justification and illustration of the approach in a different $N = 1$ context).

As for the crucial uncorrelated errors (internal validity) question, if the proper randomization scheme and associated units can be identified, an appropriate randomization test will follow. In particular, as Edgington (e.g., 1975a) has correctly argued, a randomization analysis (or, for that matter, any other analysis that is "statistical-conclusion" valid) depends on a random assignment—or blocked random assignment—of treatments to phases. This, of course, is not the case if A always precedes B (see our previous discussion). Yet, in certain $ABAB$ designs, random assignment may indeed be possible. For example, in the baseline (A) versus treatment (B) situation an initial A phase could be designated as an adaptation or "warmup" phase, not to be included in the analysis. It might then be possible to randomly assign two A and two B conditions to four successive phases to constitute the analysis proper. In other instances A and B may represent two different experimental treatments (rather than a baseline and a treatment), in which case random assignment may be more reasonable. (Note that under the proper randomization scheme, it is possible to come up with two consecutive phases of the same type.)

A word in defense of randomization tests, as applied to systematic (rather than randomized) $ABAB$ designs, should be included here. Fortunately there is good reason to believe that they will nonetheless prove to be appropriate insofar as closely approximating what would have been obtained under optimal conditions. [For a more detailed argument in a related context, see Bradley's (1968) discussion of the Irwin-Fisher test.] Thus, randomization tests are to be used in conjunction with systematic $ABAB$ designs with these thoughts in mind.

Finally, while it is true that classical statistical procedures could also follow from the identification of proper randomization schemes and units, they would be used merely as time-saving approximations to the exact randomization tests that could have been performed—rather than as tests dependent on random sampling. Thus, their function would be quite unlike that typically conceived and, moreover, as was mentioned previously, their justification depends on a fairly large number of units (phases in the $N = 1$ framework).

With this rationale then, let us consider some possible data analysis solutions to the $ABAB$ design in particular. As was noted at the outset, the present discussion is not meant to exhaust all possibilities, and specifically the work of Kazdin (1976) and Edgington (e.g., 1975a) should be consulted.

III. Examples of Randomization Tests in Small-Sample Behavior Change Experiments

A. Basic Rationale

Before proceeding to develop in detail a randomization approach to the analysis of $AB \cdots AB$-type designs, an important distinction concerning nonparametric inference models should be pointed out. [For a more complete treatment of these concepts, the reader is referred to Lehmann's (1975) definitive text.]

As a simple example, consider the nonparametric analog (based on ranks) to the independent-samples t test. The "null" distribution underlying the associated test statistic can be justified in one of two ways. The first strategy requires the assumption that the two groups have the same population distribution. In turn, this assumption implies, given the actual values of the k observations in Group 1 and the $n - k$ observations in Group 2, that each group of k observations from the total sample of size n had the same a priori chance of appearing in Group 1. This approach can be referred to as the *population* model, since we use as a secondary fact the implication that all $\binom{n}{k}$ samples of size k are equally likely under the explicit null hypothesis of equal population distributions.

A second strategy, based on what may be called the *randomization* model, involves no population assumption at all and merely asks whether an observed sample of size k could have been obtained by a random selection from the total sample of size n. Since both approaches finally use the same tables for testing the significance of the test statistic, they are equivalent practically but distinct conceptually. In fact, the theoretical success of nonparametric statistics is due in part to the equivalence of the two procedures from a practitioner's point of view.

Unfortunately, in applying a randomization model to the analysis of $AB \cdots AB$-type designs, the appropriate population model that would correspond to and justify the analysis may be unclear. Granted, one can apply the randomization model without regard to an equivalent population analog. However, it is very easy to construct simple population models for the time-series problem that could be considered logical "null" models but would produce a corresponding null distribution different from that obtained under a randomization model (e.g., a simple first-order autoregressive process). In particular, what would be "equally likely" under a randomization model would not be equally likely under a population model.

To develop a closer correspondence between population and randomization models in $N = 1$ designs, one could define summary measures (e.g., means) based on a group of observations within a phase. As we will see shortly, under certain conditions the use of summary phase statistics may lead to approximately independent, or at least uncorrelated, random variables that are identically distributed even though the population model itself generates dependent observations. There is some precedent for desiring this, since population models defined by independent and identically distributed random variables are consistent with randomization counterparts in standard nonparametric analyses of trend (see, for example, Conover, 1971). Moreover, researchers interested in employing randomization procedures for their data but who are reluctant to do so due to the lack of a clearly defined population counterpart, may be reassured. In particular, at least an approximate population analog can be constructed by defining the summary statistics in an appropriate manner.[3]

In the data analysis stage then, one assumes that the summary measures associated with the experimental units are *fixed*, and merely divided between or among conditions in all possible permissible ways. For the sake of argument, let us return to our previously mentioned $ABAB$ design in which each phase consists of 24 successive observations. For this experiment there would be 4 experimental units, and for each unit a mean based on the 24 associated data points could be computed.

As an important aside, let us return to our classroom analogy. We previously argued that the statistical-conclusion validity of an experiment in which treatments are randomly assigned to intact classrooms depends

---

[3] Unless otherwise specified, hereafter we will use the generic term "randomization" to refer exclusively to the *data analysis* strategy that is employed by the researcher according to both Lehmann (1975) models.

on an analysis that preserves classrooms as the units. In terms of our analogy, phases correspond to classrooms, and thus the analysis must be carried out at the phase level. However, there is still a major distinction between the two situations that must be discussed. In the classroom context, it is reasonable to view the resulting class summary measures (e.g., class means) as independent random variables as long as no between-class sources of mutual influence are present (see Cook & Campbell, 1975). In such cases the usual ANOVA models (when large numbers of classrooms are administered each treatment) or nonparametric analogs such as those to be presented here (when smaller numbers of classrooms are employed), are completely appropriate.

Unfortunately, in the $N = 1$ context the summary measures based on phases (e.g., phase means) are generally correlated since they are formed from subsets of data points chosen from a process defined by a sequence of (usually) dependent random variables. And within our to-be-developed nonparametric framework, this correlation among *summary measures* (as opposed to *errors* in the ANOVA model) may be a relevant consideration. In particular, the distinction between Lehmann's (1975) "population" and "randomization" nonparametric models, discussed prrviously, is an important one. For while as Edgington (personal communication, November, 1976) has noted, correlated summary measures will not affect the validity of the approach under the randomization model—assuming that treatments have been assigned to phases in the strict random sense mentioned earlier— they will have a bearing on statistical inference according to the population models. Fortunately for population model subscribers, however, although the correlation between summary measures may initially appear to invalidate our present justification vis-à-vis the classroom analogy, it can be argued that the summary phase statistics will typically be correlated only to a trivial (negligible) degree.

To illustrate this, suppose that the underlying process being observed consists of a sequence of K identically distributed but dependent variables, $X_1, X_2, \ldots, X_K$, where X_i and X_j are observed at the ith and jth time points. Furthermore, a reasonable model that can be applied is one in which the correlation between X_i and X_j is $\rho^{|i-j|}$ (where $\rho \geq 0$), implying that the correlation between observations is positive and decreases as a function of the distance between X_i and X_j in the sequence (see, for example, Elashoff, 1968). If the K variables are subdivided into phases consisting of k random variables each, and means are used as summary statistics for the various phases, the maximum correlation between phases is attained for those that are temporally adjacent. But, as Table 3.1 indicates, this correlation is essentially 0 for ρ not too close to 1.00 (e.g., for $\rho \leq .50$, which is reasonable in time-series experiments of this kind—see Glass *et al.*, 1975) and for moderate values of k (e.g., for $k > 6$).

TABLE 3.1
Correlations between Adjacent Phase Means Based on k
Observations Apiece and Assuming a Model With
$$\rho_{x_i, x_j} = \rho^{|i-j|}$$

				Value of ρ					
k	.10	.20	.30	.40	.50	.60	.70	.80	.90
3	.036	.079	.132	.198	.278	.377	.495	.637	.804
6	.017	.037	.062	.094	.138	.202	.299	.445	.666
9	.012	.024	.040	.059	.087	.129	.199	.323	.556
12	.009	.018	.029	.043	.062	.092	.144	.245	.469
15	.007	.014	.023	.034	.049	.071	.111	.193	.400
18	.006	.012	.019	.028	.040	.058	.090	.157	.344
21	.005	.010	.016	.024	.033	.049	.075	.131	.299
24	.004	.009	.014	.021	.029	.042	.064	.112	.262

In short, the use of phase means provides a set of analysis units that may be considered uncorrelated (or independent if a further assumption of normality is assumed for the original random variables in the sequence). Taking the implications of this fact one step further: These negligible correlations among the phase means permit a direct analysis of an $N = 1$ experiment via randomization procedures that may be justified even according to a nonparametric "population" model.

It is worth mentioning at this juncture that any of a number of summary measures could be similarly computed to represent each unit. Indeed, in certain situations something other than a mean based on all k within-phase observations would be desirable. For example, anticipating considerable fluctuation in a series at the beginning of a phase, or substantial change from the beginning to the end, one may elect to compute a summary measure based only on the *middle k*, or the *last k*, observations within each phase. The respective extremes of these points of view would be to consider only the median observation, or the last observation, within each phase (but then, balanced consideration must be given to the greater unreliability of a single observation).[4] It is beyond the scope of this chapter to advocate a scheme for selecting a *particular* summary measure; rather, it is up to the behavior change researcher to make a rational choice. (For some possibilities, including measures reflecting variability and slope, see Edgington, 1975a and Kazdin, 1976.) Whatever scheme one adopts, however, can be easily fit

---

[4] Our previous discussion of uncorrelated phase statistics applies here as well, in even more dramatic fashion. For example, the correlation between *individual* observations from two adjacent phases with $k = 6$ and assuming $\rho_{x_i, x_j} = .50$ would be a mere .015 according to the model adopted here.

into our proposed framework. The single most important issue in this regard is that the researcher's choice of a summary measure be made on a priori logical grounds, rather than on after-peeking-at-the-data "logical" grounds. For if the latter course of action is taken, probability statements associated with the statistical test(s) performed are completely invalidated. The same issue is pertinent to our discussion of hypothesis testing when "postdictions"—rather than predictions—about various outcomes are made (see also Lehmann, 1975).

Returning from our digression, then, suppose that we use the mean of the 24 observations at each of the 4 phases to represent our units. Viewing these 4 means as fixed and determined, we then examine all possible assignments of them to conditions A and B *under the assumption that two must go to each condition* (consistent with the way in which the experiment was actually executed). This, of course, is a simple combinatorial problem from which all possible assignments of 2 things out of 4 may be represented as $\binom{4}{2} = 6$.[5]

Let us demonstrate this for an $N = 1$ $ABAB$ experiment that produces within-phase means of 2.0, 7.0, 3.0, and 8.0 respectively. Given these means, one could assign the following pairs to one of the treatments (let us say A), where order is not important:

2.0 and 7.0	7.0 and 3.0
2.0 and 3.0	7.0 and 8.0
2.0 and 8.0	3.0 and 8.0

for a total of six, as previously mentioned. (Once assignment of a pair of means to *one* of the treatments has been achieved, the means going to the other treatment are completely determined, which is why only one treatment needs to be considered. The more-than-two-treatment problem is obviously more complex but is nonetheless handled within the same framework.)

For each of these six possible assignments to a particular treatment (here A), a sum of the two measures is then computed:

$2.0 + 7.0 = 9.0$	$7.0 + 3.0 = 10.0$
$2.0 + 3.0 = 5.0$	$7.0 + 8.0 = 15.0$
$2.0 + 8.0 = 10.0$	$3.0 + 8.0 = 11.0$

---

[5] An alternative randomization approach is available in which the first A and the first B are viewed as a paired unit, as are the second A and the second B. However, it can be shown that for behavior change experiments based on the designs discussed here, this approach will prove considerably more inefficient than the one we adopt.

and based on these sums a probability distribution is defined as

Sum	Probability
5.0	1/6
9.0	1/6
10.0	2/6
11.0	1/6
15.0	1/6

Hereafter, we will refer to the randomization test associated with this procedure as our *basic* randomization test.

Now, if in the experiment, the baseline phases (A) produced generally lower responses than the treatment phases (B), low values in this distribution should be associated with A. With $A > B$, high values in this distribution would be associated with A. For an experiment in which it has not been predicted in advance whether $A < B$ or $A > B$, one outcome from each extreme in the probability distribution, 5.0 and 15.0, would be selected with corresponding probability $1/6 + 1/6 = 1/3$. This value represents the Type I error probability (α) or level of significance associated with the to-be-performed statistical test; and it is worth remembering that since random sampling need not be assumed, α typically refers to the likelihood that *for these data* a total as extreme as 5.0 or 15.0 could have been produced under the assumption that all possible assignments of means to conditions were equally likely. Of course, in the random-sampling situation extreme sums associated with one condition are taken as evidence of a treatment effect and the same rationale applies here.

In the present experiment the sum of the means associated with A actually turned out to be $2.0 + 3.0 = 5.0$, which permits rejection of a conditional no-difference hypothesis with $\alpha = 1/3 = .3\overline{3}$. Unfortunately, there is good reason to believe that a significance level of $.3\overline{3}$ would (and should) meet with disfavor among most researchers steeped in the .05 tradition. But for the $N = 1$ $ABAB$ design and a nondirectional ("better or worse than") alternative hypothesis, this is the best one can do. The design and hypothesis also bear on the important question of statistical power where, in a field such as behavior change research with its small N's, power is usually low—especially when weak treatments are employed.

Fortunately there are some options available to the behavior change researcher to improve the just-mentioned α and power concerns. As might be suspected, this can be accomplished by increasing the number of units in the experiment, which in turn can be accomplished by employing $N > 1$ or by adding more phases to the design. Solutions of this kind will be discussed later, but first let us consider some possibilities that do not change the design at all, but rather the sensitivity associated with the alternative hypothesis one formulates.

B. Strengthening the Alternative Hypothesis

1. WEAK PREDICTIONS

In the previous section, hypothesis testing was discussed in a non-directional (two-tailed) sense. Certainly in many behavior change experiments, the researcher has a notion of whether A should be higher or lower than B, especially when A represents baseline performance. In such cases— and if it is unimportant to detect outcomes in the direction opposite to expectation—a directional (one-tailed) test is clearly appropriate. The consequences of this would be to select outcomes from only one side of the probability distribution in establishing a decision rule.

As was mentioned in the context of choosing an appropriate summary measure, any so-called one-tailed hypothesis must be formulated in advance of data collection. Not to do so is deceptive in two senses: (1) with respect to the subsequent probability statements that can rightfully be made, and (2) with respect to the researcher's behavior directed toward the scientific community, evoking issues of ethicality. It has already been argued that behavior change researchers should attempt to maximize the sensitivity of the hypothesis-testing operation as much as possible. This can be readily accomplished through a careful consideration of the hypothesis being tested and the kinds of outcomes likely to be obtained (see also Bradley, 1968, pp. 134–138). Our basic theme is to get researchers to *think* about what they are doing and what ought to happen as a result. But the thinking process must occur before, and not after, the experiment has been performed, or else a rationale can give way to a rationalization. With a little forethought and planning, not only will the probability cycle be run in the right direction, but the procedures used in analyzing $N = 1$ data will be strengthened considerably. We hope to illustrate this latter point in the following pages.

Returning to the present example, if it were predicted ahead of time that $A < B$, then one would be entitled to consider outcomes on only the lower side of the probability distribution. Thus, the single sum of 5.0 would be included to yield an α of $1/6$ or $.1\bar{6}$. But even with this strategy, an α of .16 is still too high by traditional standards. Let us present therefore some additional hypothesis-strengthening strategies for the $N = 1$ $ABAB$ design that will bring α into the realm of respectability. [As J. Elashoff has remarked in a personal communication (December, 1976), the following discussion depends on the reader's familiarity with the notion of planned contrasts in the analysis of variance. The relatively uninitiated should refer to texts such as Hays (1963) or Kirk (1968) for an introduction.]

2. STRONGER PREDICTIONS

In certain situations, it may be possible to specify a predicted rank ordering among a set of summary measures. [For a justification of this approach, refer to Marascuilo and McSweeney's (1977) discussion of trend analysis applied to the Kruskal–Wallis test.] For instance, with regard to the present example, it might be argued on logico-substantive grounds (a priori, of course) that the A_1 baseline phase should produce the lowest performance level of the four, A_2 should also be low (but not as low as A_1 due to starting at an initially higher level and incomplete extinction following Treatment B_1), B_1 should be next as result of the treatment, and B_2 should be highest given a similar improvement from A_1 to B_1 but starting at an initially higher level than A_2. Thus, one would predict $B_2 > B_1 > A_2 > A_1$ for the above argument. (It should be noted that weaker predicted orderings such as B_1 and $B_2 > A_2 > A_1$ can also be handled within this framework, but with corresponding losses. For an example, see Chapter 6, this volume.) Given this prediction, once the data have been collected, the ordinal ranks 1 through 4 may be applied to the four summary measures in the following manner. The highest measure is multiplied by a factor of 4, the next highest by a factor of 3, and so on. The resulting summed products value is then referred to the probability distribution defined by all possible arrangements of ranks and obtained outcomes. For example, with four phases there are $4! = 24$ possible conditional arrangements, presented in Table 3.2 with reference to the hypothetical means given previously. The probability distribution summarizing these operations is presented in Table 3.3.

It can be seen that the largest possible "summed products" value of 61 has an associated probability of $1/24 = .042$, which represents (at last!) an $\alpha < .05$. It will also be noted that in our hypothetical experiment, the *observed* rank-ordering $B_2 > B_1 > A_2 > A_1$ was in fact the one resulting in the largest value of 61, which would permit one to reject a conditional no-differential hypothesis with $\alpha = .042$. Thus, even though our observed data have not changed from one analysis strategy to the next, the more sensitive ordinal approach permitted a more conservative level of significance ($\alpha = .042$) in comparison to the basic test with its associated one- and two-tailed alternatives ($\alpha = .167$ and .333, respectively).

The situation is completely analogous to Glass et al.'s (1975) notions about no, weak, and strong predictions using time-series analysis (p. 45).

TABLE 3.2
All Possible Permutations and Summed Products of
Ranks 1–4 and the Obtained Phase Means

Permutation	Means				Summed products
	2.0	7.0	3.0	8.0	
1	1	2	3	4	57
2	1	2	4	3	52
3	1	3	2	4	61
4	1	3	4	2	51
5	1	4	2	3	60
6	1	4	3	2	55
7	2	1	3	4	52
8	2	1	4	3	47
9	2	3	1	4	60
10	2	3	4	1	45
11	2	4	1	3	59
12	2	4	3	1	49
13	3	1	2	4	51
14	3	1	4	2	41
15	3	2	1	4	55
16	3	2	4	1	40
17	3	4	1	2	53
18	3	4	2	1	48
19	4	1	2	3	45
20	4	1	3	2	40
21	4	2	1	3	49
22	4	2	3	1	39
23	4	3	1	2	48
24	4	3	2	1	43

Generally speaking, the more one is willing to specify a priori, the more sensitive one's test becomes (see also Lehmann, 1975, p. 39). This sensitivity statement in turn relates to the comparative statistical power of two tests that should be assessed with α held constant (which was not done here). In the present context, the magnitude of the power advantage (of the stronger over the weaker tests) will depend on such factors as the number of experimental subjects and units, as well as on the within-condition interphase variability. With regard to the latter point, when a particular treatment is expected to yield quite different performance levels at different experimental phases, an alternative hypothesis that addresses this variability directly will lead to a more sensitive test than one that ignores it.

In certain situations, one can do even better in predicting outcomes than by using the ordinal weighting scheme just described. Consider once

TABLE 3.3
Probability Distribution Representing
the 24 Permutations of Table 3.2

Summed products	Probability
39	1/24
40	2/24
41	1/24
43	1/24
45	2/24
47	1/24
48	2/24
49	2/24
51	2/24
52	2/24
53	1/24
55	2/24
57	1/24
59	1/24
60	2/24
61	1/24

again our hypothetical data. While it is certainly true that the means trace out the ordinal pattern $B_2 > B_1 > A_2 > A_1$, they do more than that. In particular, the two A means are quite close together, as are the two B means— at least in comparison to the distance between the combined A and the combined B means. Interestingly, we can build such a *predicted* pattern into our statistical test. Suppose we predicted a priori that the means would order the way they did *and* would be separated from one another either (1) by the distances, or (2) by the proportions that they actually were. The former case can be referred to as an *interval* weighting scheme, and rather than utilizing the weights 1–4 as in the *ordinal* case, one could assign weights 1, 6, 2, and 7 for A_1, B_1, A_2, and B_2 respectively (where distances between predicted means are purposely made unequal). Alternatively, employing a *ratio* weighting scheme (the latter case), one could assign the weights 1, 3.5, 1.5, and 4 to the four respective means.

What are the advantages in adopting an interval or ratio, as opposed to an ordinal, weighting scheme? The issue boils down to one of statistical power and sensitivity: If the true unknown phase means were actually unequally separated, and in a fashion congruent with that specified by the interval or ratio weights, then in many situations—apart from the trivial case in which the singlemost extreme outcome is obtained—the more sensitive (interval and ratio) procedures will detect differences where the other (ordinal) will not. On the other hand, it is important to mention the "something you can't get for nothing" associated with doing this. Apart from the potentially greater difficulty in specifying precise distances in contrast to rank orders, if in reality the actual differences between means were all equal, an interval–ratio weighting scheme would prove *less* sensitive than an ordinal one. In some cases, only ordinal predictions will be a safe bet; but in others, where "groupings" of means are clearly indicated, more complex schemes of the kind described here would be advocated. Once again, however, the onus is on the investigator to behave with rationality and with caution.

The most dramatic example of the tradeoffs involved in selecting an appropriate statistical test and/or alternative may be illustrated in what might be termed a *rigid* version of the just-mentioned weighting schemes. According to this approach, one would specify an a priori ordinal relationship among phases (here, $B_2 > B_1 > A_2 > A_1$). If, in fact, the *exact* predicted ordering occurred among the obtained summary measures, the prediction would be confirmed with $\alpha = 1/n!$ (here, $\alpha = \frac{1}{24} = .042$). Note that this particular approach is very parsimonious (especially from a computational–data analysis standpoint) yet at the same time, as mentioned above, very rigid (read "risky") in its decision-making ability. That is, unless the sole stated ordering occurs among the given phase summary statistics, the predicted pattern cannot be confirmed—*even when the observed pattern is very close to that predicted.* This is not a problem with any of the previously discussed approaches, however, where *very close* is *very good* from a prediction–confirmation standpoint. [For further discussion, see Bradley (1968).]

Despite the espoused value of behavior change researchers behaving in a predict–confirm/do not confirm mode (see our previous arguments), one must be aware of an important difference in adopting this logic in contrast to that underlying a direct comparison of two conditions (say, by our basic randomization test). The statistical confirmation of a *predicted ordering* need not be indicative of the statistical confirmation of a *treatment effect.* To use an extreme example, suppose that a researcher predicted that $A_1 < B_1 < B_2 < A_2$ and that, in fact, this pattern was statistically confirmed in the data on the basis of our ordinally keyed permutation test. One would certainly not take this as convincing evidence of a difference between A and B per se, inasmuch as it would be possible with this pattern for the sum of the two A means to equal exactly the sum of the two B means. The moral here is that predictions, as well as interpretations of statistically significant findings, must be closely tied to the logico-substantive considerations alluded to earlier (see also Edgington, 1975b).

Finally, it should be mentioned with regard to all of the techniques just presented that extensions are immediately apparent. As was discussed earlier, in some cases A and B may represent two different treatments rather than a treatment and baseline. Or several different treatments might be compared, rather than only two. The important thing is that once the "units" are correctly identified and, hopefully, randomly assigned to phases, appropriate randomization distributions can be derived and probabilities specified. This will frequently result in increased conceptual and computational labor, however, and so various aids (especially for the latter, to be discussed later) may have to be recruited.

C. Increasing the Number of Experimental Units

While one way to increase the sensitivity of randomization tests is to strengthen the alternative hypothesis, another is to increase the number of experimental units included in the design. And, as was mentioned earlier, this can generally be accomplished by one of two (non-mutually exclusive) strategies: (1) increasing the number of phases, or (2) increasing the number of subjects beyond $N = 1$. Let us discuss each of these strategies briefly, while noting the specific statistical solutions that are called for within the present framework.

1. INCREASING THE NUMBER OF PHASES

It was previously suggested that whenever a behavior could be expected to reveal itself within k' observation intervals (where $k' < k$), then for a fixed number of *total* observation intervals a researcher would do well to increase the number of baseline and treatment phases, at the expense of reducing k within each phase (but see our previous discussion of the correlation between successive summary measures, which may be relevant when one is employing the "population" model with very small values of k). The rationale for this is simply that many behavior change experiments suffer from within-phase "observation overkill," whereas an appropriate statistical analysis will be helped considerably (in terms of statistical power) if those unneeded within-phase observations were used in the interest of extending the number of phases (essentially replicating the experiment). To see what this recommendation buys us in the present example, instead of four phases consisting of $k = 24$ observations apiece, suppose the experimenter extended the design by including an additional baseline condition (A). This was done since it was decided a priori that $k = 19$ observations per phase would be sufficient to assess the consequences of the treatment (B). Ironically, by increasing just the number of *baseline* phases, from two ($ABAB$) to three ($ABABA$), a researcher will have increased his or her probability of detecting an effect due to *treatment* should it exist. (For a discussion of certain *implementation* issues associated with doing this, see Chapter 1, this volume.)

In terms of the basic randomization test discussed initially, the most extreme outcome would now have associated one- and two-tailed probabilities of $\alpha = 1/\binom{5}{3} = .10$ and $\alpha = 2/\binom{5}{3} = .20$ in contrast to the previous $.1\bar{6}$ and $.3\bar{3}$, respectively. Of more moment, however, are the stronger permutation tests (ordinal-, interval-, and ratio-weighted) where now with their $5! = 120$ associated permutations, not just *the* most extreme outcome but the *six* most extreme outcomes would lead to rejection of the conditional no-difference hypothesis with $\alpha = .05$. The consequence of this latter fact is, of course, to permit an investigator to formulate less than *completely correct* a priori predictions and yet still be able to detect a treatment difference. (Naturally this is not possible with the *rigid* approach, as previously discussed.) Because of this, it might be argued that the "risks" associated with making fairly strong predictions are not really as great as what first meets the eye.

With the addition of one or more treatment phase (i.e., *ABABAB*) power continues to increase (provided, of course, that the within-phase k—here, 16—is also sufficient to give the treatment enough time to "work"). In terms of the various analyses, with six alternating A and B phases all will now be able to produce conventional ($\alpha \leq .05$) levels of significance. For the basic randomization test, the one-tailed value is exactly $\alpha = .05 = \frac{1}{\binom{6}{3}} = \frac{1}{20}$

(eight alternating A and B phases are required to produce a two-tailed α less than or equal to .05, namely .028). And, with six alternating A and B phases the stronger tests would be able to include the 36 most extreme one-sided outcomes (out of 720) in the rejection region.

2. INCREASING THE NUMBER OF SUBJECTS

Including an additional subject (or subjects) in the *ABAB* design is equivalent to performing an independent replication of the experiment. Because of this, methods for combining data based on independent replications would be appropriate. Marascuilo and McSweeney (1977) discuss several possibilities that could be considered, and due to present space limitations, the interested reader is referred to that source. In any case, the statistical procedures outlined here could be applied to each subject separately before combining the evidence. If this is done, the conditional nature of the resulting probability distribution must be recognized, and statistical conclusions must be stated accordingly. Naturally, the revelation of a similar treatment effect or pattern in two more subjects could be taken as evidence regarding the external validity of the research. However, without a random sampling of subjects from some well-defined population, there is no statistical basis for such an argument.

As a final possibility—and one that fits well with our notion of testing *precise* hypotheses—if there is reason to believe that patterns will generalize across individuals, and if $N > 1$ subjects are available, consider the following plan: Treat the first subject (or first few subjects) as *exploratory* in the sense of using him or her (them) to observe relationships among phases. On the basis of this initial experimentation, derive weights of the kind described earlier. Then, apply these weights in a prediction *confirmatory* sense to the remaining one or more subjects to be treated. Such a procedure could be viewed as an $N = 1$ analog to cross-validation studies using multiple-regression models.

D. Aids in Performing Randomization Tests

In the example presented here with two baseline and two treatment phases, the amount of computational labor required to perform the analysis was not overwhelming. However, in other situations (where phases or subjects are increased, as discussed in the previous section) it may well be. For this reason, three general courses of action available to an investigator will be mentioned here.

1. TABLES

A potentially desirable modification of the basic randomization test is to convert the summary data to *ranks* prior to conducting the analysis. If this is done, the familiar two-sample Wilcoxon (or Mann–Whitney) test is produced (see Marascuilo & McSweeney, 1977). The advantage associated with doing this lies in the extensive tables that are available for this and other rank tests, while the corresponding loss in efficiency is not great.

For our stronger tests, the two summed-products statistics actually turn out to be unstandardized correlation coefficients (see Hubert & Levin, in press). Applying such weights to the data actually obtained in various experiments would create an infinite number of possible totals; consequently, tables do not exist for these tests. However, if the obtained summary measures are converted to ranks and then weighted by the ordinal scheme, unstandarized values of Spearman's rank-order correlation coefficient (rho) will be produced. After applying the appropriate transformation given in Hubert and Levin (in press), one could then refer to tables of Spearman's rho (e.g., Owen, 1962).

2. COMPUTER

A second alternative that exists is the computer. Two different tasks, relevant to present purposes, could be assigned to this electronic aid. First, one could have generated the complete permutation distribution associated with each of the procedures we have discussed. Then, by referring to the most extreme values, a researcher (or the computer) could decide whether or not an obtained value was significant.

In many situations, however, generating complete distributions will be quite uneconomical, even for a computer. (Note that with 10 alternating phases there are 3,628,800 possible permutations, which would require an extravagant amount of computer time.) Thus, a second assignment of the computer could be to execute the interesting approach discussed by Hope (1968) and Edgington (1969). The approach is essentially a Monte Carlo approximation to the true permutation distribution, and it has been found that 100 randomly sampled permutations will usually suffice (see Hubert & Levin, 1977, for an illustration).

3. APPROXIMATIONS BASED ON THE NORMAL DISTRIBUTION

Finally, and as usual, one can generally rely on the normal distribution when in need. In particular, normal approximations to the exact permutation tests are to be recommended when the number of units in the experiment is moderately large. What "moderately large" means will be discussed below.

It should be initially pointed out that our basic randomization test can be related directly to the familiar two-sample t test. However, the earlier recommended conversion to ranks (i.e., to a Wilcoxon statistic) is to be preferred for a "moderate" number of phases associated with *each* condition (eight or more). This is because a normal approximation to the rank tests can be depended on for comparatively lower sample sizes (when parametric assumptions are in doubt). The appropriate large-sample approximation to the Wilcoxon test is discussed in most nonparametric statistic books, including Marascuilo and McSweeney (1977).

Let us now provide and illustrate a convenient approximation to the more powerful tests discussed in this chapter. (Since these procedures are not as readily accessible, they will be presented in more detail here.) Following Kendall (1970) and Hubert and Levin (in press), if we let Γ represent the summed products (based on either ordinal, interval, or ratio weights), then the expected value and variance of Γ are given by

$$E(\Gamma) = \frac{1}{n}\left(\sum_{i=1}^{n} x_i\right)\left(\sum_{i=1}^{n} y_i\right)$$

$$\text{Var}(\Gamma) = \frac{1}{n-1}\left[\sum_{i=1}^{n} (x_i - \bar{x})^2\right]\left[\sum_{i=1}^{n} (y_i - \bar{y})^2\right]$$

where n is the total number of phases, and x and y represent the weights and summary measures respectively, as well as their corresponding means based on the n phases ($\bar{x}$ and $\bar{y}$).

With at least four phases within *each* condition (i.e., when $n \geq 8$), an obtained summed products value Γ may be substituted into the formula

$$z = [\Gamma - E(\Gamma)]/[\text{Var}(\Gamma)]^{1/2}$$

and reasonably referred to the standard normal distribution as an approximation to the exact permutation probability.

To illustrate this approach, let us suppose that eight alternating control (A) and treatment (B) phases are administered to a single subject. Suppose further that the researcher specifies an a priori lowest to highest ordering of the four A phases in their temporal sequence, followed by a similar ordering of the four B phases. Thus, it is posited that

$$A_1 < A_2 < A_3 < A_4 < B_1 < B_2 < B_3 < B_4$$

In terms of the actual sequence of events, the appropriate ordinal weights are as follows:

$$
\begin{array}{cccccccc}
A_1 & B_1 & A_2 & B_2 & A_3 & B_3 & A_4 & B_4 \\
1 & 5 & 2 & 6 & 3 & 7 & 4 & 8
\end{array}
$$

Let us now suppose that, following the experiment, the means associated with each of the eight phases actually ordered as follows (note that the summary measures have been converted to ranks—a possibility mentioned earlier—merely to simplify the present illustration):

$$
\begin{array}{cccccccc}
A_1 & B_1 & A_2 & B_2 & A_3 & B_3 & A_4 & B_4 \\
1 & 3 & 4 & 8 & 2 & 5 & 6 & 7
\end{array}
$$

The exact cumulative probabilities associated with the largest summed products (Γ) are given in Table 3.4, having been obtained via a transforma-

TABLE 3.4
Exact and Approximate Cumulative Probabilities
for the Largest Values of Γ

Value of Γ	Cumulative probability	
	Exact	Approximate
204	.0000	.0040
203	.0002	.0049
202	.0006	.0059
201	.0011	.0070
200	.0023	.0084
199	.0036	.0099
198	.0054	.0117
197	.0077	.0138
196	.0109	.0162
195	.0140	.0188
194	.0184	.0219
193	.0229	.0254
192	.0288	.0294
191	.0347	.0339
190	.0415	.0389
189	.0481	.0446
188	.0575	.0507
187	.0661	.0577
186	.0756	.0653
185	.0855	.0737
184	.0983	.0830
183	.1081	.0929
⋮	⋮	⋮

tion of a measure based on Spearman's rho as discussed previously.[6] The approximate cumulative probabilities, derived from the formulas presented earlier, are also shown in Table 3.4 for purposes of comparison. That is, the expected value and variance of this distribution are given by

$$E(\Gamma) = \frac{36(36)}{8} = 162.00$$

$$\mathrm{Var}(\Gamma) = \frac{42(42)}{7} = 252.00$$

and the z formula may then be applied to each obtained value of Γ.

---

[6] It should be mentioned that if the a priori ordinal predictions are applied to the obtained ranked summary data in a somewhat different fashion, Kendall's tau coefficient could be

The important thing to note here is that (as with most normal approx-imations to exact distributions) even though the extreme tail probabilities do not match up closely, for the conventional levels of significance (say $\alpha = .01, .05,$ and $.10$), the matchup is not too bad. For example, using the normal approximation a researcher would decide that Γ would have to equal at least 189 in order for α to be less than or equal to .05. Precisely the same value of Γ is required according to the exact distribution. In the present example, Γ may be computed to be 193, which provides support for the predicted ordering with both exact and approximate $\alpha \le .05$. [It should also be noted that our weaker basic randomization test (i.e., the Wilcoxon two-sample test) would *not* permit us to conclude that there was a treatment effect with a one-tailed $\alpha \le .05$.]

IV. A Few Final Words

Let us close on a similar note to how we began. There is much con-troversy surrounding the use of inferential statistics in $N = 1$ experimental designs. In our own minds we keep returning to the basic issue of why one would want to analyze such data *statistically* in the first place, rather than evaluating them *clinically* with respect to the question: Did a particular treatment change *this* subject's behavior from Level X to Level Y? How-ever, to the extent that statistical inference is desired by behavior change researchers (or by editors of behavior change journals?), the issue boils down to one of choosing a correct unit for analysis. In this regard, we noted: (1) that the issue has been ignored by previous authors offering traditional large-sample statistical analyses for $N = 1$ data; (2) that nonparametric randomization tests are appropriate in cases where units have been randomly assigned to phases; and (3) in the case of systematic (rather than random) assignment of units to phases, randomization tests may be viewed as an appropriate approximation. As is mentioned throughout the chapter, such tests are viewed as conceptually and computationally simple data analysis alternatives for applied behavioral researchers to consider.

---

obtained. As with Spearman's rho, tabled probabilities associated with this permutation dis-tribution exist and, and in fact, are quite extensive. When tied ranks are present, the normal approximation must be depended upon since tables are not available. In such cases, Kendall's tau may afford an especially attractive option inasmuch as there is some evidence (Kendall, 1970) that the distribution of tau approaches normality at a faster rate than does the distribu-tion of Spearman's rho (see Marascuilo & McSweeney, 1977, for further discussion).

We have also distinguished between examining the data for correlated errors as opposed to examining them for correlated observations. While it is true that if errors are correlated so will be observations, the converse is *not* necessarily true. The demonstrated existence or nonexistence of such correlations is useful in allowing a researcher to select an appropriate method of analysis.

The sampling of potentially useful randomization tests that we presented was just that, namely, a sampling. In considering others, however, one must keep in mind the "units" issue and other interal validity issues as well. We would surely be remiss in concluding without mentioning the exciting application of randomization tests to the analysis of $N = 1$ data recently reported by Edgington (1975a). With the problem turned around and viewed in a novel manner—as Edgington has done—a whole new armament of powerful randomization procedures for small-sample experiments is likely to emerge.

ACKNOWLEDGMENTS

Part of this chapter was written while the first author was visiting the Foundations of Education Department at the University of Houston. The constructive feedback of Drs. Thomas Kratochwill, Eugene Edgington, and Janet Elashoff, based on an earlier draft of the chapter, is gratefully acknowledged.

REFERENCES

Box, G. E. P., & Jenkins, G. M. *Time series analysis: Forecasting and control*. San Francisco: Holden-Day, 1970.

Bracht, G. H., & Glass, G. V. The external validity of experiments. *American Educational Research Journal*, 1968, *5*, 437–474.

Bradley, J. V. *Distribution-free statistical tests*. Englewood Cliffs, NJ: Prentice-Hall, 1968.

Campbell, D. T., & Stanley, J. C. *Experimental and quasi-experimental designs for research*. Chicago: Rand McNally, 1966.

Conover, W. J. *Practical nonparametric statistics*. New York: John Wiley & Sons, 1971.

Cook, T. D., & Campbell, D. T. The design and conduct of quasi-experiments and true experiments in field settings. In M. D. Dunnette & J. P. Campbell (Eds.), *Handbook of industrial and organizational research*. Chicago: Rand McNally, 1975.

Edgington, E. S. Statistical inference from $N = 1$ experiments. *Journal of Psychology*, 1967, *65*, 195–199.

Edgington, E. S. Approximate randomization tests. *Journal of Psychology*, 1969, *72*, 143–149.

Edgington, E. S. Randomization tests for one-subject operant experiments. *Journal of Psychology*, 1975, *90*, 57–68. (a)

Edgington, E. S. Randomization tests for predicted trends. *Canadian Psychological Review*, 1975, *16*, 49–53. (b)

Elashoff, R. M. Effects of errors in statistical assumptions. In D. L. Sills (Ed.), *International encyclopedia of the social sciences* (*Vol. 5*). Macmillan and The Free Press, 1968.

Gentile, J. R., Roden, A. H., & Klein, R. D. An analysis of variance model for the intrasubject replication design. *Journal of Applied Behavior Analysis*, 1972, *5*, 193–198.

Glass, G. V., Peckham, P. D., & Sanders, J. R. Consequences of failure to meet assumptions underlying the fixed effects analysis of variance and covariance. *Review of Educational Research*, 1972, *42*, 237–288.

Glass, G. V., Willson, V. L., & Gottman, J. M. *Design and analysis of time series experiments*. Boulder: University of Colorado Press, 1975.

Hartmann, D. P. Forcing square pegs into round holes: Some comments on "An analysis-of-variance model for the intrasubject replication design." *Journal of Applied Behavior Analysis*, 1974, *7*, 635–638.

Hays, W. L. *Statistics for psychologists*, New York: Holt, Rinehart, & Winston, 1963.

Hersen, M., & Barlow, D. H. *Single case experimental designs: Strategies for studying behavior change*. New York: Pergamon, 1976.

Hope, A. C. A. A simplified Monte Carlo significance test procedure. *Journal of the Royal Statistical Society*, 1968, *30*, 582–598.

Hubert, L. J., & Levin, J. R. A general statistical framework for assessing categorical clustering in free recall. *Psychological Bulletin*, 1976, *83*, 1072–1080.

Hubert, L. J., & Levin, J. R. Evaluating priority effects in free recall. *British Journal of Mathematical and Statistical Psychology*, in press.

Hubert, L. J., & Levin, J. R. Inference models for categorical clustering. *Psychological Bulletin*, 1977, *84*, 878–887.

Kazdin, A. E. Statistical analysis for single-case experimental designs. In M. Hersen & D. H. Barlow, *Single case experimental designs: Strategies for studying behavior change*. New York: Pergamon, 1976.

Kendall, M. G. *Rank correlation methods*. London: Griffin, 1970.

Keselman, H. J., & Leventhal, L. Concerning the statistical procedures enumerated by Gentile et al.: Another perspective. *Journal of Applied Behavior Analysis*, 1974, *7*, 643–645.

Kirk, R. E. *Experimental design: Procedures for the behavioral sciences*. Belmont, CA: Brooks/Cole, 1968.

Kratochwill, T. R., Alden, K., Demuth, D., Dawson, D., Panicucci, C., Arntson, P., McMurray, N., Hempstead, J., & Levin, J. A further consideration in the application of an analysis-of-variance model for the intrasubject replication design. *Journal of Applied Behavior Analysis*, 1974, *7*, 629–633.

Kratochwill, T. R., Levin, J. R., & Benjamin, L. S. *On the applicability of the Benjamin special Latin square design to single-subject research*. Paper presented at the annual meeting of the American Educational Research Association, New York, April, 1977.

Lehmann, E. L. *Nonparametrics: Statistical methods based on ranks*. San Francisco: Holden-Day, 1975.

Marascuilo, L. A., & McSweeney, M. *Nonparametric and distribution-free methods for the social sciences*. Monterey, CA: Brooks/Cole, 1977.

Nicolich, M. J., & Weinstein, C. S. *Time series analysis of behavioral changes in an open classroom*. Paper presented at the annual meeting of the American Educational Research Association, New York, April, 1977.

Owen, D. B. *Handbook of statistical tables.* Reading, MA: Addison-Wesley, 1962.

Page, E. B. *Recapturing the richness within the classroom.* Paper presented at the annual meeting of the American Educational Research Association, Chicago, February, 1965.

Peckham, P. D., Glass, G. V., & Hopkins, K. D. The experimental unit in statistical analysis. *Journal of Special Education,* 1969, *3,* 337–349.

Shine, L. C., & Bower, S. M. A one-way analysis of variance for single-subject designs. *Educational and Psychological Measurement,* 1971, *31,* 105–113.

4

Analysis of Interrupted
Time-Series Experiments

JOHN M. GOTTMAN
UNIVERSITY OF ILLINOIS

GENE V GLASS
UNIVERSITY OF COLORADO

I. Introduction

Since the publication of Glass, Willson, and Gottman's *Design and Analysis of Time-Series Experiments* (1975), we have observed a variety of reactions to the statistical procedures developed for the analysis of time-series data. We have both served on symposia on methodological issues related to the analysis of the interrupted time-series experiment. We have been surprised by some of the debate these procedures have generated. Some of these issues are illustrated by the following comments of a referee arguing for rejection of a manuscript submitted to a journal that publishes applied behavioral research. This anonymous review was sent to us by the author of the rejected manuscript. The reviewer wrote:

> Applied behavior analysis doesn't need sensitive statistics to salvage small effects. The field needs basic effects, that is, effects that are large, reliable, powerful, clear,

and durable. Such basic effects will give us strong principles. The field doesn't need dubious, small, and sometime but statistically significant results, because these would result in the development of more and weaker principles. Behavior modification became a technology by ignoring small effects. The sort of eyeball analysis that has been done has acted as a filter, weeding out the small effects. Are we far enough along in the development of the field that we can afford to lose this filter? The reviewer doesn't think so. In the reviewer's opinion, the development of sensitive statistics appropriate for the research designs of applied behavior analysis would be bad for the field.

We are indebted to this reviewer for succintly raising several issues we would like to address in this chapter. We would also like briefly to review our work, to underscore some points that have been misunderstood, and to update the Glass *et al.* (1975) volume.[1]

II. Issues in the Statistical Analysis of Behavioral Data: The Insufficiency of "Eyeballing" Graphs

What sense is to be made of the anonymous reviewer's opinions? Are they mere atavistic yearnings for a simpler time when no one was commending complicated statistical methods to their attention? Or is the reviewer defending a logically consistent behavioral methodology from the seductive overtures of statisticians who would colonize one of the few native sciences left outside their domain?

Purged of their predominant wishful qualities, the reviewer's comments impart a single substantive point: accepting effects not obvious to the unaided eye threatens to misdirect a science that takes pride in large effects. Operant psychologists particularly seek large effects; indeed they sometimes act as though they have proprietary rights to large effects and will refuse to sully their journals with anything but large effects (Michael, 1974). But we suspect that the large effects that operant psychologists are accustomed to detecting readily in their graphs are a unique phenomenon of the experimental laboratory. An animal is apt to respond with gross and exaggerated shifts in behavior when it has been starved to three-fourths its normal body weight or when it is conditioned in an environment made sterile to force its attention to the controlling stimulus. In a prison or a school, such manipulation would be cruel and repugnant. The experimenter controls only a few of the rewards his subjects desires, and the setting is a

---

[1] Since this reference will be cited repeatedly in the following text, we shall shorten it to GWG.

complex pattern of stimuli few of which can be controlled. One has every reason to expect small effects outside the laboratory, and a comparison of the findings published in the *Journal of Experimental Analysis of Behavior* (the "laboratory" journal) and in the *Journal of Applied Behavior Analysis* (the "applied" journal) will bear out this expectation.

By what logic would one *want* to overlook small effects that are actually present but somewhat obscured by uncontrolled error? One may not be satisfied with small effects, but rejecting them as inadequate is different from not seeing them at all. If effects are small, one tries to increase them if one can; or one lives with them, if one must. Small effects detectable by sensitive statistical procedures but undetectable by mere inspection of graphs might be strengthened by reasonable changes in experimental manipulations. On the contrary, absence of an effect might well indicate that substantial effects lie in a different region, with different operants and reinforcers. But to decide whether to attempt to strengthen a small effect or look elsewhere probably requires the assistance of modern statistical methods, as we shall attempt to show with the following example.

Thirteen graduate students studying in a seminar on time-series analysis were asked to inspect various graphs and to judge whether or not an intervention effect was present. The graphs were taken from a study by Komechak (1974) on the control of anxious thoughts. After a few baseline days, subjects were rewarded for maintaining anxiety-free thoughts. Each student was asked to judge whether the series was significantly deflected or displaced at the point of intervention of reward. The same data were analyzed by the methods outlined in GWG and a t-statistic was obtained for each intervention effect. Two graphs, reproduced as Fig. 4.1, will illustrate the results.

The data for Person A in Fig. 4.1 show a fairly erratic and nonstationary pattern of response. When analyzed with the proper statistical techniques (namely, as a first-order integrated moving-averages process), the shift upward in the series at the point of intervention of reward—between the tenth and eleventh days—proved to be highly statistically significant ($t = 3.08$, $df = 29$, $p < .001$). But of the 13 judges, only 7 considered the observed shift to be statistically reliable for Person A. The findings are even more remarkable for Person B. This second series showed no statistically significant ($t = .21$, $df = 19$) shift at the point of intervention—between the ninth and tenth days—yet 11 of the 13 judges felt there was a significant upward shift in the series coincident with instituting rewards for anxiety-free thoughts. Clearly, the "eyeball test" gives results that vary from judge to judge and that can conflict sharply with the findings of statistical tests.

It might be argued that the judges in this little study were not experienced operant psychologists. In their defense, it can be noted that each judge had substantial experience in inspecting and analyzing all manner of data, much

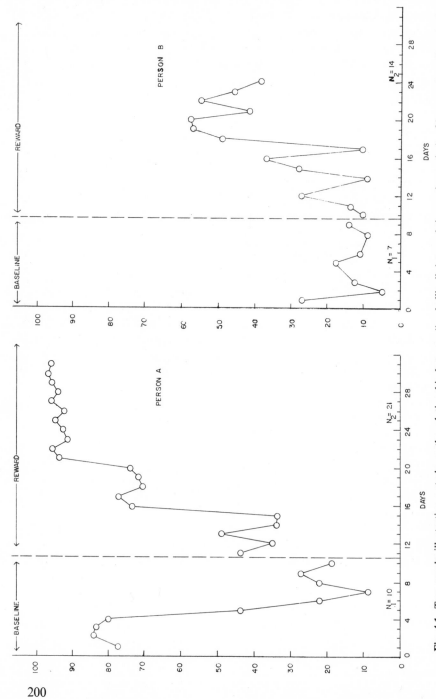

Fig. 4.1. Two graphs illustrating a study on the relationship between "eyeballing" data and time-series analysis of intervention effects in the interrupted time-series experiment. [Data from Komechak, 1974.]

200

of it from operant psychology, for intervention shifts. We are not suggesting that operant psychologists turn responsibility for data interpretation over to the computer and let their faculties atrophy. But those faculties laboriously developed and of which they can be justifiably proud can be refined and made more discriminating if exercised along with statistical methods.

A. The Problem of Autocorrelation

There is a basic problem in estimating intervention effects if a time-series is autocorrelated. Autocorrelated time-series are those in which the present value of the series is to some extent predictable from past values. If there were no autocorrelation in a series of observations, then a simple graphical procedure developed by Shewart (1931) for industrial quality control would provide an adequate test of the significance of an intervention effect. In Shewart's procedure two standard deviation bands are drawn around the mean level of the series; when successive points drift outside the bands, the series has significantly changed its level.

If the data are autocorrelated a t-test will produce results that are in error. Scheffé (1959) showed that for large n, Type I error is underestimated for positive autocorrelation and overestimated for negative autocorrelation. Gastwirth and Rubin (1971) found similar results for small n when the time-series follows a model known as first-order autoregressive. Padia (1973) studied more complex models with large n and found similar results. Table 4.1 shows the probability of a Type I error for a first-order autoregressive

TABLE 4.1
**Probability of Type I Error for First-Order Autoregressive Process
for Various Nominal α Levels**[a]

ρ_1 or ϕ_1	Actual probability of a Type I error for		
	Nominal $\alpha = .01$	Nominal $\alpha = .05$	Nominal $\alpha = .10$
.50	.1362	.2584	.3422
.40	.0910	.2006	.2846
.30	.0474	.1498	.2262
.20	.0348	.1074	.1802
.10	.0204	.0768	.1388
.00	.0100	.0500	.1000
−.10	.0044	.0300	.0702
−.20	.0016	.0168	.0444
−.30	.0004	.0074	.0224
−.40	.0001	.0026	.0118
−.50	.0000	.0006	.0040

[a] From Padia (1973).

process when the data are considered independent. This work was continued by Padia (1975).

The point is simply that one cannot ignore autocorrelation or assume that it does not exist in proposing an alternative solution for estimating intervention effects in the interrupted time-series experiment. First, a model is fit to the data. The model is identified from a general class of models proposed by Box and Jenkins (1970). Box and Jenkins's models are more useful for applications with fewer observation points than are needed for spectral time-series analysis. Once the data are fit by a particular model, a transformation proposed in GWG is used, which leaves an uncorrelated residual from the original series. This transformation then creates a matrix equation in the form of the general linear model. The GWG solution is conceptually a simple solution to the problem of autocorrelation. We will now examine alternative solutions that have been proposed.

B. Analysis of Variance Alternatives

In 1974, a series of papers was published in the *Journal of Applied Behavior Analysis* in which was discussed the use of an analysis of variance procedure applied to single-subject data by Gentile, Roden, and Klein (1972). Gentile *et al.* had applied recommendations made previously by Shine and Bower (1971), who had suggested viewing a subject as "a response generator the responses of which to a particular stimulus are statistically independent and normally distributed about a central response value [p. 112]." The reader will recall this assumption as the basic condition needed to apply a Shewart (1931) chart to time-series data. Shine and Bower also suggested estimating the variance by using the differences between successive observations across odd trials only. This is certainly a reasonable estimate for constructing Shewart bands. Notice, however, that Shine and Bower's solution to the problem of autocorrelation is no solution at all. They simply assume that there is none.

Kratochwill *et al.* (1974) demonstrated that behavioral data similar to those of Gentile *et al.*, are very different from the fair tosses of a coin assumed by Gentile *et al.* to characterize their data. In a study of a student's time on task, they found that the probability of the subject's behavior being the same on two consecutive observations was .87, compared to .42 for the two consecutive coin tosses being the same. GWG (p. 117) investigated 95 nonseasonal time series. Of these 95 series, only 16 were not autocorrelated. Thus the Kratochwill *et al.* (1974) experiment is fairly typical of behavioral data.

Gentile *et al.* (1972) further complicated matters by collapsing baseline and return to baseline periods and collapsing first onset and second onset of treatment periods. They were correctly criticized by Hartmann (1974), who also pointed out that this procedure will greatly increase the magnitude of the error term and decrease power to detect a treatment effect. Hartmann recommended some tests of the lag-one autocorrelation coefficient within conditions, and the cross correlations over different conditions as tests of independence. Thoresen and Elashoff (1974) pointed out that Hartmann's suggestion does not consider autocorrelation at lags greater than one. Hartmann's suggestions would be appropriate for first-order autoregressive or first-order moving average time-series in which the autocorrelation decays as a function of lag or truncates after lag one, respectively (see GWG, p. 99).

Kesselman and Leventhal (1974) suggested considering repeated observations as a factor in a repeated-measures analysis of variance under baseline and experimental conditions. They also recommended using the caution of an experiment-wise protection rate against a Type I error similar to those used in unplanned comparisons of means in an analysis of variance design. The problem with their suggestions is that the F-ratio for conditions tests many other hypotheses that the hypothesis of interest about the intervention effect. For example, the conditions effect (e.g., baseline versus reinforcement) will be significant if there is an uninterrupted increasing or decreasing trend; also, it may be nonsignificant if there is a reversal of trend with no mean difference across conditions. The analysis of variance using repeated measures, therefore, does not reject the null hypothesis for the right reasons, nor does it reflect the logic of the time-series design (see also the discussion in GWG, pp. 72–74).

C. Regression Analysis Alternatives

The application of linear regression to the analysis of the interrupted time-series experiment is illustrated by a study cited by Kaestner and Ross (1974, p. 51). The procedure is illustrated in Fig. 4.2. An increasing linear trend is projected from the baseline period into the experimental period. The data in the experimental period lie below the projected line. Kaestner and Ross point out that "the figure is visually impressive, and the summary report from which the figure is drawn states that the change is statistically significant . . . [p. 51]."

Kelly, McNeil, and Newman (1973) proposed a technique that has been cited as an appropriate procedure, but one that is in error. GWG wrote,

Kelly, McNeil, and Newman (1973) were likewise heedless of the problems entailed by statistical dependence among observations in a time-series when they presented a series of "statistical models for research in behavior modification."

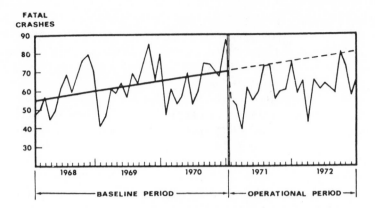

Fig. 4.2. Total fatal crashes for 2 years of program operation. [Data from Kaestener and Ross, 1974.]

Their proposed techniques, based on the general linear model with assumptions of independence of "errors," are, in large part, equivalent to techniques devised previously in econometrics (e.g., Johnston, 1966, pp. 227 ff.; Kmenta, 1971, pp. 419–425). Kelly *et al.* (1973) confused "random sampling" with "statistical independence" in stating the assumptions of the normal theory general linear model, and thus obscured the issue to which the bulk of the remainder of this text is addressed. The "robustness" literature which they cited does not support their disregard of statistical dependence. Furthermore, these authors committed the common error of assuming that problems of "repeated measures" designs are adequately resolved if "persons," upon whom measures are repeated across trials or treatment conditions, is included as a random factor in the model and interactions of persons with other factors are used as error terms. Such inclusion is necessary, but not sufficient to resolve the difficulties with repeated measures [p. 73].

The use of the procedure Kaestner and Ross cited illustrates some confusion about the confidence interval drawn around the linear regression line. This confidence interval is not constant about the center of the baseline period, but diverges from the center of the period. Suppose that we have derived a regression equation

$$\hat{Y}_i = \hat{\alpha} + \hat{\beta}X_i + e_i$$

Then the Gauss–Markov theorem states that within the class of linear unbiased estimators of β or α, the least-squares estimator has minimum variance. That is, when $\hat{\alpha}$ and $\hat{\beta}$ are selected such that $\Sigma e_i^2 = S^2$ is a minimum, the estimators $\hat{\alpha}$ and $\hat{\beta}$ have minimum variance. The 95% confidence interval for predicting an individual Y_0 from the regression line is given by

$$Y_0 = \hat{\mu}_0 + (t_{.025})s\left(\frac{1}{n} + \frac{X_0^2}{\Sigma x_i^2} + 1\right)^{1/2}$$

with the *t*-distribution having $(n - 2)$ degrees of freedom, and assuming that the mean of the X_i is zero (see Wonnacott & Wonnacott, 1970, p. 31). This means that as the point X_0 moves away from the mean of the interval, the confidence interval increases. This is illustrated in Fig. 4.3. Thus, the further away one moves from the center of the baseline period, the less confidence one can have in the baseline regression line.

A second problem with regression solutions is the fact that the errors e_i are likely to be autocorrelated. In the case of classical linear regression, the regression equation can be expressed in matrix form as

$$Y = XB + E$$

where the expected $\epsilon(E) = 0$ and $\epsilon(E'E) = \sigma_e^2 I$, where I is the identity matrix. The least-squares solution is well known:

$$\hat{E} = (Y - X\hat{B})$$

$$\hat{E}'\hat{E} = (Y - X\hat{B})'(Y - X\hat{B})$$

$$= Y'Y - Y'X\hat{B} - (X\hat{B})'Y + (X\hat{B})'X\hat{B}$$

Taking the derivative of $\hat{E}'\hat{E}$ with respect to $\hat{B}$ and setting it equal to zero (the condition for the residual to be minimized) gives

$$\partial(\hat{E}'\hat{E})/\partial\hat{B} = 0 - 2X'Y + 2X'X\hat{B} = 0$$

which is true for

$$\hat{B} = (X'X)^{-1}X'Y$$

However, when the residuals are uncorrelated, $\epsilon(E'E) = \sigma_e^2 \Omega$, where Ω is *not* the identity matrix, but

$$\Omega = \begin{bmatrix} \epsilon(E_1 E_1) & \epsilon(E_1 E_2) & \epsilon(E_1 E_3) \dots \epsilon(E_1 E_\tau) \\ \epsilon(E_2 E_1) & \epsilon(E_2 E_2) & \epsilon(E_2 E_3) \dots \epsilon(E_2 E_\tau) \\ \vdots & \vdots & \vdots & \vdots \\ \epsilon(E_\tau E_1) & \epsilon(E_\tau E_2) & \epsilon(E_\tau E_3) \dots \epsilon(E_\tau E_\tau) \end{bmatrix}$$

which is simply the autocovariance matrix

$$\Omega = \begin{bmatrix} 1 & \gamma_1 & \gamma_2 & \gamma_3 & \cdots \gamma_{\tau-1} \\ \gamma_1 & 1 & \gamma_1 & \gamma_2 & \cdots \gamma_{\tau-2} \\ \gamma_2 & \gamma_1 & 1 & \gamma_1 & \cdots \gamma_{\tau-3} \\ \gamma_3 & \gamma_2 & \gamma_1 & 1 & \cdots \gamma_{\tau-4} \\ \vdots & \vdots & \vdots & \vdots & \vdots \\ \gamma_{\tau-1} & \gamma_{\tau-2} & \gamma_{\tau-3} & \gamma_{\tau-4} & \cdots 1 \end{bmatrix}$$

where[2] γ_j = the lag-j autocovariance = $\epsilon(\hat{E}_\tau \hat{E}'_{\tau+j})$.

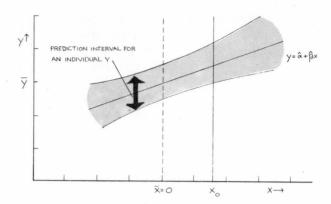

Fig. 4.3. Confidence intervals in predicting a single observation as a function of distance from the mean of the observation period.

In the autocorrelated case it can easily be shown (see, for example, Hibbs, 1974) that the variance of the regression estimates is

$$\text{Var}(\hat{B}) = \sigma_e^2 (X'X)^{-1} X'\Omega X (X'X)^{-1}$$

and often leads to spurious attributions of significance to independent variables (Hibbs, 1974, p. 257).

The best unbiased estimates when the residuals are autocorrelated[3] is

$$\hat{B}^* = (X'\Omega^{-1}X)^{-1} X'\Omega^{-1}Y$$

$\hat{B}^*$ is unbiased with variance

$$\text{Var}(\hat{B}^*) = \sigma_e^2 (X'\Omega^{-1}X)^{-1}$$

The problem in doing regression analysis when the residuals are auto-correlated is to do time-series model fitting on the residuals in order to estimate Ω. For example, if the residuals are fit by a first-order autoregressive process,

$$e_t = \phi e_{t-1} + u_t, \qquad u_t \sim NID(0, \sigma_u^2)$$

then it can be shown that $\gamma_k = \phi^k \gamma_0$, and Ω is estimated from the sample data.[4]

---

[2] This assumes stationarity of the time-series.

[3] Hibbs (1974) showed that classical linear-squares estimators are biased to the extent that the trace of the matrix$[(X'X)^{-1}X'\Omega X]$ differs from the trace of the identity matrix (pp. 258–259).

[4] After classical regression, a time-series model is fit to the residuals.

To appreciate the extent to which the problem of autocorrelated residuals is a serious problem, suppose that both the X_i and the residuals are fit by the first-order regressive process above. That is, assume that

$$Y_t = \beta X_t + e_t$$

where

$$e_t = \phi e_{t-1} + u_t, \qquad u_t \sim NID(0, \sigma_u^2)$$

$$X_t = \lambda X_{t-1} + w_t, \qquad w_t \sim NID(0, \sigma_w^2)$$

Then it can be shown that

$$\text{Var}(\hat{\beta}) = \frac{\sigma_e^2}{\Sigma_t X_t^2} \left[\frac{1 + \phi\lambda}{1 - \phi\lambda} \right]$$

instead of

$$\text{Var}(\hat{\beta}) = \frac{\sigma_e^2}{\Sigma_t X_t^2}$$

If $\phi = \lambda = .8$ the bracketed ratio is 4.56, and classical linear regression underestimates the true variance of $\hat{\beta}$ by 456% and inflates the t-ratio by more than 200%. This equation reduces to $\sigma_e^2 (X'X)^{-1}$ when there is no autocorrelation.

However, when there is autocorrelation in the residuals, as will be the case for most applications, the least-squares estimates provide biased estimates of the regression coefficient variances. Hibbs (1974) wrote, "Since the bias is generally negative, the estimated variances and standard errors understate, perhaps very seriously, the true variances and standard errors. This produces inflated t-ratios, a false sense of confidence in the precision of the parameter estimates [p. 257]."

Hibbs (1974) presents an example of the reanalysis of a time-series regression of presidential popularity from Truman to Johnson originally analyzed by Mueller (1970). The residuals were fit by a first-order autoregressive process. Hibbs' reanalysis indicated "that substantively non-trivial modifications of Mueller's conclusions are in order [p. 288]," and that the corrected

estimate of 84.6 percent for the starting point of Truman's first-term popularity rating ... provides a much better fit to the empirical data than does the [classical regression] estimate of 72.4 percent. Indeed, Mueller's analysis of the [classical regressive] residuals led him to make special note of the poor performance of the model in accounting for Truman's extremely high initial popularity in the aftermath of Roosevelt's death [p. 289].

Time-series models are also not free of the problem of a diverging confidence interval around the estimate. Box and Jenkins (1970, pp. 126–170), in their discussion of forecasting, point out that the variance of the forecast error increases as the time elapses from the last observation. If a time-series Z_t is represented as an infinite moving-average process,

$$z_t = \sum_{j=0}^{\infty} \psi_j a_{t-j}$$

then the variance of the forecast error $V(l)$ as a function of the lead time l away from the tth observation is

$$V(l) = (1 + \psi_1^2 + \psi_2^2 + \cdots + \psi_{l-1}^2)\sigma_a^2$$

where σ_a^2 is the variance of the random errors a_j. This fact is illustrated by Fig. 4.4.

Both the autoregressive and the moving-averages components of an autoregressive integrated moving-average (ARIMA) model affect the forecast function. The autoregressive operator determines the mathematical *form* of the forecast function, and the moving-averages operator determines how the form chosen is fitted to the data (see Box and Jenkins, 1970, p. 139).

To summarize, classical regression solutions ignore the problem of autocorrelation and also face the problem of increasing variance of the forecast error and diverging confidence bands. These solutions, therefore, are likely to be acceptable only very near the center of the baseline period and very near the intervention point. We also refer the reader to Kazdin's (1976) discussion.

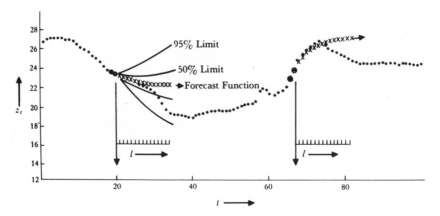

Fig. 4.4. Forecast for two series illustrating change in confidence interval away from last data entry point. [Data from Box and Jenkins, 1970.]

III. Time-Series Analysis

We will sketch the outlines of interrupted time-series analysis and emphasize some aspects of the analysis that have been overlooked.

A. Stationary Time-Series Models

A time-series $\{z(t)\}$ is said to be stationary if two conditions are met: (1) $\epsilon[z(t)] = \mu$ is independent of t, and (2) $\epsilon([z(t) - \mu][z(t + k) - \mu]) = \gamma(k)$ is independent of historical time t and depends only on the relative lag time k. A stationary series thus has no trend and has the same probability structure throughout its historical time. By the same probability structure, we thus mean that the autocorrelations are not changing with historical time, and therefore that *the correlogram* (the plot of the autocorrelation as a function of lag k) is consistent throughout the series.

The simplest time-series is called a *white noise* process $\{a_t\}$:

$$\epsilon(a_t) = 0$$

$$\epsilon(a_t, a_{t+k}) = \begin{cases} \sigma_a^2 & \text{if} \quad k = 0 \\ 0 & \text{if} \quad k \neq 0 \end{cases}$$

White noise processes are thus uncorrelated processes with fixed mean of zero and a stable variance of σ_a^2. White noise processes are, of course, stationary.

It is easy to show that the weighted sum of any finite set of stationary processes is also a stationary process. Thus a special class of time-series models, *moving-average models*, which are simply a weighted sum of white noise processes, are always sure to be stationary. A moving-average process of order q is denoted $MA(q)$.

$$MA(q): \quad z_t = a_t + \theta_1 a_{t-1} + \theta_2 a_{t-2} + \cdots + \theta_q a_{t-q}$$

Another important class of processes are called *autoregressive processes*. An autoregressive process is one in which we can predict an observation at time t from the past of the series. This means that if we were to calculate some weighted sum of, say, the p previous observations

$$\phi_1 z_{t-1} + \phi_2 z_{t-2} + \cdots + \phi_p z_{t-p}$$

and subtract this from the current observation z_t, we would obtain a white noise process:

$$z_t - [\phi_1 z_{t-1} + \phi_2 z_{t-2} + \phi_3 z_{t-3} - \cdots - \phi_p z_{t-p}] = a_t$$

A useful notation for time-series is obtained by defining two operations:
1. Backward shift operator:

$$Bz_t = z_{t-1}, \qquad B^2 z_t = z_{t-2}, \qquad B^3 z_t = z_{t-3}, \quad \ldots, \quad B^p z_t = z_{t-p}$$

2. Difference operator:

$$\nabla = 1 - B, \qquad \nabla z_t = z_t - z_{t-1}$$

These operators make it possible to rewrite the autoregressive and moving-average models as follows:

$$MA(q): \quad z_t = a_t + \theta_1 a_{t-1} + \theta_2 a_{t-2} + \cdots + \theta_q a_{t-q}$$

$$= a_t + \theta_1 B a_t + \theta_2 B^2 a_t + \cdots + \theta_q B^q a_t$$

$$= (1 + \theta_1 B + \theta_2 B^2 + \cdots + \theta_q B^q) a_t$$

$$= \theta(B) a_t$$

where $\theta(B) = 1 + \theta_1 B + \theta_2 B^2 + \cdots + \theta_q B^q$.

$$AR(p): \quad z_t = \phi_1 z_{t-1} + \phi_2 z_{t-2} + \cdots + \phi_p z_{t-p} + a_t$$

$$= (\phi_1 B + \phi_1 B^2 + \cdots + \phi_p B^p) z_t = a_t, \qquad \phi(B) z_t = a_t$$

where $\phi(B) = 1 - \phi_1 B - \phi_2 B^2 - \cdots - \phi_p B^p$.

Rewriting the moving-average and autoregressive time series in this way makes it possible for us to discuss the stationarity of autoregressive processes. The reader will recall that moving-average processes are always stationary. However, this is not necessarily true for autoregressive series. For example, consider the series

$$z_t = z_{t-1} + a_t$$

which is known as a *random walk* process. One realization of the series is formed as follows. We start with a white noise process a_t that is normally, independently distributed with mean zero and variance one:

$$a_1 = .464, \quad a_2 = .137, \quad a_3 = 2.455, \quad a_4 = -.323, \quad a_5 = -.068,$$

$$a_6 = .296, \quad a_7 = -.288, \quad a_8 = 1.298, \quad a_9 = .241, \ldots$$

This series was taken from a table of random normal numbers. If we have an initial starting value of $z_0 = 1.000$, the series

$$\{z_t\} = \{z_0 = 1.000, z_1 = 1.000 + .464 = 1.464, z_2 = 1.601, z_3 = 4.056,$$

$$z_4 = 3.733, z_5 = 3.665, z_6 = 3.961, z_7 = 3.673, z_8 = 4.971, z_9 = 5.212\}$$

We can see that this series drifts away from a mean level, and thus violates the first condition of stationarity.

In fact, it can be shown that the autoregressive process of order p,

$$AR(p): \quad \phi(B)z_t = a_t$$

is only stationary if all the roots of the equation $\phi(B) = 0$ lie outside the unit circle. For a first-order autoregressive process,

$$AR(1): \quad (1 - \phi B)z_t = a_t, \quad z_t = \phi z_{t-1} + a_t$$

This is true only when $|\phi| < 1$. This can be verified as follows. For an $AR(1)$ process,[5]

$$z_t = \phi z_{t-1} + a_t$$

Substituting for z_{t-1} gives

$$z_t = \phi(\phi z_{t-2} + a_{t-1}) + a_t$$

and continuing gives

$$z_t = a_t + \phi a_{t-1} + \phi^2 a_{t-2} + \cdots + \phi_k a_{t-k+1} + \phi^k z_{t-k}$$

Taking the expected value,

$$\epsilon\left(z_t - \sum_{j=0}^{k} \phi^j a_{t-j}\right)^2 = \phi^{2k}\epsilon(z_{t-k}^2)$$

which approaches zero as k goes to infinity if and only if $|\phi| < 1$.

Note that in this case we can write

$$z_t = \sum_{j=0}^{\infty} \phi^j a_{t-j}$$

in the least-squares sense of convergence. This means that the first-order autoregressive process,

$$AR(1): \quad z_t = \phi z_{t-1} + a_t$$

is an infinite-order moving-average process:

$$MA(\infty): \quad z_t = (a_t + \phi a_{t-1} + \phi^2 a_{t-2} + \cdots)$$

$$= \sum_{j=0}^{\infty} \phi^j a_{t-j}$$

---

[5] We assume that z_t has been transformed so that its mean level is subtracted, $z_t = z_t - \bar{z}$.

The reverse is also true, namely, that a finite-order moving-average process is an infinite-order autoregressive process. A useful class of time-series models are the combined autoregressive moving-average models (ARMA):

$$ARMA(p, q): \quad \phi(B)z_t = \theta(B)a_t$$

$$z_t - \phi_1 z_{t-1} - \phi_2 z_{t-2} - \cdots - \phi_p z_{t-p}$$

$$= a_t + \theta_1 a_{t-1} + \theta_2 a_{t-2} + \cdots + \theta_q a_{t-q}$$

B. Nonstationary Time-Series Models

One of the major contributions of Box and Jenkins (1970) was the extension of autoregressive and moving-average processes to nonstationary time series. A nonstationary time-series may be differenced by applying the differencing operator until the residual is a stationary, albeit auto-correlated series. For example, for the random walk process

$$z_t = z_{t-1} + a_t$$

first differencing gives

$$\nabla z_t = z_t - z_{t-1} = a_t$$

a white noise process. The degree of differencing d to obtain a stationary series is no greater than 2 for most applications (Box and Jenkins, 1970), and for 95 series considered by GWG, 51 had $d = 0$, and 38 had $d = 1$.

The integrated autoregressive moving-average model, $ARIMA(p, d, q)$ is thus given by an $ARMA(p, q)$ model fit to the series after it has been differenced d times, that is $\nabla^d z_t$ is fit by an $ARMA(p, q)$ model. Hence the general $ARIMA(p, d, q)$ model is given by

$$ARIMA(p, d, q): \quad \phi_p(B)\nabla^d z_t = \theta_q(B)a_t$$

The first step in time-series analysis of the interrupted time-series experiment is *model identification*, that is, finding the values p, d, and q.

C. Model Identification

With the first-order autoregressive model one assumes that it is possible to predict the value z_t of a series at time t from a knowledge of the immediately preceding value, z_{t-1}. The model is

$$(z_t - L) = \phi_1(z_{t-1} - L) + a_t$$

where the value L represents the mean level of this stationary series, ϕ_1 represents the degree of dependency between adjacent observations, and the $\{a_t\}$ are a set of values normally and independently distributed with mean zero and variance σ_a^2. Note that these $\{a_t\}$ are what we wish we had in the first place, namely, a stationary, independent set of observations.

Notice that if we define a transformation $Z_t' = Z_t - \phi_1 Z_{t-1}$, then the Z_t' would also be normally and independently distributed. This is a useful point since it means that identifying a model also identifies a transformation that carries an autocorrelated series into an uncorrelated residual series. The general $ARIMA(p, d, q)$ model

$$\phi_p(B)\nabla^d z_t = \theta_q(B)a_t$$

can be rewritten

$$a_t = \theta_q^{-1}(B)\phi_p(B)\nabla^d z_t \quad \text{or} \quad a_t = \psi(B)z_t$$

where

$$\psi(B) = \theta_q^{-1}(B)\phi_p(B)(1 - B)^d$$

The autocorrelation of the first-order autoregressive process as a function of the lag k is given by ϕ_1^k, and therefore for stationary $AR(1)$ processes the correlogram decays exponentially as a function of lag.

In general, we use both the autocorrelation function and a rather complex function called the partial autocorrelation function to identify autoregressive and moving-averages components in a stationary time series. The partial autocorrelation function is the autocorrelation of a series with the effects of previous time points "partialed out" (see Padia, 1975, p. 31). In fact, the partial autocorrelation is defined as follows. If the time-series is presumed to be a realization of an $AR(p)$ process, it is written as

$$\boxed{z_t} = \boxed{\phi_1 z_{t-1} + \cdots + \phi_{p-k+1} z_{t-k+1}} + \boxed{\phi_{p-k} z_{t-k}} + a_t$$

The partial autocorrelation function (PACF) ϕ_{kk} is the correlation of the two circled terms, holding the term in the box constant.[6] The autocorrela-

---

[6] Another way of understanding the partial autocorrelation function is in terms of the duality between autoregressive and moving-average models. Any time-series model can be written as an infinite autoregressive model,

$$\pi(B)(z_t - \bar{Z}) = a_t$$

writing $z_t - \bar{Z} = \tilde{z}_t$, this gives

$$\tilde{z}_t = \pi_1 \tilde{z}_{t-1} + \pi_2 \tilde{z}_{t-2} + \cdots + a_t.$$

The partial autocorrelation function is approximately $\phi_{kk} \cong \pi_k$.

tion function (ACF) and the partial autocorrelation function (PACF) are a team that is useful in model identification. They are both necessary and useful because of the duality between autoregressive and moving-average processes. Any finite autoregressive model that is stationary can be written as an infinite moving-average process, and any finite moving-average process that is invertible can be written as an infinite autoregressive process. We also difference the time series d times to eliminate all trend from the data. First differencing eliminates linear trend, second differencing eliminates quadratic trend, and so on.

To summarize, the general ARIMA model is given by

$$\phi_p(B)\nabla^d(Z_t - L) = \theta_q(B)a_t$$

where L is the location of the series at $t = 0$. This rather formidable expression is actually quite simple. The $\phi_p(B)$ is the autoregressive component, the ∇^d is the differencing component, and the $\theta_q(B)$ is the moving-averages component (see GWG, p. 82). Model identification refers to the specification of p, d, and q. Note that this only specifies the *orders* of the autoregressive, differencing, and moving-averages components. It does not specify the values of the model parameters. Rather than review the mathematical components of the model identification process, it may be helpful to provide a summary of a "consumer's guide" of model identification taken from GWG (pp. 112–118).

In general, it is difficult to identify most processes with any confidence with fewer than 50 observations. Box and Jenkins (1970, Chap. 6) suggest that the ACF and PACF only be calculated to lags less than $N/4$, where N is the number of observations. For mixed processes there are $(q - p)$ anomalous points on the correlogram, i.e., points that do not satisfy the form of the ACF (see Box and Jenkins, 1970, p. 175). Hence, with $N = 16$, we can only calculate three values of the ACF, which limits the class of models we can confidently identify. In the case of fewer observations an intelligent guess about the model will thus have to be made. If the data are seasonal, the problem is worse, and still longer series are required. For practice in identification with examples of actual time-series the reader is referred to Anderson (1975) as a supplement to Box and Jenkins (1970). *Note, however, that the need for a long series has nothing to do with the statistical power of tests of intervention effects.* Once we select a model, by whatever process, the N for testing intervention effects may be much less than 50.

It is more essential to identify correctly the degrees of differencing than to identify the correct degree of the autoregressive or moving average component. Either underdifferencing or overdifferencing is bad. The former leaves dependence in the series, which should have been removed; the latter introduces unwanted dependence into the data. Padia (1975), using Monte

Carlo simulation techniques, found that "In general, failure to difference a non-stationary time-series results in a gross underestimate of Type I error and power. Over-differencing a stationary time-series results in large overestimates of Type I error and power [p. 2]."

The results of identifying 116 series are presented in Table 4.2. These series varied over the unit observed (person, city, nation) and the time-series variable (alpha brain waves, crime rates, examination scores, stock prices, learning curves, etc.). Twenty-one of these series were identified as cyclical and possess no simple expression in terms of the basic ARIMA model. The remaining 95 series were fit with low orders of p, d, and q. Fifty-one series required no differencing ($d = 0$); 38 required only first differencing ($d = 1$), and only 6 required second differencing ($d = 2$). Ninety-three were fit with models that had zero or first-order autoregressive terms ($p = 0$ or 1), and 85 were fit with models that had zero or first order moving-averages terms ($q = 0$ or 1). To summarize, approximately 75% of the series were non-seasonal; these series were covered primarily by four models: white noise, $ARIMA(0, 0, 0)$, 18%; first-order autoregressive, $ARIMA(1, 0, 0)$, 23%; white noise after first differencing, $ARIMA(0, 1, 0)$, 11%; and the integrated moving-averages process, $ARIMA(0, 1, 1)$, 23%.

A computer program called CORREL has been developed by Bower, Padia, and Glass that computes autocorrelations and partial autocorrelations for raw data and several differencings of the data. The program gives

TABLE 4.2
Results of Identification of Time-Series Models for Social-Behavioral Data

Order of moving-averages, q	Order of autoregression, p	Order of differencing, d			Totals	
		0	1	2		
0	0	16	9	2	$q = 0: 51; p = 0: 71$	
0	1	21	1	0		
0	2	2	0	0		
1	0	10	22	2	$q = 1: 34; p = 1: 22$	
1	1	0	0	0		
1	2	0	0	0		
2	0	2	4	2	$q = 2: 8; \ p = 2: 2$	
2	1	0	0	0		
2	2	0	0	0		
3	0	0	2	0	$q = 3: 2$	
3	1	0	0	0		
3	2	0	0	0		
Totals		51	38	6	95	95

standard errors for each coefficient as well as a chi-square test of whether the series or the differenced series is white noise, that is, unautocorrelated. This program and a manual for its use are available from the second author upon request. Table 4.3 is useful, assuming that the data have been properly differenced to eliminate trend. An autoregressive term is indicated by an autocorrelation function that dies out slowly and a moving-averages function is indicated by a partial autocorrelation function that dies out slowly. Table 4.3 gives some indication of the *duality between AR and MA processes.* This duality only exists under stationarity conditions for the AR operator and invertibility conditions for the MA operator. Under these conditions a finite AR process is the same model as a specific infinite MA process. An AR model of order p

$$AR(p): \quad \phi_p(B)z_t = a_t$$

is an infinite MA model [if $\phi_p(B)$ is stationary]:

$$MA(\infty): \quad z_t = \phi_p^{-1}(B)a_t$$

and the converse is true for an MA model:

$$MA(q): \quad z_t = \theta_q(B)a_t$$

can be rewritten [if $\theta_q(B)$ is invertible]

$$AR(\infty): \quad \theta_q^{-1}(B)z_t = a_t$$

Just as all MA processes are stationary (but not necessarily invertible), all AR processes are invertible (but not necessarily stationary). The duality is completed by the partial autocorrelation function (PACF), which dies out when the autocorrelation function (ACF) truncates and truncates when the PACF dies out. The stationarity conditions for the AR operator are that all roots of $\phi_p(B) = 0$ lie outside the unit circle, and the invertibility conditions for the MA operator are that all roots of $\theta_q(B) = 0$ lie outside the unit circle. The duality between the ACF and the PACF will be useful in model identification.

TABLE 4.3

Identification of the Autoregressive and Moving Average Components of an ARMA (p,q) Series

	Autocorrelation	Partial autocorrelation
$AR(p)$	dies out slowly	cuts off after lag p
$MA(q)$	cuts off after lag q	dies out slowly
$ARMA(p,q)$	dies out slowly	dies out slowly

The first step in model identification is finding the degree of differencing d to achieve stationarity. The stationary differenced series varies about a mean level and has a stable autocorrelation (one that varies only with lag and not starting point). In practice this means that the autocorrelation function dies out at relatively large lags. If the autocorrelation function stays large, the series is probably under- or overdifferenced.

The second step involves identifying the degree of the autoregressive component p and the degree of the moving-average component q. Figure 4.5 illustrates the forms of the autocorrelation and partial autocorrelation functions for various AR and MA models.

D. General Guidelines for Identification

Usually the cases we examine may be fit by more than one model. However, recall that the duality of autoregressive and moving average processes will usually mean that these models are extremely similar. The flowchart in Fig. 4.6 is our general summary of what we do to identify a model in practice. The first step is to select the degree of differencing such that the ACF dies off quickly. We then examine anaomalous terms in the ACF of the differenced series (see Appendix 1); the number of anomalous terms, that is, terms that do not decay or show damped sine wave oscillation, equals $(q - p)$. The number of anomalous terms in the PACF equals $(p - q)$.

The third step is to examine whether the ACF cuts off after lag q, which suggests that the differenced series is a pure moving-average series. If the PACF cuts off after lag p, the differenced series is a pure autoregressive series. Otherwise, it is a mixed ARMA model.

To decide whether the PACF and ACF cut off, we need estimates of the standard errors of the autocorrelation and partial autocorrelation as a function of lag.

To obtain standard errors for the ACF and PACF, we consider two hypotheses:

H_1: $\rho_k = ACF = 0$ for lags $k > q$, which implies an $MA(q)$ process

H_2: $\phi_{kk} = PACF = 0$ for lags $k > p$, which implies an $AR(p)$ process

Under H_1,

$$\hat{\sigma}(r_k) = \frac{1}{N^{1/2}}\{1 + 2(r_1{}^2 + \cdots + r_q{}^2)\}^{1/2}, \quad k > q$$

$|r_k|/\hat{\sigma}(r_k)$ is distributed normally, so, if $|r_k|/\hat{\sigma}(r_k) < u_\alpha$ (read from a table of normal distribution) then we accept H_1.

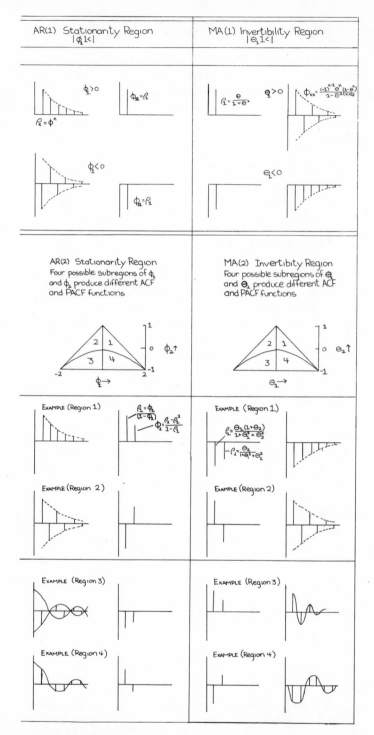

Fig. 4.5. Theoretical autocorrelation and partial autocorrelation functions for various stationary AR and MA processes.

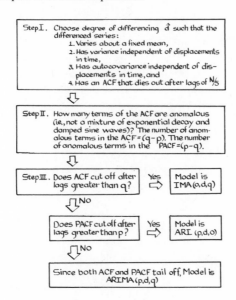

Fig. 4.6. Flowchart for model identification.

Under H_2, if $|\phi_{kk}|/\hat{\sigma}(\hat{\phi}_{kk}) < u_\alpha$ we accept H_2:

$$\hat{\sigma}(\hat{\phi}_{kk}) = 1/N^{1/2} \quad \text{for} \quad k > p$$

Usually, we will draw a 2 S.D. band around zero for the PACF.

E. Examples of Identification

We will present several examples that follow the general guidelines for model identification.

EXAMPLE 1

Holtzman (1963) presented data due to Mefferd gathered from a from a simple schizophrenic patient. Figure 4.7 depicts these data. The patient's "perceptual speed" was observed for 60 days under baseline conditions; on Day 61 the patient was placed on chlorpromazine, a first generation tranquilizer; on Day 121 electroshock treatment was added; both treatments were suspended on Day 181 and baseline conditions were reinstated for the final 60 days.

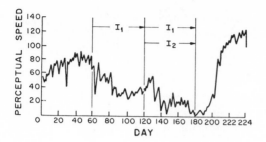

Fig. 4.7. Effects of a tranquilizer (Chlorpromazine) (I_1) and electroshock (I_2) on the perceptual speed of a single schizophrenic patient.

A correlogram was calculated for the preintervention data, for the series, and for first and second differences.

Lag	z	$(1 - B)z$	$(1 - B)^2 z$
1	.43	−.47	−.61
2	.39	−.14	.03
3	.47	.12	.14
4	.40	−.05	−.13
5	.43	.18	.23
6	.24	−.26	−.29
7	.35	.16	.19
8	.27	.02	.05
9	.17	−.25	−.31
10	.32	.37	.42
11	.11	−.23	−.28
12	.15	.02	.08
13	.15	.02	.02
14	.09	−.06	−.11
15	.18	.22	.27

The standard errors of the autocorrelations are above approximately .13 at Lag 1 and rise to .22 at Lag 15. We can see that for the preintervention data the ACF does not die out. Hence the series is nostationary. First differencing, $(1 - B)z$, gives an ACF that dies out. *We must be careful not to continue differencing.* For example, in the random walk process, which is nonstationary,

$$z_t = z_{t-1} + a_t$$

first differencing gives white noise,

$$\nabla z_t = (1 - B)z_t = z_t - z_{t-1} = a_t$$

Second differencing, however, produces another nonstationary series:

$$\nabla^2 z_t = (1 - B)^2 z_t = (1 - 2B + B)^2 z_t = 1 - 2z_{t-1} + z_{t-2}$$

$$= 1 - 2(z_{t-2} + a_t) + z_{t-2} = 1 - z_{t-2} + a_t$$

Nonstationarity has crept back into the series in the form of the z_{t-2} term. Second differencing in the Mefferd case adds no gain over first differencing in the decay of the ACF; hence the model may be an $ARIMA(p, 1, q)$. Nothing in the correlogram suggests the exponential decay associated with autoregressive terms; thus p will be taken to be zero. Finally, only the Lag 1 autocorrelation of the first differences appears significantly nonzero; therefore, the model that will be adopted will be $ARIMA(0, 1, 1)$, the integrated moving-averages model.

EXAMPLE 2 [7]

The preintervention observations were:

$z_1 = 55$	$z_{21} = 53$	$z_{41} = 70$
$z_2 = 56$	$z_{22} = 63$	$z_{42} = 88$
$z_3 = 48$	$z_{23} = 80$	$z_{43} = 88$
$z_4 = 46$	$z_{24} = 65$	$z_{44} = 85$
$z_5 = 56$	$z_{25} = 78$	$z_{45} = 87$
$z_6 = 46$	$z_{26} = 64$	$z_{46} = 63$
$z_7 = 59$	$z_{27} = 72$	$z_{47} = 91$
$z_8 = 60$	$z_{28} = 77$	$z_{48} = 94$
$z_9 = 53$	$z_{29} = 82$	$z_{49} = 72$
$z_{10} = 58$	$z_{30} = 77$	$z_{50} = 83$
$z_{11} = 73$	$z_{31} = 35$	$z_{51} = 88$
$z_{12} = 69$	$z_{32} = 79$	$z_{52} = 78$
$z_{13} = 72$	$z_{33} = 71$	$z_{53} = 84$
$z_{14} = 51$	$z_{34} = 73$	$z_{54} = 78$
$z_{15} = 72$	$z_{35} = 77$	$z_{55} = 75$
$z_{16} = 69$	$z_{36} = 76$	$z_{56} = 75$
$z_{17} = 68$	$z_{37} = 83$	$z_{57} = 86$
$z_{18} = 69$	$z_{38} = 73$	$z_{58} = 79$
$z_{19} = 79$	$z_{39} = 78$	$z_{59} = 75$
$z_{20} = 77$	$z_{40} = 91$	$z_{60} = 87$

The program CORREL will give ACF and PACF values, useful for lags less than $60/4 = 15$. The ACF for the series is approximately

$r_1 = .43$	$r_5 = .43$	$r_9 = .17$
$r_2 = .39$	$r_6 = .24$	$r_{10} = .32$
$r_3 = .47$	$r_7 = .35$	$r_{11} = .11$
$r_4 = .40$	$r_8 = .27$	$r_{12} = .15$

---

[7] This example is taken from Bower, Padia, and Glass (1974).

The standard error of each ACF is

Lag 1 = .13	Lag 5 = .20	Lag 9 = .23
Lag 2 = .15	Lag 6 = .22	Lag 10 = .24
Lag 3 = .17	Lag 7 = .22	Lag 11 = .24
Lag 4 = .19	Lag 8 = .23	Lag 12 = .24

We can therefore see that ACF does not die out quickly and this suggests that first differencing is in order. For first differencing the first terms of the ACF and the standard errors are

$$r_1 = -.47, \quad \text{Lag 1} = .13$$
$$r_2 = -.14, \quad \text{Lag 2} = .16$$
$$r_3 = .12, \quad \text{Lag 3} = .16$$
$$r_4 = -.05, \quad \text{Lag 4} = .16$$
$$r_5 = .18, \quad \text{Lag 5} = .16$$
$$r_6 = -.26, \quad \text{Lag 6} = .16$$
$$r_7 = .16, \quad \text{Lag 7} = .16$$
$$r_8 = .02, \quad \text{Lag 8} = .17$$

After Lag 1 the ACF is effectively zero, which suggests an IMA (1) process, i.e., $ARIMA(0, 1, 1)$ of order $p = 0$, $d = 1$, $q = 1$. This can be checked to see if the PACF dies out for the first differenced series. We get

$$\phi_{11} = -.47 \quad \text{Std. Error} = .13$$
$$\phi_{22} = -.46$$
$$\phi_{33} = -.34$$
$$\phi_{44} = .01$$
$$\phi_{55} = .16$$
$$\phi_{66} = -.24$$

This is not quite an exponential decay, but it is close. Viewing this series as truncating after Lag 3 [which suggests an integrated autoregressive process $ARI(3, 1, 0)$, $p = 3$, $d = 1$, $q = 0$] would give a less parsimonious model than the $ARIMA(0, 1, 1)$ identified earlier.

EXAMPLE 3 [8]

Sample values of Series A (chemical process concentration readings taken every two hours) are read down:

---

[8] This example is taken from Box and Jenkins (1970, Series A).

17.0	16.8	17.2	17.4	17.4
16.6	17.4	17.4	16.8	17.6
16.3	17.1	17.4	17.1	17.4
16.1	17.0	17.0	17.4	17.3
17.1	16.7	17.3	17.4	17.0
16.9	17.4	17.2	17.5	17.8

Values of the ACF are (read across)

$$.57 \quad .50 \quad .40 \quad .36 \quad .33 \quad .35$$

for zero differencing, suggesting $d > 0$. For first differencing the ACF values are

$$-.41 \quad .02 \quad -.07 \quad -.01 \quad -.07$$

which Box and Jenkins suggest are "small after the first lag. This suggests that this time series might be described by an IMA $(0, 1, 1)$ process. However, from the autocorrelation function of z, it is seen that *after lag* 1 the correlations do decrease fairly regularly. Therefore, an alternative possibility is that the series is a mixed one of order $(1,0,1)$ (p. 179)." The PACF can be examined to test this possibility. If the model is a mixed one, with $d = 0$, then the PACF of z should truncate for lags $k > 2$. We get, for the PACF of z,

$$.57 \quad .25 \quad .08 \quad .09 \quad .07$$

which supports the notion that the model is $ARIMA(1, 0, 1)$. However, Box and Jenkins (1970) wrote, "We shall see later that the two possibilities result in virtually the same model (p. 179)."

F. Model Parameters

The next step in model fitting is the estimation of the values of the model parameters. To illustrate this process consider the integrated moving-averages process $ARIMA(0, 1, 1)$. Assume also that an intervention has occurred between time $t = n_1$, and $t = n_1 + 1$, which has produced a sudden and constant increase in level δ. Prior to intervention the model is

$$z_t = L + (1 - \theta_1) \sum_{i=1}^{t-1} a_i + a_t$$

θ_1 is the model parameter we want to estimate $(-1 < \theta_1 < 1)$. After the intervention, the model is

$$z_t = L + \delta + (1 - \theta_1) \sum_{i=1}^{t-1} a_i + a_t$$

To transform the model to the general linear model, define a new series $y_1, y_2, y_3, \ldots,$ by

$$y_1 = z_1$$

$$y_2 = z_2 - z_1 + \theta_1 y_1$$

$$y_3 = z_3 - z_2 + \theta_1 y_2$$

$$\vdots$$

$$y_t = z_t - z_{t-1} + \theta_1 y_{t-1}$$

The logic of this transformation is that the y can be expressed as

$$
\begin{bmatrix} y_1 \\ y_2 \\ \vdots \\ y_{n_1} \\ \hline y_{n_1+1} \\ \vdots \\ y_n \end{bmatrix}
=
\begin{bmatrix} 1 & 0 \\ \theta_1 & 0 \\ \vdots & \vdots \\ \theta_1^{n_1-1} & 0 \\ \hline \theta_1^{n_1} & 1 \\ \vdots & \theta_1 \\ & \theta_1^2 \\ & \vdots \\ \theta_1^{n-1} & \theta_1^{n_2-1} \end{bmatrix}
\begin{bmatrix} L \\ \delta \end{bmatrix}
\begin{bmatrix} a_1 \\ a_2 \\ \vdots \\ a_n \end{bmatrix}
$$

The above formulation can be expressed [9] as a matrix equation:

$$Y = X^*\beta + a$$

which is in the form of the general linear model.

The least-squares solution of estimates to L and δ is given by

$$\begin{bmatrix} \hat{L} \\ \hat{\delta} \end{bmatrix} = (X^{*\prime}X^*)^{-1}X^{*\prime}Y$$

---

[9] The symbol X^* is used to denote the "design" matrix for the transformed variable y to distinguish it from a design matrix X for the original variable z.

The sum of squared estimated errors for particular values of L and δ is given by $SS(\theta_1|Z) = \hat{a}'\hat{a}$, where $\hat{a} = Y - X^*\hat{\beta}$. We can vary θ_1 in small steps between -1 and $+1$ and find the value of θ_1 that minimizes the quantity $SS(\theta_1|z)$.

Using normal theory for the random variables a_i, the distribution of the least-squares estimates is given by

$$(\hat{L} - L)/S_a(C^{11})^{1/2} \sim t_{n-2},$$

$$(\hat{\delta} - \delta)/S_a(C^{22})^{1/2} \sim t_{n-2}$$

where

$$s_a^2 = \frac{\hat{a}'\hat{a}}{n-2} = \frac{SS(\theta_1|z)}{n-2}$$

C^{jj} is the jth diagonal entry in $(X^{*\prime}X^*)^{-1}$ and t_{n-2} is Student's t with $n - 2$ degrees of freedom, where $n = n_1 + n_2$ total observations, n_1 before and n_2 after intervention.

GWG presented a generalization of this transformation procedure using psi-weights for estimating and testing intervention effects in the general $ARIMA(p, d, q)$ model. Their approach arrived at a solution similar to that obtained by Kepka (1972), who used a different method. The $ARIMA(p, d, q)$ can be expressed as

$$z_t = \psi_0 a_t + \psi_1 a_{t-1} + \psi_2 a_{t-2} + \cdots$$

which is an infinite moving-average process. A set of recursive relationships can be derived for obtaining the ψ_j from the $ARIMA(p, d, q)$ model.

The transformation to the y is given recursively by

$$y_t = z_t - \sum_{j=1}^{t-1} \psi_j y_{t-j}$$

The transformed variable y_t is a linear function of L, the level of the series at time zero, and any number of parameters δ_i reflecting the effects of an intervention into the series. The general equation is

$$\begin{bmatrix} y_1 \\ y_2 \\ \vdots \\ y_N \end{bmatrix} = \begin{bmatrix} X^*_{11} & X^*_{12} \cdots \\ X^*_{21} & X^*_{22} \cdots \\ \vdots & \vdots \\ X^*_{N1} & X^*_{N2} \cdots \end{bmatrix} \begin{bmatrix} L \\ \delta_1 \\ \delta_2 \\ \vdots \end{bmatrix} + \begin{bmatrix} a_1 \\ a_2 \\ \vdots \\ a_N \end{bmatrix},$$

or $Y = X^*\beta + a$, in matrix form. The δ_i are intervention effects parameters.

The reader is referred to GWG for details of the derivation with worked examples.

G. Examples of Interrupted Time-Series Analysis

For the Mefferd data discussed above as Example 1 of model identification, we use the $ARIMA(0, 1, 1)$ to test the intervention effect, testing the baseline 60 days to the chloropromazine 60 days. One hundred successive calculations by the TSX program are performed, varying θ_1, the model parameter in the $ARIMA(0, 1, 1)$ model, from -1 to $+1$ in steps of .02. For each possible value of θ_1, the observations are transformed into the y using the transformation given above. The y variable is then expressed as a special case of the general linear model, which makes it possible to do least-squares analyses. Each of the hundred least-squares analyses produce a residual error variance s_a^2, from which the maximum likelihood estimate of θ_1 is found. The relevant portion of the hundred calculations is as shown in the accompanying tabulation.

θ_1	s_a^2	$\hat{L}$	$t(\hat{L})$	$\hat{\delta}$	$t(\hat{\delta})$
⋮	⋮	⋮	⋮	⋮	⋮
.70	94.30	53.54	7.72	-20.82	-3.00
.72	93.80	53.66	7.98	-21.14	-3.15
.74	93.44	53.83	8.28	-21.48	-3.30
*.76	93.25	54.06	8.61	-21.83	-3.48
.78	93.29	54.37	9.00	-22.22	-3.68
.80	93.62	54.76	9.43	-22.63	-3.90
.82	94.34	55.26	9.94	-23.09	-4.15
⋮	⋮	⋮	⋮	⋮	⋮

The maximum likelihood estimate of θ_1 is approximately .76, since that value corresponds to the minimum residual error variance. For $\theta_1 = .76$, the estimated level of the series at "time 0" is 54.06, which is quite significantly different from zero ($t = 8.61$, $df = 118$). But more important, the estimated intervention effect is -21.83, also highly significantly different from zero ($t = -3.48$, $df = 118$, $p < .001$). Hence the introduction of the tranquilizer brought about a statistically significant downward shift in level of the series. GWG note that:

A "naked eye" examination of Figure 8 would have seemed to have indicated such a shift, although the level of the series was dropping for about ten days prior to the intervention, and it is not obvious that the drop in the series after intervention is quite unexpected from an unaltered ARIMA(0, 1, 1) process. However, the statistical analysis demonstrates emphatically that the post-I level of the series is not the normal progression of the pre-I process.

It is interesting to note here that the results of the analysis are quite sensitive to the value of θ_1. If θ_1 were taken to be zero, the analysis would reduce to an independent groups t-test between the pre-I and post-I, for which $\hat{\delta}$ is -21.00 but the associated t-statistic fails to surpass conventional levels of statistical significance ($t = -1.72$, $df = 118$). Furthermore, if θ_1 were taken to be $-.80$, $\hat{\delta}$ would have equaled $+6.59$ with the associated t-statistic being 0.434! [p. 140].

H. Model Adequacy

The adequacy of the identified model can be assessed by analyzing the correlogram of the residual series and using a test statistic developed by Box and Pierce (1970), which under some conditions is distributed as chi-square. Among other conclusions, Box and Pierce showed that an overall test for the adequacy of an ARIMA process is obtained by calculating, *for the residual series,* for a particular set

$$\hat{r}_1, \hat{r}_2, \ldots, \hat{r}_m$$

of these autocorrelations, the number

$$N \sum_{k=1}^{m} \hat{r}_{k^2}$$

which could be referred to x^2 distribution with $(m - p - q)$ degrees of freedom. Of course, model parameters should also usually be significantly different from zero (or the original correlogram would have indicated a stationary, independent random series), and the residual sum of squares should be less than that of alternative ARIMA models.

I. Modeling Intervention Effects

Transforming the autocorrelated data z into the form of the general linear model permits all the flexibility in model construction afforded by linear models. One first specifies a model of the nature of intervention effects in terms of the original variable z. For example, assume that an intervention appears at point $n_1 + 1$ and disappears after three points in time. The matrix representation of this model in terms of z, which is assumed to be an $ARIMA(p, d, q)$ model, can be written

$$z = \sum_{j=0}^{t} \psi_{t-j} a_j + \begin{bmatrix} \begin{array}{cc} 1 & 0 \\ 1 & 0 \\ \vdots & \vdots \\ & 0 \\ \hline 1 & 1 \\ 1 & 1 \\ 1 & 1 \\ 1 & 1 \\ 1 & 0 \\ \vdots & \vdots \\ 1 & 1 \end{array} \end{bmatrix} \begin{bmatrix} L \\ \delta \end{bmatrix}$$

where $\psi_0, \psi_1, \ldots, \psi_t$ are the psi-weights corresponding to the appropriate $ARIMA(p, d, q)$ process.

Denoting the design matrix by X, this formulation of the intervention effect in terms of z takes the form

$$\mathbf{z} = \sum_{j=0}^{t} \psi_{t-j} a_j + X\boldsymbol{\beta}$$

which is not in the form of the general linear model since each z_t is a function of more than one error a_i. The data z must be transformed into y by a transformation that eliminates from z_t all errors a_i except a_t. This transformation will ensure that y is in the form of the general linear model. Note, however, that the transformation of z also transforms $X\boldsymbol{\beta}$. We shall denote the transformed design matrix by X^*; hence

$$\mathbf{y} = X^*\boldsymbol{\beta} + \mathbf{a}$$

The psi-weight transformation appropriate for taking z into y has been worked out for the general $ARIMA(p, d, q)$ model (see GWG, Chap. 7). The transformation has been programmed for electronic computer so that z and X can be entered and y and X^* will result. Thus the user may enter the appropriate computer program with the original data and a specification of an intervention model X, and y, X^*, and the corresponding least-squares estimate of $\boldsymbol{\beta}$ can be routinely obtained.

Zimrig (1975) presented data collected in an evaluation of the Gun Control Act of 1968. He assumed that the intervention should have an accretive effect on the scarcity of gun supplies since enforcement officers were added gradually. The design matrix was altered so that the full impact of the intervention would be felt in the following proportions: January 0, February 1/6, March 2/6, April 3/6, May 4/6, June 5/6, July 6/6. A drop-off of 1/6 effectiveness every two months after July was also predicted since enforcement measures were gradually phased out.

The design matrix X for this formulation of the intervention effect was as follows:

$$X\boldsymbol{\beta} = \begin{bmatrix} 1 & 0 \\ \cdot & \cdot \\ \cdot & \cdot \\ \cdot & \cdot \\ \cdot & 0 \\ \cdot & 1/6 \\ \cdot & 2/6 \\ \cdot & 3/6 \\ \cdot & 4/6 \\ \cdot & 5/6 \\ \cdot & 1 \\ \cdot & 5/6 \\ \cdot & 4/6 \\ \cdot & 3/6 \\ \cdot & 2/6 \\ \cdot & 1/6 \\ \cdot & 0 \\ \cdot & \cdot \\ \cdot & \cdot \\ \cdot & \cdot \\ 1 & 0 \end{bmatrix} \begin{bmatrix} L \\ \delta \end{bmatrix}$$

When δ was estimated with the preceding design matrix its values was larger than when the intervention effect was estimated with a model that specified an immediate and permanent effect δ (a reduction of 9.61 murders per month in the former case versus 8.59 in the latter).

As an illustration in greater detail of the flexible use of the design matrix X, consider the problem posed by the data in Fig. 4.8. There appear the ratings on a scale called "irritability" of a woman for a month surrounding the onset of menstruation. It was hypothesized on the basis of the woman's personal history and in advance of examining these data that the irritability rating would rise for the 2 days following the onset of vaginal bleeding. Vaginal bleeding appeared on the fourteenth day of the series. Thus, the statistical question is whether the fourteenth and fifteenth data points in the series (those points circumscribed by the rectangle in Fig. 4.8) lie significantly off the pre-I and post-I series. Asked equivalently, is there a significant intervention effect of two days duration?

The series in Fig. 4.8 appears to be nonstationary, wandering considerably across the first 13 days. The correlogram for this rather short series tends to bear out this supposition, the lagged autocorrelations remaining relatively large even for large lags. When the data are differenced, i.e., when $z_t - z_{t-1}$ is formed, the lag_1 autocorrelation is $-.48$ and the autocorrelations for higher lags are not negligibly different from zero. The graph and the pattern of autocorrelations suggest that an $ARIMA(0, 1, 1)$ model is appropriate for the data. Accordingly the data in Fig. 4.8 were analyzed with the integrated moving averages model, and the following design matrix was constructed in accord with the hypothesized intervention effect:

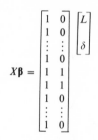

$$X\beta = \begin{bmatrix} 1 & 0 \\ 1 & 0 \\ \vdots & \vdots \\ 1 & 0 \\ 1 & 1 \\ 1 & 1 \\ 1 & 0 \\ \vdots & \vdots \\ 1 & 0 \end{bmatrix} \begin{bmatrix} L \\ \delta \end{bmatrix}$$

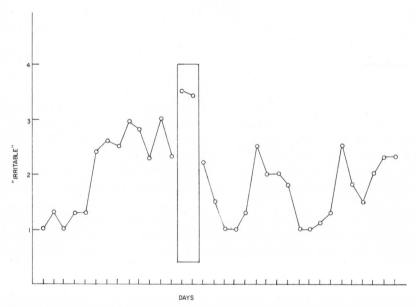

Fig. 4.8. A single subject's self-ratings of irritability before and after the onset of menstruation.

The observed data z_t were transformed by means of the equation

$$y_t = z_t - z_{t-1} + \theta y_{t-1}$$

for values of θ from -1 to $+1$ in steps of .02. For each value of θ, the linear model $y = X^*\beta + a$ was fit and estimates of L, δ, and a obtained. That value of θ for which $\Sigma\hat{a}^2$ is minimized is the maximum likelihood solution for θ, L, and δ. This solution was obtained for $\theta = .14$. The following estimates resulted in the vicinity of $\theta = .14$:

θ	$\hat{\sigma}_a^2$	$\hat{L}$	$t(\hat{L})$	$\hat{\delta}$	$t(\hat{\delta})$
⋮	⋮	⋮	⋮	⋮	⋮
.02	.266	1.01	1.95	1.20	3.29
.04	.265	1.01	1.97	1.20	3.30
.06	.264	1.02	1.98	1.20	3.36
.08	.264	1.02	2.00	1.20	3.31
.10	.264	1.03	2.01	1.21	3.32
.12	.264	1.03	2.03	1.21	3.33
.14	.263	1.04	2.04	1.21	3.34
.16	.264	1.04	2.06	1.21	3.35
.18	.264	1.05	2.07	1.22	3.35
.20	.265	1.05	2.09	1.22	3.36
⋮	⋮	⋮	⋮	⋮	⋮

The estimate of the initial level of the series (at time $t = 0$) was found to be 1.04 at $\theta = .14$. This value is statistically significantly different from zero ($t = 2.04$ with $df = 32$), although the hypothesis that $L = 0$ is neither very plausible nor very interesting. A meaningful curiosity centers on $\hat{\delta}$ and the significance of its deviation from zero. The value of $\hat{\delta}$ for $\theta = .14$ is 1.21, indicating that the self-rating is estimated to be displaced about 1.2 units above the series for the 2-day period following the onset of vaginal bleeding. The t-statistic associated with the test of the significance of the difference between 1.21 and 0 is 3.34 with 32 degrees of freedom, a value significant at any reasonable level. Thus the series is significantly deflected above the normal course of the series for 2 days immediately following the onset of vaginal bleeding.

Further specific worked examples will not be presented in this chapter since they are available in GWG and in a manual written for the computer programs CORREL and TSX by Bower, Padia, and Glass (1974), available from the second author.

IV. Conclusion

The major contribution of time-series analysis is that it introduces a forgotten dimension—time—into the study of change processes. The methodology has only begun to be applied; we wish to point out that even at this juncture it can make a unique contribution in the construction of research questions. Time-series analysis is not merely a footnote in the analysis of variance or a statistical slap on the wrist to those who ignore autocorrelation in their data. Ignoring serial dependency among observations is not merely an error, but a lost opportunity.

The opportunity is one that focuses our attention on the *form of change* over time. The modeling of intervention effects can provide a powerful test for specifically hypothesized forms of change. Some change effects may be small, some ephemeral. The initial detection of these kinds of effects for important problems recalcitrant to our current best efforts is one applied contribution of time-series analysis. The detection of specific forms of change process is a valuable theoretical contribution of time-series analysis.

Another aspect of the opportunity is the potential time-series analysis poses for the study of change within an individual. The applied aspect of this opportunity is that it opens the door to quasi-experimentation and program evaluation with single units—patients, classrooms, programs, schools, cities, and countries. Time-series analysis also makes it possible to study groups of subjects *N*-of-one-at-a-time. This application has potential for revealing scientific principles by generalizing from single-subject experiments (see Chapter 1, this volume).

Any tool has its uses and limitations. We suggest that time-series analysis will take its place as a conceptual method to aid scientific investigation.

Appendix 1.   Anomalous Values

For an $ARMA(p,q)$ process there are three possible cases:

1. $q > p$:   The series of correlations of the ACF are

$$\underbrace{\rho_q, \quad \rho_{q-1}, \ldots, \quad \rho_{q-p+1},}_{\substack{\text{These follow the pattern} \\ \phi(B)\rho_k = 0}} \quad \underbrace{\rho_{q-p}, \ldots, \quad \rho_0}_{\substack{\text{These show an} \\ \text{anomalous pattern}}}$$

2. $q < p$:   In this case all correlations of the ACF will follow the pattern $\phi(B)\rho_k = 0$.

3. $q = p$:   Only ρ_1 is anomalous, which can be used to discover that $q = p$. For example, consider an $ARMA(1, 1)$ process

$$(1 - \phi, B)\rho_k = 0 \qquad k \geq 2$$
$$\rho_k = \phi\rho_{k-1} \qquad k \geq 2$$

One initial value: we need ρ_1 and so

$$\tilde{z}_t = \phi_1\tilde{z}_{t-1} + a_t - \theta_1 a_{t-1} \qquad (*)$$

Multiply (*) by $\tilde{z}_t$ and take expectations of both sides:

$$\gamma_0 = \phi_1\gamma_1 + \sigma_a^2 - \theta_1(\phi_1\sigma_a^2 - \theta_1\sigma_a^2)$$

or

$$\gamma_0 = \phi_1\gamma_1 + \sigma_a^2(1 - \theta_1\phi_1 + \theta_1^2)$$

Multiply (*) by $\tilde{z}_{t-1}$ and take expectations of both sides:

$$\gamma_1 = \phi_1\gamma_0 - \theta_1\sigma_a^2$$

Solve for ρ_1 and get

$$\rho_1 = \frac{(1 - \phi_1\theta_1)(\phi_1 - \theta_1)}{1 + \theta_1^2 - 2\phi_1\theta_1}$$

$$\rho_k = \phi_1^{k-1}\rho_1$$

Hence, the ACF follows the pattern determined by $(1 - \phi_1 B)\rho_k = 0$ after ρ_1, which is determined by the sign of $(\phi_1 - \theta_1)$

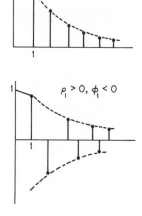

234   John M. Gottman and Gene V Glass

Anderson, O. D. *Time series analysis and forecasting: The Box-Jenkins approach.* London: Butterworths, 1975.

Bower, C. P., Padia, W. L., & Glass, G. V TMS: Two Fortran IV programs for the analysis of time-series experiments. Boulder, CO: Laboratory of Educational Research, 1974.

Box, G. E. P., & Jenkins, G. M. *Time-series analysis: Forecasting and control.* San Francisco: Holden-Day, 1970.

Box, G. E. P., & Pierce, D. A. Distribution of residual autocorrelations in autoregressive integrated moving average models. *Journal of the American Statistical Association,* 1970, *65,* 1509–1526.

Gastwirth, J. L., & Rubin, H. Effect of dependence on the level of some one-sample tests. *Journal of the American Statistical Association,* 1971, *66,* 816–820.

Gentile, J. R., Roden, A. H., & Klein, R. D. An analysis of variance model for the intrasubject replication design. *Journal of Applied Behavior Analysis,* 1972, *5,* 193–198.

Glass, G. V., Willson, V. L., & Gottman, J. M. *Design and analysis of time-series experiments.* Boulder, CO: Colorado Associated University Press, 1975.

Hartmann, D. P. Forcing square pegs into round holes: Some comments on an analysis-of-variance model for the intrasubject replication design. *Journal of Applied Behavior Analysis,* 1974, *7,* 635–638.

Hibbs, D. A., Jr. Problems of statistical estimation and causal inference in time-series regression models. In H. A. Costner (Ed.), *Sociological Methodology 1973–1974.* San Francisco: Jossey-Bass, 1974.

Holtzmann, W. Statistical models for the study of change in the single case. In C. W. Harris (Ed.), *Problems in measuring change.* Madison: University of Wisconsin Press, 1963.

Johnston, J. *Econometric methods.* New York: McGraw-Hill, 1966.

Kaestner, N. F., & Ross, H. L. Highway safety programs: How do we know they work? *North Carolina Symposium on Highway Safety,* 1974, *10,* 1–67.

Kazdin, A. E. Statistical analyses for single-case experimental designs. In M. Hersen & D. Barlow (Eds.), *Single case experimental designs: Strategies for studying behavior change in the individual.* New York: Pergamon, 1976.

Kelly, F. J., McNeil, K., & Newman, I. Suggested inferential statistical models for research in behavior modification. *Journal of Experimental Education,* 1973, *41,* 54–63.

Kepka, E. J. Model representation and the threat of instability in the interrupted time-series quasi-experiment. Unpublished doctoral dissertation, Northwestern University, June, 1972.

Kesselman, H. J., & Leventhal, L. Concerning the statistical procedure enumerated by Gentile et al.: Another perspective. *Journal of Applied Behavior Analysis,* 1974, *7,* 643–646.

Kmenta, J. *Elements of econometrics.* New York: Macmillan, 1971.

Komechak, M. G. The effect of thought detection on anxiety responses. Unpublished doctoral dissertation. North Texas State University, December, 1974.

Kratochwill, T., Alden, K., Demuth, D., Dawson, D. L., Panicucci, C., Arntson, P., McMurray, N., Hempstead, J., & Levin, J. A further consideration in the application of an analyses-of-variance model for the intrasubject replication design. *Journal of Applied Behavior Analysis,* 1974, *7,* 629–634.

Michael, J. Statistical inference for individual organism research: some reactions to a suggestion by Gentile, Roden, and Klein. *Journal of Applied Behavior Analysis,* 1974, *7,* 627–628.

Mueller, J. E. Presidential popularity from Truman to Johnson. *American Political Science Review,* 1970, *64.*

Padia, W. L. Effect of autocorrelation on probability statements about the mean. Masters Thesis, Laboratory of Educational Research, University of Colorado, 1973.

Padia, W. L. The consequence of model misidentification in the interrupted time-series experiment. Unpublished doctoral dissertation, University of Colorado, 1975.

Scheffé, H. *The analysis of variance.* New York: John Wiley & Sons, 1959.

Shewart, W. A. *The economic control of the quality of manufactured product.* New York: Macmillan, 1931.

Shine, L. C., II., & Bower, S. M. A one-way analysis of variance for single-subject designs. *Educational and Psychological Measurement,* 1971, *31*, 105–113.

Thoresen, C. E., & Elashoff, J. D. "An analysis of variance model for intrasubject replication design": Some additional comments. *Journal of Applied Behavior Analysis,* 1974, *7*, 639–642.

Wonnacott, R. J., & Wonnacott, T. H. *Econometrics.* New York: John Wiley & Sons, 1970.

Zimrig, F. E. Firearms and federal law: The gun control act of 1968. *The Journal of Legal Studies,* 1975, *6*, 133–191.

5

Sequential Analysis of Observational Data Using Markov Chains

JOHN M. GOTTMAN
UNIVERSITY OF ILLINOIS

CLIFF NOTARIUS
CATHOLIC UNIVERSITY OF AMERICA

I. Introduction

This chapter is an attempt to speak to a growing sense among researchers who observe interacting organisms, for example, ethologists who study signal and response systems between organisms (e.g., Wilson, 1975), that the characteristics of either organism alone may not be adequate for understanding the process that has taken place between them. A great deal of observational research has focused only on the response rates of various coding categories rather than on the sequential patterning of behavior over time. This focus on rates clearly ignores the dimension of time and ignores the importance of sequence. An additional benefit is that an attention to sequence will make it possible to use statistics in the study of interacting organisms one dyad at a time, rather than requiring group data for estimates of variability in statistical comparisons.

We need some conceptualization of what an interacting *system* means if words like "communication" and "reciprocity" are to be more than metaphors we allude to in discussion sections. In the act of defining sequential dependency and cross-sequential dependency, it may be possible to provide some clarity to these intuitively appealing concepts.

In 1949, Miller and Frick published a paper that directed the attention of behavioral scientists to the sequential analysis of behavior displayed by an organism. They suggested that the patterning of responses could be determined by models based on the sequential dependencies between categories of behavior. Miller and Frick were recommending the study of response patterns and response sterotypy with techniques of information analysis (Shannon & Weaver, 1949).

Since 1949, there have been many applications of the techniques Miller and Frick suggested for the study of response patterning in one organism. However, in the last decade it has been interest in the study of social interaction that has led ethologists, sociobiologists, and developmental, social, and clinical psychologists to search for methodologies for analyzing observational data. This search has led researchers in extremely diverse fields to look for solutions to the same analytic problems. A valuable by-product of this interest in the observational study of social interaction may be an increase in communication between the biological and social sciences.

We will begin this chapter with a presentation of some mathematical concepts in Markov chain analysis and illustrate these concepts with specific examples. We begin by assuming that at a set of discrete times, $t = 1, 2, 3, \ldots$, we can observe a system and decide that it is in one of a set of states, $1, 2, 3, \ldots, k$. Considerable ingenuity can go into defining an observational problem so that this is the case, and clearly there is more than one way to define a set of states. The basic data of the Markov chain are thus a set of codes that tell us what state was observed at each time.

Suppose we observe a system using two codes, A and B. If we observe a sequence $AABABABBABAB$, we can describe nonsequentially by tallying the frequency of A as 6 and the frequency of B as 6. The unconditional probability of A is thus $p(A) = 6/12 = .50$, and the unconditional probability of B is $6/12 = .50$. The conditional probability of the occurrence of B, given that A has occurred just prior to B is the proportion of times that B occurs right after A; A occurs 6 times, and of those six times B occurs after A 5 times. Hence the conditional probability of B given A, is $5/6 = p(B|A) = .83$. We thus reduce the uncertainty in state B's occurrence by knowing that the immediately preceding state of the system was A. The history of the system thus is useful in predicting the future of the system. This is essentially the line of reasoning we pursue in any sequential analysis. Some examples will further describe this line of reasoning and provide an introduction to the language of Markov chain analysis.

Example

Jaffe and Feldstein (1970) recorded a 1 whenever a subject was observed to be speaking, and a 0 when silence was observed. They obtained a sequence of ones and zeros: 1111111110001111 . . .

Suppose that we characterize a system as having three possible states. For example, for dialogues Jaffe and Feldstein defined three states: State 0, both people are silent; State 1, A is speaking; State 3, B is speaking. The fourth possible state of simultaneous speech was so infrequent that it was dropped for some of their analyses.

If a system has three states 0, 1, and 2, we can describe the system in part by specifying how likely the system is to make transitions between states. These probabilities can be arranged in a matrix called the *transition matrix P*:

$$\text{state at time } t + 1$$

$$
P = \text{state at time } t \quad
\begin{array}{c}
0 \\
1 \\
2
\end{array}
\begin{bmatrix}
p_{11} & p_{12} & p_{13} \\
p_{21} & p_{22} & p_{23} \\
p_{31} & p_{32} & p_{33}
\end{bmatrix}
$$

The rows of this matrix sum to one, and each entry gives the conditional probability that the system, which was in one state at time t, will be in some other specified state at time $t + 1$:

p_{ij} = probability of a transition from state i to state j
        within one time interval

We are saying that we can characterize the system's movement over time with only knowledge of the immediately preceding event. A markov chain is called *stationary* if this transition probability of going from State i to State j does not depend on where in the chain ($t = 1, 2, 3, \ldots$) the step is being made (for an example of a test of stationarity see Lichtenberg & Hummel, 1976). The most common way of representing a Markov process is the *state transition diagram* (see Fig. 5.1). Each of the arrows gives the probability of a one-step transition.

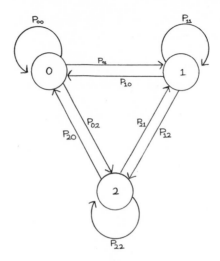

Fig. 5.1. State transition diagram for system with three states.

Example

The Jaffe and Feldstein monologue example of a system with two states yielded the following one-minute sequence of codes:

11111111100011111111111111111111111111111111111111111111111
11111111111111111111100000000000000000111111111111111111111
11111111111111100111111111111111111001111111111111111111111
111111111111101000000001111111

This sequence produced the following frequency matrix:

State at time $t + 1$

		0	1	Total
State at time t	0	25	6	31
	1	6	162	168
				199

When we divide the frequencies by the row totals, we obtain the transition matrix:

$$P = \begin{bmatrix} P_{00} & P_{01} \\ P_{10} & P_{11} \end{bmatrix} = \begin{bmatrix} .81 & .19 \\ .04 & .96 \end{bmatrix}$$

Note that the rows necessarily sum to 1.0. We can also calculate the *initial unconditional probability vector*:

$$v = [p(0), p(1)] = [.16, .84]$$

This vector gives the probability that the system will be observed in each of the states.

To summarize, we have an initial state probability vector

$$p^{(0)} = [p_1^{(0)}, p_2^{(0)}, p_3^{(0)}]$$

The superscript zeros symbolize the initial $t = 0$ nature of this vector. We also have an initial one-step conditional transition matrix:

$$P = \begin{bmatrix} p_{11} & p_{12} & p_{13} \\ p_{21} & p_{22} & p_{23} \\ p_{31} & p_{32} & p_{33} \end{bmatrix}$$

Suppose we want to describe the system after n steps. Since we know how the system is likely to move from time t to time $t + 1$, and we know the initial state vector $p^{(0)}$, we can logically derive the probability vector after n steps, denoted $p^{(n)}$:

$$p_1^{(n)} = p_1^{(n-1)}p_{11} + p_2^{(n-1)}p_{21} + p_3^{(n-1)}p_{31}$$

$$p_3^{(n)} = p_1^{(n-1)}p_{12} + p_2^{(n-1)}p_{22} + p_3^{(n-1)}p_{32}$$

$$p_3^{(n)} = p_1^{(n-1)}p_{13} + p_2^{(n-1)}p_{23} + p_3^{(n-1)}p_{33}$$

Example

Gottman, Markman, and Notarius (1977) coded the nonverbal behavior of distressed and nondistressed married couples. They used a hierarchical rule in which a speaker's facial expressions, voice tone, and specific body positions and movements were coded positive, negative, or neutral. The following transition matrix was obtained for distressed couples:

	$H0$	$H+$	$H-$	$W0$	$W+$	$W-$
$H0$	.00	.05	.09	.57	.01	.17
$H+$	.24	.00	.02	.30	.37	.07
$H-$	.26	.02	.00	.35	.04	.34
$W0$	.68	.03	.08	.00	.10	.11
$W+$	.47	.19	.06	.27	.00	.01
$W-$	.47	.03	.27	.22	.01	.00

$P =$

In this example, H refers to husband, W to wife, and 0 is neutral, $+$ positive, and $-$ negative. This matrix can be used with the assumption that a first-order Markov model is adequate to describe the system, an assumption that we shall see is testable. Suppose we wish to describe the lag-two transition probabilities. For example, suppose we wish to calculate the transition probability of $H0 \rightarrow W0$ after two lags. There are several ways of getting from $H0$ through the branches of the state transition diagram to arrive at $W0$ after two lags:

			product
$p(H0 \rightarrow H0)$ = .00	and then	$p(H0 \rightarrow W0) = .57$	.00
$p(H0 \rightarrow H+)$ = .05	and then	$p(H+ \rightarrow W0) = .30$	.02
$p(H0 \rightarrow H-)$ = .09	and then	$p(H- \rightarrow W0) = .35$	.03
$p(H0 \rightarrow W0)$ = .57	and then	$p(W0 \rightarrow W0) = .00$	.00
$p(H0 \rightarrow W+)$ = .12	and then	$p(W+ \rightarrow W0) = .27$	.03
$p(H0 \rightarrow W-)$ = .17	and then	$p(W- \rightarrow W0) = .22$	.04
		sum =	.12

The $p(H0 \rightarrow W0$ in two lags) = .12. The actual lag-two transition probability was .10, which is a close approximation to that obtained assuming a first-order Markov model.

The procedure above would be repeated for each transition. It can be summarized in one simple matrix equation:

$$\text{lag-2 transition matrix} = P \times P = P^2$$

To test the assumption that a first-order Markov model is adequate, actual transitional probabilities at lag-k would be compared to $P^{(k)}$ (see Jaffe and Feldstein, 1970).

The Chapman–Kolmogorov equations can be written neatly using matrix algebra, and we now digress for a few fundamentals on matrices and how to multiply them.

II. Matrices

For an excellent introduction to matrix algebra the reader is referred to Finkbeiner (1966). This chapter will only summarize a few elementary properties of matrices. A matrix is a rectangular array of numbers, for example,

$$A = \begin{bmatrix} a_{11} & a_{12} & a_{13} & \cdots & a_{1n} \\ a_{21} & a_{22} & a_{23} & \cdots & a_{2n} \\ \vdots & \vdots & \vdots & & \vdots \\ a_{m1} & a_{m2} & a_{m3} & \cdots & a_{mn} \end{bmatrix}$$

$$A = \begin{bmatrix} +1 & -2 & 0 \\ 0 & +1 & 2 \end{bmatrix}$$

The subscripts on the a_{ij} simply tell you which row (row i) and which column (column j) the element a_{ij} is in. The notation above is standard. In the second matrix, $a_{11} = 1$, $a_{12} = -2$, $a_{13} = 0$, $a_{21} = 0$, $a_{22} = 1$, $a_{23} = 2$.

It is possible to define the sum, difference, and product of two matrices. The sum of two matrices is simply the sum of corresponding elements

$$A = \begin{bmatrix} 3 & 5 \\ 1 & 0 \end{bmatrix}, \qquad B = \begin{bmatrix} 12 & 1 \\ 6 & 2 \end{bmatrix}$$

$$A + B = \begin{bmatrix} 3 + 12 & 5 + 1 \\ 1 + 6 & 0 + 2 \end{bmatrix} = \begin{bmatrix} 15 & 6 \\ 7 & 2 \end{bmatrix}$$

Therefore, it does not make sense to add and subtract matrices that are of different sizes.

Matrix multiplication is very useful for simplifying sets of equations. Its definition is a little bit more complicated than addition and subtraction. The way you would multiply A and B above is as follows. The product $C = AB$ is obtained by multiplying the rows of A by the columns of B. The first element of C, c_{11},

$$C = AB \begin{bmatrix} 3 & 5 \\ 1 & 0 \end{bmatrix} \begin{bmatrix} 12 & 1 \\ 6 & 2 \end{bmatrix} = \begin{bmatrix} 66 & 13 \\ 12 & 1 \end{bmatrix}$$

is the product $3 \times 12 + 5 \times 6 = 66$. The second element c_{12} is the product of row 1 of A with column 2 of B: $3 \times 1 + 5 \times 2 = 13$. In the second row of C, the first element c_{21} is the product of the second row of A and the first row of B: $1 \times 12 + 0 \times 6 = 12$. The second element of the second row of C, c_{22}, is the product of the second row of A and the second column of B: $1 \times 1 + 0 \times 2 = 1$.

In general, if $A = (a_{ik})$ represents the $m \times n$ matrix

$$A = \begin{bmatrix} a_{11} & a_{12} & \cdots & a_{1n} \\ a_{21} & a_{22} & \cdots & a_{2n} \\ a_{m1} & a_{m2} & \cdots & a_{mn} \end{bmatrix}$$

and $B = (b_{kj})$ represents the $n \times p$ matrix

$$B = \begin{bmatrix} b_{11} & b_{22} & \cdots & b_{1p} \\ b_{21} & b_{22} & \cdots & b_{2p} \\ \vdots & \vdots & & \vdots \\ b_{n1} & b_{n2} & & b_{np} \end{bmatrix}$$

then the product $C = (c_{ij})$, where

$$c_{ij} = \sum_{k=1}^{n} a_{ik}b_{kj}$$

The size of C is $m \times p$.

This definition may seem a bit overwhelming right now, but it will help us rewrite the Chapman–Kolmogorov equations as follows:

$$p^{(n)} = [p_1^{(n)}, p_2^{(n)}, p_3^{(n)}] \quad \text{and} \quad P = \begin{bmatrix} p_{11} & p_{12} & p_{13} \\ p_{21} & p_{22} & p_{23} \\ p_{31} & p_{32} & p_{33} \end{bmatrix}$$

Then the equations can be summarized in matrix form as

$$p^{(n)} = p^{(n-1)}P$$

and therefore

$$p^{(n)} = P^{(n-2)}P \times P = p^{(n-2)}P^2$$

$$p^{(n)} = p^{(n-3)}P \times P^2 = p^{(n-3)}P^3$$

$$p^{(n)} = p^{(0)}P^n$$

What this last equation says is that we can derive the unconditional state transition vector of the system after n steps by multiplying the state transition matrix P by itself n times and then multiplying P^n by the initial state probability vector.

Example 1

Suppose

$$\begin{array}{cc} & \begin{array}{cc} 1 & 2 \end{array} \\ P = \begin{array}{c} 1 \\ 2 \end{array} & \begin{bmatrix} \frac{2}{3} & \frac{1}{3} \\ \frac{1}{2} & \frac{1}{2} \end{bmatrix} \end{array}$$

Then, by matrix multiplication

$$P^2 = \begin{array}{c} 1 \\ 2 \end{array}\begin{array}{cc} 1 & 2 \\ \begin{bmatrix} .611 & .389 \\ .583 & .417 \end{bmatrix} \end{array}, \qquad P^3 = \begin{array}{c} 1 \\ 2 \end{array}\begin{array}{cc} 1 & 2 \\ \begin{bmatrix} .602 & .398 \\ .597 & .403 \end{bmatrix} \end{array}$$

Note that the number .389 in P^2 gives the probability of a transition from state 1 to state 2 after two steps. The number .602 in P^3 is the probability of a return from state 1 to state 1 after three steps.

Example 2

For the Jaffe and Feldstein monologue data, they found

$$P = \begin{bmatrix} .81 & .19 \\ .04 & .96 \end{bmatrix} \qquad P^{14} = \begin{bmatrix} .18 & .82 \\ .15 & .85 \end{bmatrix}$$

$$P^2 = \begin{bmatrix} .66 & .34 \\ .06 & .94 \end{bmatrix} \qquad P^{18} = \begin{bmatrix} .16 & .84 \\ .15 & .85 \end{bmatrix}$$

$$P^6 = \begin{bmatrix} .33 & .67 \\ .12 & .88 \end{bmatrix} \qquad P^{26} = \begin{bmatrix} .16 & .84 \\ .16 & .84 \end{bmatrix}$$

$$P^{10} = \begin{bmatrix} .22 & .78 \\ .14 & .86 \end{bmatrix} \qquad P^{27} = \begin{bmatrix} .16 & .84 \\ .16 & .84 \end{bmatrix}$$

Note that the last matrix is identical to the previous matrix, so that

$$\begin{bmatrix} .16 & .84 \\ .16 & .84 \end{bmatrix} \times \begin{bmatrix} .84 & .19 \\ .04 & .96 \end{bmatrix} = \begin{bmatrix} .16 & .84 \\ .16 & .84 \end{bmatrix}$$

$$P^{26} \times P = P^{26}$$

We have reached a *steady state* stationary distribution. In general, it is possible to show that if

$$P = \begin{bmatrix} 1 - a & a \\ b & 1 - b \end{bmatrix}$$

P^n approaches a steady state matrix as n increases:

$$\begin{bmatrix} b/(a + b) & a/(a + b) \\ b/(a + b) & a/(a + b) \end{bmatrix}$$

III. Types of Markov Chains

Two states are said to intercommunicate if after some number of transition steps there is a nonzero transition probability (in both directions) from one state to the other. Symbolically, two states i and j intercommunicate if, for some $n \geq 0$, $p_{ij}^{(n)} > 0$, and for some $m \geq 0$, $p_{ji}^{(m)} > 0$.
The Markov chain

$$
\begin{array}{c}
\begin{array}{ccc} 1 & 2 & 3 \end{array} \\
P = \begin{array}{c} 1 \\ 2 \\ 3 \end{array}\begin{bmatrix} 1 & 0 & 0 \\ 0 & \frac{1}{2} & \frac{1}{2} \\ \frac{1}{3} & \frac{1}{3} & \frac{1}{3} \end{bmatrix}
\end{array}
$$

can be drawn as shown in Fig. 5.2. It has an *absorbing state*, State 1. Once the system makes a transition to State 1, it can never leave. Notice that State 1 does not intercommunicate with other states. In any chain with an absorbing state the process is always eventually absorbed. If all pairs of states intercommunicate, the chain is called irreducible.

A cyclic chain is illustrated by the transition matrix (see also Fig. 5.3)

$$
\begin{array}{c}
\begin{array}{cccc} 1 & 2 & 3 & 4 \end{array} \\
P = \begin{array}{c} 1 \\ 2 \\ 3 \\ 4 \end{array}\begin{bmatrix} 0 & 1 & 0 & 0 \\ 0 & 0 & 1 & 0 \\ 0 & 0 & 0 & 1 \\ 1 & 0 & 0 & 0 \end{bmatrix}
\end{array}
$$

This chain could be generalized by a representation

$$
P = \begin{bmatrix} 0 & P_1 & 0 & \cdots \\ 0 & 0 & P_2 & \cdots \\ \vdots & \vdots & \vdots & \\ P_d & 0 & 0 & \cdots \end{bmatrix}
$$

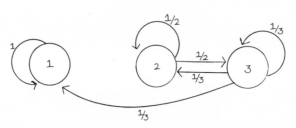

Fig. 5.2. State transition diagram for a system with an absorbing state.

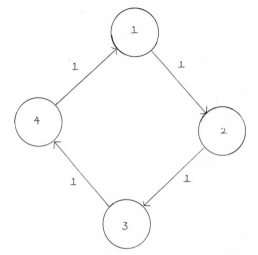

Fig. 5.3. State transition diagram
for cyclic chain.

in which each P_i is a submatrix representing a disjoint family of intercom-
municating states. This system moves from State 1 to some subfamily of
states P_1, reverberates there for awhile, and then makes a transition to
family P_2, and so on, until it returns to State 1. This representation has a
fairly complex kind of periodicity.

An important subclass of Markov processes are called random walk
processes. The analog for generating this matrix is a drunkard hanging
onto a lampost at time zero. At any time the drunkard has a probability
of moving to the right, to the left, or remaining stationary. It is essential
to realize that the random walk requires some *ordinal relation among the
states*. We must be able to think of states as neighboring states in some sense.
An example of a random walk chain is

$$P = \begin{matrix} & \begin{matrix} 1 & \ \ 2 & \ \ 3 \end{matrix} \\ \begin{matrix} 1 \\ 2 \\ 3 \end{matrix} & \begin{bmatrix} 0 & \frac{1}{2} & \frac{1}{2} \\ \frac{1}{2} & 0 & \frac{1}{2} \\ \frac{1}{2} & \frac{1}{2} & 0 \end{bmatrix} \end{matrix}$$

Here the drunkard will never stay in the same spot, but has an equal probability of moving to the right or to the left. We can throw in an open manhole
at State 3 as an absorbing state:

$$P = \begin{matrix} & \begin{matrix} 1 & \ \ 2 & \ \ 3 \end{matrix} \\ \begin{matrix} 1 \\ 2 \\ 3 \end{matrix} & \begin{bmatrix} 0 & \frac{1}{2} & \frac{1}{2} \\ \frac{1}{2} & 0 & \frac{1}{2} \\ 0 & 0 & 1 \end{bmatrix} \end{matrix}$$

once the drunkard arrives at State 3, the process is absorbed.

The general random walk process is given by the matrix

$$\begin{bmatrix} r_0 & p_0 & 0 & 0 & \cdots \\ q_1 & r_1 & p_1 & 0 & \cdots \\ 0 & q_2 & r_2 & p_2 & \cdots \\ \vdots & \vdots & \vdots & \vdots & \end{bmatrix},$$

where $q_n + r_n + p_n = 1$, $q_n > 0$, $p_n > 0$, $r_n > 0$, for $n = 1, 2, \ldots$, $r_0 + p_0 = 1$, $p_0 > 0$, $r_0 > 0$.

This chapter will make a suggestion for hypothesis testing that utilizes the random walk process (see Appendix 2).

For further presentation of the application of matrix algebra to Markov chains the reader is referred to Appendix 1.

IV. Occupation Times

One interesting aspect of Markov chains is the calculation of the periodicities of various states.

Let k be a recurrent state whose recurrence time has a finite mean $m_{k,k}$ and a finite variance $\sigma_{k,k}^2$. Then Parzen (1967) showed that if $N_k(n)$ is the number of times State k is visited in the first n transitions,

$$E[N_k(n)] = n \frac{1}{m_{k,k}}, \qquad \text{Var}[N_k(n)] = n \frac{\sigma_{k,k}^2}{(m_{k,k})^3}$$

and $N_k(n)$ is approximately normally distributed.

We can also calculate the mean number of steps N_j to reach an absorbing state, starting from State j. If a transition probability matrix P has absorbing states we can write P in a canonical form suggested by Kemeny, Snell, and Thompson (1966):

$$r \text{ states} \quad s \text{ states}$$

$$P = \begin{matrix} r \\ s \end{matrix} \left[\begin{array}{c|c} I & O \\ \hline R & Q \end{array} \right]$$

where I is an $r \times r$ identity matrix, O is an $r \times s$ matrix of zeros, R is an $s \times r$ matrix, and Q is an $s \times s$ matrix. The first r states are absorbing and the last s states are nonabsorbing. The P^n is of the form

$$P^n = \begin{bmatrix} I & 0 \\ * & Q^n \end{bmatrix}$$

where the asterisk stands for an $s \times r$ matrix. It can be shown that $Q^n \to 0$ since the probability of being in nonabsorbing states must eventually be zero. Thus the matrix $(I - Q)^{-1}$ exists and is called the *fundamental matrix* of the absorbing chain by Kemeny *et al.* If the matrix $N - (n_{ij})$ is the expected number of times that the chain is in State j if it starts in State i for two nonabsorbing States i and j, then it can be shown that $N = (I - Q)^{-1}$ (see Appendix 2).

Example 1

(From Kemeny *et al.*, 1966, p. 285)

$$
\begin{array}{cc}
I & O \\
\end{array}
$$

$$
\begin{array}{c}
\quad\, 0 \;\; 4 \quad 1 \;\; 2 \;\; 3 \\
\begin{array}{c}
0 \\
4 \\
1 \\
2 \\
3
\end{array}
\left[
\begin{array}{cc|ccc}
1 & 0 & 0 & 0 & 0 \\
0 & 1 & 0 & 0 & 0 \\
\frac{1}{2} & 0 & 0 & \frac{1}{2} & 0 \\
0 & 0 & \frac{1}{2} & 0 & \frac{1}{2} \\
0 & \frac{1}{2} & 0 & \frac{1}{2} & 0
\end{array}
\right] \\
\quad\;\; R \qquad\quad\; Q
\end{array}
$$

$$
I - Q =
\begin{bmatrix}
1 & -\frac{1}{2} & 0 \\
-\frac{1}{2} & 1 & -\frac{1}{2} \\
0 & -\frac{1}{2} & 1
\end{bmatrix}
$$

$$
\begin{array}{c}
\qquad\qquad\qquad 1 \quad 2 \quad 3 \\
N = (I - Q)^{-1} =
\begin{array}{c}
1 \\
2 \\
3
\end{array}
\begin{bmatrix}
\frac{3}{2} & 1 & \frac{1}{2} \\
1 & 2 & 1 \\
\frac{1}{2} & 1 & \frac{3}{2}
\end{bmatrix}
\end{array}
$$

The expected number of times in each nonabsorbing state is given by the elements of matrix N. For example, starting in State 2, the number of times in State 1 before absorption is 1; the number of times in State 2 before absorption is 2; and, the number of times in State 3 before absorption is 1. Therefore, the number of steps before absorption, starting at State 2, is $1 + 2 + 1 = 4$.

Example 2

Jaffe and Feldstein (1970) used the theory of absorbing states to calculate the average number of periods before the floor switches from one
speaker to another. The floor switch away from a particular speaker was
arbitrarily designated an absorbing state. This makes it possible to look at
all states of Speaker A before a floor switch (the absorbing state) to obtain
mean utterance lengths for each speaker (See Jaffe & Feldstein, 1970, p. 80).
The "utterance domain" of states for Speaker A include State 0 (both silent),
State 1 (A vocalizing), and State 3 (simultaneous speech). The absorbing
state is State 3 (B vocalizing). Jaffe and Feldstein calculated the correlations
between actual counts of floor switches and the frequency of switches estimated from the Markov chain model. The correlations ranged from .90 to
.96. They wrote, "The high correlations support the appropriateness of the
first-order model."

V. Nth Order Models

The Markov assumption that the behavior of a system at time t depends
only on its behavior at time $t - 1$ may seem to many researchers to be an
extremely limiting assumption. However, it is possible to generalize the
Markov model to diadic, triadic, quartic, etc., sequences. It is, in fact, even
possible to test each successive model to decide when to stop, that is, when
the next-order model adds essentially no new information.

These suggestions were made in Miller and Frick's original paper, but
it remained for the application by Altmann in 1965 to the behavior of
rhesus monkeys to demonstrate the potential of these methods.

Very few researchers will have as many states as they have codes in an
observation category system. An exception is Altmann (1965), whose
transition probability matrix had 14,400 cells. He wrote, "However, this
matrix, which measures about 6 × 9 feet, would be difficult to publish; it
is available from the author on request [p. 503]." Many dyads (i.e., pairs of
behaviors) fortunately were never observed by Altmann, and he was easily
able to publish the transition probability matrix of the dyads seen at least
once.

Altmann, following Miller and Frick (1949), called a zero-order model
one in which each behavior code is equally likely. The first-order model
estimates the relative frequency of each behavior code. The first-order model
is thus the unconditional state probability vector. The second-order model
estimates transitional probabilities and is thus what we have been calling a
Markov chain.

The null hypothesis Altmann used to test the second-order model is that the behavior of the monkeys is independent of the immediately preceding event, $p_{jk} = p(j)p(k)$. Altmann compared obtained transition probabilities with those calculated from this null hypothesis and concluded,

> Such comparisons quickly reveal that the behaviour of the monkeys does, in fact, depend in part upon the immediately preceding event. Therefore, we discarded our former model, consisting of independent probabilities and replaced it with a model that specifies the probability that any behaviour pattern will occur, given that some specified behaviour pattern has just preceded [p. 503].

Altmann then continued this process, examining third- and fourth-order models. The third-order model is not a Markov chain. Probabilities are calculated for transition from a pair (i, j) to a third state k. Again, the adequacy of the third-order model is compared to the second-order model. To test the amount of information gain in each successive order model, Altmann used the definition of uncertainty by Shannon and Weaver (1949). We will now discuss these concepts of information and the notion of reduction in uncertainty provided by each model of increasing order.

VI. Reduction in Uncertainty

The reader is referred to two introductions to information theory, Attneave (1959) and Quastler (1958), from which much of the following discussion is drawn.

Suppose we want to guess the location of a specific square out of the 64 squares on a checkerboard, and we can ask yes–no questions. How many questions would be necessary to locate the target square? The answer is six questions. The first question would ask something like, "Is it one of the 32 squares on the left half of the board?" The answer reduces the number of alternatives in half. The next question, which could be, "is it one of the 16 in the upper half of the remaining 32 squares? The answer again reduces the number of remaining alternatives in half.

Each answer gives us *one bit*, a binary unit of information. Thus the uncertainty to the question, "What square of the checkerboard am I thinking of?" amounts to six bits of information.

How do we quantify this? It is equivalent to saying that if each alternative is equally likely, the information is equal to the logarithm to the base 2 of the number of alternatives. Sixty-four squares is 2^6, and the number of bits is $\log_2(2^6) = 6$. The information is thus

$$H = \log_2 m$$

where m is the number of equiprobable alternatives. If each alternative has probability $p = 1/m$, this means

$$H = \log_2 \frac{1}{p} = -\log_2 p$$

When the alternatives are not equally likely, the formula can be generalized to a weighted average. If each of i alternatives has probability p_i, then

$$H = \sum_i p_i \log_2\left(\frac{1}{p_i}\right)$$

If we had a biased coin that came up heads 90% of the time, then the uncertainty or information associated with a throw of this coin is

$$H = \sum_i p_i \log_2\left(\frac{1}{p_i}\right)$$
$$= .90 \log_2\left(\frac{1}{.90}\right) + .10 \log_2\left(\frac{1}{.10}\right)$$
$$= (.90)(.15) + (.10)(3.32) = .47 \text{ bits}$$

Note that the uncertainty associated with an unbiased coin is

$$H = .50 \log \frac{1}{.50} + .50 \log \frac{1}{.50}$$
$$= .5(1.00) + .5(1.00) = 1.00$$

The toss of the unbiased coin is more uncertain than the toss of the biased coin.

Suppose we have a sequence of codes that is redundant to some order, containing unknown sequential dependencies. The first-order estimate of H

$$\hat{H}_1 = \sum_i p_i \log\left(\frac{p_1}{p_i}\right)$$

assumes the absence of redundancy of higher orders.

The second-order estimate $\hat{H}_2$ considers the possibility that there is some information in pairs of consecutive codes, which is calculated as if every pair were a separate code

$$H(\text{pairs}) = \sum p(\text{pairs}) \log\left[\frac{1}{p(\text{pairs})}\right]$$

The second-order estimate of H takes the difference between $\hat{H}(\text{pairs})$ and $\hat{H}_1$:

$$\hat{H}_2 = \hat{H}(\text{pairs}) - \hat{H}_1$$

This quantity being nonzero is equivalent to the requirement that the conditional probabilities exceed the unconditional probabilities, which is a common test in sequential analysis. This requirement means that knowledge of one event A reduces uncertainty in the occurrence of another event B, compared to a prediction that would be made simply by knowledge of the unconditional frequency of B, that is,

$$p(B/A) > p(B)$$

Let us consider one application, the transmission of information in which we would be interested in the accurate transmission of information. This analysis compares information that is the input to a communication channel with the information of the output following transmission. Since the transmission process is usually not perfect, the input is not equal to the output. The relevant measures are the average information input $H(x)$, the average information output $H(y)$, the average amount of information transmitted T, the information that is input but not output $Hy(x)$, the information that is output without having been input $Hx(y)$, and the total amount of information in the system $H(x,y)$. These relationships are portrayed diagrammatically (from Miller, 1953) in Fig. 5.4.

In the sequential analysis application we can examine preceding behaviors as a basis for predicting what will occur.

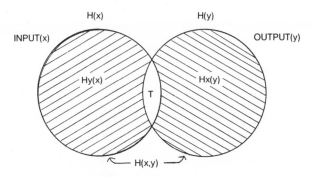

Fig. 5.4. The transmission of information.

Example 1 [1]

Suppose an observer codes a set of behaviors of one animal (called the signals, x_1, x_2, ...) and the set of behaviors of another animal (called the *responses*, y_1, y_2, ...). Table 5.1 presents the steps in the calculation of each of the following quantities (see Fig. 5.5):

$$H(x) = - \sum_i p(i) \log(p(i)) = 1.92 \text{ bits} \qquad \text{(Source Info)}$$

$$H(y) = - \sum_j p(j) \log(p(j)) = 2.00 \text{ bits} \qquad \text{(Receiver Info)}$$

$$Hy(x) = - \sum_j p(j)H_j(i) = 1.70 \text{ bits} \qquad [\text{Equivocation (Source)}]$$

$$Hx(y) = - \sum p(i)H_i(j) = 1.78 \text{ bits} \qquad [\text{Ambiguity (Receiver)}]$$

$$T(x, y) = H(x) - Hy(x)$$

$$= H(y) - Hx(y) = .22 \text{ bits}$$

$$H_j(i) = \sum_i p_j(i) \log p_j(i)$$

$$H_i(j) = \sum_j p_i(j) \log p_i(j)$$

TABLE 5.1

Computation of Signal Information, Receiver Information, Equivocation, and Ambiguity[a]

	$y_j =$	y_1	y_2	y_3	y_4	y_5	y_6	$p(i)$	$-p(i) \log_2 p(i)$
Action (signal) $x_i = x_1$		—	.001	—	—	—	—	.001	.01
x_2		.001	.007	.006	.001	—	—	.015	.09
x_3		.005	.022	.060	.027	.005	—	.119	.37
x_4		.004	.042	.156	.152	.039	.001	.394	.53
x_5		—	.009	.075	.175	.095	.010	.364	.53
x_6		—	.001	.011	.035	.039	.010	.096	.32
x_7		—	—	—	.003	.006	.002	.011	.07
$p(j)$		.010	.082	.308	.393	.184	.023	1.000	$\sum = 1.92$
$-p(j) \log_2(p(j))$		.07	.30	.52	.53	.45	.13	$\sum = 2.00$	

[a] From Wilson (1975), after Quastler (1958).

---

[1] This example is taken from Wilson (1975, pp. 196–197).

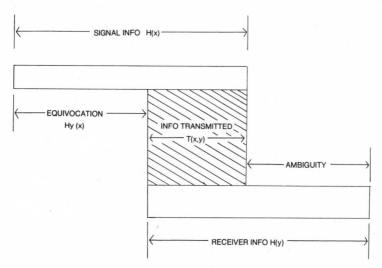

Fig. 5.5. Graphical representation of information functions. [Source: Quastler, H. A primer on information theory. In H. P. Yockey, R. L. Platman, & H. Quastler (eds.), *Symposium on information theory in biology.* New York: Pergamon, 1959.]

EXPLANATION

To calculate the equivocation of the signal we take each behavior Y_j and note the conditional probabilities of the X_i that evokes it. For example, when Y_1 is evoked X_2 is responsible $.001/.010 =$ entry/column total $= .1$, or 10% of the time; X_3 is responsible $.005/.010 = .5$, or 50% of the time, and X_4 is responsible $.004/.010 = .4$, or 40% of the time:

$$H_j(i) = -\sum p_j(i) \log p_j(i)$$

$$H_1(i) = -p_1(1) \log p_1(1) - p_1(2) \log p_1(2) - \cdots$$

$$= -.1 \log(.1) - .5 \log(.5) - .4 \log(.4)$$

$$= .33 + .50 + .53 = 1.36 \text{ bits}$$

Now multiply $H_1(i)$ by $p(1)$:

$$p(1) = .001 + .005 + .004 = .010 \text{ (column total)}$$

$$(.010)(1.36) = .0136$$

Do this for $j = 2, 3, \ldots, 6$.

WBWWBBBWBWBBWWWBBBWWBBWBBBWW
BBWBBWWWBWWBBWWBWWWWBWWWBBWW
WBWWBBWWBWWBBBWWBWWBBBBWWBWW
WWBBBWBWBWWWBWWWBWWBWWBWWWBW
WWWBE˜WBWWWBWWBBBWWWBWBBWWB
WBBWWWBWWWBBWWBBWWBBWWWBBWWB
BWBBBWWBBBWWBBWBBWWBBWWWBWWBB
WWBBBBW...

Fig. 5.6. Code sequence of draws of black and white balls from an imaginary urn. [Source: Attneave, F. *Applications of Information Theory to Psychology*. New York: Holt, 1959, p. 22.]

Example 2 [2]

Suppose we have a series of 203 codes as shown in Fig. 5.6. We can tabulate the frequencies (n_i) of all the tetragrams, trigrams, digrams, and codes as shown in Table 5.2. Note we tabulated *overlapping* tegragrams: first in the sequence was *WBWW*, second was *BWWB*, third was *WWBB*, etc.

To find $H = \sum p_i \log(1/p_i)$ for any N-gram, we can use the computational formula

$$H = \log n - \frac{1}{n} \sum n_i \log n_i$$

Values of $n_i \log n_i$ are given in a table in Attneave (1959). The Nth order estimate of H is

$$\hat{H}_N = \hat{H}(N\text{-gram}) - \hat{H}(\overline{N-1}\text{-gram})$$

We can plot $\hat{H}_N$ as a function of the order of estimation N (Fig. 5.7).

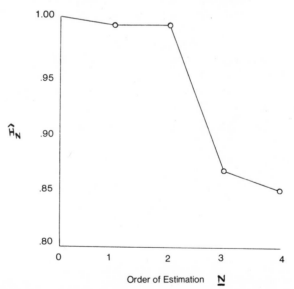

Fig. 5.7. Estimated information in a guess, as a function of order of estimation. [Source: Attneave, F. *Applications of Information Theory to Psychology*. New York: Holt, 1959, p. 25.]

[2] This example is taken from Attneave (1959, pp. 22–25).

Table 5.2

Tetragram	n_i	$n_i \log n_i$	Trigram	n_i	$n_i \log n_i$	Digram	n_i	$n_i \log n_i$	Symbol	n_i	$n_i \log n_i$
$WWWW$	3	4.755	WWW	19	80.711	WW	58	339.763	W	100	737.732
$WWWB$	16	64.000	WWB	39	206.131						
$WWBW$	15	58.603									
$WWBB$	24	110.039	WBW	20	86.439	WB	51	289.294			
$WBWW$	16	64.000									
$WBWB$	4	8.000	WBB	22	98.108						
$WBBW$	22	98.108									
$WBBB$	9	28.529	BWW	39	206.131	BW	50	289.193			
$BWWW$	16	64.000									
$BWWB$	23	104.042	BWB	11	38.054				B	91	592.209
$BWBW$	4	8.000									
$BWBB$	7	19.651	BBW	30	147.207	BB	41	219.660			
$BBWW$	23	104.042									
$BBWB$	7	19.651	BBB	11	38.054						
$BBBW$	9	28.529									
$BBBB$	2	2.000									
Sum	200	785.949	Sum	200	956.307	Sum	200	1130.910	Sum	200	1329.941

$\hat{F}(\text{tetragram})$

$= 7.644 - \frac{1}{200} \times 785.949$

$= 3.71$

$\hat{F}_4 = \hat{F}(\text{tetragram}) - \hat{F}(\text{trigram})$
$= 3.714 - 2.862$
$= .852$

$\hat{F}(\text{trigram})$

$= 7.644 - \frac{1}{200} \times 956.307$

$= 2.862$

$\hat{F}_3 = \hat{F}(\text{trigram}) - \hat{F}(\text{digram})$
$= 2.862 - 1.989$
$= .873$

$\hat{F}(\text{digram})$

$= 7.644 - \frac{1}{200} \times 1130.910$

$= 1.989$

$\hat{F}_2 = \hat{F}(\text{digram}) - \hat{F}_1$
$= 1.989 - .995$
$= .994$

$\hat{F}_1 = \log n - \frac{1}{n} \sum n_i \log n_i$

$= \log 200 - \frac{1}{200} \times 1329.941$

$= 7.644 - 6.649$

$= .995$

257

Example 3

The organization of song in rose-breasted grosbeaks was studied by Lemon and Chatfield (1973). They wrote,

> The calculation yield for grosbeak #1, $\hat{H}_1 = 4.08$ bits, and $\hat{H}_2 = 1.09$ bits, while for grosbeak #2, $\hat{H}_1 = 3.62$ bits and $\hat{H}_2 = 1.03$ bits. The large drops in uncertainty from $\hat{H}_1$ to $\hat{H}_2$ are comparable to such drops in cardinals, especially in individual called Chambers which sang more continuously because of his unmated condition. In conclusion the results indicate that there is much less uncertainty about a syllable when the previous syllable is known and hence confirm the earlier conclusion that successive syllables are not independent [p. 33].

They then compared tetrads to triads and concluded that, for most cases, the first-order Markov model is adequate.

Example 4

Hazlett and Estabrook (1974) studied the agnostic behavior of spider-crab *Microphrys bicornutus*. They wrote,

> The behavior of these crabs was influenced much more during an interaction by the behavior of the other crab, than by any of the "static" characters mentioned above. For example, the uncertainty of act III was reduced 1.00 bits (31.5%) by knowing act II. This means that 1.00 bits of information are apparently transmitted from crab to crab by their behavior patterns (more information may be transmitted, but it is not apparent in the behavior of recipient crab). . . . The percentage of uncertainty reduction rose throughout the fight, to where knowing the next-to-last act almost completely eliminated uncertainty about how the fight would end. This was due to "low body" posture (by the losing crab) always being followed by the less common (18% of fights) last act—"pass on by." . . . Some acts by one crab tended to be followed by the same act by the other crab (high body, double cheliped spread, maxilliped beating), while other strong aggressive patterns were directive . . . toward submission (double cheliped slap followed by low body) or retreat (single ambulatory raise, single cheliped spread) [pp. 139–140].

Example 5

Baker (1973) studied the foraging behavior of six species of migratory shorebirds in winter and summer. Figure 5.8 shows the percentage reduction of uncertainty for all species for the winter and summer. Baker concluded that,

> Over all orders of estimation winter uncertainties usually decrease more rapidly than in summer, meaning stereotypy is greater in winter foraging behavior . . .

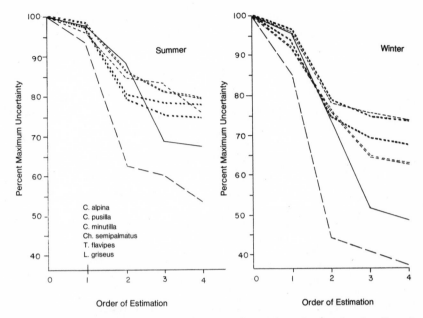

Fig. 5.8. Mean reduction of uncertainty over four orders of estimation for all species. [Source: Baker, M. C. Stochastic processes of the foraging behavior of six species of migratory showbirds. *Behaviour*, 1973, *47*, 241–270.]

most species in both seasons seem to exhibit behavior that is Markovian to a significant degree . . . examination of two events allows much better prediction of the next event than just knowing the identity of one previous event [p. 260].

Example 6 (Worked Summary Example)

The following summary may be helpful in clarifying the calculations involved in uncertainty reduction analyses. Suppose we have a situation in which three antecedent events can occur, A_1, A_2, and A_3. To each of these antecedents any one of three consequents may occur, C_1, C_2, C_3. The following tabulation represents these conditions, with hypothetical observed frequencies of the joint occurrence of each antecedent–consequent pair.

		Antecedent (A_i)			
		A_1	A_2	A_3	
Consequent (C_j)	C_1	40	10	5	55
	C_2	10	40	5	55
	C_3	0	0	40	40
		50	50	50	150

The first quantity we are interested in is the amount of information available per antecedent, $H(x)$. Following from the basic concepts,

$$H(x) = \sum_i p_i \log(1/p_i)$$

Since all antecedents (A_i) are equally likely, $H(x) = \log_2 3 = 1.59$. Next we would like to know the estimated information per response, $H(y)$. Since our data are in frequencies, we can rewrite the basic equation

$$H(y) = \sum_i P_j \log_2 \frac{1}{P_j}$$

$$= \log_2 n - \frac{1}{n} \sum_j n_j \log_2 n_j$$

$$= \log_2 150 - \frac{1}{150} (55 \log 55 + 55 \log 55 + 40 \log 40)$$

$$= 1.64$$

To obtain an information measure of the joint occurrence of an antecedent and a response we consider the observed frequencies of each cell:

$$H(x, y) = \sum_{i,j} p_{ij} \log \frac{1}{p_{ij}}$$

$$= \log_2 n - \frac{1}{n} \sum_{i,j} n_{ij} \log_2 n_{ij}$$

$$= \log_2 150 - \frac{1}{150} [3(40 \log_2 40) + 2(10 \log_2 10) + 2(5 \log_2 5)]$$

$$= 2.37$$

Notice that the values for $H(x)$ and $H(y)$ differ by only .05 bits. It is evident that the consequents contain nearly as much information as the antecedents. This is in contrast to the case when the consequent carries no information, or uncertainty (as would be the case if only one consequent occurred) and $H(y)$ would be equal to 0 bits.

It is also important to note that although the amount of information in $H(x)$ and $H(y)$ is nearly the same, it cannot be concluded that the information is the same. To assess the shared or transmitted information between antecedent and consequent (T), calculate

$$T(x;y) = H(x) + H(y) - H(x,y)$$

In our example,

$$T(x;y) = 1.59 + 1.64 - 2.37 = .86$$

which is the estimate of information transmitted from antecedent to consequent, out of a possible maximum of 1.59 bits. The measure T is a measure of relatedness or association.

The function $Hy(x)$ specifies the amount of antecedent information that is lost, or simply it is the uncertainty of the antecedent when the consequent is known. It is called the stimulus *equivocation* and is defined as

$$Hy(x) = H(x,y) - H(y) = H(x) - T(x;y)$$

We can also specify the uncertainty of the consequent given the antecedent, $Hx(y)$. This uncertainty has been called the consequent equivocation and is defined as

$$Hx(y) = H(x,y) - H(x) = H(y) - T(x;y)$$

Thus for the data presented,

$$Hy(x) = .73, \qquad Hx(y) = .78$$

If a Markov model reduces uncertainty, then we should expect $Hx(y)$ to be less than $H(y)$. In our example $Hx(y)$ is considerably less than $H(y)$, supporting our intuitive impressions from visual inspection of the data matrix. We might mention the limiting case of perfect transmission in which each antecedent evokes its own unique consequent. In this case

$$Hx(y) = 0 = Hy(x), \qquad T(x;y) = H(x) = H(y) = H(x,y)$$

VII. Multivariate Informational Analysis

The preceding discussion was based on only two variables for conceptual clarity. However, the technique is easily extrapolated to n variables. Thus in addition to testing the reduction in uncertainty available when the antecedent is known, we might further ask if we can gain greater reduction in uncertainty when both the antecedent and, let us say, the source of the antecedent are *also* accounted for. This third variable might just as easily be the situation of the events observed, the eye color of the antecedent person, the hair color of the consequent person, etc.

The formulas for the three-variable cases are identical with those previously derived. Thus the information associated with the third variable is specified as

$$H(w) = \log_2 n - \frac{1}{n} \sum_k n_k \log_2 n_k$$

Likewise,

$$H(x, y, w) = \log_2 n - \frac{1}{n} \sum_{i,j,k} n_{i,j,k} \log_2 n_{i,j,k}$$

and is equal to the total information per observation. Following through a test of the adequacy of a Markov model, we may calculate the amount of information two variables share with a third:

$$T(w, x; y) = H(w, x) + H(y) - H(x, y, w)$$

Remaining consistent with our notation, we are asking how much information is shared when accounting for the antecedent and a third variable (e.g., the situation).

Recall that the function T is always a symmetrical measure of shared information, $T(y;x) = T(x;y)$. Since our topic is focused on the extent to which a Markov model reduces uncertainty, we are interested particularly in the reduction of uncertainty that can be derived from knowledge of the antecedent, either alone or in combination with other variables in the multivariate case. A measure available for this is the coefficient of constraint, D (Newman & Gerstman, 1952). The coefficient D is a measure of relatedness that is not symmetrical and can be interpreted as the percentage reduction of uncertainty of specified variables. In other words, $D(y;x)$ is directly analogous to a simple correlation ratio. With two variables $D(x;y) = T(x;y)/H(y)$. With three variables,

$$D(x, w, : Y) = T(x, w : y)/Hx(y)$$

which is analogous to multiple correlation and

$$D_x(w:y) = T_x(w:y)/Hx(y)$$

which is analogous to partial correlation.

Raush (1965) used this statistic to investigate affectional behavior exchanged between different groups of children in several diverse situations. A primary question for Raush was the extent to which an observed affectional behavior was determined by the immediate antecedent behavior, the situation, or the individual factors associated with group membership. Through the use of the ratio $D_x(y:z)/[1 - D(x:z)]$ Raush was able to estimate the proportion of remaining variance that was accounted for by a particular variable, when the variance of other elements was removed. This procedure permitted Raush to conclude that antecedent acts were the primary determinants of immediately consequent behaviors. The situation and individual factors contributed smaller independent effects. Thus classification by the situation or by the group does not permit as great a reduction of uncertainty of the consequents as does the immediate antecedent.

In another application, Raush, Barry, Hertel, and Swain (1974) applied multivariate informational analysis to the study of marital conflict. They coded couples interaction on different tasks, preserving the sequential nature of the dialogue. The informational analyses permitted an assessment of the relative strengths situation, sex, antecedent, and/or couple contributed to the reduction of uncertainty about possible outcomes. For example, the questions posed are of the type, Does knowing that the speaker is female reduce uncertainty about the manner in which she will act? Does knowing both the sex of speaker and the immediate antecedent reduce the uncertainty of the consequent? What is the effect of the antecedent on the consequent, when sex is held constant? To answer these questions, the appropriate measure is the amount by which the uncertainty of the consequent response (c) is reduced by knowledge or control of other variables, namely, situation, sex, antecedent, and/or couple. Thus the criterion is always the consequent C. Table 5.3 reproduces their results. From the table it is apparent

TABLE 5.3
Informational Analyses of Couples Conflict[a]

Source	$U(C)$ (%)	Source	$U(C)$ (%)
$I;C$	3.64	$I_S;C$	7.36
$S;C$	.18	$I_A;C$	6.30
$A;C$	4.24	$S_I;C$	3.89
$P;C$	4.71	$S_A;C$	.32
$I,S;C$	7.54	$A_I;C$	6.90
$I,A;C$	10.54	$A_S;C$	4.38
$S,A;C$	4.56	$P_S;C$	6.62
$P,S;C$	6.80	$P_A;C$	7.56
$P,A;C$	11.79	$S_P;C$	2.09
$I,S,A;C$	10.89	$A_P;C$	7.08
$P,S,A;C$	16.37	$P,S_A;C$	9.15
		$P,A_S;C$	14.15
		$S,A_P;C$	6.91
		$A_{PS};C$	9.57
		$P_{SA};C$	11.81
		$S_{PA};C$	4.58

[a] Notation: I, situation; S, sex; A, antecedent; P, couple; $I,S;C$, joint effects of situation and sex on consequent act; I_SC_j, effects of situation on consequent act with sex held constant.

that the couple interaction style offers the single greatest percentage reduction in uncertainty, 4.71, as compared to 3.64 for situation, .18 for sex, and 4.24 for the antecedent. When accounting for the effects of more than one variable, Raush *et al.* determined that 16.37% of the consequent uncertainty can be reduced by knowledge of the couple, the sex of the speaker, and the immediate antecedent. Note that an account of joint effects of these three variables increases the reduction of uncertainty more than might be expected from summation of the independent effects (16.37 versus 9.13). In addition, it is apparent that couples respond differently to a given antecedent. For example, the reduction of uncertainty afforded when couple was accounted for is 4.7% compared with 7.6% when the effects of couple were assessed for each antecedent (antecedent held constant).

We might summarize this presentation by noting the informational analysis does not describe the detail of the communication process, but rather the patterns that govern it. Thus comparison of $P;C$ with $P_A;C$ does not tell us how the couples respond differently to a specific antecedent, only that they do. Inspection of the coding categories makes it clear that a non-distressed couple is much less likely to follow a complaint with another complaint than is a distressed couple. Hence, the informational analysis permits analysis of the qualitative data generated by a coding system and requires no assumptions about the metric of the criterion variable as is required by analysis of variance techniques.

A. Significance Tests

There are a variety of procedures[3] used in hypothesis testing in connection with sequential analysis, although many of the papers we have read and would have liked to discuss in this chapter present transitional probability matrices only and do no hypothesis testing.

B. Binomial Test

Bakeman (1976) discussed the data analysis of transition probabilities and wrote that, "It would be pleasing to offer some sort of automatic analytic device: observation data would be fed into one end, and test statis-

---

[3] Other analytic techniques for testing the adequacy of Markov models are presented in Appendix C in Jaffe and Feldstein (1970) and in Appendices I and II of Lemon and Chatfield (1971). For other analytic techniques applied to Markov processes, see Howard (1960), Hoel, Port, and Stone (1972), and Isaacson and Madsen (1976).

tics, neatly labeled as to significance, would emerge from the other. Instead, the sort of analysis recommended here is neither particularly new nor automatic nor even particularly complicated [p. 10]." Bakeman uses binomial Z-scores of conditional probabilities to indicate the extent to which the probabilities exceed predicted values.

Suppose an infant had his eyes open 53.7% of the overall time, but 66.3% of the time when feeding. The question is, are these percentages enough to establish feeding/eyes open as a behavioral pattern? The z index is designed to assess whether behaviors co-occur more or less frequently than their simple probabilities would predict. The index is

$$z = (x - NP)/(NPQ)^{1/2}$$

where x is observed joint frequency of feeding and eyes open ($x = 533$ for Bakeman's data), NP is predicted joint frequency (frequency of feeding = $N = 834$,[4] probability of eyes open $P = .537$), and NPQ is the variance of the difference between predicted and observed ($Q = 1 - P$, $NPQ = 834 \times .537 \times .463$). In this example, $z = 7.29$. Bakeman uses an index in excess of 2 as sufficient to establish a behavior pattern. In the sample of 45 infants, the unconditional probability for eyes open was .432, while the mean conditional probability for eyes open given concurrent feeding was .582. This binomial test assumes stationarity of the unconditional probabilities remains relatively constant throughout the interaction stream. This assumption can be made a null hypothesis of an appropriate chi-square test. For an excellent summary of these tests, see Castellan (1976). The conditional probability exceeded the unconditional probability for 33 of the 45 infants ($p < .01$ by sign test).

C. Chi-Square Tests

We refer the reader to two recent excellent treatments of the various chi-square tests of significance related to sequential analysis. Castellan (1976) reviews chi-square tests related to tests for the order of the Markov model and assumptions of stationarity. Bishop, Feinberg, and Holland (1975) review log-likelihood models for analyzing N-dimensional contingency tables; Chapter 7 focuses on Markov matrices. For a simple introduction to chi-square tests, we review Slater, who also (1973) recommends a chi-square test. Suppose there are three states, A, B, and C, and the observed frequency matrix is

---

[4] If N is less than 25, see Siegel (1956, pp. 36–40).

$$
\begin{array}{c c c}
 & A \quad B \quad C & \\
\begin{array}{c} A \\ B \\ C \end{array}
\begin{bmatrix}
10 & 20 & 5 \\
15 & 4 & 6 \\
10 & 2 & 8 \\
\overline{35} & \overline{26} & \overline{19}
\end{bmatrix}
&
\begin{array}{c}
35 \\
25 \\
20 \\
\overline{80}
\end{array}
\end{array}
$$

The null hypothesis expected frequency matrix can be calculated as the (row total × column total)/(grand sum):

$$
\begin{array}{c c c}
 & A \quad\; B \quad\; C \\
\begin{array}{c} A \\ B \\ C \end{array}
\begin{bmatrix}
15.3 & 11.4 & 8.3 \\
10.9 & 8.1 & 6.0 \\
8.8 & 6.5 & 4.7
\end{bmatrix}
\end{array}
$$

Then

$$
\chi^2 = \sum_{i,j} \frac{(O_{ij} - E_{ij})^2}{E_{ij}}
$$

Slater's recommendation deals with what has been called the "base-rate problem." The base-rate problem occurs when we examine differences between transition probabilities for two groups without considering differences in unconditional probabilities between the two populations. Slater's recommendation is applicable to single-subject or single-dyad data. An example where we might be concerned with a base-rate problem might be Baker's (1973) study of the differences between the foraging behavior of migratory shorebirds in winter and summer. If some behaviors are less frequent in the winter than in summer, these differences need to be taken into account when looking at differences in transitional probabilities.

When we compare two groups, however, more powerful tests of differences in transition probabilities are available by using analysis of variance techniques, by using unconditional probability as a covariate. The covariance test may also control for possible ceiling and floor effects in base-rate differences between the groups (for an application see Gottman, Notarius, Markman, Bank, Yoppi, & Rubin, 1976).

When the researcher does information theory analysis of the data, there is a simple relationship between $\hat{T}$, the estimate of shared information between one model and another, and χ^2 (Attneave, 1959, p. 29):

$$
\chi^2 \cong 2(\log_e 2)n\hat{T} = 1.3863n\hat{T}
$$

($n = \sum n_i$, i.e., the number of coding symbols used in the Nth-order model).

Example[5]

Suppose we want to test the hypothesis that probabilities using three preceding symbols are actually no different from first-order probabilities. We would then expect any pair of tetragrams that differ only in the last symbol, such as $WWBB$ and $WWBW$ to have frequencies proportional to the first-order frequencies of B and W (91 and 109 respectively), within the limits of sampling error. The observed matrix is

$WWWW$	$WWBW$	$WBWW$	$WBBW$	$BWWW$	$BWBW$	$BBWW$	$BBBW$
3	15	16	22	16	4	23	9

$WWWB$	$WWBB$	$WBWB$	$WBBB$	$BWWB$	$BWBB$	$BBWB$	$BBBB$
16	24	4	9	23	7	7	2

The expected matrix for a cell is

$$\frac{\text{(row total)} \times \text{(column total)}}{(N = \text{grand total})}.$$

For example, for the $WWWW$ cell the expected frequency is $(108) \times (19)/200 = 10.3$

$$\chi^2 = \sum \frac{(O - E)^2}{E} = 37.52 \quad \text{with} \quad df = (8 - 1)(2 - 1) = 7$$

Calculating χ^2 with the approximation formula we use $\hat{T} = .143$, and again $n = 200$, which gives $\chi^2 = 39.60$, a fairly good approximation to 37.52. The value of $\hat{T}$ was obtained by the formula for shared information between fourth- and first-order models:

$$\hat{T} = \hat{H}_1 - \hat{H}_4 = .995 - .852 = .143$$

(See Table 5.2.)

For χ^2 tests with degrees of freedom larger than one, fewer than 20% of the cells should have an expected frequency of less than 5, and no cell should have an expected frequency of less than 1 (Cochran, 1954). If these conditions are not met, the researcher must combine categories to increase expected frequencies. This can be guarded against if the number of observations is large.

---

[5] This example is from Attneave (1959, pp. 28–29).

VIII. The Sackett Alternative to Markov Chain Analysis

Sackett (1974) proposed an extremely elegant alternative to Markov chain analysis. Suppose that a set of coding categories A, B, C, D are used to describe the behavior of an organism or socially interesting dyad. Suppose further that the data are gathered such that it is possible for a code to follow itself. Usually such a stream of codes would be called *time-sequential* data with some unitized time such as six seconds during which one and only one code is recorded. Bakeman (1976) and Bakeman and Dabbs (1976) have extended the work that we will describe to other kinds of data types such as *multiple-event-sequential* data in which more than one code can occur in any time block. Time need not be the only way of unitizing a behavior stream. For example, Gottman, Markman, and Notarius (1977, footnote 1) use utterance segments of a verbatim transcript of husband/wife speech as basic units for coding verbal and nonverbal behaviors. The procedures presented here can be easily modified for the *event-sequential* case in which a code does not follow itself (see Sackett, 1974).

Suppose we have two individuals interacting and that the observed record is

Behavior$_1$ A B B A B D C A B C B A B

Behavior$_2$ B A B C D A C B A B C A D

The Sackett analysis is called *lag-sequential* analysis. Two kinds of analyses are possible, *autologs* and *cross lags*.

A. Autolags

The autolag analysis involves a plot of the conditional probability of a behavior following itself at each lag. For the behavior of Individual 1 we see that A occurs 4 times out of 13 times, so its unconditional probability is $4/13 = .31$. At Lag 1, A never follows itself, so the conditional probability of A following A at Lag 1 is zero. Thus A acts to inhibit its own occurrence. At Lag 2, the same result obtains. At Lag 3, A occurs once out of a possible 3 times since it is not possible to use the last A to calculate Lag 3 probabilities. Hence the probability of A occurring after itself at Lag 3 is $1/3 = .33$, which is very close to its unconditional level. In the autolag analysis we plot the unconditional probability of A and use the standard deviation of the expected probability $\{p(A)[1 - p(A)]/N\}^{1/2}$ to test the null hypothesis that the conditional probability at each lag does not exceed the unconditional. Note that the confidence bands around the unconditional probability get larger with increasing lag because N gets smaller with increasing lag, since there are fewer instances of A that can go into a calculation of the transitional probabilities. Five out of 100 autolags can be expected to fall outside the confidence bands by chance alone.

Sackett (personal communication) has identified several types of autolag functions. Figure 5.9 illustrates the variety of patterns observed. The first graph shows a *damping function;* the dashed line shows an inhibited refractory period, and the solid line shows an excited period in which the occurrence of Code A makes its subsequent occurrence less or more likely, respectively.

The second graph illustrates an *on/off function* in which the behavior code A is either inhibited (solid line) or excited (dashed line) for a specific number of lags before returning to expected levels. The behavior's occurrence in these cases acts like a switch to turn the behavior off for a while or, alternatively, on at heightened levels for a while.

The third graph indicates a *cyclic function* with alternate periods of inhibition and excitation. Most of the cyclic functions observed to date in Sackett's experience are *damped cyclic functions* in which the cycling only lasts for some portion of the lags.

Using Bakeman's Z-score we can calculate a Z-score for each autolag.

EXAMPLE

Gottman, Markman, and Notarius (1977) coded the nonverbal behaviors of husbands and wives. They coded the behavior of the listener as well as the behavior of the speaker as neutral, positive, or negative. For the $H0$-code, the autolag follows an on-off pattern, with a Z-score greater than 1.96 only at Lag 3. For the $H00$ code, the pattern is cyclic, with periods of inhibition alternating with periods of excitation (see Table 5.4).

B. Cross Lags

Andersson (1974) presented a graphical procedure for studying the agonistic and courtship activities of the Great Skua bird. He graphed the proportion of observation units that contained a specific behavior X when the criterion behavior C was observed at time zero. For example, if the criterion behavior is attack, Andersson graphed the proportion of units before and after the attack for which the behavior $X =$ upright posture was observed. In Fig. 5.10 we see a plot of the expected value of association between behaviors X and C if they are assumed to be independent events. Confidence intervals are computed from the 2×2 chi-square table (see Andersson, 1974, pp. 40–41).

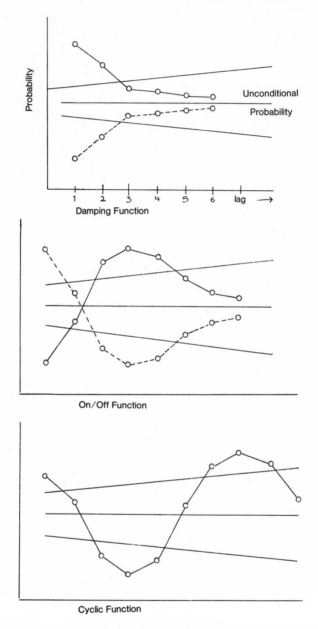

Fig. 5.9. Patterns of autolag.

TABLE 5.4

Behavior	Lag					
	1	2	3	4	5	6
$H0-$: Husband's speaking is neutral while wife's listening is negative (unconditional prob. = .02)			Pattern: on/off			
Conditional probability	.00	.06	.09	.06	.03	.06
Z-Score	.00	1.84	3.15	1.84	.53	1.84
$H00$: Husband's speaking is neutral while wife's listening is neutral (unconditional prob. = .31)			Pattern: cyclic			
Conditional probability	.00	.60	.15	.47	.22	.41
Z-Score	.00	15.48	-8.42	8.59	-4.40	7.11

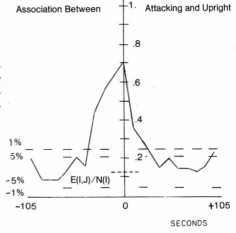

N(I)=48   N(J)=193   N=1563   NS=1

E(I,J)=5.927

Association Between   Attacking and Upright

Fig. 5.10. Association between upright posture and attacks toward other individuals. [Source: Andersson, M. Temporal Graphic Analysis of Behavior Sequences. *Behaviour*, 1974, *61*, 38–48.]

This method is extended by Sackett (1974). Sackett observed a crab-eating macaque mother and infant dyad. The behaviors observed were such behaviors as "infant active," "mother pat–stroke–jiggle," "mother nurse," "mother groom," and "infant explore."

Sackett's analysis begins by designating one behavior as the "criterion behavior." This procedure can be repeated so that all behaviors may serve as the criterion. Then a set of conditional probability profiles are constructed, one profile for each of the other behaviors. For each of the other behaviors we graph the conditional probability of that behavior given the criterion occurred, at each lag from the criterion. This procedure is illustrated in Fig. 5.11. Peaks in the conditional probability profile indicate lag-sequential positions with respect to the criterion at which the given behavior is more

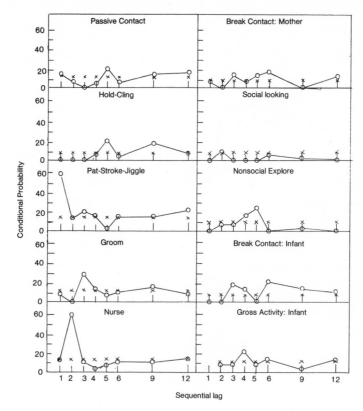

Fig. 5.11. Lagged conditional probabilities when the criterion behavior is gross activity by the infant. [Source: Sackett, 1974.]

likely to occur. If a likely sequence *ABC* is identified following a particular criterion behavior *A*, one would also examine the most likely sequence obtained with *B* as a criterion to determine whether behavior *C* showed a higher than unconditional probability at Lag 1 from *B*. The extent to which observed and predicted values differ can be assessed with *Z*-scores.

The set of profiles can be examined together to suggest possible sequences, even though actual sequences are not studied for more than two behaviors at once (the criterion and the other behavior). The pattern in Fig. 5.3 suggests the sequence infant active, mother pat–stroke–jiggle, mother nurse, mother groom. The sequence can be checked by having other behaviors in the chain as the criterion (see Sackett, 1974).

Sckett's cross-lag method was applied by Gottman, Markman, and Notarius (1977) to identify sequences of interactions in distressed and nondistressed couples. Table 5.5 presents some of their results. The initial most likely sequence identified by Gottman *et al.* for nondistressed couples involved one spouse expressing feelings about a problem (*PF*) with the other spouse agreeing. This sequence is called "validation" in Table 5.5. For distressed couples the most likely initial sequence observed was one spouse expressing feelings about a problem followed by the other spouse expressing his or her feelings about the problem, a sequence called "cross-complaining" in Table 5.5.

The Sackett alternative provides several advantages over Markov chain analysis. First, it does not test the same hypothesis, namely, in general, how much information is gained by each additional order model. This is usually not the kind of question the investigator has in mind in a sequential analysis. The questions usually concern the identification of pattern, cycles, and cross correlations that allow one to predict from the behavior of one organism to the behavior of another.

Second, the Sackett alternative is far less overwhelming than a set of output that looks at all possible sequences of all the codes. The lag-sequential analysis is more manageable and more appropriate for the sequential analysis of categorical data in discrete time. Computer programs for these analyses are currently available.[6]

---

[6] Computer programs for lag sequential analysis are available from Dr. Gene Sackett, Department of Psychology, University of Washington, Seattle, Washington; and from Dr. Roger Bakeman, Department of Psychology, Georgia State University, Atlanta, Georgia. A program for Markov matrix analysis has been written by Larry Fitzpatrick, Institute of Child Development, University of Minnesota, Minneapolis, Minnesota.

TABLE 5.5

Sackett's Method Applied to Identify the Most Likely Sequence Following a Spouse's Expression of Feelings About a Problem[a] in Clinic and Nonclinic Couples

	Lag						State transition diagram
	1	2	3	4	5	6	
	Criterion = HPFo						
Nonclinic							
WPFo	.24	.13	.18	.16	.17	.18	(PFo) → (AG)
WAGo	.30[a]	.05	.19	.09	.15	.11	
HPFo	.00	.38	.14	.26	.17	.22	←
HAGo	.02	.11	.07	.07	.08	.07	
Z-score	9.77	10.31	5.11	3.57	2.38	[a]	"validation"
Clinic							
WPFo	.23[a]	.11	.17[a]	.14	.16[a]	.12	(PFo) → (PFo)
WAGo	.16	.03	.08	.05	.06	.09	
HPFo	.00	.33	.15	.25[a]	.17	.20[a]	←
HAGo	.01	.07	.05	.06	.06	.07	
Z-score	3.90	9.11	2.50	5.02	1.86	2.10	"cross-complaining"
	Criterion = WPFo						
Nonclinic							
WPFo	.00	.28[a]	.15	.18	.18	.16	(PFo) → (AGo)
WAGo	.02	.17	.07	.16[a]	.07	.14	
HPFo	.31[a]	.12	.24[a]	.17	.23	.21	
HAGo	.19	.05	.10	.08	.07	.08	
Z-score	3.34	6.30	2.10	2.69	[a]	[a]	
Clinic							
WPFo	.00	.26	.13	.18[a]	.13	.17[a]	(PFo) → (PFo)
WAGo	.01	.12	.03	.07	.06	.07	
HPFo	.29[a]	.09	.23[a]	.15	.22	.15	←
HAGo	.14	.03	.06	.05	.08	.06	
Z-score	4.76	6.89	3.51	2.84	3.02	2.31	

[a]Problem description phase of marital discussion lag sequential analysis with PFo (feelings or information about a problem) as initial criterion code. (Only probabilities > .07 are included.) Z-scores refer to conditionals that have the symbol [a], that is, these are most likely with $Z > 1.96$.

IX. Special Applications

Markov chain models have been used for studying several kinds of questions that may be of interest to readers. These examples are given here to illustrate the range of potential application of Markov models.

A. The Mix of Aggressive and Nonaggressive Boys

Raush (1965) studied the social interaction of aggressive and non-aggressive children. In a paper in 1972 he asked the question, "What would happen if the hyperaggressive boys of the example above were to interact successively with normal boys? [p. 284]." This experiment never actually took place, but Raush answered this question using the Markov matrices of the interaction between the two groups of boys and cross-multiplying transition matrices successively.

In the early phase of treatment of the hyperaggressive boys "the patients would wind up more friendly than before—but only by 4 percent; the normal boys would wind up considerably less friendly—a drop of 24 percent. In a sense then, theoretically, continuous interaction would not do much for reform of the very disturbed children but would do a great deal for corruption of the normal children [p. 284]."

B. Identifying Stimuli that Control Behavior

Patterson (1974) presented data of the repeated observation of one family with a $6\frac{1}{2}$-year-old boy, Karl, who was referred "for treatment because of his extremely high rate of noxious behaviors [p. 902]."

Patterson constructed a set of decision rules for identifying controlling stimuli that had to do with differences between unconditional and conditional probabilities. He argued that

> Even though identified as "significant" a controlling stimulus's contribution to ongoing behavior might be trivial. If, for example, the A_i stimulus was itself a low-base-rate event, then its general contribution would be severely limited. To take this into account, the base rate $p(A_i)$ for a controlling stimulus was combined with $p(R_i/A_i)$. The resulting compound probability $(p(R_i/A_i))(p(A_i))$ describes how much of the information contained in $p(R_i)$ one can account for by taking into account the single variable A_i. If the summed compound probability for the network of significant stimuli accounts for only a small portion of $p(R_i)$, then one might assume that the most relevant antecedents had not originally been built into the code system. Summing the compound probabilities for all 29 categories would, of course, account for all of the information in $p(R_i)$ [p. 905].

Patterson identified the specific behaviors of mother, father, and sister that controlled initiations and maintenance of Karl's noxious behaviors. The noxious responses yell, whine, and disapproval were under control of antecedent events in the immediately preceding time interval. Using this information to predict Karl's behavior with a new set of observation data,

Patterson found that information about prior "facilitating stimuli" doubled the predictions about hostility that could be made from the unconditional hostility base rate alone. It is interesting that although the hostility base rate decreased from .1196 to .0773 in three months, which "presumably reflects the result of the family intervention program which had taken place during this period [p. 907]," the dynamics of control of the hostile behavior remained the same.

C. The Monitoring and Evaluation of Intervention Programs

Raush (1972) conducted the same hypothetical mix experiment of hyperaggressive and normal boys using the Markov matrices taken later in treatment. Raush concluded that, "If the same patients later in treatment were combined in hypothetical interaction with the same normal boys, the friendliness of the patients would increase by 7 percent and that of the normal boys would decrease by 11 percent—a more equitable balance [p. 284]."

Stuart (1971) assessed the effectiveness of a contracting program with a 16-year-old girl by calculating the day-to-day transition probabilities of positive to positive, positive to negative, negative to negative, and negative to positive behaviors for three weeks in treatment.

The first week initial transition probability from positive to negative was .40; this probability was .15 in the second month of treatment, and upon follow-up nine months later was .04. The initial transition matrix

$$
\begin{array}{cc}
+ & - \\
\end{array}
$$
$$
\begin{array}{c} + \\ - \end{array}
\begin{bmatrix}
.60 & .40 \\
.75 & .25
\end{bmatrix}
$$

would tend toward a steady state of

$$
\begin{array}{cc}
+ & - \\
\end{array}
$$
$$
\begin{array}{c} + \\ - \end{array}
\begin{bmatrix}
.65 & .35 \\
.65 & .35
\end{bmatrix}
$$

without intervention (see Section II). The steady state matrix can be taken as the basis for calculating expected frequencies, and this matrix compared to the obtained matrix $[\chi^2(1) = 96.06, p < .001]$ of

$$
\begin{array}{cc}
+ & - \\
\end{array}
$$
$$
\begin{array}{c} + \\ - \end{array}
\begin{bmatrix}
.96 & .04 \\
1.00 & .00
\end{bmatrix}
$$

D. The Problem of What Time Interval to Choose

A paper by Delius (1969) on the maintenance behavior of skylarks considered various kinds of stochastic analyses of sequential observations. One issue raised by Delius is what time interval to use in a stochastic analysis. He correlated six behaviors and plotted the correlations as a function of the time unit for the observations. Figure 5.12 depicts his results. He concluded that

> It is obvious that the correlations are as a rule functions of the sampling unit and that these functions can take quite different forms from case to case, monotonously increasing as in the case of bodyshake-preening, decreasing like in scratching-flying, or non-monotonous as in scratching-flying, or non-monotonous as in scratching-wing and leg stretch. Even more, for given behaviour patterns pair correlations may be zero for one unit while positive for another, i.e., scratching-both wing stretch, or positive correlations may turn negative at another sampling unit duration, i.e., scratching-flying.
>
> This indicates that the correlations matrices based on a given time unit are of restricted value in typifying the relationship between behavioural variables [pp. 161–162].

Delius's conclusion is, of course, correct. However, the dependence of correlations on the time unit used in sampling may be informative. For example, it may be useful to know at what time unit the correlation between two behaviors is a maximum. This knowledge may say something about the *periodicity* of dependency between two behaviors as a function of time lags.

Nelson (1964) specifically tested for the independence of events separated by time intervals $m \Delta t$, $m = 1, 2, 3, \ldots$. Nelson investigated the courtship behavior from species of Glandulocaudine fishes. He found that,

> At the five percent level of significance,[7] events following quivering and shaking are independent of it after ten seconds, and those following extending only after 15. But in this example events following twitching are evidently still dependent on it even after a full 40 seconds has elapsed . . . [p. 100].

Nelson used these results to define a *sequence* of courtship as one in which an intersequence interval separates events. The separation is defined in terms of statistical independence. A sequence was defined as a series of statistically dependent events bounded at each end by an intersequence interval.

It should be noted that Delius and Nelson are talking about two different statistics: product moment correlations, and transition probabilities, respectively. Nonetheless, the point is that the search for the least chunking

---

[7] Using a binomial test as in Bakeman (1976).

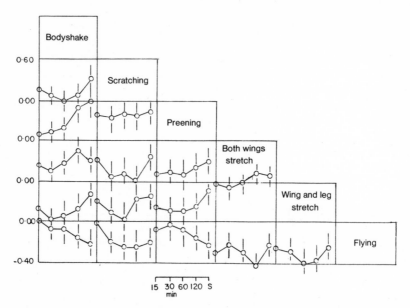

Fig. 5.12. Frequency correlations as functions of the unit observation periods [Source: Delius, J. A. Stochastic analysis of the maintenance behavior of skylarks. *Behaviour*, 1969, *33*, 137–178.]

period in terms of statistical dependency of sequences may be informative, and need not be a fly in the ointment. The appropriate chunk of time to use for punctuating a stream of behavior may, however, vary as a function of the subject or interacting system. For example, a mother may seem to be un-responsive to her infant with a three-second chunking interval—there is a high probability that she will continue to be in the same state in the next interval regardless of the infant's behavior. However, with a larger time period she may appear responsive; this dyad may have a rhythmicity of responsiveness longer than 3 seconds.

X. Conclusion

This chapter has presented methods for conceptualizing the single relationship. The statistical concepts suggest *a particular definition of communication,* namely, that *a particular behavior of one organism communicates if its occurrence reduces undertainty in the behavior of another organism.* The identification of patterns of communication was the subject of this chapter.

Markov models permit description of how far back into the dyad's history it is necessary to go to reduce uncertainty in the dyad's current behavior. Parsimonious models of first-order are observed with some regularity, but we must not assume that interaction patterns are that simple for more complex coding systems and for more complex species.

Information theory provides us with a language that can be used for the description of dyadic interaction patterns. One important generalization we wish to make in description is about lag relationships independent of historical time, and our null hypothesis here is stationarity. Information theory provided us with a crude swipe at sequential patterning. We are, however, usually interested in finer questions than the degree of stereotypy in signal and response systems, and Sackett's lag-sequential analysis provides an alternative for identifying pattern and interconnectedness between interacting organisms. This chapter was written to encourage researchers in human behavior to describe their observations of social interaction in richer detail than we currently obtain by presenting rates of behavior. We feel strongly that our science has underplayed the importance of the descriptive phase of scientific investigation. Somehow it seems logical that the interaction of organisms must be described by attention to pattern and sequence. Once we have good descriptive data, we may identify new phenomena that enrich our theories.

Appendix 1. Matrix Analysis Applied to Markov Chains

If A is a $K \times K$ matrix, we can diagonalize A by a series of elementary row and column operations. The elements of the diagonal representation of A will be the eigenvalues of A. The matrix A is a linear transformation operating on a vector space. We can find vectors that are invariants of A. If x is such a vector, then $Ax = \lambda x$, where λ is a scalar value; x is called a right eigenvector. If $xA = \lambda x$, x is callèd a left eigenvector.

If there exists a linearly independent set of right eigenvectors, $\phi^{(1)}$, ..., $\phi^{(n)}$ and a linearly independent set of left eigenvectors $\psi^{(1)}, \ldots, \psi^{(n)}$, then the sets of vectors are orthogonal:

$$(\phi^{(i)}, \psi^{(j)}) = \sum_{k=1}^{n} \phi_{ik}\psi_{jk} = \delta_{ij} = \begin{cases} 1, & i = j \\ 0, & i \neq j \end{cases}$$

and A is diagonalizable as $A = \Phi\Lambda\psi$, where

$$\Phi = \begin{bmatrix} \phi_{11} \cdots \phi_{n1} \\ \cdots\cdots\cdots \\ \phi_{n1} \cdots \phi_{nn} \end{bmatrix} \qquad \Psi = \begin{bmatrix} \Psi_{11} \cdots \Psi_{n1} \\ \cdots\cdots\cdots \\ \Psi_{1n} \cdots \Psi_{nn} \end{bmatrix}$$

$$\Lambda = \begin{bmatrix} \lambda_1 & 0 & \cdots & 0 \\ 0 & \lambda_2 & \cdots & 0 \\ \vdots & \vdots & & \vdots \\ 0 & 0 & \cdots & \lambda_n \end{bmatrix} = \mathrm{diag}(\lambda_1, \ldots, \lambda_n)$$

Then we can also show that

$$A^m = \Phi\Lambda^m\Psi$$

where

$$\Lambda^m = \mathrm{diag}(\lambda_1{}^m, \lambda_2{}^m, \ldots, \lambda_n{}^m)$$

If A is a Markov transition probability matrix, we have a convenient representation of the mth step transition probability matrix (see Karlin, 1968, for more detail).

If A has k linearly independent eigenvectors $x_1, x_2, \ldots, x_k$, with eigenvectors $\lambda_1, \lambda_2, \ldots, \lambda_k$, then A is similar to a diagonal matrix and its representation is somewhat simple:

$$A = \mathsf{L}^{-1}\Lambda\mathsf{L}, \qquad A^m = \mathsf{L}^{-1}\Lambda^m\mathsf{L}$$

where

$$\mathsf{L} = \begin{bmatrix} x_1 \\ x_2 \\ \vdots \\ x_k \end{bmatrix} = \begin{bmatrix} x_{11} & x_{12} \cdots x_{1k} \\ x_{21} & x_{22} \cdots x_{2k} \\ \vdots & \vdots & \vdots \\ x_{k1} & x_{k2} \cdots x_{kk} \end{bmatrix}$$

and $\Lambda = \mathrm{diag}(\lambda_1, \ldots, \lambda_k)$. A necessary and sufficient condition for A to be similar to a diagonal matrix is for all the eigenvalues to be distinct. All the characteristic vectors are also then independent (Finkbeiner, 1966).

Appendix 2. Derivation of $N = (I - Q)^{-1}$ (from Parzen, 1967, p. 238)

Let a Markov chain have state space S, with subspace T denoting the set of nonrecurrent states in the chain.

Let n' denote the time before absorption:

$$n' = \sum_{j \in T} N_j(\infty)$$

which is the number of steps the chain spends among nonrecurrent states before being absorbed. The time to absorption is $N = N' + 1$. Let

$$m_j = E(N \mid X_0 = j) = 1 + E(N' \mid X_0 = j)$$

be the mean time to absorption given that the chain started at state j:

$$m_j = 1 + \sum_{i \in T} \sum_{n=1}^{\infty} p_{j,i}(n) = \sum_{i \in T} n_{j,i}$$

$$m_j = 1 + \sum_{k \in T} p_{j,k} m_k, \qquad j \in T$$

$$I\mathbf{m} = 1 + Q\mathbf{m} \qquad \mathbf{i} = \begin{bmatrix} 1 \\ 1 \\ \vdots \\ 1 \end{bmatrix}$$

$$(I - Q)\mathbf{m} = 1$$

if

$$N = (I - Q)^{-1} = I + Q + Q^2 + \cdots + Q^n + \cdots$$

Appendix 3. Random Walk as Null Hypothesis

For some applications it is possible to define a set of states such that we can speak of neighboring states. For example, in the study of parent–infant interaction we can define the following states:

State 1:   Both parent and child silent, no eye contact.
State 2:   Child or parent vocalize, no eye contact.
State 3:   Both child and parent vocalize, no eye contact.
State 4:   Both child and parent vocalize with eye contact.

These four states are ordered in terms of increasing reciprocal contact.
A random walk process for these four states would be

$$
P = \begin{array}{c} \\ 1 \\ 2 \\ 3 \\ 4 \end{array}
\begin{array}{cccc} 1 & 2 & 3 & 4 \\ \end{array}
\begin{bmatrix}
\frac{1}{2} & \frac{1}{2} & 0 & 0 \\
\frac{1}{3} & \frac{1}{3} & \frac{1}{3} & 0 \\
0 & \frac{1}{3} & \frac{1}{3} & \frac{1}{3} \\
0 & 0 & \frac{1}{2} & \frac{1}{2}
\end{bmatrix}
$$

The system can stay in the same state or move to a neighboring state with equal likelihood. The random walk is a reasonable null hypothesis, which is an alternative hypothesis to Slater's (1973) suggestion for applications when states can be rank ordered.

We need a procedure for comparing the steady state obtained transition matrix (after n steps) with the steady state random walk matrix (after n steps). Karlin (1968) presented a general method for calculating the transition probabilities of a random walk process after n steps.

The general random walk process is given by the transition probability matrix:

$$P = \begin{bmatrix} r_0 & p_0 & 0 & 0 & \cdots \\ q_1 & r_1 & p_1 & 0 & \cdots \\ 0 & q_2 & r_2 & p_2 & \cdots \\ \vdots & \vdots & \vdots & \vdots & \end{bmatrix}$$

where

$$q_n + r_n + p_n = 1, \qquad q_n > 0, \quad p_n > 0, \quad r_n \geq 0 \quad \text{for} \quad n = 1, 2, \ldots$$

$$r_0 + p_0 = 1, \qquad p_0 > 0, \quad r_0 \geq 0$$

Consider the following system of equations:

$$xQ_k(x) = q_k Q_{k-1}(x) + r_k Q_k(x) + p_k Q_{k+1}(x), \qquad k = 1, 2, \ldots$$

with initial specifications $Q_0(x) = 1$, $Q_1(x) = (x - r_0)/p_0$. Since $p_n > 0$ for all n, $Q_n(x)$ is determined recursively, $n \geq 2$, and $Q_n(x)$ is a polynomial in x of exact degree n.

There exists a function $\sigma(x)$, $x\epsilon[-1, 1]$, that is nondecreasing and not constant such that

$$\int_{-1}^{1} Q_k(x)Q_s(x) \, d\sigma(x) = \begin{cases} 0 & \text{if} \quad k \neq s \\ >0 & \text{if} \quad k = s \end{cases} \qquad k = 0, 1, 2, \ldots$$

Namely, the $Q_k(x)$ are orthogonal polynomials w.r.t. $\sigma(x)$ over the interval $[-1, +1]$. The function $\sigma(x)$ is unique up to an addative constant:

$$xQ_k(x) = \sum_{r=0}^{\infty} P_{kr} Q_r(x), \qquad k = 0, 1, \ldots$$

Multiply both sides by x and substitute:

$$x^2 Q_k(x) = \sum_{r=0}^{\infty} P_{kr} \sum_{s=0}^{\infty} P_{rs} Q_s(x) = \sum_{s=0}^{\infty} P_{ks}^2 Q_s(x), \qquad k = 0, 1, \ldots$$

Proceeding in this manner, we get

$$x^n Q_k(x) = \sum_{r=0}^{\infty} P_{kr} Q_r(x), \qquad k = 0, 1, \ldots, \quad n = 1, 2, \ldots$$

Multiplying both sides by $Q_s(x)$ and integrating over $[-1, 1]$ w.r.t. $d\sigma(x)$ gives (because of orthogonality)

$$\int_{-1}^{1} x^n Q_k(x) Q_s(x) \, d\sigma(x) = \sum_{r=0}^{\infty} P_{kr}^n \int_{-1}^{1} Q_r(x) Q_s(x) \, d\sigma(x)$$

$$= P_{ks}^n \int_{-1}^{1} Q_s^2(x) \, d\sigma(x)$$

$$\therefore \quad P_{ks}^n = \int_{-1}^{1} x^n Q_k(x) Q_s(x) \, d\sigma(x) \bigg/ \int_{-1}^{1} Q_s^2(x) \, d\sigma(x)$$

The procedure is similar to a diagonalization method. The procedure asserts that the vector $(Q_0(x), Q_1(x), \ldots)$ is an eigenvector of P for the eigenvalue x. One choice for the $Q_k(x)$ is

$$Q_k(x) = \cos k(\text{arc} \cos x), \qquad k = 0, 1, \ldots$$

$$d\sigma(x) = \rho(x) \, dx$$

where

$$\rho(x) = (1/2\pi)(1 - x^2)^{-1/2}$$

$$\int_{-1}^{1} Q_k(x) Q(x) \rho(x) \, dx = \int_{0}^{\pi} \cos k\Theta \cos l\Theta \, d\Theta = 0, \qquad \text{if} \quad k \neq l$$

ACKNOWLEDGMENT

The authors wish to thank William Timberlake for suggesting valuable references in the ethological literature.

REFERENCES

Altmann, S. A. Sociobiology of Rhesus monkeys. II: Stochastics of social communication. *Journal of Theoretical Biology*, 1965, *8*, 490–522.

Andersson, M. Temporal Graphical Analysis of behavior sequences. *Behaviour*, 1974, *51*, 38–48.

Attneave, F. *Applications of information theory to psychology.* New York: Holt, Rinehart, & Winston, 1959.

Bakeman, R. Untangling streams of behavior: Sequential analysis of observation data. A paper presented at a conference entitled, "Application of Observational-Ethological Methods for the Study of Mental Retardation," University of Washington, Seattle, Washington, Summer, 1976.

Bakeman, R., & Dabbs, Jr., J. M. Social interaction observed: Some approaches to the analysis of behavior streams. *Personality and Social Psychology Bulletin, 3,* 1976, *2,* 335–345.

Baker, M. C. Stochastic properties of the foraging behavior of six species of migratory shorebirds. *Behaviour,* 1973, *47,* 241–270.

Bishop, Y. M. M., Feinberg, S. E., & Holland, P. W. *Discrete multivariate analysis.* Cambridge, MA: Massachusetts Institute of Technology Press, 1975.

Castellan, Jr., N. J. The analysis of behavior sequences. Unpublished manuscript, Indiana University, Bloomington, Indiana, 1976.

Cochran, W. G. Some methods for strengthening the common χ^2 tests. *Biometrics,* 1954, *10,* 417–451.

Delius, J. A. Stochastic analysis of the maintenance behaviour of skylarks. *Behaviour,* 1969, *33,* 137–178.

Finkbeiner, D. T. *Introduction to matrices and linear transformations.* San Francisco: W. H. Freeman, 1966.

Gottman, J., Markman, H., & Notarius, C. The topography of marital conflict: A sequential analysis of verbal and nonverbal behavior. *Journal of Marriage and Family,* 1977, *39,* 461–477.

Gottman, J., Notarius, C., Markman, H., Bank, S., Yoppi, B., & Rubin, M. E. Behavior exchange theory and marital decision making. *Journal of Personality and Social Psychology,* 1976, *34,* 14–23.

Hazlett, B. A., & Estabrook, G. F. Examination of agonistic behavior by character analysis. I. The spider crab (*Microphrys bicornutus*). *Behaviour,* 1974, *48,* 131–144.

Hoel, P. G., Port, S. C., & Stone, C. J. *Introduction to stochastic processes.* Boston: Houghton Mifflin, 1972.

Howard, R. A. *Dynamic programming and Markov processes.* Cambridge, MA: The Massachusetts Institute of Technology Press, 1960.

Isaacson, D. L., & Madsen, R. W. *Markov chains: Theory and applications.* New York: John Wiley & Sons, 1976.

Jaffe, J., & Feldstein, S. *Rhythms of dialogue.* New York: Academic Press, 1970.

Karlin, S. *A first course in Stochastic Processes.* New York: Academic Press, 1968.

Kemeny, J. G., Snell, J. L., & Thompson, G. L. *Introduction to finite mathematics.* Englewood Cliffs, NJ: Prentice-Hall, 1966.

Lemon, R. E., & Chatfield, C. Organization of song in cardinals. *Animal Behaviour,* 1971, *19,* 1–17.

Lemon, R. F., & Chatfield, C. Organization of song of rose-breasted grosbeaks. *Animal Behaviour,* 1973, *21,* 28–44.

Lichtenberg, J. W., & Hummel, T. J. Counseling as stochastic process: Fitting a Markov chain model to initial counseling interviews. *Journal of Counseling Psychology,* 1976, *23,* 310–315.

Miller, G. A. What is information measurement? *American Psychologist,* 1953, *8,* 31–11.

Miller, G. A., & Frick, F. C. Statistical behavioristics and sequences of responses. *Psychological Review,* 1949, *56,* 311–324.

Nelson, K. The temporal patterning of courtship behaviour in the glandule caudine fishes. *Behaviour,* 1964, *24,* 90–146.

Newman, E. B., & Gerstman, L. S. A new method for analyzing printed English. *Journal of Experimental Psychology*, 1952, *44*, 114–125.

Parzen, E. *Stochastic processes*. San Francisco: Holden-Day, 1967.

Patterson, G. R. A basis for identifying stimuli which control behaviors in natural settings. *Child Development*, 1974, *45*, 900–911.

Quastler, H. A primer on information theory. In H. P. Yockey, R. L. Platzman, & H. Quastler (Eds.), *Symposium on information theory in biology*. New York: Pergammon Press, 1958.

Ruash, H. L. Interaction sequences. *Journal of Personality and Social Psychology*, 1965, *2*, 487–499.

Raush, H. L. Process and change: A Markov model for interaction. *Family Process*, 1972, *11*, 275–298.

Raush, H. L., Barry, W. A., Hertel, R. K., & Swain, M. A. *Communication, conflict and marriage*. San Francisco: Jossey-Bass, 1974.

Sackett, G. P. A nonparametric lag sequential analysis for studying dependency among responses in observational scoring systems. Unpublished manuscript, University of Washington, 1974.

Shannon, C. E., & Weaver, W. *The Mathematical theory of communication*. Urbana: The University of Illinois Press, 1949.

Siegel, S. *Nonparametric statistics*. New York: McGraw-Hill, 1956.

Slater, P. J. B. Describing sequences of behavior. In P. P. G. Bateson & P. H. Klopfer (Eds.), *Perspectives in ethology*, 1973.

Stuart, R. B. Behavioral contracting within the families of delinquents. *Journal of Behavior Therapy and Experimental Psychiatry*, 1971.

Wilson, E. O. *Sociobiology: The new synthesis*. Cambridge, MA: Belknap Press of Harvard University Press, 1975.

6

Choosing a Statistical Method for Analysis of an Intensive Experiment

JANET D. ELASHOFF
UNIVERSITY OF CALIFORNIA, LOS ANGELES

CARL E. THORESEN
STANFORD UNIVERSITY

The nature of the relationship between empirical data and statistical inference has always been stormy. Squalls and showers have chronically prevailed, sometimes precipitating noisy thunderstorms. Pressure zones have ranged widely—from strategical arguments for and against using *any* type of inference based on statistical logic to tactical problems about such issues as null hypothesis testing, confidence intervals, and prior probabilities. In Chapters 1–5 a variety of approaches to the analysis of intensive experiments have been suggested. In this chapter we discuss some of these approaches and provide suggestions about what the researcher might do given a particular problem. Two examples will be used to illustrate some of the basic issues in choosing a statistical analysis.

I. Some Introductory Comments

The fundamental issue clearly centers around *evaluating observed changes*. What criteria should be used? Typically, the question has been answered in terms of the type of experimental design used. It is generally believed that "true" experiments yield the most valid basis for evaluating observed changes.

It is important to note that the meaning of a true experiment has evolved over time. Since the late 1930s, the orthodox view defines the true experiment as a situation in which subjects or units are *randomly sampled from a population* and then *randomly assigned* to two or more groups or conditions (cf. Campbell & Stanley, 1966; Boruch & Reicksen, 1974; Underwood, 1957). Change is evaluated primarily by comparing the mean or average change *between* groups. Yet the key characteristics—randomization and comparisons between groups—have not always been a part of the term experiment as a concept (Boring, 1954; Cochran, 1974). Indeed, the logic of randomization is a fairly new notion, first becoming popular during the late 1930s (Fisher, 1935).

The argument for randomization is straightforward: when little is known about all the variables that might influence changes in one group compared to another, the best remedy is to balance or equalize their possible effects. This can be done by allowing each subject "equal opportunity" of being in either group.[1] In addition, randomization provides a check on the experimenter, preventing unwitting bias in assigning subjects to treatment groups. Randomization is also essential to the assumptions underlying certain statistical tests used to evaluate differences between groups; randomization guarantees a valid way of computing an error value. But randomization was most strongly advocated by Fisher (1935) because of its presumed efficiency; with a proper plan in advance one could study effects of several factors simultaneously. Replication could also be built into the same experiment.

The notion of making comparisons between groups (comparative observations) has a much older tradition than randomization, dating back to the Old Testament (Daniel 1:10–16). Yet it was not until the late eighteenth century that much attention was given to carefully *controlled comparisons between groups (treatments) using numerical procedures.* An early example is provided by P. C. A. Louis, a French physician in the early 1800s interested in studying the natural history of diseases. Louis (1834) suggested ways for comparing the effects of various treatments.[2] It was Louis whose compara-

---

[1] Use of very small samples seriously limits the power of randomization to equalize or balance the possible effects of unknown factors.

[2] Comparative observations (designs) had been suggested almost a thousand years earlier by Avicenna (A.D. 980–1037), the Arab scholar who had proposed intensive time-series studies

tive data on blood letting *refuted* this widely used treatment. He showed that for several medical problems, blood letting was not associated with improved outcomes in comparison with patients not receiving this treatment. Louis noted the critical value and the difficulty of making "exact observations," commenting on the very careless ways researchers collected and interpreted data. Such problems obviously remain.

Another example of making comparisons based on careful observations is offered by Arthur Young (1771), a scholarly English farmer, concerned with different planting methods (i.e., methods of sowing, type of soil, drainage, planting, climate). Young sternly criticized his research peers for not using controlled observations. His solution was to use the same field, dividing it into plots or sections. He strongly cautioned against overgeneralizing results since too many factors could influence the yield on a particular farm.

Young's approach remains quite modern: systematic replication across varying conditions based on precise and reliable measurement. Young's keen sense of how researchers often "misbehave" anticipated a current issue. He believed most researchers hold steadfast to strong biases, trying to confirm in a very selective fashion what they already believe to be true," adapting a favorite notion, and then forming experiments to confirm it." Such behavior, he noted, "gave me a disgust of favorite hypotheses." His refreshing conclusion was to be distrustful of favorite hypotheses, especially one's own.[3]

We bring up randomization, comparative observations, and the true experiment because these concepts play major roles, often unrecognized, in discussions of what types of designs and analytic methods to use in making inferences about the meaning of results. The clearcut popularity of between-group designs in the behavioral and medical sciences is based on assumptions about variability, experimental control, generalizations, and causality. The basic logic underlying intensive or time-series studies hinges on beliefs about effective ways to study and understand observed variability, better ways to exercise experimental control, and what types of replication are most relevant in establishing the generality of findings. The issues in deciding which kinds

---

with a few cases (e.g., selecting contrasting cases and studying how they changed over time). Unfortunately, his empirical position, stressing controlled replication and the power of refutation, went unheeded by medieval scholars, who relied almost entirely on the theory and logic of authoritative tradition (Thoresen, in press).

[3] The "subjective" behavior of scientists, compared with the stereotyped "objective" version presented in most research texts, is highly relevant to the problems of how researchers go about selecting and justifying criteria to evaluate change. The topic is not addressed here. See Kuhn (1970) and Mahoney (1976) for a critical discussion of the subjectivity of science and the limits of confirming theory based on statistical inferences.

of designs will be most useful for which kinds of problems are many and are unlikely to be resolved on strictly logical or polemical grounds.[4]

Cook and Campbell (1976) in speaking of how to evaluate the validity of experimental designs noted: "Estimating the internal validity of a relationship is a deductive process in which the investigator has to be *his own most trenchent critic* and has to systematically think through how each of the threats have influenced his data [p. 229, italics added]."

The authors in this text offer perspectives bearing on the analysis of single case experiments—from the need to avoid all inferential statistics as judgmental aids (relying instead on visual inspection) to the use of complex autoregressive integrative moving average statistical methods. There are no clearcut rules to follow in choosing among these methods. Instead one must rely on a careful appraisal and thoughtful analysis of each situation. Seldom is there only one way or even any best way of proceeding. Usually there are several possibilities, each with its own set of advantages and limitations.

We believe that doctrinaire positions that unequivocably advocate just one strategy and condemn others (e.g., "all experiments require randomized groups" or "applied time-series data must avoid any inferential statistics") do far more harm than good. Any statistical method, descriptive or inferential, serves as a tool that may or may not be useful, *depending on the task at hand.* We concur with the concerns voiced by Cronbach (1975) that far too much reliance has been placed on routine null hypothesis testing rather than a careful analysis of the structure of the data. We also agree with Michael (1974) that excessive reliance on group statistics keeps the investigator away from a better understanding of individual performance. Development of better experimental control can suffer if the attention is focused too much on techniques of statistical control.

Similarly, we agree that there is an important distinction between a "clinically significant" effect, such as the treatment goal of completely eliminating destructive tantrums over time in a disturbed ten year old, and a "statistically significant" difference, such as the average loss of six pounds in one community compared to another community in a comparative field experiment.

What seems to be in order is a goodly amount of experimentation—controlled observation and careful analysis of different ways to design and analyze problems. Especially needed is a willingness to learn from making

---

[4] We note that some writers have argued against any type of "justificationist" position, that is, where the investigator attempts to prove or confirm hypotheses (theory) from observed data using probability statements (Mahoney, 1976; Weimar, 1976; Bartley, 1962; Kuhn, 1970; Popper, 1972). Instead a type of critical rationalism is urged in which the utility and adequacy of competing theories are analyzed using a variety of methods.

informative errors (Popper, 1972). Undoubtedly, such behavior will gradually reveal what are the relative strengths and weakness of alternatives. Perhaps we may find ways of synthesizing positive features of various methods. It is unlikely, however, that such progress will be made unless more investigators experiment with more options.

II. Commentary on Suggested Analytic Methods

A. Visual Analysis

Parsonson and Baer (Chapter 2 of this volume) build a case for the exclusive use of careful graphing and visual analysis methods. Visual methods do have much to recommend them. Ease of use is an important feature of any proposed analytic method, and the design and understanding of visual displays does not require special mathematical expertise on the part of the experimenter or the reader. Carefully designed visual displays are vital in the exploratory phases of data analysis; they encourage the investigator and the reader to examine the data closely. The eye is one of the best tools known for detecting time patterns or unusual data features. Visual impressions are a very useful aid in formulating explicit questions to ask of the data and hypotheses about the nature of intervention effects; they are also useful in reminding the investigator that any preconceived ideas he may have about the nature of the response variable need to be reexamined in light of the data.

We regret, however, the implication by Parsonson and Baer that visual displays and statistical descriptions and tests are mutually exclusive, "either–or" propositions. *Statistical and visual methods should be partners in the analytic endeavor.* Even when pure description is of interest, it is often helpful to compute statistical summaries such as averages, trend lines, and correlation coefficients to aid the eye and provide for more objective comparisons.

But it is in the confirmatory phase of data analysis, at the time when one asks questions such as, "Is an observed result significant? Could it have been due to chance? Is it likely to be confirmed upon replication?" that explicit and formal methods of inference are needed. To make an inference one must be explicit about the pattern of baseline data and about prediction of the type of intervention effect expected—an immediate jump in level, an upward trend, fewer very low points, etc.

Parsonson and Baer recommend looking for intervention effects that are "clearly evident and reliable." But what exactly is meant by this? The eye is notoriously easy to mislead, and visual inspection alone, so helpful when we wish to note any type of change in the exploratory mode, can make one forget the importance of having predicted that particular kind of change in the confirmatory stage of inquiry. Time dependency or serial correlation in the response measure is especially hard to assess or take account of by visual inspection, as Gottman and Glass (Chapter 4 of this volume) point out.

Parsonson and Baer argue that only large intervention effects are of interest; if effects are large they will be "clearly evident" through visual methods; use of statistical methods might turn up undesirable or obscure small effects. Assuming that we restrict our attention to large effects, this is not a reason to reject statistical procedures. Statistical tests are designed to help answer the questions: Could this observed effect have been due to chance? Will it be likely to stand up to replication? It is then up to the investigator to assess whether the size of the effect is likely to be of interest. There are really two separate questions: (1) Is the effect large? (2) Are we likely to find this effect again in a replication? No matter how large the apparent effect, it is unlikely to be of interest if it will not stand up to replication.

If the experimenter can produce large effects through increase in experimental control without losing the possibility of applying techniques outside the laboratory, he should do so. But many interventions will not have "slam-bang" effects and it will be important to measure small effects reliably. Gilbert, Light, and Mosteller (1975) state it aptly: "Once small effects are found and documented, it may be possible to build improvements upon them. The banking and insurance businesses have built their fortunes on small effects—effects the size of interest rates. Ten percent per year doubles the principal in a little over seven years. Similarly, a small effect that can be cumulated over several periods—for example, the school life of a student— has the potential of mounting up into a large gain." Detection and measurement of small effects requires the careful and informed use of statistical methods as well as replication of the experiment to be sure that observed effects are not due to the particular characteristics of the individual or to other factors, such as historical effects, or changes in instrumentation.

B. Markov Chain Analysis

Gottman and Notarius (Chapter 5 of this volume) present methods of investigating the time dependency among nominal categories of events. The methods they describe are intermediate in ease of understanding and application. Gottman and Notarius illustrate how Markov methods can be used to discover repetitive patterns of behavior and to exhibit differences in patterns under varying conditions; they also discuss methods for assessing the interrelationships between parallel time sequences of events; they do not, however, emphasize methods for testing the significance of intervention effects.

These methods have the advantage that they bring examination of the structure of the data, and especially of time dependency into the forefront of exploratory analysis. A major limitation is that they make no use of any ordinal information about categories that might exist.

C. Time Series Methods

Gottman and Glass (Chapter 4 of this volume) illustrate the application of autoregressive moving average models to continuous time-series data. These methods attempt to model the serial dependency in the data thereby focusing attention on the details of the behavior of the response measure over time. However, the methods are difficult to understand, and require the computer to apply. In addition, there are problems with using the same data to choose a model and then to test an intervention effect. Further, tests on correlation coefficients are not sensitive in small to moderate size samples and, unfortunately, as illustrated by Gottman and Glass, results may sometimes be very sensitive to the exact model chosen.

Tests based on such time-series analyses may be more sensitive for detection of small interventions but the researcher pays for this increased sensitivity by (1) being forced to make some rather stringent assumptions about the underlying structure of the data, (2) needing a long preintervention (baseline) period, and (3) having to learn a complicated technique. The user will also find it difficult in general to describe results to the reader.

D. Randomization Tests

Levin, Marascuilo, and Hubert (Chapter 3 of this volume) recommend focusing on a single descriptive summary measure, such as the mean within each phase. The researcher must make a prediction about the rank ordering of these phase summaries and then make an inference about the effects of intervention. The inference is based on the agreement between observed and predicted ranks, conditional on the observed set of summaries. The methods are relatively easy to understand and use. They are not especially useful in the exploratory phase of data analysis because they essentially ignore issues of (1) the structure of the response variable, (2) the correlational structure of the data, and (3) the choice of an appropriate summary measure within each phase. The stress laid on a priori predictions is especially important in the confirmatory phase; the tests they recommend are sound and conservative for such purposes. These methods require, however, a fairly large number of phases and would be unduly conservative if the data structure was simple or known to follow a specific pattern since all within-phase data except the summary measure is ignored.

III. Exploratory and Confirmatory Data Analysis

The development of a model describing the structure of the data is the basis for choosing a statistical procedure. An analytic approach to the data should be selected when the experiment is being planned. The type of analysis anticipated has implications for the design of the experiment—the necessary number and ordering of phases and the number and timing of within-phase observations. The actual design used will limit the analytic options available. To illustrate several points in selecting an appropriate statistical model we will use two examples. The first focuses attention on the appropriateness of alternate analytic methods. It is the experiment by Klein *et al.* (1972) in which on-task–off-task recordings were made at 10 second intervals under several baseline and token reward conditions. The second example is a record of several variables relating to the sleeping problems of an adult female, such as latency of sleep onset, hours slept per night, and number of nighttime awakenings (Coates, Thoresen, Friedman, & Phillips, 1977).

We have chosen to discuss one example with discrete data and one with continuous responses since analytic methods are generally aimed specifically at one or the other data type. The reader should remember however that classifying the response variable itself as being discrete or continuous must always be somewhat arbitrary. Discrete data like the on-task–off-task records become continuous when they are summarized by reporting percentages of on-task behavior in 5 minute periods. Continuous data like minutes latency to sleep onset can easily be dichotomized as, say, shorter than 15 minutes, and 15 minutes or longer.

Perhaps the single most crucial question in deciding how to analyze the results is whether the experiment should be considered exploratory or confirmatory. Is the experiment the first of its type? Will the observations need to be carefully examined to determine what response pattern is characteristic of the baseline period? That is, have several other studies provided reliable information on what to expect before treatment is begun or is this one of the first intensive studies? Are several different types of intervention effect possible—an immediate jump or step effect in behavior, a delayed but gradual change in response, an abrupt change in level but none in trend? If answers to these questions are yes, then the analysis should be carried out in an exploratory way; definitive tests of whether or not the intervention has a statistically significant effect must await the performance of a second intensive experiment. An investigator who does not have firm expectations about the experimental outcome needs to concentrate on exploring the data. A single experiment can not serve both as vehicle for choosing an appropriate inferential test and for making sound conclusions based on the results of that test.

Only after an investigator has gained experience with a response and an intervention and can make detailed predictions about the structure of the data and the expected effects of the intervention prior to the running of the experiment can he expect to be able to apply and report statistical conclusions as to the significance of the intervention effect. The development of a model describing the structure of the data is the basis for choosing a statistical test.

To help develop a model for the structure of the data and subsequently choose a method of analysis, the investigator must ask several questions about the nature of the experiment and the response measure:

1. What are the relevant response measures?
2. What is the baseline pattern in terms of level, variability, and trend?
3. What is the correlation between successive responses?
4. What is the pattern likely to be without intervention?
5. What is the desired or expected pattern due to intervention?

IV. Selecting an Analytic Approach in Practice

A. James and Lynn: On-Task, Off-Task Behavior

Klein, Roden, Gentile, Resnick, Reynolds, and Bachmeyer (1972) observed the behavior of three kindergarten children during a 1 hour "conceptual" period each day. Throughout the entire experiment each child was given a total of five tokens for the successful completion of each designated task. Each child was observed for a five minute period; a W was recorded for on-task and an O for off-task behavior for each 10 second interval (up to 3 seconds of off-task were allowed within an on-task W interval). Each child was observed an average of twice during each day.

The A phase (baseline) was 10 days. During the 4 days of the first intervention (the B phase) teacher attention to the target children was increased but the tokens were given as during the baseline. During the 5 days of the C phase the same number of tokens were given for each task but they were administered contingently as rewards for on-task behavior *during* the task.

These periods were followed by a 2 day withdrawal of treatment (return to baseline conditions, A_2) and then another three days of contingent reward for being on-task (C_2).

1. EXAMINING THE BASELINE-EXPLORATORY ANALYSES

The summary data for two of the children are shown in Table 6.1. We first ask: What is the response measure of interest? What are the characteristics of these strings of 10-second on-task–off-task records? How could they be summarized most effectively? To answer these questions, we need to examine the basic 5-minute strings of 30 records. The authors do not provide these, but Kratochwill *et al.* (1972) obtained and reported a record made in a similar way (see Table 6.2). In this 10-minute record, we note that there are 30 Ws and 30 Os, so half the time was spent on-task and half the time off-task. Next, we may note that there were four on-task periods, one of 150 seconds, one of 100 seconds, one of 30 seconds, and one of 20 seconds. The five off-task periods lasted 30, 80, 10, 50 and 130 seconds, respectively.

To look more closely at the structure of this record, we may adopt the notion of Markov chain transition matrices from Chapter 5. We note that since there were 50% Os and 50% Ws in this particular string of 60 observations, there should be about 50% Os and 50% Ws following a W and the same following an O *if* the successive 10-second records were independent of each other as in a binomial trial. However, we find about 86% of the time that a W is followed by a W and an O is followed by an O (see Table 6.3). If we did a χ^2 test of "independence" in such a table we would find a very significant result. This is not surprising. The nature of the behavior being observed is such that the expected duration of either on-task or off-task behavior is longer than the 10-second recording interval; we therefore expect to find the patterns WW and OO more frequently than the patterns WO or OW.

A number of tests of whether the order of symbols in a string is random have been developed. We illustrate here the runs test (Dixon & Massey, 1969, p. 342). Any unbroken sequence of one character is called a *run*. In this record there are four runs of Ws and five of Os, for a total of nine runs (see Table 6.2). We reject the hypothesis of random (or independent) arrangement of Ws and Os if there are too few or too many runs. For 30 Ws and 30 Os randomly ordered, we would expect between 22 and 39 runs in 95% of such experiments (Table A-11, Dixon & Massey, 1969). Clearly the number of runs observed here is much lower than expected with random ordering.

One could also use the concepts of uncertainty to investigate the inter-relationships among successive behavior records. As done in Table 5.2 of Chapter 5 we have looked at single codes, digrams, trigrams, and tetragrams

TABLE 6.1
**Mean Proportions of On-Task Behavior and Numbering of Recording
Intervals for Each Phase**[a]

Student	A_1 (Baseline) 10 days	B (Teacher attention) 4 days	C_1 (Tokens) 5 days	A_2 (Baseline) 2 days	C_2 (Tokens) 3 days
James p	.286	.331	.372	.219	.202
n	974	610	529	210	282
Lynn p	.260	.446	.381	.266	.301
n	1023	480	565	90	143

[a] From Klein *et al.* (1972).

TABLE 6.2
**Ten Minute String of On-Task (W) and Off-Task (O) Records Made at
10-Second Intervals (Grouped in Triples for Convenience)**[a]

OOO	WWW	WWW	WWW	WWW	WWW
OOO	OOO	OOW	WWW	WWW	WWW
OWW	WOO	OOO	WWO	OOO	OOO
OOO	OOO				

[a] From Kratochwill *et al.* (1972).

TABLE 6.3
**Transition Matrix for 60 10-Second Recordings of
On-Task (W) or Off-Task (O)**

		Observation t		
		W	O	
Observation	W	26	4	30
$t - 1$	O	4	25	29
		30	29	59

(see Table 6.4). Note that the estimated uncertainty $\hat{H}$ is markedly reduced by knowing the preceding symbol ($\hat{H}_1 = 1.00$, $\hat{H}_2 = .58$), but that it is not reduced much more by knowing the preceding three symbols ($\hat{H}_3 = .57$, $\hat{H}_4 = .45$).

Now that we have a better idea of the behavior in question, we must decide how to summarize it. What aspect of the on-task versus off-task behavior do we wish to influence? For this problem, it is probably most

TABLE 6.4

Information Analysis[a]

(W = on-task, O = off-task)

Tetragram	n_i	Trigram	n_i	Digram	n_i	Symbol	n_i
OOOO	17	OOO	20	OO	23	O	27
OOOW	3						
OOWO	0	OOW	3				
OOWW	3						
OWOO	0	OWO	0	OW	4		
OWOW	0						
OWWO	1	OWW	4				
OWWW	3						
WOOO	3	WOO	3	WO	4	W	30
WOOW	0						
WOWO	0	WOW	1				
WOWW	1						
WWOO	3	WWO	4	WW	26		
WWOW	1						
WWWO	3	WWW	22				
WWWW	19						

[a] n_i = number of k-grams of this type

$$\hat{H}(k\text{-gram}) = \log_2 n - \frac{1}{n} \Sigma n_i \log_2 n_i$$

$$\hat{H}_k = \hat{H}(k\text{-gram}) - \hat{H}((k-1)\text{-gram})$$

$\hat{H}(\text{tetragram}) = 2.60 \quad \hat{H}(\text{trigram}) = 2.15 \quad \hat{H}(\text{digram}) = 1.58 \quad \hat{H}(\text{symbol}) = 1.00$

$\hat{H}_4 = 2.60 - 2.15 = .45 \quad \hat{H}_3 = .57 \qquad \hat{H}_2 = .58 \qquad \hat{H}_1 = 1.00$

appropriate to begin by summarizing each 5 minute period and examining the behavior of this 5 minute response variable. The authors chose to examine only the total proportion of time on task but alternatives do exist. One might ask what was the length of the longest on-task interval in the 5 minute time block or how many off-task periods were there or how long was the longest off-task period? (It may be that one or two long on-task periods are more efficient than many short ones.)

Given the decision to use proportion of time on-task as the summary for each 5-minute period, the next step is to examine these 5-minute time blocks across the baseline period. This is the point at which a visual display could prove helpful. What is the mean proportion and the standard deviation of these proportions? Is there any time trend? Are the two 5 minute blocks in the same day more similar than those in different days? Are there any effects due to day of week, for example, are Monday proportions lower than those of other days? Is there a tendency for records on two successive days to be more similar than records several days apart? Here, also, is the place to examine carefully the reasons for the varying lengths of the observation periods between phases and across children for their possible effects on the results. All these questions bring us back to ways of dealing with continuous data, which we will defer until the next example.

2. INTERVENTION EFFECTS—CONFIRMATORY ANALYSES

Once the pattern in the baseline period is established we can ask if it is reasonable to expect this pattern to continue in the absence of baseline. A steady pattern with no trend and no other changes, besides that of an intervention, would make this a reasonable assumption. A trend up or down in frequency of the behavior in the baseline period makes it more difficult to know what would have happened in the absence of intervention.

One next needs to ask if the intervention can be expected to result in an immediate jump or step in the frequency of on-task responses, a slow trend upward, a quick trend upward, or a shift in the structure of the data (such as in transition matrices), or a change in the stability of frequency. The way one chooses to summarize data in the intervention period depends on the answers to such questions.

In this example we might specify the structure of baseline data by recording the percentage of time on-task, first, second, third, and higher transitions, and probabilities of "runs" of various lengths of on-task versus off-task behavior. Intervention might be expected to change the total percentage of time on-task or the time duration of the maximum on-task period (i.e., minimum or maximum duration). After these characteristics of the response measure have been considered and examined, the investigator is in a position to look through various statistical approaches to see which *fits his problem*.

For the data as summarized by Klein *et al.* (1972), only one approach to its analysis seems possible since it is unlikely that the 10-second intervals in each phase can be treated as independent binomial trials with constant probability values. To analyze the data as summarized, we must assume that the outcome measure of interest is proportion of time on-task and that we expect intervention to make an immediate and stable shift in this proportion (i.e., we do not want to discard time intervals immediately after intervention has started or allow for a trend).

To apply the nonparametric randomization tests outlined by Levin *et al.* in Chapter 3, we must predict an ordering for the outcomes of the five phases. The five phases are A_1, first baseline; B, teacher attention with tokens; C_1, contingent token rewards, A_2, second baseline, and C_2, contingent token rewards. Klein *et al.* (1972) predicted that proportions of on-task behavior would be lowest in the baseline phases, intermediate in the B phase, and highest in the C phases. No predictions about differences between A_1 and A_2, between C_1 and C_2, or about magnitude of differences were made. Recall that this design was one in which phases were conducted in systematic rather than in random order; however, Levin *et al.*, (Chapter 3 of this volume) argue that randomization tests may still provide a useful approximation for systematic designs.

The investigators predicted that the proportion of time on-task in each of the five phases would satisfy the inequalities: $A_1 < B$, $A_2 < B$, $B < C_1$, $B < C_2$. To construct a nonparametric randomization test for James' data, we begin with the five observed proportions for James, .286, .331, .372, .219, .202 (see Table 6.1). Under the null hypothesis of no intervention effects, there are 120 ($5! = 5 \times 4 \times 3 \times 2 \times 1$) possible and equally likely outcomes of the experiment (assignments of observed proportions to phases). Four of these 120 possible assignments of proportions to phases would satisfy the investigators' prediction; that is, if we write the observed proportions in the order A_1, A_2, B, C_1, C_2, the four possible outcomes

.202,   .219,   .286,   .331,   .372   .219,   .202,   .286,   .331,   .372
.202,   .219,   .286,   .372,   .331   .219,   .202,   .286,   .372,   .331

would all satisfy the predicted inequalities, while none of the other 116 possible outcomes would do so. Thus, we could construct a test of the null hypothesis which would reject in favor of the investigators' hypothesis at the level $p = 4/120 = .033$ if we rejected the null hypothesis only when one of these four outcomes was observed. For James, we actually observed, $A_1 = .286$, $A_2 = .219$, $B = .331$, $C_1 = .372$, and $C_2 = .202$ which does not satisfy the prediction. Thus, using this randomization test, we would not be able to reject the null hypothesis for James. We could apply the same test procedure to Lynn's data, and, again, would not reject the null hypothesis since the two largest proportions did not occur in the C phases.

Suppose we wish to construct a more liberal test and reject the null hypothesis if an outcome close to that predicted occurs. To do this, we must be more explicit about the predicted response pattern. Assume that we predict that the difference between proportions in phases A and B will be the same size as that between proportions in phases B and C. Then we could construct a contrast among the phase proportions by assigning weights -1 and -1 to the two baseline phases, 0 to the B phase, and $+1$ and $+1$ to the two C phases. This contrast will be large and positive for outcomes consistent with the investigators' prediction. For any of the four most extreme outcomes, we have $-.202 - .219 + .331 + .372 = .282$. The next most extreme value of the contrast is $-.202 - .219 + .286 + .372 = .237$. Each of these contrast values will occur for four different experimental outcomes, thus, for a one-sided test at the .066 level (8/120), the investigator would reject the null hypothesis if the value of the contrast were .237 or .282. The observed value of the contrast for James is $-.286 - .219 + .372 + .202 = .069$, not in the critical region. Table 6.5 summarizes the outcomes for which the contrast value is positive. Each line in the table represents 4 of 120 outcomes (1/30) obtainable by interchange of A subscripts and/or interchange of C subscripts. Note that line 1 of the table corresponds to the four outcomes listed above which satisfy the investigators' prediction; all of these four outcomes lead to the same contrast value. We see that a contrast as large or larger than that observed for James would be expected to occur 30% of the time under the null hypothesis.

For the Klein $et\ al.$ (1972) data as summarized, the only analytic approach discussed in this book that can be used to test for intervention effects is that of nonparametric randomization tests. However, the investigators have ignored a wealth of possibly informative detail in their data by proceeding directly to these summaries. The methods of Chapter 5 would be useful in exploring the behavior of the strings of 10-second on-task and off-task records for details of children's baseline behavior and possible shifts in these patterns with intervention. Summaries of the 5-minute recording periods, perhaps proportions of time on-task, could be studied through visual displays, or possibly by using time-series methods. When so

TABLE 6.5
James's Data

Coefficient -1	-1	B 0	$+1$	$+1$	Value of contrast	Probability under null hypothesis
.202	.219	.286	.331	.372	.282	1/30
.202	.219	.331	.286	.372	.237	1/30
.202	.286	.219	.331	.372	.215	1/30
.286	.219	.202	.331	.372	.198	1/30
.202	.219	.372	.331	.286	.196	1/30
.202	.331	.219	.286	.372	.125	1/30
.331	.219	.202	.286	.372	.108	1/30
.202	.286	.331	.219	.372	.103	1/30
.286	.219	.331	.202	.372	.069	1/30
.202	.286	.372	.219	.331	.062	1/30
.202	.331	.286	.219	.372	.058	1/30
.202	.372	.219	.286	.331	.043	1/30
.286	.219	.372	.331	.202	.028	1/30
.372	.219	.202	.331	.286	.026	1/30
.331	.219	.286	.202	.372	.025	1/30

The top column headers read: "A phase" spanning the first two coefficient columns (Coefficient -1 and -1), "B" over the middle column, and "C phase" spanning the two $+1$ columns.

much time and effort have been spent on the data collection, the investigator should use all the tools at his disposal to study the results in depth.

B. Helen: Problems with Sleeping

A 58-year-old woman with insomnia of 20 years duration participated in an exploratory intervention study (Coates, Thoresen, Friedman, & Philips, 1977). She was asked to self-record several things about her sleep for a 1 week-baseline period. Intervention followed with 12 days of progressive relaxation training, 10 days of cognitive focusing training, 14 days of time management, and finally 54 days of positive self-evaluation and focused relaxation training. A 6-day follow-up was conducted 3 months later; 7 months after that a 23-day follow-up took place. Variables recorded were date, minutes to fall asleep (latency to sleep onset) the preceding night, number of awakenings in the night, minutes awake during the night after awakening (wake after sleep onset), and ratings on the Stanford Sleepiness Scale, a depression adjective checklist, and a daily activity–pleasantness log.[5]

1. EXAMINING THE BASELINE—EXPLORATORY ANALYSES

Analysis should first focus on the outcome measure of major concern to the patient. Here we have arbitrarily chosen to examine minutes latency to sleep onset and total sleep time. We begin by characterizing the response pattern during the baseline period. Unfortunately, a one week baseline period is a rather short one to establish a firm pattern. Baseline results for these two variables are presented in Tables 6.6 and 6.10.

For minutes latency we first note that the subject tends to round to the nearest 10 minutes, and so the data are not so continuous as they might first seem. Second, median latency is 30 minutes with a minimum of 20 and a maximum of 80. The minimum occurred on Saturday night and the two high latencies on Sunday and Monday nights. The behavior of this variable suggests that there may be "day of the week" effects; mean values may not describe the data well. Alternatives would include such things as classifying latencies as short or long and reporting frequency of long latencies in a week, reporting the single longest latency, and summarizing by using the median. We should also think of this problem in terms of what we would like the

---

[5] The Stanford Daily Sleep Questionnaire provides data on the first five variables. In this study eight all night polygraphic recordings of Helen's sleep were also collected (electroencephalogram, electroculogram, electromyogram, and actogram). These data are not discussed here.

TABLE 6.6
Minutes Latency by Treatment Day and Day of Week

Phase	Days	Fri. night	Sat. night	Sun. night	Mon. night	Tue. night	Wed. night	Thu. night
Baseline	1–7						30	30
		30	20	60	80	30		
Progressive	8–16						10	10
relaxation		10	5	50	5	180	10	15
		5	70	10				
Cognitive	18–30				10	10	10	20
focus		5	5	25	15	3	120	70
Time	31–44	10	5	20	10	65	2	90
management		2	30	30	250	1	2	2
Positive	45–100	5	5	35	20	5	5	5
evaluation		2	5	5	5	5	2	110
and focused		30	30	—	15	80	15	20
relaxation		10	5	100	5	5	2	5
		15	2	210	15	15	30	15
		15	10	60	15	70	70	15
		15	15	15	10	15	2	45
		10	10	15	10	10	15	5
Three-month	192–198	30	30	15	5	60	5	2
follow-up								
12-Month	393–402						30	10
follow-up		10	5	5	5	5	5	5
		5						
	412–416				5	15	15	90
		2						

treatment to influence—median latency, maximum weekly latency, number of weekly latencies greater than 45 minutes, and so on.

Since these data are clearly exploratory we may examine the rest of the record to see what patterns hold up across treatments. The full record is shown in Table 6.6. An initial scan of the data reveals that there is a trend toward shorter latencies as the trial proceeds but that one or two long latencies a week continue to appear—these tend to fall during the week rather than on Friday or Saturday nights. A few simple tabulations will help clarify these observations.

Suppose we arbitrarily classify latencies as short (less than or equal to 15 minutes), moderate (20 through 45 minutes), long (more than 45 but less than 120 minutes), and very long (120 minutes or longer). Then we may tabulate latency lengths by week and by day of week (see Tables 6.7 and 6.8). We see that of 18 long or very long latencies 13 occurred on Sunday,

Tuesday, or Thursday nights (we would expect 8 if they were evenly distributed in the week) and only 1 occurred on a Friday or Saturday night (we would expect 5). Only 5 of the 14 Sunday nights had a short latency while at least 9 of the latencies on each of the other days were short. At the beginning of the study there were generally two long latencies a week, this dropped to one, and there were several weeks at the end with no long latencies. Examination of maximum weekly latencies shows that variability within each phase remains high throughout. Table 6.7b shows the means and standard deviations of latencies for each phase; we see how much larger the means are than the medians due to the occasional long and very long latencies; the standard deviations often exceed the means.

It is clear that the nightly latencies exhibit a type of serial correlation. If we were to try to guess the latency on a particular night it would help to know the median latency for that week. It would also help to know the day of the week and whether there were any long latencies in the rest of the week. If the long latencies occurred in a regular weekly pattern we would expect to see high serial correlations at lags of 7 days, 14 days, 21 days, etc. We could then construct a model for the data with terms accounting for this periodicity. However, the pattern found is sufficiently irregular that study of serial correlations is unlikely to reveal it; it would thus be difficult to build a time-series model reflecting this time pattern adequately. Table 6.9 shows serial correlations up to Lag 18 calculated for the first 44 days of the time record up to the start of the positive evaluation treatment. The correlations are small and variable in sign. There is a slight tendency for correlations with large absolute values to occur for lags that are multiples of three. Although one can detect a pattern visually—one immediately guesses that Monday, Wednesday, and Friday create anticipatory stresses—the data are sufficiently variable and irregular that analysis of the *daily* latency records by the time-series methods discussed in Chapter 4 is unlikely to prove satisfactory.

We can see from this kind of preliminary inspection of the latency data that the most appropriate model for analysis is not readily obvious. Given the weekly pattern for the latency data, analysis might focus more profitably on a weekly summary value, such as the maximum or median weekly latency (see Table 6.7). We discuss the possible effects of intervention on latency after a review of the daily record for total sleep.

Total sleep time in hours was the second variable explored (see Table 6.10). The pattern is similar to that seen for minutes latency, with a short sleep time about once a week, especially on Sunday and Tuesday nights. The shortest sleep time in the week often coincides with the longest latency in the week. Again, weekly minimum or median sleep time is probably the most useful way to summarize the data. Table 6.11 presents the minimum and median hours of sleep for each phase.

TABLE 6.7a
Maximum and Median Weekly Latencies (in Minutes)

Phase (total days)	Maximum latency for week	Median latency for week	Median latency for phase
Baseline (7)	80	30	30
Progressive relaxation (11)	180	10[a]	10
Cognitive focus (11)	120	15[a]	10
Time management (14)	90	10	10
	250	2	
Positive evaluation and	35	5	15
focused relaxation (56)	110	5	
	80	30	
	100	5	
	210	15	
	70	15	
	45	15	
	15	10	
Three-month follow-up (7)	60	15	15
12-Month follow-up (14)	10[a]	5	5

[a] Only complete week used; see Table 6.6.

TABLE 6.7b
Phase Means, Medians and Standard Deviations for Latency

Phase (no. of days)	Mean	Median	Standard deviation
Baseline (7)	40	30	22
Progressive relaxation (11)	34	10	53
Cognitive focusing (11)	21	10	33
Time management (14)	42	10	67
Positive evaluation and focused relaxation (56)	23	15	35
Three-month follow-up (7)	21	15	21
12-Month follow-up (14)	14	5	22

TABLE 6.8a
Length of Latency by Day of Week

	Fri.	Sat.	Sun.	Mon.	Tue.	Wed.	Thu.
Short	12	10	5	12	9	12	9
Mod	3	4	4	1	1	2	4
Long	0	1	4	1	4	1	3
Very Long	0	0	1	1	1	1	0
Total	15	15	14	15	15	16	16

TABLE 6.8b
Number of Long or Very Long Latencies by Week
(Complete Weeks Fri.–Thu.)

Week	No. of long latencies	Week	No. of long latencies
1	2	9	1
2	2	10	1
3	1	11	1
4	2	12	3
5	2	13	0
6	1	14	0
7	0	15	1
8	1	16	0

TABLE 6.9
Serial Correlations ($n = 44$)

Lag	Minutes latency	Total sleep
1	−.12	−.18
2	−.05	.12
3	−.26	−.38
4	.17	.29
5	−.18	−.29
6	.08	.17
7	−.11	.03
8	.09	.22
9	−.08	−.25
10	−.14	−.13
11	.16	.01
12	.30	−.09
13	−.17	−.01
14	−.18	.07
15	.16	.19
16	−.02	−.22
17	−.05	.12
18	−.12	−.38

2. INTERVENTION EFFECTS—CONFIRMATORY ANALYSES

After inspecting baseline measures and deciding how best to summarize the data, we focus on what the expected effect of intervention is likely to be. For data of this sort one would clearly have to follow the patient for at least

TABLE 6.10
Total Sleep by Treatment Day and Day of Week (in Hours)

Phase	Fri.	Sat.	Sun.	Mon.	Tue.	Wed.	Thu.	Min. hours	Median hours
Baseline						4.8	6.7		
	6.9	2.9	4.8	6.1	7.1			2.9	6.1
Progressive relaxation						8.1	5.1		
	6.3	8.3	5.7	7.6	4.3	8.1	5.3		
	10.1	4.8	8.8					4.3	6.3
Cognitive focusing				6.3	8.4	6.8	7.1		
	9.0	6.7	5.1	6.3	7.0	2.5	5.2	2.5	6.3
Time management	8.1	9.3	4.1	7.0	4.2	7.3	2.8	2.8	7.0
	11.1	8.9	6.5	1.8	6.1	4.9	7.4	1.8	6.5
Positive evaluation and	6.1	6.9	5.6	4.3	6.6	6.3	4.6	4.3	6.1
focused relaxation	12.5	9.9	8.2	5.9	4.8	5.0	4.8	4.8	5.9
	6.3	8.2	—	5.1	6.5	6.8	7.0	5.1	6.7
	6.4	7.5	3.8	6.0	6.9	7.4	7.5	3.8	6.9
	5.8	8.0	3.5	7.3	7.6	6.8	8.5	3.5	7.3
	8.0	7.3	6.6	8.0	6.0	6.0	6.8	6.0	6.8
	6.3	7.2	7.0	8.9	3.1	7.0	6.5	3.1	7.0
	5.6	7.7	6.7	6.3	7.0	6.5	7.7	5.6	6.7
Three-month follow-up	6.7	7.0	8.6	8.9	5.8	6.9	7.0	5.8	7.0
12-Month follow-up						10.0	8.6		
	10.7	8.5	9.4	7.5	5.3	8.3	8.5		
	10.3								
				9.0	8.5	7.0	9.3		
	9.3							5.3	8.5

TABLE 6.11
Minimum and Median Values for Total Sleep Time by Phases (in Hours)

Phase (days)	Minimum (hours)	Median (hours)
Baseline (7)	2.9	6.1
Progressive relaxation (11)	4.3	6.3
Cognitive focusing (11)	2.5	6.7
Time management (14)	1.8	6.7
Positive evaluation and focused relaxation (56)	3.1	6.8
Three-month follow-up (7)	5.8	7.0
12-Month follow-up (14)	5.3	8.6

an entire week to assess an intervention. In addition since the patient is being gradually trained in the practice of several techniques, each added to those preceding, one would probably expect to see a steady improvement over the intervention periods.

In looking at maximum latency to sleep onset or median or minimum total sleep time we see an apparent slow trend across the weeks. For minutes latency the Spearman rank correlation is $-.59$ between maximum latency and treatment weeks (ignoring all partial weeks). If the weekly maximum latencies could be considered independent of each other this would be significant at $p < .05$. The Spearman rank correlation between minimum hours of sleep and treatment weeks is .74 ($p < .05$ if we can assume independence). For median hours of sleep, the correlation with treatment week is .70.

In this example, the 7-day baseline period is not long enough to preclude the possibility that the weekly trend occurred before the start of treatment. Perhaps latency and total sleep time vary slowly over time in a wavelike fashion. However, Helen's reports of 20 years of disrupted sleep make it unlikely that a gradual improvement would have occurred in the absence of treatment.

One way to try to assess whether weekly summary scores can be considered independent is to look at the first order serial correlations of the residuals after the trend has been removed. (The presence of trend in the data will tend to create a positive Lag 1 serial correlation even when successive observations are independent apart from trend.) For minutes latency the first-order serial correlation of residuals from the least-squares regression line of rank of maximum weekly latency on treatment week number is $-.34$. Similarly, for minimum weekly hours sleep, we find $-.25$. Since these serial correlations are based on a sample of only 15 weeks, neither is significant at the 5% level but their negative values reflect the tendency for large ups and downs across weeks in addition to the slow improving trend.

If the data are summarized by treatment phase and predictions made about the ordering of outcomes by phases, the nonparametric randomization tests can be applied. (Note that treatments were given in systematic rather than random order.) Based on the nature of the treatment, we predict that sleep time will be lowest in the baseline phase, longer in the combined Phases 2–4, longer in Phase 5 (positive evaluation and focused relaxation) and longest in the posttreatment Phases 6 and 7. For these four periods, median hours of sleep are 6.1, 6.7, 6.8, and 8.5, respectively. There are $4! = 24$ possible assignments of these four median scores to treatment periods. Under the randomization model, the probability of their occurring in increasing order is $1/24 = .04$. Since the observed median sleep times are in increasing order, we could reject the null hypothesis at the one-sided 4% level. (A two-sided test would reject at the 8% level.)

V. Concluding Comments

In an initial intensive experiment we should look carefully at the data and try to answer these questions:

1. What are the relevant response measures?
2. What is the baseline pattern in terms of level, variability, and trend?
3. What is the correlation between successive responses (Lag 1, Lag 2, etc.)?
4. What is the pattern likely to be without intervention (if baseline were continued)?
5. What is the desired or expected pattern due to an intervention effect?

When these questions have been answered with some degree of confidence, another experiment can be planned in which this information is used as the basis for choosing a statistical test to assess intervention effects. Using only one piece of data (the same single-case experiment) to suggest statistical models *and* to test hypotheses can lead to rejecting the null hypothesis more frequently than the nominal significance level would indicate (Type I error). More importantly, the failure to carry out controlled observation studies, prior to intervention, seriously limits the utility and the validity of intensive designs in research. The basic argument is that each unit under study—person, classroom, family agency—serves as "its own control." Yet such control cannot be exercised without an adequate background of information on that unit. Put in general terms, interrupted (planned interventions) time-series should as a rule be preceded by uninterrupted (controlled observation) time-series designs (Thoresen, in press).

The investigator can help understand the issue of whether successive observations are independent or correlated by asking questions such as:

1. What is the typical length of a behavior in relation to the recording interval?
2. What do I know about possible inertia in the system?
3. What is the likelihood of periodic or systematic effects due to hour of the day, day of the week, week of the month, or season of the year?

Think of the issue in terms of prediction. Any increase in the predictability of a particular response gained by having information in addition to mean or trend level implies some lack of independence or homogeneity in the data.

Even though the investigator may wish to test intervention effects for each unit separately, we can and should take advantage of all comparable experiments in trying to assess the structure of the data. The baselines from several different single-case experiments with different individuals may allow examination of the data for possible periodicities or serial correlations which are impossible to evaluate in a single 2- or 3-week record. In addition, we can gradually come to have a good deal more faith in a model that seems to fit several similar pieces of data than in one constructed on just a single case. This of course argues directly for replication, not only for demonstrating experimental effects but for building a basis for selecting valid and useful statistical models. If the assumptions necessary to the analytic technique chosen do not fit the data, the results may be seriously overstated or obscured.

In-depth examination of the structure of the data is crucially important to the intelligent choice of an analytic method for testing intervention effects. "Sufficient unto the day is the labour thereof." We hope that the work of researchers will reflect the intensive labor needed to expand the use of appropriate statistics. The day has clearly arrived.

REFERENCES

Bartley, W. W. *The retreat to commitment*. New York: Knopf, 1962.
Boring, E. G. Psychological factors in the scientific process. *American Scientist*, 1954, *42*, 639–645.
Boruch, R. F., & Riecken, H. W. *Social experimentation: A method for planning and evaluating social intervention*. New York: Academic Press, 1974.
Campbell, D. T., & Stanley, J. C. *Experimental and quasi-experimental designs for research*. Chicago: Rand McNally, 1966.
Coates, T. J., Thoresen, C. E., Friedman, L. T., Phillips, R. L. *Behaviorial self-management in treating insomnia: A four year study*. Unpublished manuscript. Stanford University, 1977.
Cochran, W. G. Early development of techniques in comparative experiments. Technical Report 44, July, 1974, Dept. of Statistics, Harvard University.
Cronbach, L. J. Beyond the two disciplines of scientific psychology. *American Psychologist*, 1975, *30*, 116–127.
Dixon, W. J., & Massey, F. J., *Introduction to statistical analysis*, 3rd ed. New York: McGraw Hill, 1969.
Fisher, R. A. *The design of experiments*. Edinburgh: Oliver & Boyd, 1935.
Gilbert, J. P., Light, R. J., & Mosteller, F., Assessing social innovations: An empirical base for policy. In C. A. Bennett & A. A. Lumsdaine (Eds.), *Evaluation and experiment*. New York: Academic Press, 1975.
Klein, R. D., Roden, A. H., Gentile, J. R., Resnick, L. B., Reynolds, L. J., & B. Bachmeyer, The effects of a systematic manipulation of contingencies upon overt work behavior in a primary classroom. Unpublished Technical report. Learning Research and Development Center, University of Pittsburgh, 1972.
Kratochwill, T., Alden, K., Demuth, D., Dawson, D., Panicucci, C., Arnston, P., McMurray, N., Hempstead, J., & Levin, J. A further consideration in the application of an analysis of variance model for the intrasubject replication design. *Journal of Applied Behavior Analysis*, 1974, *7*, 629–633.
Kuhn, T. S. Logic of discovery or psychology of research. In I. Lakatos & A. Musgrave (Eds.), *Criticism and the growth of knowledge*, Cambridge: University Press, 1970, 1–23.

Louis, P. C. A. *Essay on clinical instruction* (Translated by P. Martin). London: S. Highley, 1834.

Mahoney, M. J. *Scientist as subject: The psychological imperative.* Cambridge, MA: Ballinger, 1976.

Michael, J. Statistical inference for individual organism research: some reactions to a suggestion by Gentile, Roden, and Klein. *Journal of Applied Behavior Analysis*, 1974, *7*, 629–634.

Popper, K. R. *Objective knowledge: An evolutionary approach.* London: Oxford University Press, 1972.

Thoresen, C. E. *Let's get intensive: Studying change over time.* Englewood Cliffs: Prentice-Hall, in press.

Underwood, B. J. *Psychological research.* New York: Appleton, 1957.

Weimer, W. B. *Psychology and the conceptual foundations of science.* Hillsdale, NJ: Lawrence Erlbaum, 1976.

Young, A. *A course of experimental agriculture.* Dublin: E. X. Shaw, et al., 1771.

Index

313

A
B
C 8
D 9
E 0
F 1
G 2
H 3
I 4
J 5